X 1027250

GRADE

11

VOLUME 1

5 6 7 8 9 10 1468   29 28 27 26 25 24 23

4500864798

r9.22

Program Consultants:

Kylene Beers

Martha Hougen

Tyrone C. Howard

Elena Izquierdo

Carol Jago

Weston Kieschnick

Erik Palmer

Robert E. Probst

GRADE

11

VOLUME 1

Program Consultants

Kylene Beers

Nationally known lecturer and author on reading and literacy; coauthor with Robert Probst of *Disrupting Thinking, Notice & Note: Strategies for Close Reading,* and *Reading Nonfiction;* former president of the National Council of Teachers of English. Dr. Beers is the author of *When Kids Can't Read: What Teachers Can Do* and coeditor of *Adolescent Literacy: Turning Promise into Practice,* as well as articles in the *Journal of Adolescent and Adult Literacy.* Former editor of *Voices from the Middle,* she is the 2001 recipient of NCTE's Richard W. Halle Award, given for outstanding contributions to middle school literacy.

Martha Hougen

National consultant, presenter, researcher, and author. Areas of expertise include differentiating instruction for students with learning difficulties, including those with learning disabilities and dyslexia; and teacher and leader preparation improvement. Dr. Hougen has taught at the middle school through graduate levels. Dr. Hougen has supported Educator Preparation Program reforms while working at the Meadows Center for Preventing Educational Risk at The University of Texas at Austin and at the CEEDAR Center, University of Florida.

Tyrone C. Howard

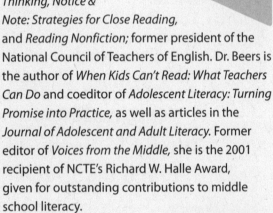

Veteran teacher, author, and professor in the Graduate School of Education and Information Studies at UCLA. Dr. Howard is the inaugural director of the UCLA Pritzker Center for Strengthening Children and Families, a campus-wide consortium examining academic, mental health, and social and emotional experiences and challenges for the most vulnerable youth populations. Dr. Howard has published over 75 peer-reviewed journal articles and several bestselling books, including, *Why Race & Culture Matters in Schools* and *Black Male(d): Peril and Promise in the Education of African American Males.* He is considered one of the premier experts on educational equity and access in the country.

Elena Izquierdo

Nationally recognized teacher educator and advocate for English language learners. Dr. Izquierdo is a linguist by training, with a Ph.D. in Applied Linguistics and Bilingual Education from Georgetown University. She has served on various state and national boards working to close the achievement gaps for bilingual students and English language learners. Dr. Izquierdo is a member of the Hispanic Leadership Council, which supports Hispanic students and educators at both the state and federal levels.

Carol Jago

Teacher of English with 32 years of experience at Santa Monica High School in California; author and nationally known lecturer; former president of the National Council of Teachers of English. Ms. Jago currently serves as Associate Director of the California Reading and Literature Project at UCLA. With expertise in standards assessment and secondary education, Ms. Jago is the author of numerous books on education, including *With Rigor for All* and *Papers, Papers, Papers*; and she is active with the California Association of Teachers of English, editing its scholarly journal *California English* since 1996. Ms. Jago also served on the planning committee for the 2009 NAEP Reading Framework and the 2011 NAEP Writing Framework.

Weston Kieschnick

Author, award-winning teacher, principal, instructional development coordinator, and dean of education. Mr. Kieschnick has driven change and improved student learning in multiple capacities over his educational career. Now, as an experienced instructional coach and Senior Fellow with the International Center for Leadership in Education (ICLE), Mr. Kieschnick shares his expertise with teachers to transform learning through online and blended models. He is the author of *Bold School: Old School Wisdom + New School Innovation = Blended Learning that Works* and co-author of *The Learning Transformation: A Guide to Blended Learning for Administrators*.

Erik Palmer

Veteran teacher and education consultant based in Denver, Colorado. Author of *Well Spoken: Teaching Speaking to All Students* and *Digitally Speaking: How to Improve Student Presentations*. His areas of focus include improving oral communication, promoting technology in classroom presentations, and updating instruction through the use of digital tools. He holds a bachelor's degree from Oberlin College and a master's degree in curriculum and instruction from the University of Colorado.

Robert E. Probst

Nationally respected authority on the teaching of literature; Professor Emeritus of English Education at Georgia State University. Dr. Probst's publications include numerous articles in *English Journal* and *Voices from the Middle,* as well as professional texts including (as coeditor) *Adolescent Literacy: Turning Promise into Practice* and (as coauthor with Kylene Beers) *Disrupting Thinking, Notice & Note: Strategies for Close Reading,* and *Reading Nonfiction*. He has served NCTE in various leadership roles, including the Conference on English Leadership Board of Directors, the Commission on Reading, and column editor of the NCTE journal *Voices from the Middle.*

Foundations and Encounters Page 1

? ESSENTIAL QUESTIONS

What connects people to certain places?

What values and beliefs shape who we are?

What does it mean to be a stranger in a strange land?

What happens when cultures collide?

KEY LEARNING OBJECTIVES

- Determine and analyze theme
- Analyze plot
- Analyze and evaluate structure
- Determine central idea
- Synthesize information
- Paraphrase
- Compare themes

READER'S CHOICE

SHORT READS

from **The Way to Rainy Mountain**
Memoir by N. Scott Momaday

Mother Tongue
Essay by Amy Tan

from **La relación**
Historical Narrative by Álvar Núñez Cabeza de Vaca

from **The General History of Virginia**
Historical Narrative by John Smith

Voyage
Poem by Carmen Tafolla

Available
online

ⓔEd

LONG READS

The Namesake
Novel
by Jhumpa Lahiri

**An Indigenous
People's History
of the United
States**
Nonfiction
by Roxanne Dunbar-Ortiz

**The Moor's
Account**
Novel
by Laila Lalami

Recommendations

UNIT 1 TASKS

ⓔEd

Go online for
Unit and Selection Videos
Interactive Annotation and Text Analysis
Selection Audio Recordings
SAT® Exam / ACT® Test Prep
Collaborative Writing

Writable

Building a Democracy Page 126

? ESSENTIAL QUESTIONS

What does oppression look like?
How do we gain our freedom?
How can we share power and build alliances?
How do we reach our goals?

KEY LEARNING OBJECTIVES

- Analyze argument
- Determine and analyze themes
- Analyze media
- Analyze point of view
- Analyze and evaluate structure
- Analyze author's purpose
- Analyze and compare tone

READER'S CHOICE

Available online

🙂Ed

Recommendations

UNIT 2 TASKS

🙂Ed

Go online for
Unit and Selection Videos
Interactive Annotation and Text Analysis
Selection Audio Recordings
SAT® Exam / ACT® Test Prep
Collaborative Writing

Writable

The Individual and Society Page 248

ESSENTIAL QUESTIONS

How can we be true to ourselves?

How do we relate to the world around us?

What do we secretly fear?

When should we stop and reflect on our lives?

Available online

KEY LEARNING OBJECTIVES

- Analyze structure and purpose
- Analyze figurative language
- Summarize
- Compare main ideas
- Analyze symbols
- Analyze mood
- Analyze allegory

© Houghton Mifflin Harcourt Publishing Company

COLLABORATE & COMPARE

READER'S CHOICE

Available online

🙂*Ed*

Recommendations

UNIT 3 TASKS

🙂*Ed*

Go online for
Unit and Selection Videos
Interactive Annotation and Text Analysis
Selection Audio Recordings
SAT® Exam / ACT® Test Prep
Collaborative Writing

Writable

?
ESSENTIAL QUESTIONS

When is self-determination possible?
What causes divisions between people?
How do we respond to defeat?
What is the price of progress?

KEY LEARNING OBJECTIVES

- Analyze and evaluate arguments
- Evaluate sources
- Analyze plot
- Analyze rhetoric
- Compare arguments
- Analyze speaker
- Compare structure

READER'S CHOICE

SHORT READS

Letter to Sarah Ballou
Letter by Sullivan Ballou

from **The Fortunes**
Novel by Peter Ho Davies

from **What to the Slave Is the Fourth of July?**
Speech by Frederick Douglass

Go Down, Moses
Follow the Drinking Gourd
Swing Low, Sweet Chariot
Spirituals

Imagine the Angels of Bread
Poem by Martín Espada

Available online

ⓔEd

LONG READS

Their Eyes Were Watching God	**Born a Crime**	**Homegoing**
Novel	Autobiography	Novel
by Zora Neale Hurston	by Trevor Noah	by Yaa Gyasi

Recommendations

UNIT 4 TASKS

WRITING

SPEAKING & LISTENING

© Houghton Mifflin Harcourt Publishing Company

ⓔEd

Go online for
Unit and Selection Videos
Interactive Annotation and Text Analysis
Selection Audio Recordings
SAT® Exam / ACT® Test Prep
Collaborative Writing

Writable

America Transformed Page 516

 ESSENTIAL QUESTIONS

How much do we control our lives?

Why do humans cause harm?

What are the consequences of change?

What makes a place unique?

KEY LEARNING OBJECTIVES

- Analyze setting
- Analyze tone
- Analyze counterarguments
- Analyze point of view
- Analyze irony
- Analyze author's purpose
- Compare genres

READER'S CHOICE

SHORT READS

Ode to Cheese Fries
Poem by José Olivárez

The Men in the Storm
Short Story by Stephen Crane

A Journey
Short Story by Edith Wharton

Glass-Lung
Short Story by Anjali Sachdeva

**Healthy Eaters, Strong Minds:
What School Gardens Teach Kids**
Article by Paige Pfleger

Available
online

ᵒⒺd

LONG READS

**The Great
Gatsby**
Novel
by F. Scott Fitzgerald

**Escape to Gold
Mountain:
A Graphic
History
of the Chinese
in North America**
Graphic Novel
by David H.T. Wong

**How the García
Girls Lost Their
Accents**
Novel
by Julia Álvarez

Recommendations

UNIT 5 TASKS

WRITING

ᵒⒺd

Go online for
Unit and Selection Videos
Interactive Annotation and Text Analysis
Selection Audio Recordings
SAT® Exam / ACT® Test Prep
Collaborative Writing

Writable

Modern and Contemporary Voices Page 640

? ESSENTIAL QUESTIONS

How do we deal with rejection or isolation?

Can anyone achieve the American Dream?

When should personal integrity come before civic duty?

What would we do if there were no limits?

KEY LEARNING OBJECTIVES

- Analyze characters
- Evaluate interpretations of a drama
- Analyze structure
- Analyze literary devices
- Analyze development of ideas
- Analyze perspective
- Compare ideas across genres

© Houghton Mifflin Harcourt Publishing Company

COLLABORATE & COMPARE

Compare Ideas Across Genres

READER'S CHOICE

SHORT READS

Poems of the Harlem Renaissance
   The Weary Blues by Langston Hughes
   Song of the Son by Jean Toomer
   From the Dark Tower by Countee Cullen
   A Black Man Talks of Reaping by Arna Bontemps

Martin Luther King Jr.: He Showed Us the Way
Essay by César Chávez

Ten Kliks South
Short Story by Phil Klay

Poetry
Poem by Marianne Moore

YouTube Stars Stress Out, Just Like the Rest of Us
Article by Neda Ulaby

Available online
ⓄEd

LONG READS

One Hundred Years of Solitude
Novel
by Gabriel García Márquez

They Called Us Enemy
Graphic Memoir
by George Takei, Justin Eisinger, Steven Scott, and Harmony Becker

The Things They Carried
Fiction
by Tim O'Brien

Recommendations

UNIT 6 TASKS

WRITING

ⓄEd

Go online for
Unit and Selection Videos
Interactive Annotation and Text Analysis
Selection Audio Recordings
SAT® Exam / ACT® Test Prep
Collaborative Writing Writable

Selections by Genre

© Houghton Mifflin Harcourt Publishing Company

© Houghton Mifflin Harcourt Publishing Company

DRAMA

MEDIA STUDY

HMH | (into) **Literature™ Online**

 Experience the Power of *HMH Into Literature*

Find your units and lessons

Quickly browse for texts and resources

Tools for Today—All in One Place

Whether you're working alone or collaborating with others, it takes effort to analyze the complex texts and competing ideas that bombard us in this fast-paced world. What will help you succeed? Staying engaged and organized. The digital tools in this program will help you take charge of your learning.

Engage!

Spark Your Learning

These activities kick-start the unit and help get you thinking about the unit theme.

Engage Your Brain

Before you read, take some time to do a fun activity designed to rev up your brain and connect to the text.

Interact with the Texts

- As you read, highlight and take notes to mark the text in your own customized way.

- Use interactive graphic organizers to process, summarize, and track your thinking as you read.

- Play the audio to listen to the text read aloud. You can also turn on read-along highlighting.

Choices

Choose from engaging activities, such as writing an advice column, creating a podcast, or participating in a debate, to demonstrate what you've learned.

Stay Involved!

Collaborate with and Learn from Your Peers

- Watch brief **Peer Coach Videos** to learn more about a particular skill.

- Flex your creative muscles by digging into **Media Projects** tied to each unit theme.

- Bring your writing online with **Writable,** where you can share your work and give and receive valuable feedback.

Read On!

Find helpful **Reader's Choice** suggestions with each unit, and access hundreds of texts online.

Writable

No Wi-Fi? No Problem!

With HMH *Into Literature,* you always have access; download when you're online and access what you need when you're offline.

The Positive Disrupter

Dr. Kylene Beers

Dr. Robert E. Probst

Reading is Change: Thoughts by Two Teachers

by **Dr. Kylene Beers** and **Dr. Robert E. Probst**

Here you are, in the last years of high school, and for more of your school years than you might care to remember you've probably been told not to be disruptive. Sit still. Listen. Keep quiet. But now we're going to tell you to be a disrupter.

Sometimes, of course, you should be still and listen, learn, ponder. But sometimes you should speak up to make a change, to influence those around you, to cause a disruption. We're not encouraging you to misbehave. We're encouraging something much bigger than that.

Disruptions That Bring Change and Growth

Throughout our nation's history, we've grown due to technological disruptions: the horse and buggy eventually became the electric car, the telegram evolved into the text, and the rabbit-eared, three-channel TV became a three-hundred-channel smart device. We've also grown due to social and political disruptions. Women demanded the right to vote; African Americans fought for their freedom; and at one point reading and writing were things reserved for the privileged—ordinary people had to fight to upset that imbalance of power.

Disruptions are a part of life. Some will be positive: new and faster ways to communicate, better ways to grow food, easier ways to clean water. And some will be negative. One of the greatest disruptions we've faced as a nation and world was the COVID-19 pandemic of 2020. The "stay home, stay safe" order disrupted everyone's life. The questions we must ask are, "What did we learn" and "What will we carry forward?"

Other disruptions will affect only you, or you and your family or friend community. You may decide that your religious or political views differ from those of your friends or family. You may choose to be a musician though your parents wanted you to be a pharmacist, or a soldier though your parents wanted you to be a farmer. And there will be other personal choices that you will have to make.

Or others will make them for you. You are going to have to deal with those disruptions and the changes they will bring. You, and others your age, will make the decisions. It's important that you decide what you think. If you don't read and learn, the decisions will be made for you by those who do, or by those who are simply louder.

Some groups of people have always withheld power from others by making sure they know less. One of the most powerful ways of doing that is to ensure groups can't read or write. In some countries today, girls are denied schooling. And, too many who do learn to read and write fail to realize that the more they read, the more able they will be to use reason and evidence to question the world around them and influence their own futures. Too many choose not to read.

The Path to Positive Disruption

The texts you will read this year take on some of the issues every human must face: love, greed, hope, death, injustice, equity, and our relationship with nature, to name a few. Read these selections carefully. Though the story might have taken place in another time with a different group of people, the human emotions and issues remain relevant. Decide what matters to you. Wonder what the issues mean in your life today. And as you decide, think of the world that you will help to shape. You are tomorrow's builders, scientists, politicians, artists, teachers, and nurses. You are our brave soldiers who will defend this country, and our curious thinkers who will change it. And you will change it only by disrupting, slightly or significantly, what it is now.

To do that you need to read well—attentively and thoughtfully. We'll help you do that with some tools we call the **Notice & Note Signposts**, explained throughout this program (see the chart on the next two pages). Recognizing signposts will help you better understand what you're reading and thus, what you're thinking.

Reading—smart reading—gives you the opportunity to weigh a thought, a value, a belief, and decide whether to hold onto it, change it, or dispose of it. If you don't decide for yourself, then someone else will. And if you allow that, then you no longer have much influence over the shape of the world in which you live. Don't be that person. Be a person with power, a positive disrupter.

Shape the world in which you live.

COLLABORATIVE DISCUSSION

What is something you'd like to disrupt? How might reading help you do that?

**Notice & Note Handbook
Peer Coach Videos**

When you notice a signpost in your reading, mark the text with its initials.

LITERARY TEXTS

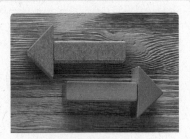

CONTRASTS AND CONTRADICTIONS *CC*

A sharp contrast between what we would expect and what we observe the character doing; behavior that contradicts previous behavior or well-established patterns

When you notice this signpost, ask:

Why would the character act (feel) this way?

AHA MOMENT

A sudden realization of something that shifts a character's actions or understanding of self, others, or the world

When you notice this signpost, ask:

How might this change things?

TOUGH QUESTIONS *TQ*

Questions characters raise that reveal their inner struggles

When you notice this signpost, ask:

What does this question make me wonder about?

WORDS OF THE WISER *WW*

The advice or insight about life that a wiser character, who is usually older, offers to the main character

When you notice this signpost, ask:

What is the life lesson, and how might this affect the character?

AGAIN AND AGAIN *AA*

Events, images, or particular words that recur over a portion of the story

When you notice this signpost, ask:

Why might the author bring this up again and again?

MEMORY MOMENT *MM*

A recollection by a character that interrupts the forward progress of the story

When you notice this signpost, ask:

Why might this memory moment be important?

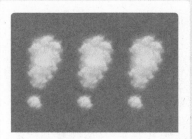

INFORMATIONAL TEXTS

BIG QUESTIONS BQ

It's important to take a **Questioning Stance** or attitude when you read nonfiction.

- *What surprised me?*
- *What did the author think I already knew?*
- *What changed, challenged, or confirmed what I already knew?*

CONTRASTS AND CONTRADICTIONS CC

A sharp contrast between what we would expect and what we observe happening; a difference between two or more elements in the text

When you notice this signpost, ask:

What is the difference, and why does it matter?

EXTREME OR ABSOLUTE LANGUAGE XL

Language that leaves no doubt about a situation or an event, allows no compromise, or seems to exaggerate or overstate a case

When you notice this signpost, ask:

Why did the author use this language?

NUMBERS AND STATS NS

Specific quantities or comparisons to depict the amount, size, or scale; or the writer is vague and imprecise about numbers when we would expect more precision

When you notice this signpost, ask:

Why did the author use these numbers or amounts?

QUOTED WORDS QW

Opinions or conclusions of someone who is an expert on the subject or someone who might be a participant in or a witness to an event; or the author might cite other people to provide support for a point

When you notice this signpost, ask:

Why was this person quoted or cited, and what did this add?

WORD GAPS WG

Vocabulary that is unfamiliar to the reader—for example, a word with multiple meanings, a rare or technical word, a discipline-specific word, or one with a far-removed antecedent

When you notice this signpost, ask:

Do I know this word from someplace else? Does this seem like technical talk for experts on this topic? Can I find clues in the text to help me understand the word?

© Houghton Mifflin Publishing Company • Image Credits: (tl)©Yakobchuk Vasyl/Shutterstock; (tc) ©Radachynskyi Serhii/Shutterstock; (tr) ©aslysun/Shutterstock; (bl) ©concept w/Shutterstock; (bc) ©space_heater/Shutterstock; (br) ©Adriana/Adobe Stock

Social & Emotional Learning

The Most Important Subject Is You!

by **Carol Jago**

You have essays to turn in. You have quizzes to take. You have group projects to complete. Your success in those areas depends on more than your understanding of the academic skills they cover. It also depends on how well you understand yourself, and how well you're able to extend that understanding to others. This might seem obvious, but there's an actual term for that type of learning—it's called **Social and Emotional Learning.**

Why It Matters

But doing well in school is not the only benefit to understanding yourself and others. When it comes to Social and Emotional Learning, the answer to the question, "When will I actually use this in my life?" is clear: every single day, forever. Whether you are with your family, your community, your friends, at a workplace, or by yourself on a deserted island, you will have a better chance of achieving satisfaction and making positive contributions if you're able to do things like the following:

- ✓ identify your emotions
- ✓ make smart choices
- ✓ set reasonable goals
- ✓ recognize your strengths
- ✓ have empathy
- ✓ manage your reactions
- ✓ evaluate problems and solutions
- ✓ show respect for others

Where Literature Comes In

English Language Arts classes can provide some of the best opportunities to develop these skills. That's because reading literature allows you to imagine yourself in different worlds and to understand what it's like to be in a wide range of situations. You can think through your own feelings and values as you read about various characters, conflicts, historical figures, and ideas, and you can become more aware of why others might act and feel as they do.

Throughout this book, you will find opportunities for Social and Emotional Learning in the Choices section of many lessons. But you don't need to wait for a special activity to practice and learn. Reading widely and discussing thoughtfully is a natural way to gain empathy and self-knowledge. The chart below shows the five main areas of Social and Emotional Learning and tells how reading can help you strengthen them.

Areas of Social and Emotional Learning	How Reading Can Help
If you have **self-awareness,** you're conscious of your own emotions, thoughts, and values, and you understand how they affect your behavior.	Understanding why characters act the way they do can increase your understanding of your own responses and motivations.
If you're good at **self-management,** you are able to control your emotions, thoughts, and behaviors in different situations.	Paying attention to why characters explode in tumultuous ways or how they keep calm under pressure can help you recognize what to do and not to do when faced with stressful situations in your own life.
If you have **social awareness,** you can empathize with others, including people who are different from you.	Reading about people with different life experiences can help you understand the perspectives of others.
If you have well-developed **relationship skills,** you can get along with different kinds of people and function well in groups.	Reflecting on the conflicts between characters can help you gain insight into what causes the conflicts in your life and how to reach mutual satisfaction.
If you are good at **responsible decision-making,** you make good choices that keep you and others safe and keep you moving toward your goals.	Evaluating the choices characters make and thinking about what you would do in their place can help you understand the consequences of your decisions.

Having the Hard Conversations

The more widely and deeply you read, the more you'll strengthen your social and emotional skills, and the more likely you are to encounter ideas that are different from your own. Some texts might bring up strong reactions from you, and you'll need to take a step back to understand how you're feeling. Or, your classmates might have responses that are dramatically different from yours, and you'll need to take a breath and decide how to engage with them. Remember: it's okay to disagree with a text or with a peer. In fact, discussing a difference of opinion can be one of the most powerful ways to learn.

Tips for Talking About Controversial Issues

> The reason I think so is because I've noticed that I . . .

> So what I hear you saying is . . .
> Did I get that right?

Communicate clearly.
Speak honestly and carefully, rather than for dramatic effect. Notice if the person listening seems confused and give them room to ask questions.

Listen actively.
Try your best to understand what the other person is saying, and why they might think or feel that way. If you don't understand, ask questions or rephrase what you thought you heard and ask them if you're getting it right.

> When you use that word I have a negative reaction because it sounds like you are saying you think that person isn't smart.

> I'm sorry. That's not what I meant.

Take a stand against name-calling, belittling, stereotyping, and bias.
Always try exploring ideas further rather than making personal attacks. If someone feels hurt by something you said, listen to them with an open mind. Perhaps you expressed bias without realizing it. Apologize sincerely if that happens. And if you are hurt by a comment or hear something that could be interpreted as hurtful, calmly let the person who said it know why you feel that way.

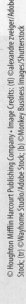

> I need to take a break from this conversation now.

Pay attention to your feelings.
Recognize the topics or situations that make it hard for you to stay calm. Try to separate your strong feelings from what the person is saying. If you need to, excuse yourself from the conversation and find a place where you can help yourself relax.

> We see this really differently, so let's move on for now.

Consider the relationship.
It's likely that the people you're in class with are people you will be seeing regularly for years. You don't have to be friends with them or agree with their point of view, but you do have to get an education alongside each other. Speaking respectfully even if you're on opposite sides of an issue will make it easier to work together if you ever have to collaborate. Try to assume the best about them rather than the worst. Acknowledge that our experiences affect our points of view.

Agree to disagree.
Even after listening carefully and being listened to, you still might not agree. That's okay. You can acknowledge your differences, remain respectful, and exit the conversation.

> I don't agree with you, but I understand why it looks that way from your perspective.

Learning, growing, and working with others isn't always easy. If you read widely and deeply and try your best to speak honestly, you're likely to gain the understanding and compassion that can help you manage the stresses, challenges, and opportunities that life brings your way.

"I'm happy to say that America is still the great melting pot—maybe a chunky stew rather than a melting pot at this point, but you know what I mean."

—Philip Glass

Early American Literature

Foundations and Encounters

? As you read the texts in this unit, think about how they explore these **Essential Questions**.

What connects people to certain places?
When Europeans first came to North America, they fought to take the land from Native Americans. Consider what connects people to the places they live, work, and fight to preserve.

What values and beliefs shape who we are?
America's early explorers valued glory, riches, adventure, and trade—usually at great risk to their own safety and well-being. Think about the values that are important to you.

What does it mean to be a stranger in a strange land?
The first European settlers faced a challenging environment and unfamiliar people as they forged a new life for themselves in America.

What happens when cultures collide?
English Puritans and Native Americans lived peacefully at first, but conflicts arose as many more Europeans arrived.

ANALYZE THE IMAGE
How does the artist represent an encounter between different cultures?

Explore unit themes and build background.
Stream to Start Video

Spark Your Learning

Here are some opportunities to think about issues related to **Unit 1: Foundations and Encounters.**

As you read, you can use the **Response Log** (page R1) to track your thinking about the Essential Questions.

Think About the Essential Questions

Review the Essential Questions on page 1. Which question is most intriguing to you? Perhaps it relates to something you have read or reminds you of a personal experience. Write down your thoughts.

Make the Connection

Consider the quotation by Philip Glass that introduces the unit on the opening page.

- What is the difference between a melting pot and a chunky stew?

- Which description best represents your school or community?

Discuss your ideas with a partner.

Build Academic Vocabulary

You can use these Academic Vocabulary words to write and talk about the topics and themes in the unit. Which of these words do you already feel comfortable using when speaking or writing?

Prove It!

Use one of the Academic Vocabulary words in a sentence in which you give someone advice about visiting a place they have never been before.

	I can use it!	I understand it.	I'll look it up.
adapt			
coherent			
device			
displace			
dynamic			

Preview the Texts

Review the images, titles, and descriptions of the texts in the unit.

Mark the title of the text that interests you most.

The World on the Turtle's Back

Myth by **Iroquois storytellers**

In this creation myth, two boys' differences bring balance to the world.

Balboa

Short Story by **Sabina Murray**

A Spanish explorer reflects on the awesomeness of his achievements.

A Desperate Trek Across America

Nonfiction Narrative by **Andrés Reséndez**

On the coast of Florida in 1528, a group of conquistadors face starvation, disease, and enslavement.

New Orleans

Poem by **Joy Harjo**

The speaker ponders the history of this great American city.

Coming of Age in the Dawnland

History Writing by **Charles C. Mann**

The writer discusses how the European settlers viewed Native American customs.

from **Of Plymouth Plantation**

Historical Narrative by **William Bradford**

The Puritans arrive in North America and meet the native peoples for the first time.

Here Follow Some Verses Upon the Burning of Our House, July 10th, 1666

Poem by **Anne Bradstreet**

The speaker grieves after her home is destroyed in a fire.

World, in hounding me . . .

Poem by **Sor Juana Inés de la Cruz** translated by **Alan S. Trueblood**

The speaker questions society's values and expectations.

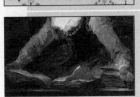

Foundations and Encounters

Over five hundred years ago, European explorers first set foot in the Americas. They encountered a rich variety of native cultures with strongly different customs, speaking about 300 different languages and living in diverse environments. For tens of thousands of years at least, millions of Native Americans had lived on the land, in small villages and in large cities, such as the Aztec capital of Tenochtitlán, the site of present-day Mexico City.

The Meeting of Two Worlds

Christopher Columbus's 1492 arrival in the Caribbean marked the beginning of European conquest and colonization of the Americas. Spain, Portugal, England, France, and the Netherlands all staked claims in the

1492
Columbus lands at Hispaniola, in the Caribbean.

1521
Cortés conquers the Aztecs at Tenochtitlán (Mexico City).

1400

1513
While in Panama, Balboa "discovers" the Pacific Ocean.

1539–41
De Soto explores the region between Florida and the Mississippi River.

Americas. At first, some Native Americans were helpful to the Europeans, but it soon became clear that the newcomers intended to take control of the land. However, firearms were not the most dangerous weapons the Europeans brought with them; they also brought new diseases that killed millions of Native Americans.

In the early 1500s, Spain conquered the great Aztec and Inca empires and claimed Mexico, most of South America, and large portions of what is now the United States. The first French settlements in New France were founded in the early 1600s by fur traders along the St. Lawrence River. Eventually, French holdings included the Great Lakes region and most of the land along the Mississippi River, which was named Louisiana.

From Colonies to a Country

The English settlers were eager to establish a colony in North America and to prevent the northward expansion of the Spanish colony in Florida. A private trading company, the Virginia Company of London, established the first permanent English settlement at Jamestown, Virginia, in 1607. In 1619, the first Africans were brought to Virginia as enslaved persons to work for white slaveholders.

The original settlers of New England were Pilgrims, Protestant reformers who wanted to separate from the Church of England. Among them was William Bradford, who helped organize the voyage of the *Mayflower*, bringing nearly a hundred people to Massachusetts in 1620. Another group who settled in New England were the Puritans, who wanted to "purify" the Church of England. The Puritans' religious beliefs influenced all

EXTEND

Think of a question you have about a topic, an event, or a person from the historical period. Then, research the answer and add it as an entry to the timeline.

1607
The English establish their first permanent settlement in Jamestown, Virginia.

1676
English settlers defeat Native Americans in King Philip's War.

1700

1620
Mayflower Pilgrims found Plymouth colony in Massachusetts.

1682
France claims the Mississippi River valley and names it Louisiana.

Pilgrims arrive at Plymouth Rock, 1620.

In 1898, a Shoshone chief named Washakie created this painting on an animal hide. The painting shows American Plains Indians on a buffalo hunt.

aspects of their lives, and their values of hard work and thrift led to financial success. The English settlements in New England and Virginia became the thirteen colonies that later formed the United States.

Native American Tales and Traditions

All Native American cultures possessed rich oral traditions. Across generations, they transmitted ideas and art through speech, storytelling, and song. Creation stories—ways to explain how the universe and humans came into being—can be found in every Native American culture. Other forms include trickster tales, dream visions, healing ceremonies, and legendary histories tracing the migration of peoples or the deeds of cultural heroes.

Tragically, much of this literature did not survive after so many Native Americans died from European diseases. The surviving works, however, show that diverse Native American groups explored common themes in their spoken literature, including a reverence for nature and the worship of many gods. Contemporary Native American writers, such as Joy Harjo, often incorporate elements of these traditional tales in their writing.

Explorers and Settlers Report Back

While Native American literature offers us a glimpse into the ways and values of America's indigenous peoples, much of our understanding of pre-colonial America comes from the first-person accounts of its early explorers, settlers, and colonists. One of the founders of Jamestown, John Smith, wrote about conflicts with Native Americans, but he also described the "New World" as a paradise with great economic potential. William Bradford, governor of Plymouth Plantation, described North America as "a hideous and desolate wilderness, full of wild beasts and wild men."

Bradford and other colonial writers were motivated by their beliefs about their role in God's plan. Their writings included historical narratives, sermons, and poems written in a generally plain style.

Anne Bradstreet was one of the first poets in the American colonies. A volume of her poetry was published in England in 1650 as *The Tenth Muse*. Some of her best work is on personal themes, such as childbirth and the death of a grandchild.

COLLABORATIVE DISCUSSION

In a small group, review the essay and timeline. Discuss which literary or historical events had the most impact and why.

Assessment Practice

Choose the best answer to each question.

1. What was North America like before the arrival of Europeans?
   - (A) It was an empty continent with abundant resources.
   - (B) It was a diverse land with more than 300 well-developed cultures with strongly differing customs.
   - (C) North America was a land recently settled by Native American groups that shared a single culture.
   - (D) North America was a continent ravaged by disease and warfare.

2. Which statement is an accurate description of Native American literature?
   - (A) It was a rich oral tradition focusing on creation stories and a reverence for nature.
   - (B) It was written in pictographs similar to Egyptian hieroglyphics.
   - (C) It contained many of the same myths and folktales that appear in European cultures.
   - (D) There was no literature because Native Americans did not have a written language.

3. We get most of our information about pre-colonial America from —
   - (A) modern-day scholars of the historical period
   - (B) elaborate written records from ancient civilizations
   - (C) first-person accounts of early explorers, settlers, and colonists
   - (D) Native American creation myths

Test-Taking Strategies

The World on the Turtle's Back

Myth by **Iroquois storytellers**

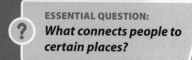

ESSENTIAL QUESTION:
What connects people to certain places?

Engage Your Brain

Choose one or more of these activities to start connecting with the myth you're about to read.

In the Beginning . . .

Think about the myths you've read. Do they recount how the world was made or why things in nature are the way they are? Do they explain human behavior or rituals? Do they teach morality or explain history? Write a list of the myths you know and what message they each convey.

Two Truths and a Lie

One of these statements about twins is false. Can you tell which one it is?

- Taller women are more likely to have twins.

- Identical twins have identical fingerprints.

- Fraternal twins can run in families, but identical twins are not genetically predetermined.

Famous Twins for Five Hundred

Famous twins are all around. Do some research to identify two famous people and their twin. Write clues in game show format and get with a partner. Take turns reading your clues and guessing the answers. Give yourselves bonus points for guessing both twins' names.

Analyze Myth

A creation myth is a particular kind of myth that describes how the universe or life began or explains the workings of the natural world. Myths often include **archetypes**—characters that represent universal examples of human nature. You will examine the twins in "The World on the Turtle's Back" and decide whether they fit the archetypes of hero and villain.

Writers of myths convey meaning by the way they develop characters and how those characters relate to the elements of the story. As you read, think about why the author presented elements of the story in this way:

- How are the twins introduced and portrayed?
- What important events contribute to their development?
- How is their conflict resolved?
- What explanations does the myth give for natural phenomena?
- Why is the setting presented the way it is? How does it change?
- What beliefs and values are reflected in the myth?

Keep track of the ways in which the elements of the creation myth are used. What does this tell you about the genre of creation myths?

Focus on Genre
↳ **Myth**

- attempts to explain the way part of the natural world works
- may include archetypes, or story elements that represent universal examples of human nature
- often expresses the values and customs of a culture

Make Inferences

An **inference** is an educated guess you make by combining information from what you read with what you already know. You can use this formula to help you determine meanings, themes, and even the values of a culture:

text evidence + prior knowledge = inference

For example, in the story it says, "Far above this unpeopled world, there was a Sky-World" (text evidence). It is widely understood that many cultures believe in an afterlife (+ prior knowledge). So a possible inference is that this "Sky-World" might be a place where the Iroquois believe they go after death (= inference). Use the chart to make inferences based on what you read:

Text evidence	Prior knowledge	Inference

Annotation in Action

Here are one student's notes about the elements of a myth. As you read, note the ways the storytellers use the elements of a myth to convey meaning.

In the beginning there was no world, no land, no creatures of the kind that are around us now, and there were no men. But there was a great ocean which occupied space as far as anyone could see. Above the ocean was a great void of air. And in the air there lived the birds of the sea; in the ocean lived the fish and the creatures of the deep. Far above this unpeopled world, there was a Sky-World. Here lived gods who were like people—like Iroquois.

The opening words suggest that this is a story of creation.

Expand Your Vocabulary

Put a check mark next to the vocabulary words that you feel comfortable using when speaking or writing.

delicacies	☐
frantically	☐
vanquish	☐
pliable	☐

Then, with a partner, write a few sentences about a creation myth you know using as many of the vocabulary words as you can. As you read "The World on the Turtle's Back," use the definitions in the side column to learn the vocabulary words you don't already know.

Background

"The World on the Turtle's Back" is an Iroquois (ĭr´ə-kwoi´) creation myth filled with conflict and compelling characters. In 1828, Iroquois author David Cusick was the first to write the story down. Today, more than 25 written versions exist.

The term **Iroquois** refers to six Native American groups that share a culture. Most of them reside in what is now New York state. They call themselves Haudenosaunee, meaning "People of the Longhouse," after the longhouses in which they lived. Between 1570 and 1600, they formed the Iroquois League and managed to remain free from European rule.

Iroquois longhouse

The World on the Turtle's Back

Myth by **Iroquois storytellers**

Notice how the storytellers introduce the twins and what you learn about them as you read.

1   In the beginning there was no world, no land, no creatures of the kind that are around us now, and there were no men. But there was a great ocean which occupied space as far as anyone could see. Above the ocean was a great void of air. And in the air there lived the birds of the sea; in the ocean lived the fish and the creatures of the deep. Far above this unpeopled world, there was a Sky-World. Here lived gods who were like people—like Iroquois.

2   In the Sky-World there was a man who had a wife, and the wife was expecting a child. The woman became hungry for all kinds of strange **delicacies**, as women do when they are with child. She kept her husband busy almost to distraction finding delicious things for her to eat.

3   In the middle of the Sky-World there grew a Great Tree which was not like any of the trees that we know. It was tremendous; it had grown there forever. It had enormous roots that spread out from

delicacy
(děl´ĭ-kə-sē) *n.* something pleasing and appealing, especially a choice food.

the floor of the Sky-World. And on its branches there were many different kinds of leaves and different kinds of fruits and flowers. The tree was not supposed to be marked or mutilated by any of the beings who dwelt in the Sky-World. It was a sacred tree that stood at the center of the universe.

4 The woman decided that she wanted some bark from one of the roots of the Great Tree—perhaps as a food or as a medicine, we don't know. She told her husband this. He didn't like the idea. He knew it was wrong. But she insisted, and he gave in. So he dug a hole among the roots of this great sky tree, and he bared some of its roots. But the floor of the Sky-World wasn't very thick, and he broke a hole through it. He was terrified, for he had never expected to find empty space underneath the world.

5 But his wife was filled with curiosity. He wouldn't get any of the roots for her, so she set out to do it herself. She bent over and she looked down, and she saw the ocean far below. She leaned down and stuck her head through the hole and looked all around. No one knows just what happened next. Some say she slipped. Some say that her husband, fed up with all the demands she had made on him, pushed her.

6 So she fell through the hole. As she fell, she **frantically** grabbed at its edges, but her hands slipped. However, between her fingers there clung bits of things that were growing on the floor of the Sky-World and bits of the root tips of the Great Tree. And so she began to fall toward the great ocean far below.

7 The birds of the sea saw the woman falling, and they immediately consulted with each other as to what they could do to help her. Flying wingtip to wingtip they made a great feathery raft in the sky to support her, and thus they broke her fall. But of course it was not possible for them to carry the woman very long. Some of the other birds of the sky flew down to the surface of the ocean and called up the ocean creatures to see what they could do to help. The great sea turtle came and agreed to receive her on his back. The birds placed her gently on the shell of the turtle, and now the turtle floated about on the huge ocean with the woman safely on his back.

8 The beings up in the Sky-World paid no attention to this. They knew what was happening, but they chose to ignore it.

9 When the woman recovered from her shock and terror, she looked around her. All that she could see were the birds and the sea creatures and the sky and the ocean.

10 And the woman said to herself that she would die. But the creatures of the sea came to her and said that they would try to help her and asked her what they could do. She told them that if they could find some soil, she could plant the roots stuck between her fingers, and from them plants would grow. The sea animals said perhaps there was dirt at the bottom of the ocean, but no one had ever been down there so they could not be sure.

ANALYZE MYTH

Annotate: In the first four paragraphs, mark words and phrases that tell you about the husband and wife.

Analyze: Explain whether the man and his wife are archetypal characters. Consider details in the text, as well as other accounts of creation you've heard or read.

frantically
(frăn´tĭ-kəl-lē) *adv.* excitedly, with strong emotion or frustration.

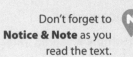

Multiple-meaning words: Mark the word *stirred* near the end of paragraph 11.

Analyze: Using context or a dictionary, what does *stirred* mean in this paragraph? Why is this definition the right one?

11   If there was dirt at the bottom of the ocean, it was far, far below the surface in the cold deeps. But the animals said they would try to get some. One by one the diving birds and animals tried and failed. They went to the limits of their endurance, but they could not get to the bottom of the ocean. Finally, the muskrat said he would try. He dived and disappeared. All the creatures waited, holding their breath, but he did not return. After a long time, his little body floated up to the surface of the ocean, a tiny crumb of earth clutched in his paw. He seemed to be dead. They pulled him up on the turtle's back and they sang and prayed over him and breathed air into his mouth, and finally, he stirred. Thus it was the muskrat, the Earth-Diver, who brought from the bottom of the ocean the soil from which the earth was to grow.

12   The woman took the tiny clod of dirt and placed it on the middle of the great sea turtle's back. Then the woman began to walk in a circle around it, moving in the direction that the sun goes. The earth began to grow. When the earth was big enough, she planted the roots she had clutched between her fingers when she fell from the Sky-World. Thus the plants grew on the earth.

13   To keep the earth growing, the woman walked as the sun goes, moving in the direction that the people still move in the dance rituals. She gathered roots and plants to eat and built herself a little hut. After a while, the woman's time came, and she was delivered of a daughter. The woman and her daughter kept walking in a circle around the earth, so that the earth and plants would continue to grow. They lived on the plants and roots they gathered. The girl grew up with her mother, cut off forever from the Sky-World above, knowing only the birds and the creatures of the sea, seeing no other beings like herself.

14   One day, when the girl had grown to womanhood, a man appeared. No one knows for sure who this man was. He had something to do with the gods above. Perhaps he was the West Wind. As the girl looked at him, she was filled with terror, and amazement, and warmth, and she fainted dead away. As she lay on the ground, the man reached into his quiver, and he took out two arrows, one sharp and one blunt, and he laid them across the body of the girl, and quietly went away.

15   When the girl awoke from her faint, she and her mother continued to walk around the earth. After a while, they knew that the girl was to bear a child. They did not know it, but the girl was to bear twins.

Annotate: Mark the phrases in paragraphs 16–18 that describe the twins' relationship.

Predict: Based on the details in these paragraphs, how do you think the twins' conflict will be resolved? Why?

16   Within the girl's body, the twins began to argue and quarrel with one another. There could be no peace between them. As the time approached for them to be born, the twins fought about their birth. The right-handed twin wanted to be born in the normal way, as all children are born. But the left-handed twin said no. He said he saw light in another direction, and said he would be born that way. The

© Houghton Mifflin Harcourt Publishing Company • Image Credits: ©PathDoc/Shutterstock right-handed twin beseeched him not to, saying that he would kill their mother. But the left-handed twin was stubborn. He went in the direction where he saw light. But he could not be born through his mother's mouth or her nose. He was born through her left armpit, and killed her. And meanwhile, the right-handed twin was born in the normal way, as all children are born.

17   The twins met in the world outside, and the right-handed twin accused his brother of murdering their mother. But the grandmother told them to stop their quarreling. They buried their mother. And from her grave grew the plants which the people still use. From her head grew the corn, the beans, and the squash—"our supporters, the three sisters."[1] And from her heart grew the sacred tobacco, which the people still use in the ceremonies and by whose upward-floating smoke they send thanks. The women call her "our mother," and they dance and sing in the rituals so that the corn, the beans, and the squash may grow to feed the people.

18   But the conflict of the twins did not end at the grave of their mother. And, strangely enough, the grandmother favored the left-handed twin.

19   The right-handed twin was angry, and he grew more angry as he thought how his brother had killed their mother. The right-handed twin was the one who did everything just as he should. He said what he meant, and he meant what he said. He always told the truth, and he always tried to accomplish what seemed to be right and reasonable. The left-handed twin never said what he meant or meant what he said. He always lied, and he always did things backward. You could never tell what he was trying to do because he always made it look as if he were doing the opposite. He was the devious one.

20   These two brothers, as they grew up, represented two ways of the world which are in all people. The Indians did not call these the right and the wrong. They called them the straight mind and the crooked mind, the upright man and the devious man, the right and the left.

21   The twins had creative powers. They took clay and modeled it into animals, and they gave these animals life. And in this they contended with one another. The right-handed twin made the deer, and the left-handed twin made the mountain lion which kills the deer. But the right-handed twin knew there would always be more deer than mountain lions. And he made another animal. He made the ground squirrel. The left-handed twin saw that the mountain lion could not get to the ground squirrel, who digs a hole, so he made the weasel. And although the weasel can go into the ground squirrel's hole and kill him, there are lots of ground squirrels and not so many

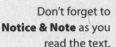

Don't forget to **Notice & Note** as you read the text.

NOTICE & NOTE

AGAIN AND AGAIN

When you notice certain images, or words being repeated in a portion of the story, you've found an **Again and Again** signpost.

Notice & Note: Mark words that associate evil, lying, and darkness with the left.

Infer: What does this tell you about beliefs the Iroquois might have had about left and right?

---

[1] **the three sisters:** Corn, beans, and squash—the Iroquois' staple food crops—were grown together. The bean vines climbed and were supported by the corn stalks, while squash, which spread across the ground and kept weeds from growing, was planted around the bean plants.

Annotate: Mark phrases in paragraphs 19–23 that describe each twin's character and behavior.

Infer: Which twin is characterized as being more admirable? What does this characterization tell you about Iroquois values?

vanquish

(văng´kwĭsh) *v.* to defeat in a contest or conflict.

weasels. Next the right-handed twin decided he would make an animal that the weasel could not kill, so he made the porcupine. But the left-handed twin made the bear, who flips the porcupine over on his back and tears out his belly.

22   And the right-handed twin made berries and fruits of other kinds for his creatures to live on. The left-handed twin made briars and poison ivy, and the poisonous plants like the baneberry and the dogberry, and the suicide root with which people kill themselves when they go out of their minds. And the left-handed twin made medicines, for good and for evil, for doctoring and for witchcraft.

23   And finally, the right-handed twin made man. The people do not know just how much the left-handed twin had to do with making man. Man was made of clay, like pottery, and baked in the fire. . . .

24   The world the twins made was a balanced and orderly world, and this was good. The plant-eating animals created by the right-handed twin would eat up all the vegetation if their number was not kept down by the meat-eating animals, which the left-handed twin created. But if these carnivorous animals ate too many other animals, then they would starve, for they would run out of meat. So the right- and the left-handed twins built balance into the world.

25   As the twins became men full grown, they still contested with one another. No one had won, and no one had lost. And they knew that the conflict was becoming sharper and sharper, and one of them would have to **vanquish** the other.

26   And so they came to the duel. They started with gambling. They took a wooden bowl, and in it they put wild plum pits. One side of the pits was burned black, and by tossing the pits in the bowl and betting on how these would fall, they gambled against one another, as the people still do in the New Year's rites.[2] All through the morning they gambled at this game, and all through the afternoon, and the sun went down. And when the sun went down, the game was done, and neither one had won.

27   So they went on to battle one another at the lacrosse[3] game. And they contested all day, and the sun went down, and the game was done. And neither had won.

28   And now they battled with clubs, and they fought all day, and the sun went down, and the fight was done. But neither had won.

29   And they went from one duel to another to see which one would succumb. Each one knew in his deepest mind that there was something, somewhere, that would vanquish the other. But what was it? Where to find it?

30   Each knew somewhere in his mind what it was that was his own weak point. They talked about this as they contested in these duels,

---

[2] **New Year's rites:** Various ceremonies to get ready for the New Year. They often included community confession of sins, the replenishing of hearths in the homes, and sacred dances, as well as the gambling ritual.

[3] **lacrosse:** a game of Native American origin wherein participants on two teams use long-handled sticks with webbed pouches to maneuver a ball into the opposing team's goal.

Don't forget to **Notice & Note** as you read the text.

day after day, and somehow the deep mind of each entered into the other. And the deep mind of the right-handed twin lied to his brother, and the deep mind of the left-handed twin told the truth.

31   On the last day of the duel, as they stood, they at last knew how the right-handed twin was to kill his brother. Each selected his weapon. The left-handed twin chose a mere stick that would do him no good. But the right-handed twin picked out the deer antler, and with one touch he destroyed his brother. And the left-handed twin died, but he died and he didn't die. The right-handed twin picked up the body and cast it off the edge of the earth. And some place below the world, the left-handed twin still lives and reigns.

32   When the sun rises from the east and travels in a huge arc along the sky dome, which rests like a great upside-down cup on the saucer of the earth, the people are in the daylight realm of the right-handed twin. But when the sun slips down in the west at nightfall and the dome lifts to let it escape at the western rim, the people are again in the domain of the left-handed twin—the fearful realm of night.

33   Having killed his brother, the right-handed twin returned home to his grandmother. And she met him in anger. She threw the food out of the cabin onto the ground and said that he was a murderer, for he had killed his brother. He grew angry and told her she had always helped his brother, who had killed their mother. In his anger, he grabbed her by the throat and cut her head off. Her body he threw into the ocean, and her head, into the sky. There, "Our Grandmother, the Moon" still keeps watch at night over the realm of her favorite grandson.

34   The right-handed twin has many names. One of them is Sapling. It means smooth, young, green and fresh and innocent,

ANALYZE MYTH

Annotate: Mark the phrases in paragraphs 32–33 that tell what happened to the left-handed twin and the grandmother.

Analyze: How does this myth explain the fact that the moon is visible mainly at night?

pliable

(plī´ə-bəl) *adj.* easily bent or shaped; easily influenced, persuaded, or controlled.

MAKE INFERENCES

Annotate: Reread paragraphs 36–38. Mark information that tells you about the right-handed twin. Then mark information that tells you about the left-handed twin.

Infer: Based on the information contained in these paragraphs, what can you infer about Iroquois customs and values?

straightforward, straight-growing, soft and **pliable**, teachable and trainable. These are the old ways of describing him. But since he has gone away, he has other names. He is called "He Holds Up the Skies," "Master of Life," and "Great Creator."

35   The left-handed twin also has many names. One of them is Flint. He is called the devious one, the one covered with boils. Old Warty. He is stubborn. He is thought of as being dark in color.

36   These two beings rule the world and keep an eye on the affairs of men. The right-handed twin, the Master of Life, lives in the Sky-World. He is content with the world he helped to create and with his favorite creatures, the humans. The scent of sacred tobacco rising from the earth comes gloriously to his nostrils.

37   In the world below lives the left-handed twin. He knows the world of men, and he finds contentment in it. He hears the sounds of warfare and torture, and he finds them good.

38   In the daytime, the people have rituals which honor the right-handed twin. Through the daytime rituals, they thank the Master of Life. In the nighttime, the people dance and sing for the left-handed twin.

?

ESSENTIAL QUESTION:
What connects people to certain places?

Review your notes and add your thoughts to your Response Log.

COLLABORATIVE DISCUSSION

With a partner, discuss what natural phenomena and other aspects of nature this myth attempts to explain. Which was the most interesting to you?

Assessment Practice

Answer these questions before moving on to the **Analyze the Text** section on the following page.

1. How does the turtle help the woman who fell from the sky?

   (A) He brings soil from the ocean floor.

   (B) He carries the woman on his back.

   (C) He breaks the woman's fall.

   (D) He makes the earth grow.

2. What happens when the twins' mother is buried?

   (A) A sacred tree grew from her head.

   (B) Man was created from her ribs.

   (C) The plants that people still use grew.

   (D) She became the light in the sky.

3. What happens to the left-handed twin?

   (A) He kills his mother and brother.

   (B) He kills his grandmother.

   (C) He becomes the Master of Life.

   (D) He becomes ruler of the underworld.

Test-Taking Strategies

Analyze the Text

Support your responses with evidence from the text.

NOTICE & NOTE

Review what you **noticed and noted** as you read the text. Your annotations can help you answer these questions.

1. **INFER** What do the Iroquois believe is different about man compared to the other beings the twins created. How do you know?

2. **ANALYZE** What characteristics and behaviors suggest that the right-handed twin is an archetypal hero? What characteristics and behaviors suggest the left-handed twin is an archetypal villain? Cite evidence from the text in the chart.

Hero archetype: Right-handed twin	Villain archetype: Left-handed twin
1	1
2	2
3	3

3. **ANALYZE** How is the conflict between the twins resolved? What does the resolution suggest about the Iroquois' view of both twins?

4. **DRAW CONCLUSIONS** What elements of the world and human nature does this creation myth explain? Cite text evidence in your response.

5. **CONNECT** Folk literature often conveys information about a people's culture. From this myth, what do you learn about the Iroquois' attitude toward nature and their view of their gods?

6. **CONNECT** What are at least two similarities that this creation myth shares with other creation myths you may have ever heard or read?

7. **DRAW CONCLUSIONS** We see **Again and Again** that the evil twin does some good, and that the good twin does some evil. Explain what you think these events could reveal about what the Iroquois believed about the nature of good and evil. Cite text evidence in your response.

Choices

Here are some other ways to demonstrate your understanding of the ideas in this lesson.

Writing
↳ Creation Myth

The fact that you are fabulous means you get to create your own world! Brainstorm and outline a creation myth that explains how your world came to be.

Ideas to consider:

- natural elements of the world that need explaining

- archetypal characters that stand for values or beliefs

- an awesome setting

- a journey or quest that a character might make

When you're ready, write your myth. Be prepared to share it with your class when it's all done.

As you write and discuss, be sure to use the **Academic Vocabulary** words.

| adapt |
| coherent |
| device |
| displace |
| dynamic |

Media
↳ Book Cover

Create a book cover for "The World on the Turtle's Back." What story elements would you include? Remember, you want to make it something people will read based on the cover alone.

1. Draw preliminary sketches that include the elements you want to feature.

2. Think about your color palette. What colors would make the story come to life?

3. Have a classmate critique your sketches and ask questions about what you've decided to include.

4. Finalize your cover and share with your classmates. If you can, display your cover around school or on a class website.

Research
↳ Comparing Creation Myths

Almost every culture has an explanation for how the world was created. Browse online to find creation myths from around the world, then choose one to compare with "The World on the Turtle's Back." Provide the name of the myth and where it comes from, then list similarities and differences between the two stories.

Expand Your Vocabulary

PRACTICE AND APPLY

Answer each question with a complete sentence to show that you understand the meaning of each vocabulary word.

1. How would you respond if you were offered a variety of **delicacies**?

2. How would you feel if you were searching **frantically** for something?

3. What might someone do to **vanquish** an enemy?

4. Would someone who is **pliable** stand firm or be willing to compromise?

Vocabulary Strategy
↳ **Multiple-Meaning Words**

Many words have more than one meaning. For example, when the word *delicacies* is used in paragraph 2 of "The World on the Turtle's Back," it means "a pleasing or appealing food choice." The word *delicacy* can also mean "fineness in appearance or construction," "frailty of bodily heath," "sensitivity to the feelings of others," or "sensitivity to small changes." When you come across a familiar word used in an unfamiliar way:

- Look at the word's context to determine its part of speech and infer the correct meaning.

- Consult a dictionary to look up all the meanings of the word.

- Compare your preliminary determination of the word's meaning to the dictionary definitions to verify the meaning of the word in context.

Interactive Vocabulary Lesson: Words with Multiple Meanings

PRACTICE AND APPLY

Each of the underlined words in the following passage has multiple meanings. For each word, state the definition of the word as it is used in the passage. Then state a definition of the word using a different meaning.

> The right-handed twin has many names. One of them is Sapling. It means smooth, young, green and fresh and innocent, straightforward, straight-growing, soft and pliable, teachable and trainable.

Watch Your Language!

Reflexive Pronouns

Reflexive pronouns are used as direct objects or indirect objects. Reflexive pronouns are used when the subject and object are the same, so they reflect on the subject of the sentence. The following words are reflexive pronouns: *myself, yourself, herself, himself, itself, ourselves, yourselves,* and *themselves.*

Reflexive pronouns can be used to provide emphasis—that the subject did something alone and not with the help of someone else. For example, *Leslie did the experiment by herself.* This sentence stresses that no one helped Leslie.

Reflexive pronouns are also used to avoid awkwardness. For example, it would be awkward to repeat the subject: *Brian made Brian a salad.* Using a reflexive pronoun eliminates the repetition: *Brian made himself a salad.*

Reflexive pronouns are used in the following ways in "The World on the Turtle's Back":

- as an indirect object to tell whom the woman said something to
- as a direct object to tell whom the woman built the hut for

> **And the woman said to <u>herself</u> that she would die.**

Interactive Grammar Lesson: Pronouns

> **She gathered roots and plants to eat and built <u>herself</u> a little hut.**

PRACTICE AND APPLY

Write your own sentences using reflexive pronouns. Use the examples from "The World on the Turtle's Back" as models. When you have finished, share your sentences with a partner.

Balboa

Short Story by **Sabina Murray**

ESSENTIAL QUESTION:
What values and beliefs shape who we are?

Engage Your Brain

Choose one or more of these activities to start connecting with the story you're about to read.

When the Old Becomes New

The colonization of the Americas resulted in a massive exchange of crops and animals between the so-called "Old World" and the American continents. Look at the plants and animals listed below. Write *E, AF, A,* or *AM* beside each one to say whether they came from Europe, Africa, Asia, or the Americas.

Alpacas	Coffee	Okra	Potatoes	Tobacco
Avocados	Corn	Peanuts	Rice	Tomatoes
Bananas	Cotton	Peppers	Sheep	Turkeys
Chickens	Cows	Pigs	Squash	Vanilla
Chocolate	Horses	Pineapple	Sugar	Watermelon

Second Thoughts

Write about a time when you had second thoughts about something you'd said or done. What about the situation made you rethink your actions or responses? Were you able to make peace with yourself and others about what happened? If so, how did you do it? If not, what would you do over?

Mirror, Mirror, on the Wall

Your eccentric great-aunt Rhiannon has given you her talking mirror that can reveal hidden aspects of your personality. You stand in front of it. What does the mirror reveal about you?

Analyze Theme

Writers of fiction often use their works to communicate insights about life or human nature called **themes**. Most themes are not directly stated; readers must infer them by looking at other elements of the work, such as characters and plot. To identify the themes in "Balboa," consider:

- **Character** How does the main character change or fail to change, and what message does this convey? What qualities does the main character possess? How do these qualities determine his or her reaction to the conflict?

- **Plot** What is the major conflict in the story? Is there a lesson to be learned from the way the conflict is resolved?

A work of fiction may have multiple themes that develop and build on each other. "Balboa" expresses a number of themes related to reality and perception, the nature of power, and what civilization means. As you read, note the different themes of the story and the details that support them.

Focus on Genre
↳ **Short Story**

- contains literary elements such as character and plot that develop the theme
- may use narrative techniques such as flashback or flash forward to build interest and suspense
- may convey more than one theme that develop and build on each other

Analyze Plot

Many stories are organized chronologically, following a tale from its beginning to its end. Sometimes, however, authors decide to present the sequence of events out of order to add interest or suspense, or to provide information that may be important to the plot. To analyze the plot of "Balboa," look at how the author uses the narrative techniques described in the chart.

Flashback	Flash Forward
A flashback is a scene that describes past events. Flashbacks can add important information to help readers understand a character and their motives, or the causes of events. You will see the protagonist in "Balboa" flash back to significant past events several times.	A flash forward gives readers a look at what will happen later in the story. A flash forward may change readers' outlook on events and characters, affect the mood, or illuminate the meaning of the work. In "Balboa," the author concludes her story with a flash forward focusing on the end of the protagonist's life.

Annotation in Action

Here are one student's notes on a theme of the story. As you read, notice how the writer develops the themes of "Balboa."

Vasco Núñez de Balboa ascends the mountain alone. His one thousand Indians and two hundred Spaniards wait at the foot of the mountain, as if they are the Israelites and Balboa alone is off to speak with God. Balboa knows that from this peak he will be able to see the western water, what he has already decided to name the South Sea. He takes a musket with him. The Spaniards have been warned that if they follow, he will use it, because discovery is a tricky matter and he wants no competition. The day is September 25, 1513.

Balboa is ambitious and arrogant— probably related to the theme.

Expand Your Vocabulary

Put a check mark next to the vocabulary words that you feel comfortable using when speaking or writing.

pristine	
protrude	
provision	
discord	
distinction	
cede	

Turn to a partner and discuss the vocabulary words you already know. Then, write a few sentences about a group of people having a disagreement using as many of the vocabulary words as you can. As you read "Balboa," use the definitions in the side column to learn the vocabulary words you don't already know.

Background

Vasco Núñez de Balboa (1475–1519) was a Spanish explorer and conquistador who first came to the Americas in 1500 as part of a voyage exploring the coast of present-day Colombia. He is most remembered for being the first European to view the Pacific Ocean (1513). This event and other facts of Balboa's life form the basis of **Sabina Murray's** story, published in her book *Tales of the New World* (2011). Murray lives in western Massachusetts, where she is on the Creative Writing faculty at the University of Massachusetts Amherst.

Balboa

Short Story by Sabina Murray

Pay special attention to the way the writer reveals Balboa's character traits.

© Houghton Mifflin Harcourt Publishing Company • Image Credits: ©Hulton Archive/Getty Images

NOTICE & NOTE

As you read, use the side margins to make notes about the text.

1   Vasco Núñez de Balboa ascends the mountain alone. His one thousand Indians and two hundred Spaniards wait at the foot of the mountain, as if they are the Israelites and Balboa alone is off to speak with God. Balboa knows that from this peak he will be able to see the western water, what he has already decided to name the South Sea. He takes a musket with him. The Spaniards have been warned that if they follow, he will use it, because discovery is a tricky matter and he wants no competition. The day is September 25, 1513.

2   Balboa ascends slowly. His musket is heavy and he would have gladly left it down below, but he doesn't trust his countrymen any more than he trusts the sullen Indians. So he bears the weight. But the musket is nothing. He is dragging the mantle[1] of civilization up the **pristine** slopes, over the mud, over the leaves that cast as much shade as a parasol[2] but with none of the charm.

ANALYZE THEME

Annotate: Mark phrases in paragraphs 1 and 2 that describe Balboa.

Infer: Based on the phrases you marked, what is a character trait that describes Balboa? What might this trait suggest about the story's theme?

pristine
(prĭs´tēn´) *adj.* pure or unspoiled.

---

[1] **mantle:** a cloak or robe worn by royalty.
[2] **parasol:** light umbrella.

Annotate: Mark details in paragraph 4 that suggest a discrepancy between who Balboa is and how he would like to be perceived.

Analyze: How would Balboa like to be viewed by others? Cite text evidence in your response.

3   Balboa is that divining line[3] between the modern and the primitive. As he moves, the shadow of Spain moves with him.

4   Balboa steps cautiously into a muddy stream and watches with fascination as his boot sinks and sinks. He will have to find another way. Upstream he sees an outcropping of rock. Maybe he can cross there. He tells himself that there is no hurry, but years of staying just ahead of trouble have left him anxiety-ridden. He would like to think of himself as a lion. Balboa the Lion! But no, he is more of a rat, and all of his accomplishments have been made with speed and stealth. Balboa places his hand on a branch and pulls himself up. He sees the tail of a snake disappearing just past his reach. The subtle crush of greenery confirms his discovery and he shrinks back, crouching. In this moment of stillness, he looks around. He sees no other serpents, but that does not mean they are not there. Only in this momentary quiet does he hear his breath, rasping with effort. He hears his heart beating in the arced fingers of his ribs as if it is an Indian's drum. He does not remember what it is to be civilized, or if he ever was. If ever a man was alone, it is he. But even in this painful solitude, he cannot help but laugh. Along with Cristóbal Colón, backed by Isabel I herself, along with Vespucci the scholar, along with the noble Pizarro brothers[4] on their way to claim Inca gold, his name will live— Balboa. Balboa! Balboa the Valiant. Balboa the Fearsome. Balboa the Brave.

5   Balboa the gambling pig farmer, who, in an effort to escape his debt, has found himself at the very edge of the world.

6   Balboa stops to drink from the stream. The water is cold, fresh, and tastes like dirt, which is a relief after what he has been drinking— water so green that the very act of ingesting it seems unnatural, as though it is as alive as he, and sure enough, given a few hours, it will get you back, eager to find its way out. He has been climbing since early morning and it is now noon. The sun shines in the sky unblinking, white-hot. Balboa wonders if it's the same sun that shines in Spain. The sun seemed so much smaller there. Even in Hispaniola,[5] the sun was Spanish. Even as he prodded his pigs in the heat, there was Spain all around, men with dice, men training roosters, pitting their dogs against each other. But here…then he hears a twig snap and the sound of something brushing up against the bushes. Balboa stands.

---

[3] **divining line:** point of separation between ideas.
[4] **Cristóbal Colón . . . Pizarro brothers:** Cristóbal Colón is the Spanish name for Christopher Columbus. Isabel I was queen of Castile (Spain) from 1474 until 1504. Amerigo Vespucci (1451–1512) was an Italian explorer and cartographer. Francisco, Gonzalo, Juan, and Hernándo Pizarro were Spanish conquistadors in Peru.
[5] **Hispaniola:** site of Columbus's first colony; the island containing modern Haiti and the Dominican Republic.

7   "I give you this one chance to turn back," he says, raising his musket as he turns. And then he freezes. It is not one of the Spaniards hoping to share the glory. Instead, he finds himself face-to-face with a great spotted cat. On this mountain, he's thought he might find his god, the god of Moses, sitting in the cloud cover near the peaks, running his fingers through his beard. But no. Instead he finds himself face-to-face with a jaguar, the god of the Indians. He knows why these primitives have chosen it for their deity. It is hard to fear one's maker when he looks like one's grandfather, but this great cat can make a people fear god. He hears the growling of the cat and the grating, high-pitched thunder sounds like nothing he has ever heard. The cat twitches its nose and two great incisors show at the corners of its mouth. Balboa raises his musket, ignites the flint,[6] and nothing happens. He tries again and the weapon explodes, shattering the silence, sending up a big puff of stinking smoke. The cat is gone for now, but Balboa knows he hasn't even injured it.

8   And now it will be tailing him silently.

---

[6] **flint:** stone used to create a spark.

© Houghton Mifflin Harcourt Publishing Company

9   There is nothing he can do about it. He should have brought an Indian with him. The Indians have all seen the South Sea before, so why did he leave them at the foot of the mountain? They have no more interest in claiming the South Sea than they do rowing off to Europe in their dug-out canoes[7] and claiming Spain. But Balboa's hindsight is always good, and no amount of swearing—which he does freely, spilling Spanish profanity into the virgin mountain air—is going to set things straight.

10   He is already in trouble. His kingdom in Darién on the east coast of the New World is under threat, and not from the Indians, whom he manages well, but from Spain. Balboa had organized the rebellion, supplanted the governor—all of this done with great efficiency and intelligence. What stupidity made him send the governor, Martín Fernández de Enciso, back to Spain? Enciso swore that he would have Balboa's head on a platter. He was yelling from the deck of the ship as it set sail. Why didn't he kill Enciso? Better yet, why didn't he turn Enciso over to some Indian tribe that would be glad to have the Spaniard, glad to have his blood on their hands? How could Balboa be so stupid? Soon the caravels[8] would arrive and his days as governor (king, he tells the Indians) of Darién will be over. Unless, Balboa thinks, unless he brings glory by being the first to claim this great ocean for Spain. Then the king will see him as the greatest of his subjects, not a troublemaking peasant, a keeper of pigs.

11   Unless that jaguar gets him first.

12   Balboa looks nervously around. The only sound is the trickle and splash of the stream that he is following, which the Indians tell him leads to a large outcropping of rock from which he will see the new ocean. Insects swoop malevolently[9] around his head. A yellow and red parrot watches him cautiously from a branch, first looking from one side of its jeweled head, then the other. Where is the jaguar? Balboa imagines his body being dragged into a tree, his boots swinging from the limbs as the great cat tears his heart from his ribs. He hears a crushing of vegetation and ducks low. He readies his musket again. "Please God, let the damned thing fire." He breathes harshly, genuflecting,[10] musket steady.

13   The leaves quiver, then part. There is no jaguar.

14   "Leoncico!" he cries out. Leoncico is his dog, who has tracked him up the slope. Leoncico patters over, wagging his tail, his great wrinkled head bearded with drool. Leoncico is a monster of a dog. His head is the size of a man's, and his body has the look of a lion—shoulders and hipbones **protruding** and muscle pulling and shifting beneath the glossy skin—which is where he gets his name. "Leoncico" means little lion.

VOCABULARY

Use Context Clues: The word *supplanted* (paragraph 10) is surrounded by other words that can help you determine its meaning.

Analyze: What does this word tell you about Balboa's motivations? Do those motivations help reveal a theme?

protrude
(prō-trōōd´) *v.* to stick out or bulge.

---

[7] **dug-out canoes:** narrow boats made by hollowing out tree trunks.
[8] **caravels:** small sailing ships with two or three masts.
[9] **malevolently:** with evil intent.
[10] **genuflecting:** bending one knee to the ground.

15   "Good dog," says Balboa. "Good dog. Good dog."

16   He has never been so grateful for the company, not even when he was hidden on board Enciso's ship bound for San Sebastian, escaping his creditors, wrapped in a sail. No one wondered why the dog had come on board. Maybe the dog had been attracted by the smell of **provisions**, the great barrels of salted meat. The soldiers fed him, gave him water. Balboa worried that Leoncico would give him away, but the dog had somehow known to be quiet. He had slept beside Balboa, and even in Balboa's thirst and hunger, the great beast's panting and panting, warm through the sailcloth, had given him comfort. When Enciso's crew finally discovered Balboa—one of the sails was torn and needed to be replaced—they did not punish him. They laughed.

provision
(prə-vĭzh´ən) *n.* food supply.

17   "The Indians massacre everyone. You are better off in a debtors' prison," they said.

18   Balboa became a member of the crew. When the boat shipwrecked off the coast of San Sebastian (they were rescued by Francisco Pizarro), Enciso had been at a loss as to where to go, and

Balboa convinced him to try Darién to the north. Once established there, Enciso had shown himself to be a weak man. How could Balboa not act? Enciso did not understand the Indians as Balboa did. He could see that the Indians were battle-hardened warriors. The Spaniards had not been there long enough to call these armies into existence. Balboa's strength had been to recognize this **discord**. He divided the great tribes, supported one against the other. His reputation spread. His muskets blasted away the faces of the greatest warriors. Balboa's soldiers spread smallpox and syphilis. His Spanish war dogs, great mastiffs and wolfhounds, tore children limb from limb. The blood from his great war machine made the rivers flow red and his name, Balboa, moved quickly, apace[11] with these rivers of blood.

19   Balboa is loved by no one and feared by all. He has invented an unequaled terror. The Indians think of him as a god. They make no **distinction** between good and evil. They have seen his soldiers tear babies from their mothers, toss them still screaming to feed the dogs. They have seen the great dogs pursue the escaping Indians, who must hear nothing but a great panting, the jangle of the dogs' armor, and then, who knows? Do they feel the hot breath on their cheek? Are they still awake when the beasts unravel their stomachs and spill them onto the hot earth? Balboa's dogs have been his most effective weapon because for them, one does not need to carry ammunition, as for the muskets; one does not need to carry food, as for the soldiers. For the dogs, there is fresh meat everywhere. He knows his cruelty will be recorded along with whatever he discovers. This does not bother him, even though one monk, Dominican—strange fish—cursed him back in Darién. He was a young monk, tormented by epileptic[12] fits. He approached Balboa in the town square in his bare feet, unarmed, waving his shrunken fist.

20   "Your dogs," screamed the monk, "are demons."

21   As if understanding, Leoncico had lunged at the monk. Leoncico is not a demon. He is the half of Balboa with teeth, the half that eats. Balboa has the mind and appetite. Together, they make one. It is as if the great beast can hear his thoughts, as if their hearts and lungs circulate the same blood and air. What did the monk understand of that? What did he understand of anything? He said that he was in the New World to bring the Indians to God. So the monk converts the Indians, and Balboa sends them on to God. They work together, which is what Balboa told the monk. But the monk did not find it funny.

---

[11] **apace:** fast enough to keep up with something.
[12] **epileptic:** caused by epilepsy, a neurological disorder.

22   How dare he find fault with Balboa? Is not Spain as full of torments as the New World? The Spaniards are brought down by smallpox at alarming rates in Seville, in Madrid. Every summer the rich take to the mountains to escape the plague, and in the fall, when they return, aren't their own countrymen lying in the streets feeding the packs of mongrels? Half of all the Spanish babies die. It is not uncommon to see a peasant woman leave her screaming infant on the side of the road, so why come here and beg relief for these savages? Why not go to France, where, one soldier tells Balboa, they butcher the Huguenots[13] and sell their limbs for food in the street? Why rant over the impaling of the Indians when Spaniards—noblemen among them—have suffered the same fate in the name of God? In fact, the Inquisition[14] has been the great educator when it comes to subduing the Indian population.

23   Why take him to task when the world is a violent place?

24   "May your most evil act be visited on you," said the monk. "I curse you."

25   The monk died shortly after that. His threats and bravery were more the result of a deadly fever than the words of a divine message. Did the curse worry Balboa? Perhaps a little. He occasionally revisits a particularly spectacular feat of bloodshed—the time Leoncico tore a chieftain's head from his shoulders—with a pang of concern. But Balboa is a busy man with little time for reflection. When the monk delivered his curse, Balboa was already preparing his troops for the great march to the west. His name had reached Spain, and the king felt his authority threatened.

26   He is the great Balboa.

27   But here, on the slope of the mountain, his name does not seem worth that much. He has to relieve himself and is terrified that some creature—jaguar, snake, spider—will take advantage of his great heaving bareness.

28   "Leoncico," he calls. "At attention."

29   Not that this command means anything to the dog. Leoncico knows "attack," and that is all he needs to know. Leoncico looks up, wags his tail, and lies down, his face smiling into the heat. Balboa climbs onto a boulder. Here, he is exposed to everything, but if that jaguar is still tracking him, he can at least see it coming. He sets his musket down and listens. Nothing. He loosens his belt and is about to lower his pants when he sees it—the flattened glimmer, a shield, the horizon. He fixes his belt and straightens himself. He stares out at the startling bare intrusion, this beautiful nothing beyond the green tangle of trees, the *Mar del Sur*, the glory of Balboa, his gift to Spain.

ANALYZE PLOT

Annotate: Mark an example of foreshadowing in paragraph 24.

Analyze: What does this example foreshadow? To what part of the story does it connect?

---

[13] **Huguenots:** French Protestants who were persecuted for their faith in the 16th and 17th centuries.

[14] **the Inquisition:** an investigation by the Roman Catholic Church to identify and punish heretics.

30   Balboa, having accomplished his goal, luxuriates in this moment of peaceful ignorance. He does not know that his days are numbered, that even after he returns to Darién with his knowledge of the South Sea, even after he has **ceded** the governorship to Pedro Arias Dávila, even after he is promised Dávila's daughter, he has not bought his safety. Dávila will see that as long as Balboa lives he must sleep with one eye open. With the blessing of Spain, Dávila will bring Balboa to trial for treason, and on January 21, 1519, Balboa's head will be severed from his shoulders. His eyes will stay open, his mouth will be slack, and his great head will roll in the dust for everyone—Indians, Spaniards, and dogs—to see.

cede
(sēd) *v.* to yield or give away.

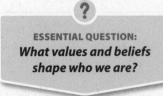

ESSENTIAL QUESTION:
What values and beliefs shape who we are?

Review your notes and add your thoughts to your Response Log.

COLLABORATIVE DISCUSSION

What words would you use to describe Balboa's character? Discuss your ideas with a partner.

Assessment Practice

Answer these questions before moving on to the **Analyze the Text** section on the following page.

1. What surprises Balboa when he drinks from the mountain stream?

   (A) a jaguar

   (B) an Indian

   (C) a thunderstorm

   (D) a Spaniard hoping to share in his glory

2. Why does Martín Fernández de Enciso dislike Balboa?

   (A) Balboa called him "weak."

   (B) Balboa led a rebellion against him.

   (C) Balboa stole money and property from him.

   (D) Balboa gave the governorship to Pedro Arias Dávila.

3. What eventually happens to Balboa?

   (A) Balboa kills Pedro Arias Dávila.

   (B) Balboa is killed by a wild animal.

   (C) Balboa goes to jail for a violent crime.

   (D) Pedro Arias Dávila executes Balboa for treason.

Test-Taking Strategies

Analyze the Text

Support your responses with evidence from the text.

NOTICE & NOTE

Review what you **noticed and noted** as you read the text. Your annotations can help you answer these questions.

(1) **ANALYZE** The story conveys the view that Balboa and the settling of the New World are bound together through statements such as "As he moves, the shadow of Spain moves with him" (paragraph 3). What theme does the story express about Balboa? What theme does it express about the New World? How are these themes related?

(2) **INTERPRET** After Leoncico surprises Balboa on the mountain, the action of the story is interrupted by a flashback. What do readers learn about Balboa from this **Memory Moment**? What theme does it suggest about the nature of power?

(3) **ANALYZE** Note the references to, and images of, dogs throughout the story. What message does the author convey through these references?

(4) **ANALYZE** What is revealed by the flash forward at the end of the story? How does this revelation affect the overall meaning of the work?

(5) **INTERPRET** Think back about the difference between who Balboa is and how he would like to be perceived. How does this contrast affect your understanding of his character?

(6) **ANALYZE** Consider what you know about plot: exposition, rising action, climax, falling action, and resolution. Mark on the plot line below where you see each of these plot points. Also fill in where there were flashbacks and flash forwards in the plot and briefly explain what you learned from the flashback or flash forward.

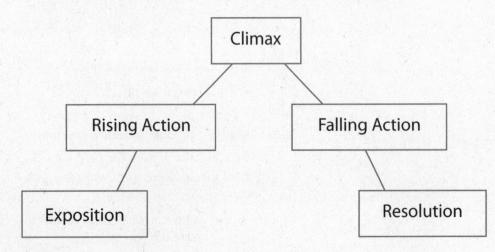

Choices

Here are some other ways to demonstrate your understanding of the ideas in this lesson.

Writing
↳ Dramatic Monologue

In Murray's story, Balboa's character stands on a ledge looking out over the Pacific Ocean, recalling all the events that got him there. Imagine that instead of thinking, he speaks out loud. Write a dramatic monologue from his point of view, expressing his thoughts as he considers this accomplishment, what it means, and what he'll do next.

Keep in mind these characteristics of a dramatic monologue:

- The structure is a speech in the form of a poem.

- The speaker—in this case, Balboa—addresses his comments to someone present but not named or heard from in the poem.

- Comments reveal the speaker's thoughts, motives, and temperament.

- To convince the unnamed listener, the speaker may lie or omit details.

When you're ready, present your monologue to your classmates. Whose Balboa is the most treacherous?

As you write and discuss, be sure to use the **Academic Vocabulary** words.

> adapt

> coherent

> device

> displace

> dynamic

Research
↳ Europeans in the Age of Exploration

In the 1400s and 1500s, European explorers set sail to gain bragging rights and pots of gold. Consider the following as candidates for being the focus of your research.

- Jacques Cartier

- Juan Ponce de León

- Hernán Cortés

- Ferdinand Magellan

- Willem Barentsz

Who were they, what did they do, and what should they not have done? Share your findings with the class.

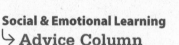

Social & Emotional Learning
↳ Advice Column

Imagine you're an advice columnist. Balboa writes to you with regrets about how he carried out his explorations. Write him back, giving him advice about being more personally aware. Use examples from the text and show him how being more aware of his feelings and his values might change how people view his actions. You may want to include these talking points:

- identifying personal strengths and weaknesses

- identifying personal values and how those values affect others

- identifying behaviors that are not respectful of others

- suggesting alternative behaviors or ways to approach a situation

Expand Your Vocabulary

PRACTICE AND APPLY

Answer each question, referring to the meaning of each vocabulary word in your response.

1. If you **cede** a toy to your younger brother, would there be **discord**?

2. If both candidates had **pristine** reputations and equal leadership experience, would it be easy to make a **distinction** between them?

3. If the children in a family took control from their parents of the grocery shopping, how would the family's **provisions** be different?

4. If the lawn has weeds **protruding** from it, is it in **pristine** condition?

Vocabulary Strategy

↳ **Context Clues**

The context of a word is the words, phrases, and sentences around it. Key words can signal a relationship between the unknown word and others that help define it.

Interactive Vocabulary Lesson: Using Context Clues

Key Words	Context Clues
such as, like, for example, including	The unknown word is followed by examples that illustrate its meaning: *We packed <u>provisions</u>, such as <u>fruit and water</u>.*
unlike, but, in contrast, although, on the other hand	The unknown word is contrasted with a more familiar word or phrase: *The tablecloth was <u>pristine</u> before dinner, <u>but it was covered with stains</u> afterward.*
also, similar to, as, like, as if	The unknown word is compared to a more familiar word or phrase: *The wad of gum <u>protruding</u> from his cheek made him look <u>as if he had the mumps</u>.*
or, that is, which is, in other words	The unknown word is preceded or followed by a restatement of its meaning: *The <u>distinction</u>, or <u>difference</u>, between the identical twins was slight.*

PRACTICE AND APPLY

With a partner, choose three unfamiliar words from "Balboa" and use context clues to define the words. Verify the meanings of the words in a dictionary, and write original sentences using the words correctly.

Watch Your Language!

Verb Tenses

Verb tense indicates the time of the action or state of being. An action or state of being can occur in the present, the past, or the future.

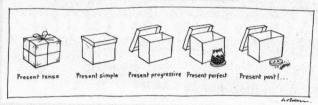

Verb Tenses		
Tense	**Use**	**Example**
Present	describe action that is happening at the present time, occurs regularly, or is constant	Balboa stops to take a drink.
Past	describe action that began and ended in the past	Balboa stopped to take a drink.
Future	describe action that will occur	Balboa will stop to take a drink.
Present Perfect	describe action that was completed at an indefinite past time or began in the past and still continues	Balboa has stopped to take a drink.
Past Perfect	describe action in the past that came before another action in the past	Balboa had stopped to take a drink.
Future Perfect	describe action in the future that will be completed before another action in the future	Balboa will have stopped to take a drink.

For the most part, "Balboa" uses present-tense verbs to tell the story. The story also uses past and future tenses to move the story around in time.

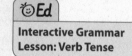

Interactive Grammar Lesson: Verb Tense

PRACTICE AND APPLY

Mark the verb and identify its tense in each sentence.

Sentence from "Balboa"	Tense
But here . . . then he hears a twig snap and the sound of something brushing up against the bushes.	
The sun seemed so much smaller there.	
Then the king will see him as the greatest of his subjects, not a troublemaking peasant, a keeper of pigs.	

Then, choose a passage in "Balboa" and rewrite it in a different tense. Share this with a partner and discuss how it affects your understanding of events in the narrative.

MENTOR TEXT

A Desperate Trek Across America

Nonfiction Narrative by **Andrés Reséndez**

Engage Your Brain

Choose one or more of these activities to start connecting with the nonfiction narrative you're about to read.

News You Can Count On

Rumor has it your favorite TV show has just been dropped, despite fantastic ratings and a devoted fan base. It can't possibly be true! Which source or sources do you trust to tell you the true story? Check all that apply.

Fan website	☐	Social media feed	☐
Evening newscasts	☐	National newspapers	☐
Tabloid newspapers or magazines	☐	Video blog	☐
A show business blog	☐	Your friends	☐

With a classmate, compare your answers. Then discuss the strengths and weaknesses of each source. Would you use the same sources to find the results of a state or national election? Why or why not?

When Life Gives You Lemons, Make Lemonade!

Most people have experienced failure of some sort. But sometimes failure can have surprising results. With a partner, talk about a time when you, or someone you know, unexpectedly benefited from what you thought was a failure.

Now What Do I Do?

Write about a time when you found yourself in strange circumstances and had to work your way through them. Were you able to achieve a positive outcome? If so, how did you do it? If not, what did you learn?

Analyze Development of Ideas

"A Desperate Trek Across America" is a nonfiction narrative, a type of informational text that chronicles the efforts of Spanish explorers of North America to recover from disaster. As the events unfold, the explorers, especially Álvar Núñez Cabeza de Vaca, are profoundly affected, as their behavior and actions will later show. As you read, track the events in the text, their impact on the explorers, and how the events and explorers shape each other.

Event	Effect
Building rafts	
Dividing the expedition to explore the coast of Florida	

Focus on Genre
↳ **Informational Text**

- includes articles, essays, and reference materials
- often describes a complex sequence of events and their effect on individuals
- may include primary source material for a particular purpose

Analyze and Evaluate Structure

Authors who describe historical events may integrate primary source material—the accounts of people who experienced the event—into their writing. In "A Desperate Trek Across America," the author structures the text by including firsthand quotations from Spanish explorers alongside his descriptions and commentary. As you read, think about what these quotations add to your understanding and how mixing primary and secondary sources adds to the text's effectiveness.

Annotation in Action

Here are notes one student took about a direct quotation in "A Desperate Trek Across America." As you read, note the author's use of quotations from primary sources and what they add to your understanding of events.

"We were in such straits that anything that had some semblance of a solution seemed good to us," wrote Álvar Núñez Cabeza de Vaca, the expedition's royal treasurer, in one of the most harrowing survival stories ever told. "I refrain here from telling this at greater length because each one can imagine for himself what could happen in a land so strange."

He is trying to find a shred of hope. The quote makes that real for me.

Expand Your Vocabulary

Put a check mark next to the vocabulary words that you feel comfortable using when speaking or writing.

straits	☐
conquistador	☐
interminable	☐
unimpeded	☐
posse	☐

Then, use the words to talk about explorers sailing the seven seas. As you read "A Desperate Trek Across America," use the definitions in the side-column to learn the vocabulary words you don't already know.

Background

From a base in Cuba, conquistadors enriched themselves and the Spanish crown by conquering the Aztec empire. This prompted Spain to seek wealth elsewhere in the Americas. In 1527, Álvar Núñez Cabeza de Vaca was second in command of a massive expedition to Florida that included five ships and 600 men. The effort ended disastrously. Two ships sank in a hurricane, and a third of the men perished or deserted. After reaching Florida in the spring of 1528, the party of about 300 men marched overland and raided the Native American settlements they encountered. **Andrés Reséndez's** chronicle begins at this point.

A Desperate Trek Across America

Nonfiction Narrative by **Andrés Reséndez**

As their expedition falls apart, Spanish explorers struggle to survive in an unknown world.

> **NOTICE & NOTE**
>
> As you read, use the side margins to make notes about the text.

Florida Panhandle, Fall 1528

1   The 250 starving Spanish adventurers dubbed the shallow estuary near their campsite the "Bay of Horses," because every third day they killed yet another draft animal, roasted it, and consumed the flesh. Fifty men had already died of disease, injury, and starvation. What was worse, after having walked the length of Florida without finding gold, those still alive had lost contact with their ships. They were stranded in an alien continent.

2   "We were in such **straits** that anything that had some semblance of a solution seemed good to us," wrote Álvar Núñez Cabeza de Vaca, the expedition's royal treasurer, in one of the most harrowing[1]

straits

(strāts) *adj.* a position of difficulty, distress, or extreme need.

---

[1] **harrowing:** referring to an experience that is extremely distressing.

survival stories ever told. "I refrain here from telling this at greater length because each one can imagine for himself what could happen in a land so strange."

Indeed, Cabeza de Vaca and the other leaders of the ill-fated venture had agreed to a desperate gamble: to trade their most effective weapons against the Indians—horses and firearms—for five makeshift vessels that might or might not be capable of carrying them to safety. Eating the horses gave them time to build the rafts. To make nails and saws, they threw their crossbows,[2] along with stirrups and spurs, into an improvised forge.

Like past **conquistadors,** Cabeza de Vaca and his men had relied on their breastplates,[3] horses, and lethal weapons to keep the Indians at bay. Such overwhelming technological advantages meant they often did not even bother to negotiate, instead simply imposing their will. By sacrificing the very tools of their supremacy, they would now have to face the New World fully exposed to its perils and hold on only by their wits.

The expedition had unraveled with frightening speed. Just months earlier, the hopeful adventurers had embarked from Cuba in four ships and a brigantine[4] and made landfall near present day Tampa Bay, intending to take possession of Florida in the name of His Most Catholic Majesty.[5] Caught up in the excitement and rush to explore, the commander rashly divided the expedition, ordering the captains to take their ships on an exploration of the coast, while the men and the horses were put ashore. They agreed to meet just a few miles north of the debarkation point. But the **interminable** and confusing coast of Florida prevented the two parties from making contact.

With their jury-rigged[6] saws they cut down trees, dragged them to the beach, lashed them together with the tails and manes of their dead horses, and fashioned sails from their tattered shirts. After five or six weeks, they slaughtered their last horse, then dragged the 15-ton rafts into the water. Fifty men crowded aboard each craft, the fifth commanded by Cabeza de Vaca. "And so greatly can necessity prevail," he observed, "that it made us risk going in this manner and placing ourselves in a sea so treacherous, and without any one of us who went having any knowledge of the art of navigation." The rafts floated only a few inches above the waterline; the waves would wash over the men as they traveled.

Little did the men on the rafts know that they were embarking on an eight-year adventure that would ultimately take their few survivors across the entire continent. After several weeks, storms separated the

---

conquistador

(kŏng-kē´stə-dôr, kŏn-kwĭs´tə-dôr) *n.* a 16th-century Spanish soldier-explorer who took part in defeating the civilizations of the indigenous peoples of Mexico, Central America, or Peru.

interminable

(ĭn-tûr´mə-nə-bəl) *adj.* seemingly endless.

ANALYZE AND EVALUATE STRUCTURE

Annotate: Mark the words and phrases in paragraph 6 that come from a primary source.

Infer: What does the primary source information add to your understanding of the explorers' situation?

---

[2] **crossbows:** weapons made by fixing a bow crosswise on a wooden base and including grooves on that base to guide the flight of the arrow.

[3] **breastplates:** pieces of armor covering the chest.

[4] **brigantine:** a two-masted sailing ship with square sails on the forward mast and a large mainsail positioned from the front to the back of the ship.

[5] **His Most Catholic Majesty:** honorary title of the king of Spain granted by Pope Alexander VI in 1494.

[6] **jury-rigged:** assembled for temporary use in an improvised way.

© Houghton Mifflin Harcourt Publishing Company • Image Credits: ©Album/Art Resource, NY

flotilla. Tormented by extreme hunger and drenched by the splashing of the waves, they were on the brink of death. "The people began to faint in such a manner that when the sun set," Cabeza de Vaca would recall, "all those who came in my raft were fallen on top of one another in it, so close to death that few were conscious." Only the helmsman and Cabeza de Vaca took turns steering the raft: "Two hours into the night, the helmsman told me that I should take charge of the raft, because he was in such condition that he thought he would die that very night." Near dawn, Cabeza de Vaca heard the surf, and later that day they landed.

8   While most of the men survived the harrowing month long passage across the Gulf, eventually washing up on the coast of what is now Texas, many more perished of exposure and hunger that winter, some even resorting to cannibalism. Fewer still withstood enslavement at the hands of the natives in the vicinity of Galveston Bay. Ultimately, only four—Cabeza de Vaca, two other Spaniards in

VOCABULARY

Foreign Words in English: English has borrowed words from many languages. The borrowed words may keep the meaning and spelling of the original word, but it's wise to check a dictionary to confirm. Mark the word *flotilla* in paragraph 7 and look up its meaning in a dictionary.

Analyze: How does the use of the word *flotilla* contribute to this account? Why might Reséndez use a foreign word here?

A Desperate Trek Across America   **45**

commanding positions, and an African slave named Estebanico—would escape their Indian masters after six years of toil. As slaves, Cabeza de Vaca and his companions were forced to cope with native North America on its own terms, bridging two worlds that had remained apart for 12,000 years or more. They lived by their wits, coming to terms with half a dozen native languages and making sense of societies that other Europeans could not even begin to fathom.

Incredibly, the four castaways used this knowledge to refashion themselves into medicine men. As Cabeza de Vaca would explain it: "we made the sign of the cross over them and blew on them and recited a Pater Noster[7] and an Ave Maria;[8] and then we prayed as best we could to God Our Lord to give them health and inspire them to give us good treatment." In one instance he revived a man who appeared to be dead. At the Indians' insistence, all four survivors performed curing ceremonies. And thus many natives came to believe that these four strange-looking beings were able to manipulate the power of nature.

This real or imagined gifts of healing enabled the four survivors to move **unimpeded,** their reputation preceding them wherever they went. Nor were their actions a mere charade to win food and respect. They believed that their curative abilities went somehow much deeper: they came to see their incredible suffering odyssey as a test to

© Houghton Mifflin Harcourt Publishing Company • Image Credits: ©MPI/Getty Images

ANALYZE AND EVALUATE STRUCTURE

Annotate: Mark words and phrases in paragraph 9 that show what the explorers did to cure people.

Evaluate: How effective is this example in showing that the explorers were adapting to their new situation?

unimpeded
(ŭn-ĭm-pēd´əd) *adj.* not delayed or obstructed in its progress.

---

[7] **Pater Noster:** a Latin phrase meaning "Our Father" that refers to the Lord's Prayer.
[8] **Ave Maria:** a Latin phrase meaning "Hail Mary" that refers to a Roman Catholic prayer.

which God had subjected them before revealing the true purpose of their existence. They viewed their sufferings as mortifications of the flesh, their beatings and extreme hunger akin to those of flagellants[9] who inflicted torment upon themselves or of monks who fasted nigh unto death.

11   Once, alone and unable to find his party's camp, Cabeza de Vaca wandered in the woods naked in dread of the approaching chill of night. "But it pleased God that I found a tree aflame, and warmed by its fire I endured the cold that night." For five days he nursed that fire, before finally finding his companions.

12   The four wanderers were no longer mere castaways; they had become explorers once again. Yet theirs was a most peculiar expedition. Four naked and unarmed outsiders were led by hundreds, even thousands, of Indians. They were fed, protected, and passed off as though prized possessions from one indigenous group to the next. They became the first outsiders to behold what would become the American Southwest and northern Mexico, the first non-natives to describe this enormous land and its peoples.

13   By the time the four reemerged from the continental interior and reached the Pacific Coast, they had been so utterly transformed by the experience that fellow Europeans could hardly recognize them.

 **NOTICE & NOTE**
QUOTED WORDS

When you notice the author has quoted someone who was a participant in or a witness to an event, you've found a **Quoted Words** signpost.

Notice & Note: Mark the quotation in paragraph 11 that tells what Cabeza de Vaca does to survive the cold night.

Infer: What does the quotation tell you about Cabeza de Vaca?

---

[9] **flagellants:** members of a Christian religious sect who publicly beat themselves with whips as an act of religious devotion and discipline.

© Houghton Mifflin Harcourt Publishing Company • Image Credits: ©MPI/Getty Images

Don't forget to Notice & Note as you read the text.

posse

(pŏs´ē) *n.* a group of civilians temporarily authorized by officials to assist in pursuing fugitives.

A **posse** of Spanish slavers[10] operating in what is now northwestern Mexico spotted potential prey: 13 Indians walking barefoot and clad in skins. On closer inspection, some of the details did not seem quite right. One was a black man. Could he be an Indian or an African emerging from the heart of the continent? Another member of the party appeared to be a haggard white man with hair hanging down to his waist and a beard reaching to his chest.

14   When Cabeza de Vaca addressed them in perfect Spanish, the slavers were "so astonished," he wrote, "that they neither talked to me nor managed to ask me anything," but bent themselves on rounding up the Indian escort. But Cabeza de Vaca and his companions would not allow it. No longer did the castaways view their companions as mere chattels,[11] the rightful prize of Christian conquest.

15   Perhaps no one understood their transformation more than the Indians themselves, who were unable to believe that Cabeza de Vaca and his three companions belonged to the same race as the slavers. The Indians had observed, he later wrote, that "we cured the sick, and they [the Spanish slavers] killed those who were well; that we came naked and barefoot, and they went about dressed and on horses and with lances; and that we did not covet anything but rather, everything they gave us we later returned and remained with nothing, and that the others had no other objective but to steal everything they found and did not give anything to anyone."

ANALYZE DEVELOPMENT OF IDEAS

Annotate: Mark what happens to Cabeza de Vaca in paragraph 16.

Analyze: As a conclusion, what do these examples add to your impression of Cabeza de Vaca?

16   Cabeza de Vaca went back to Spain, attached himself to the court of Charles V, and was able to present his ideas of a humane colonization of the New World. After years of lobbying, he was dispatched to South America, where he attempted to carry out his plans, alas with little success. He spent the last years of his life in his native Andalusia,[12] reminiscing about his adventures in another world.

---

[10] **slaver:** one who catches people to enslave them.
[11] **chattels:** enslaved persons.
[12] **Andalusia:** southernmost region of Spain.

?

ESSENTIAL QUESTION:
What does it mean to be a stranger in a strange land?

Review your notes and add your thoughts to your Response Log.

COLLABORATIVE DISCUSSION

With a partner, write a list of questions members of the Spanish court might have asked Cabeza de Vaca about the New World.

Assessment Practice

Answer these questions before moving on to the **Analyze the Text** section on the following page.

1. Why do the Spanish adventurers call the estuary near their campsite the "Bay of Horses"?

   (A) There are several herds of horses nearby.

   (B) The surrounding land is shaped like a horse's head.

   (C) They are killing, roasting, and eating their horses.

   (D) The expedition's leader raises and sells horses.

2. Why is the trip by raft so difficult for the Spaniards?

   (A) They face constant storms while traveling the Gulf.

   (B) They do not know how to navigate, and they grow weaker.

   (C) They are frequently attacked by Native Americans.

   (D) They have to travel by night for safety.

3. What does Cabeza de Vaca do after returning to Spain the first time?

   (A) He pushes for better treatment of Native Americans.

   (B) He retires and vows never to return to North America again.

   (C) He writes a report glorifying his achievements.

   (D) He argues that Spain should abandon efforts to colonize the Americas.

Test-Taking Strategies

Analyze the Text

Support your responses with evidence from the text.

NOTICE & NOTE

Review what you **noticed and noted** as you read the text. Your annotations can help you answer these questions.

1. **INTERPRET** The author includes descriptions of "makeshift vessels" manufactured using "jury-rigged" tools. How do these descriptions affect your perception of the situation?

2. **CITE EVIDENCE** In what ways were Cabeza de Vaca and the other survivors "forced to cope with native North America on its own terms"? Cite text evidence in your response.

3. **DRAW CONCLUSIONS** How does Cabeza de Vaca and the other survivors' change into medicine men relate to the other events in the text?

4. **ANALYZE** The author concludes that Cabeza de Vaca and the others "had been so utterly transformed" by their experience. What examples and evidence support this conclusion?

5. **ANALYZE** How do the **Quoted Words** from Cabeza de Vaca affect your understanding of him? Use the chart below to cite evidence and analyze the purpose of the quotes and their effectiveness.

Quotes from Text	Purpose in Text	Effective? Why or Why Not?

6. **EVALUATE** Where in the article could Reséndez have included quotes, but didn't? How would his narrative have benefited?

Choices

Here are some other ways to demonstrate your understanding of the ideas in this lesson.

Writing
↳ News Article

Cabeza de Vaca's *La relación* was a **crónica,** or historical chronicle, that narrated events in more or less the order they occurred. In the Age of Exploration, **crónicas** were the news reports of their day, even though they lacked the on-demand availability (and editability) that technology gives modern news outlets. That's where you come in! Using details from Reséndez's article, retell Cabeza de Vaca's story in the form of a modern-day news report.

Ideas to consider:

- Is this a breaking story, which will be updated frequently as more news is available?

- Is this a complete report that has been crafted over time from well-researched data?

- How many eyewitnesses will you interview, and how will you cite them?

- Is the story told from one point of view or multiple points of view?

- What text features will you include: headlines, subheads, and visual elements, such as maps?

> As you write and discuss, be sure to use the **Academic Vocabulary** words.
>
> | adapt |
> | coherent |
> | device |
> | displace |
> | dynamic |

Media
↳ Instagram Post

The explorers in Cabeza de Vaca's expedition were blown off course by a hurricane and have just landed on the shores of modern-day Florida. Create a series of Instagram posts from them that capture the novelty of the experience and their reactions to this radically different world.

Speaking & Listening
↳ Group Discussion

In a small group, discuss how you think Andrés Reséndez views his subject. Does he admire the explorers, or does he criticize them? As you discuss, consider the following:

1. the words he uses to describe the explorers and events

2. the details he includes to make his point

Use examples from the text to support your opinions. See if you can come to consensus as a group by the end of the discussion. If you can't, summarize the differences of opinion and the reasons for them.

Expand Your Vocabulary

PRACTICE AND APPLY

Mark the best answer to each question. Then explain your response.

straits	conquistadors	interminable	unimpeded	posse

1. What is someone who is **unimpeded** not likely to face?

   ○ barriers   ○ success

2. Which event is a person most likely to perceive as **interminable?**

   ○ boring lecture   ○ exciting movie

3. Which of these individuals is in dire **straits**?

   ○ first responder   ○ hurricane victim

4. Who might look to a **posse** for help?

   ○ chief of police   ○ criminal

5. Who relied on **conquistadors?**

   ○ king of Spain   ○ president of United States

Vocabulary Strategy
↳ **Foreign Words in English**

Many **foreign words** have come into the English language. Some words have kept their original spelling, while others have been modified. For example, *conquistador* is derived from a Spanish word that means "to conquer." Notice that *conquistador* begins with the same letters as the English word *conquer*. Clues like this can help you guess the meanings of foreign words and phrases. To be sure, look them up in a dictionary.

Interactive Vocabulary Lesson: Understanding Word Origins

PRACTICE AND APPLY

Define these foreign words that have come into English. Tell which language each word comes from and use each word in a sentence.

Foreign Word	Language	Sentence
conquistador	Spanish	
posse		
flotilla		

Watch Your Language!

Infinitives and Infinitive Phrases

Authors use **infinitives** and **infinitive phrases** to meet several functions in their writing. Infinitives can be used as nouns, adverbs, or adjectives. An infinitive is the base form of the verb. It is usually, but not always, signaled by the word *to*. An infinitive phrase opens with the infinitive but includes additional modifiers. Those modifiers can be just one word, as in "She hoped to finish **quickly**," or it could include multiple words, such as, "She hoped to finish **her chores quickly so she could read her book**."

- In this example from "A Desperate Trek Across America," an infinitive phrase is used as a noun. It functions in the sentence as a direct object.

> They agreed <u>to meet</u> just a few miles north of the debarkation point.

- In this example from the selection, an infinitive phrase is used as an adjective. It modifies the direct object *time*.

> Eating the horses gave them time <u>**to build the rafts**</u>.

- In this example from the selection, an infinitive phrase is used as an adverb modifying the verb *threw*.

> <u>**To make nails and saws**</u>, they threw their crossbows, along with stirrups and spurs, into an improvised forge.

It is generally not desirable to split an infinitive by placing an adverb between the *to* and the base verb form. Thus, "to wait excitedly" is preferred over "to excitedly wait."

Interactive Grammar Lesson: Infinitives and Infinitive Phrases

PRACTICE AND APPLY

Write a paragraph about Cabeza de Vaca's experience, using the examples as models. Use a mix of simple infinitives and infinitive phrases. Write one example of each type of function—noun, adjective, and adverb. When you have finished, share your sentences with a partner and compare your use of infinitives and infinitive phrases.

New Orleans

Poem by **Joy Harjo**

? **ESSENTIAL QUESTION:**
What connects people to certain places?

Engage Your Brain

Choose one or more of these activities to start connecting with the poem you're about to read.

Remember When...

Think of a time when you and your friends were talking about a shared experience and remembered it differently. How different were your accounts? Were those differences in the details or the overall experience? Why do you think that was? Discuss your thoughts and ideas with a partner.

History of the Creek

The Creek, also known as the Muscogee, are Native Americans who originally lived in what is now the Southeast. Like many other indigenous groups, they were forcibly removed from their land and relocated. Answer these questions to learn more about their story.

1. Which United States president ordered the removal of the Creek from their homeland in the Southeast?

2. Where were the Creek ordered to move to?

3. How many Creek died in a steamboat crash on the Mississippi River?

4. In what year did the forced removal of the Creek end?

5. All totaled, how many Creek were forced to leave the Southeast?

So Many Attractions, So Little Time

New Orleans boasts a fabulous tourist scene. With a small group, research things to see and do in the city. List three things you all could do if you visited, including foods you could try or festivals and attractions you could see. Share your findings with the class.

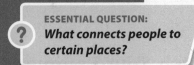

© Houghton Mifflin Harcourt Publishing Company • Image Credits: ©Ilpo Musto/Alamy

Determine Themes

A **theme** is a central idea about life or human nature. Writers usually do not explicitly state themes. It is up to the reader to infer themes from clues in the text. To determine themes, ask yourself these questions:

- What words, phrases, or ideas are repeated?
- What feelings do the imagery and figurative language evoke?
- What does the writer want me to understand?

You will have to read the entire text—often more than once—before you can determine its themes. You can use a chart to gather evidence and infer a theme.

Focus on Genre
↳ **Free Verse Poetry**

- is arranged in lines and stanzas
- has no set rhyme or rhythm
- uses figurative language and imagery to convey ideas in a few words

Evidence from the poem	Theme it supports

Analyze Figurative Language

Poets use figurative language to make readers think about ordinary things in new ways. Figurative language communicates ideas beyond the literal meanings of words. In this poem, the writer uses personification and metaphor.

- **Personification** is a figure of speech in which an object, animal, or idea is described as if it possesses human characteristics.
- **Metaphor** is a figure of speech that compares two seemingly unlike things by speaking of one as if it were the other.

When you read a poem, consider the ideas and emotions the figurative language evokes. Notice how figurative language supports the poem's themes. You can use a chart like this one to record your observations.

Example	Figurative language	Observations
"I have a memory. / It swims deep in blood, / a delta in the skin."	Personification gives "memory" the ability to "swim." Metaphor compares blood flowing through veins to water flowing through a river.	Makes me think of how powerful, active, and long-lasting memory is because water never quits flowing out of rivers.

Analyze Imagery

Writers use **imagery**—descriptive words and phrases—to re-create sensory experiences for the reader. By appealing to the senses, imagery helps readers see, hear, smell, taste, or feel what a speaker or character experiences and observes.

To analyze imagery, go back and look at the words the writer chooses to create vivid pictures. By looking at language and literary devices, you will see how the author sparks your imagination and conveys important ideas.

Annotation in Action

Here is an example of notes a student wrote about the imagery Harjo uses in "New Orleans." As you read, mark words and phrases that create vivid images.

> Near the French Market I see a blue horse
> caught frozen in stone in the middle of
> a square. Brought in by the Spanish on
> an endless ocean voyage he became mad
> and crazy. They caught him in blue
> rock, said
>   don't talk.

Caught, frozen, stone, and rock show that the horse seems trapped. Makes me feel anxious.

Background

Born in Tulsa, Oklahoma, in 1951 to a Creek father and a Cherokee French mother, **Joy Harjo** is a full member of the Muscogee (Creek) Nation. She entered college in New Mexico planning to be a painter before turning her focus to writing. Harjo has served two terms as U.S. Poet Laureate. The poem "New Orleans" is from her book *She Had Some Horses* (1983).

In this poem, Harjo brings history to life in a powerful and imaginative way. In the 1820s and 1830s, thousands of Harjo's Creek Indian ancestors were forced from their homes in Georgia and Alabama and were moved to present-day Oklahoma. Many Creek Indians traveled through New Orleans to get there. One group was put on steamboats in New Orleans. As they headed up the Mississippi, one of the boats hit a ship and over three hundred Creek Indians died in the accident.

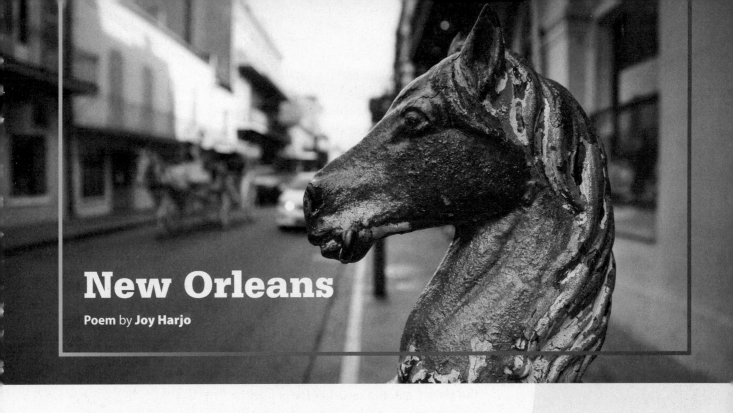

New Orleans

Poem by **Joy Harjo**

As you read, look for imagery and language that tells why New Orleans is meaningful to the speaker.

NOTICE & NOTE
As you read, use the side margins to make notes about the text.

This is the south. I look for evidence
of other Creeks, for remnants of voices,
or for tobacco brown bones to come wandering
down Conti Street, Royal, or Decatur.
5 Near the French Market I see a blue horse
caught frozen in stone in the middle of
a square. Brought in by the Spanish on
an endless ocean voyage he became mad
and crazy. They caught him in blue
10 rock, said
     don't talk.

I know it wasn't just a horse
            that went crazy.

Nearby is a shop with ivory and knives.
15 There are red rocks. The man behind the
counter has no idea that he is inside
magic stones. He should find out before
they destroy him. These things
have memory,
20   you know.

I have a memory.
            It swims deep in blood,
a delta in the skin. It swims out of Oklahoma,

2 Creeks: people belonging to a Native American group of the American South.

ANALYZE IMAGERY

Annotate: Mark a vivid image from the first four lines of the poem.

Analyze: What is the writer describing? What does this image make you think?

23 delta: the mouth of a river, where it flows into a larger body of water.

© Houghton Mifflin Harcourt Publishing Company • Image Credits: ©chatursunil/Shutterstock

New Orleans   **57**

deep the Mississippi River. It carries my
25 feet to these places: the French Quarter,
stale rooms, the sun behind thick and moist
clouds, and I hear boats hauling themselves up
and down the river.

My spirit comes here to drink.
30 My spirit comes here to drink.
Blood is the undercurrent.

There are voices buried in the Mississippi mud.
There are ancestors and future children
buried beneath the currents stirred up by
35 pleasure boats going up and down.
There are stories here made of memory.

I remember DeSoto. He is buried somewhere in
this river, his bones sunk like the golden
treasure he traveled half the earth to find,
40 came looking for gold cities, for shining streets
of beaten gold to dance on with silk ladies.

He should have stayed home.

                    (Creeks knew of him for miles
                    before he came into town.
45   Dreamed of silver blades
                    and crosses.)
And knew he was one of the ones who yearned
for something his heart wasn't big enough
to handle.
50   (And DeSoto thought it was gold.)

The Creeks lived in earth towns,
                    not gold,
        spun children, not gold.
That's not what DeSoto thought he wanted to see.
55 The Creeks knew it, and drowned him in
        the Mississippi River
                    so he wouldn't have to drown himself.

Maybe his body is what I am looking for
as evidence. To know in another way
60 that my memory is alive.
But he must have got away, somehow,
because I have seen New Orleans,
the lace and silk buildings,
trolley cars on beaten silver paths,

ANALYZE FIGURATIVE LANGUAGE

Annotate: Mark the figurative language in lines 29–31.

Analyze: How does the metaphor connect to the figurative language in the previous stanza?

37 **DeSoto:** the Spanish conquistador who explored the Mississippi River.

DETERMINE THEMES

Annotate: Beginning in line 37, the speaker shares reflections on DeSoto. Mark the lines that convey the idea that DeSoto is sorely misguided.

Infer: What message does this perspective of DeSoto's experience convey?

65 graves that rise up out of soft earth in the rain,
shops that sell black mammy dolls
holding white babies.

And I know I have seen DeSoto,
   having a drink on Bourbon Street,
70   mad and crazy
   dancing with a woman as gold
   as the river bottom.

? ESSENTIAL QUESTION:
What connects people to certain places?

Review your notes and add your thoughts to your Response Log.

COLLABORATIVE DISCUSSION

With a partner, talk about what makes New Orleans important to the speaker. Which passages reveal the speaker's attitude toward the city.

Assessment Practice

Answer these questions before moving on to the **Analyze the Text** section on the following page.

1. What inspires the speaker to travel to New Orleans?

- (A) interest in the present-day city
- (B) her ancestors' tragic experiences
- (C) distant memories from childhood
- (D) love of the Mississippi River

2. What do lace, silk, and gold represent in the poem?

- (A) beauty
- (B) memory
- (C) wealth
- (D) death

3. What do the Creeks value that DeSoto did not?

- (A) earth and life
- (B) past experiences
- (C) storytelling
- (D) gold and silver

Test-Taking Strategies

Analyze the Text

Support your responses with evidence from the text.

NOTICE & NOTE

Review what you **noticed and noted** as you read the text. Your annotations can help you answer these questions.

1 **ANALYZE** The speaker uses voices as a metaphor in lines 2 and 32. For what abstract idea are voices a metaphor? What is the significance of the voices being "remnants" and "buried in the Mississippi mud"?

2 **INTERPRET** In lines 12–13, the speaker says, "I know it wasn't just a horse / that went crazy." What does the speaker mean?

3 **INFER** Trace the development of the idea of memory through the poem. What theme about memory does the poet communicate?

4 **CITE EVIDENCE** In lines 37–42, the speaker describes DeSoto. What idea might the poet hope to convey with the color imagery that is repeated in this stanza? Use the graphic organizer to complete your response.

Color Imagery	What It Means

5 **COMPARE** How does the speaker describe DeSoto and the Creeks in lines 37–57? What do these descriptions indicate about their relationship with one another?

6 **DRAW CONCLUSIONS** In the last two stanzas, the speaker notes DeSoto "must have got away." What makes her think as she does? What can you conclude from her observations?

Choices

Here are some other ways to demonstrate your understanding of the ideas in this lesson.

Writing
↳ Literary Analysis

Reread the poem and pay special attention to all the images that evoke New Orleans. Review the notes you took as you read the poem and write an analysis about how the images in the poem convey the importance of place. Include

- an opening statement about Joy Harjo's sense of place
- details and examples from the poem that support the inferences you make about that sense of place
- an evaluation of the most effective images—why do they work?
- a conclusion that sums up your thoughts

As you write and discuss, be sure to use the Academic Vocabulary words.

- adapt
- coherence
- device
- displace
- dynamic

Speaking & Listening
↳ Presentation

In small groups, conduct a short research project to learn more about the Creek Indian Removal and its relation to the city of New Orleans. Then, reread "New Orleans" and notice how your research changes your understanding of the poem. Put together a presentation, complete with visuals, like photos or charts and graphs, to share with the class. Remember the rules of research:

1. Don't rely on just one source of information. You'll need to synthesize information from at least two sources.

2. Use reliable sources. Wikipedia is a good place to get ideas, but you're better off using sources that end in .edu or .gov. Blogs, vlogs, and YouTube are easy to search, but aren't the most accurate sources of information.

3. Cite your sources properly. Even if you decide not to quote directly, you still need to give credit to the people who gave you information. Provide a list of works cited.

Media
↳ Soundtrack

What music would you choose to accompany this poem? Create a playlist or soundtrack that includes three to five songs. At least one musician or song should be from New Orleans or represent a style of music played there.

Collaborate & Compare

Synthesize Information

Note how these authors describe encounters between Native Americans and European explorers. "Coming of Age in the Dawnland" is a secondary source, so it uses some eyewitness accounts, as well as other sources of information, to present the topic. *Of Plymouth Plantation* is a primary source, or first-hand account from someone who was there. In each, ask yourself how the author represents relations between Native Americans and Europeans and why the author chose that representation.

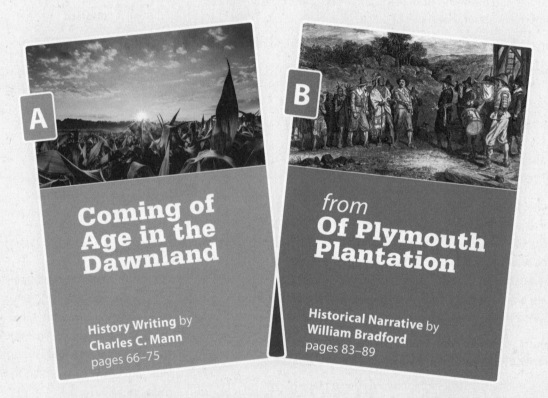

A

Coming of Age in the Dawnland

History Writing by
Charles C. Mann
pages 66–75

B

from Of Plymouth Plantation

Historical Narrative by
William Bradford
pages 83–89

When you have finished, you will get with a group to synthesize the information for a media project. You will follow these steps.

- Pick your talking points

- Fill in the gaps

- Organize your sources

- Choose your medium

- Compose

- Polish and present

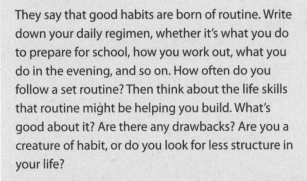
Coming of Age in the Dawnland

History Writing by **Charles C. Mann**

Engage Your Brain

Choose one or more of these activities to start connecting with the history writing you're about to read.

Day After Day

They say that good habits are born of routine. Write down your daily regimen, whether it's what you do to prepare for school, how you work out, what you do in the evening, and so on. How often do you follow a set routine? Then think about the life skills that routine might be helping you build. What's good about it? Are there any drawbacks? Are you a creature of habit, or do you look for less structure in your life?

What's in a Name?

What name would you pick to describe your most notable personality trait? What name would your friends choose for you? Get into groups and share your answers.

Well, This Could Be Interesting

You have just landed on a newly discovered planet. An inhabitant approaches. What might happen? What do you do? Think of two ways this scenario might play out, then share them with a classmate.

Determine Central Idea

The **central idea** of a text is the most important idea a writer communicates. To identify the central idea, note the details the author presents. They can be examples, descriptions, quotes from a primary source, data, statistics, or other factual evidence.

Once you've looked at the details, ask yourself how they relate to each other and what idea or ideas they support. From there, you can determine the common theme they suggest.

If it's hard to identify the central idea, try summarizing what the author says. Good summaries include only the most critical information expressed in concise terms. To summarize,

1. Highlight what you think are the main idea and supporting details.

2. Pretend to explain these ideas to someone and restate them in your own words.

3. Review your summary and omit details that aren't critical.

As you read "Coming of Age in the Dawnland," use the margins to summarize and identify the central ideas.

Focus on Genre
↳ **History Writing**

- is nonfiction writing meant to inform readers about a historical person, time, or event

- relies on facts, dates, and verifiable details to support the main ideas

- incorporates quotations from and references to experts and scholars

- uses primary sources to provide authenticity

- may use graphic features such as maps and photographs

Analyze Language

Effective writers rely on style elements like **word choice**, **tone,** and **imagery** to present their ideas. The chart below gives examples of how Mann uses language to achieve his purpose.

Word Choice	Tone	Imagery
Mann uses specialized vocabulary from the social sciences. For example, *tripartite alliance* is a political term for an agreement between three groups. He also uses Native American words like *wetu* when English words don't exist.	Mann sets his tone using words with **connotations**, or associated feelings. When he describes bedtime inside a Native American home, he uses pleasant words like *firelight* and *lullaby* to depict the scene inside the *wetu*.	Mann's descriptions bring a battle scene to life: "flash of black-and-yellow-striped bows behind trees, hiss and whip of stone-tipped arrows through the air." In this passage, the reader can "see" and "hear" the battle taking place.

As you read "Coming of Age in the Dawnland," ask yourself these questions to assess the effectiveness of Mann's language.

- How do words and phrases convey the writer's attitude toward the topic?

- How does he appeal to the readers' senses?

Annotation in Action

Here are one student's notes about the author's language in "Coming of Age in the Dawnland." As you read, note why you think Mann uses technical terms, connotations, and imagery as he describes Native American life.

Consider Tisquantum, the "friendly Indian" of the textbook. More than likely Tisquantum was not the name he was given at birth. In that part of the Northeast, *tisquantum* referred to rage, especially the rage of *manitou*, the world-suffusing spiritual power at the heart of coastal Indians' religious beliefs. When Tisquantum approached the Pilgrims and identified himself by that sobriquet, it was as if he had stuck out his hand and said, Hello, I'm the Wrath of God. No one would lightly adopt such a name in contemporary Western society. Neither would anyone in seventeenth-century indigenous society. Tisquantum was trying to project something.

Mann uses terms from Native American religion. Because he knows what these words mean, he sounds like an expert. I feel like I can trust his information.

Expand Your Vocabulary

Put a check mark next to the vocabulary words that you feel comfortable using when speaking or writing.

project	☐
settlement	☐
regimen	☐
defection	☐
stoically	☐

Then, use the words to talk about a time you set yourself a goal that was challenging to achieve. As you read "Coming of Age in the Dawnland," use the definitions in the side column to learn the vocabulary words you don't already know.

Background

In his 2005 book, *1491: New Revelations of the Americas Before Columbus*, science journalist **Charles C. Mann** (b. 1955) reviews and synthesizes the work of recent scholars who have studied early Native American societies. Christopher Columbus's voyage to the Caribbean in 1492 marked the beginning of contact between Europeans and native people in the Americas. By 1620 Native Americans in coastal New England had been trading on a limited basis with Europeans for about a hundred years. The man named Tisquantum in this excerpt from Mann's book is the person whom William Bradford called Squanto.

Coming of Age in the Dawnland

History Writing by **Charles C. Mann**

N NOTICE & NOTE

As you read, use the side margins to make notes about the text.

When European settlers arrived in the Americas, they discovered sophisticated Native American societies.

1   Consider Tisquantum, the "friendly Indian" of the textbook. More than likely Tisquantum was not the name he was given at birth. In that part of the Northeast, *tisquantum* referred to rage, especially the rage of *manitou*, the world-suffusing spiritual power at the heart of coastal Indians' religious beliefs. When Tisquantum approached the Pilgrims and identified himself by that sobriquet,[1] it was as if he had stuck out his hand and said, Hello, I'm the Wrath of God. No one would lightly adopt such a name in contemporary Western society. Neither would anyone in seventeenth-century indigenous society. Tisquantum was trying to **project** something.

project
(prə-jĕkt´) *v.* to communicate or put forth.

---
[1] **sobriquet** (sō´brĭ-kā´): nickname.

2   Tisquantum was not an Indian. True, he belonged to that category of people whose ancestors had inhabited the Western Hemisphere for thousands of years. And it is true that I refer to him as an Indian, because the label is useful shorthand; so would his descendants, and for much the same reason. But "Indian" was not a category that Tisquantum himself would have recognized, any more than the inhabitants of the same area today would call themselves "Western Hemisphereans." Still less would Tisquantum have claimed to belong to "Norumbega," the label by which most Europeans then referred to New England. ("New England" was coined only in 1616.) As Tisquantum's later history made clear, he regarded himself first and foremost as a citizen of Patuxet, a shoreline **settlement** halfway between what is now Boston and the beginning of Cape Cod.

3   Patuxet was one of the dozen or so settlements in what is now eastern Massachusetts and Rhode Island that comprised² the Wampanoag confederation. In turn, the Wampanoag were part of a tripartite alliance with two other confederations: the Nauset, which comprised some thirty groups on Cape Cod; and the Massachusett, several dozen villages clustered around Massachusetts Bay. All of these people spoke variants of Massachusett, a member of the Algonquian language family, the biggest in eastern North America at the time. (Massachusett thus was the name both of a language and of one of the groups that spoke it.) In Massachusett, the name for the New England shore was the Dawnland, the place where the sun rose. The inhabitants of the Dawnland were the People of the First Light. . . .

4   Tucked into the great sweep of Cape Cod Bay, Patuxet sat on a low rise above a small harbor, jigsawed by sandbars and shallow enough that children could walk from the beach hundreds of yards into the water before the waves went above their heads. To the west, maize hills marched across the sandy hillocks³ in parallel rows. Beyond the fields, a mile or more away from the sea, rose a forest of oak, chestnut, and hickory, open and park-like, the underbrush kept down by expert annual burning. "Pleasant of air and prospect," as one English visitor described the area, Patuxet had "much plenty both of fish and fowl every day in the year." Runs of spawning Atlantic salmon, shortnose sturgeon, striped bass, and American shad annually filled the harbor. But the most important fish harvest came in late spring, when the herring-like alewives swarmed the fast, shallow stream that cut through the village. So numerous were the fish, and so driven, that when mischievous boys walled off the stream with stones the alewives would leap the barrier—silver bodies gleaming in the sun—and proceed upstream.

DETERMINE CENTRAL IDEA

Annotate: Mark words and phrases in paragraph 2 that indicate the author is presenting new or surprising information.

Infer: What central idea does the new information suggest or support?

settlement
(sĕt´l-mənt) *n.* a small community in a sparsely populated area.

ANALYZE LANGUAGE

Annotate: Mark words with positive connotations in the first five lines of paragraph 4.

Evaluate: What feeling about Patuxet do these words create?

---

² **comprised:** made up of.
³ **hillocks:** small hills.

Annotate: Mark places on the map that correspond to places mentioned in the text.

Infer: What does the map suggest the main idea could be? Why would the author include it?

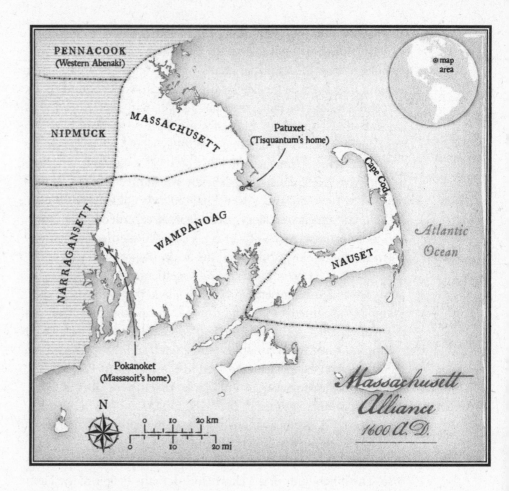

Massachusett Alliance, 1600 A.D.

DETERMINE CENTRAL IDEA

Annotate: Mark examples in paragraph 5 that describe English reactions to Patuxet homes.

Analyze: What type of source does Mann use to provide these reactions? Why are these sources important for developing a main idea?

5   Tisquantum's childhood *wetu* (home) was formed from arched poles lashed together into a dome that was covered in winter by tightly woven rush mats and in summer by thin sheets of chestnut bark. A fire burned constantly in the center, the smoke venting through a hole in the center of the roof. English visitors did not find this arrangement peculiar; chimneys were just coming into use in Britain, and most homes there, including those of the wealthy, were still heated by fires beneath central roof holes. Nor did the English regard the Dawnland *wetu* as primitive; its multiple layers of mats, which trapped insulating layers of air, were "warmer than our English houses," sighed the colonist William Wood. The *wetu* was less leaky than the typical English wattle-and-daub house, too. Wood did not conceal his admiration for the way Indian mats "deny entrance to any drop of rain, though it come both fierce and long."

6   Around the edge of the house were low beds, sometimes wide enough for a whole family to sprawl on them together; usually raised about a foot from the floor, platform-style; and always piled with mats and furs. Going to sleep in the firelight, young Tisquantum

would have stared up at the diddering[4] shadows of the hemp bags and bark boxes hanging from the rafters. Voices would skirl[5] up in the darkness: one person singing a lullaby, then another person, until everyone was asleep. In the morning, when he woke, big, egg-shaped pots of corn-and-bean mash would be on the fire, simmering with meat, vegetables, or dried fish to make a slow-cooked dinner stew. Outside the *wetu* he would hear the cheerful thuds of the large mortars and pestles[6] in which women crushed dried maize into *nokake*, a flour-like powder "so sweet, toothsome, and hearty," colonist Gookin wrote, "that an Indian will travel many days with no other but this meal." Although Europeans bemoaned the lack of salt in Indian cuisine, they thought it nourishing. According to one modern reconstruction, Dawnland diets at the time averaged about 2,500 calories a day, better than those usual in famine-racked Europe.

7   Pilgrim writers universally reported that Wampanoag families were close and loving—more so than English families, some thought. Europeans in those days tended to view children as moving straight from infancy to adulthood around the age of seven, and often thereupon sent them out to work. Indian parents, by contrast, regarded the years before puberty as a time of playful development, and kept their offspring close by until marriage. (Jarringly, to the contemporary eye, some Pilgrims interpreted this as sparing the rod.) Boys like Tisquantum explored the countryside, swam in the ponds at the south end of the harbor, and played a kind of soccer with a small leather ball; in the summer and fall they camped out in huts in the fields, weeding the maize and chasing away birds. Archery practice began at age two. By adolescence boys would make a game of shooting at each other and dodging the arrows.

8   The primary goal of Dawnland education was molding character. Men and women were expected to be brave, hardy, honest, and uncomplaining. Chatterboxes and gossips were frowned upon. "He that speaks seldom and opportunely, being as good as his word, is the only man they love," Wood explained. Character formation began early, with family games of tossing naked children into the snow. (They were pulled out quickly and placed next to the fire, in a practice reminiscent of Scandinavian saunas.) When Indian boys came of age, they spent an entire winter alone in the forest, equipped only with a bow, a hatchet, and a knife. These methods worked, the awed Wood reported. "Beat them, whip them, pinch them, punch them, if [the Indians] resolve not to flinch for it, they will not."

9   Tisquantum's **regimen** was probably tougher than that of his friends, according to Salisbury, the Smith College historian, for it seems that he was selected to become a *pniese*, a kind of counselor-bodyguard to the sachem. To master the art of ignoring pain, future *pniese* had to subject themselves to such miserable

© Houghton Mifflin Harcourt Publishing Company

ANALYZE LANGUAGE

Annotate: Mark words and images in paragraphs 8–9 that have negative connotations.

Analyze: How do these words support the idea that "Tisquantum's regimen was probably tougher than that of his friends"?

regimen
(rĕj´ə-mən) *n.* a system or organized routine of behavior.

---

[4] **diddering:** trembling.
[5] **skirl:** make a high-pitched sound, like bagpipes.
[6] **mortars and pestles:** bowl-shaped containers and blunt tools for grinding and crushing.

The exterior of a *wetu*

VOCABULARY

Specialized Vocabulary: The word *pniese* (paragraph 9) is a Native American word. You can use the words around it to get the meaning, or you can look it up in a dictionary.

Analyze: Mann uses *pniese* instead of the English translations, *advisor* or *bodyguard*. Why would using the Native American term help support Mann's central idea?

experiences as running barelegged through brambles. And they fasted often, to learn self-discipline. After spending their winter in the woods, *pniese* candidates came back to an additional test: drinking bitter gentian juice until they vomited, repeating this bulimic process over and over until, near fainting, they threw up blood.

10   Patuxet, like its neighboring settlements, was governed by a sachem, who upheld the law, negotiated treaties, controlled foreign contacts, collected tribute, declared war, provided for widows and orphans, and allocated farmland when there were disputes over it. (Dawnlanders lived in a loose scatter, but they knew which family could use which land—"very exact and punctuall," Roger Williams, founder of Rhode Island colony, called Indian care for property lines.) Most of the time, the Patuxet sachem owed fealty[7] to the great sachem

---

[7] **fealty:** obedient loyalty.

The interior of a *wetu*

in the Wampanoag village to the southwest, and through him to
the sachems of the allied confederations of the Nauset in Cape Cod
and the Massachusett around Boston. Meanwhile, the Wampanoag
were rivals and enemies of the Narragansett and Pequots to the west
and the many groups of Abenaki to the north. As a practical matter,
sachems had to gain the consent of their people, who could easily
move away and join another sachemship. Analogously, the great
sachems had to please or bully the lesser, lest by the **defection** of
small communities they lose stature.

    Sixteenth-century New England housed 100,000 people or
more, a figure that was slowly increasing. Most of those people lived
in shoreline communities, where rising numbers were beginning
to change agriculture from an option to a necessity. These bigger
settlements required more centralized administration; natural
resources like good land and spawning streams, though not scarce,
now needed to be managed. In consequence, boundaries between
groups were becoming more formal. Sachems, given more power

defection
(dē-fĕk´shŭn) *n.* the abandonment
of one social or political group in
favor of another.

11

Ground maize used to make *nokake*

and more to defend, pushed against each other harder. Political tensions were constant. Coastal and riverine New England, according to the archaeologist and ethnohistorian Peter Thomas, was "an ever-changing collage of personalities, alliances, plots, raids and encounters which involved every Indian [settlement]."

12   Armed conflict was frequent but brief and mild by European standards. The *casus belli*[8] was usually the desire to avenge an insult or gain status, not the wish for conquest. Most battles consisted of lightning guerrilla raids by ad hoc companies in the forest: flash of black-and-yellow-striped bows behind trees, hiss and whip of stone-tipped arrows through the air, eruption of angry cries. Attackers slipped away as soon as retribution had been exacted. Losers quickly conceded their loss of status. Doing otherwise would have been like failing to resign after losing a major piece in a chess tournament—a social irritant, a waste of time and resources. Women and children

 NOTICE & NOTE
WORD GAPS

When you notice vocabulary that is unfamiliar—for example, a rare or technical word, or a discipline-specific word, you've found a **Word Gaps** signpost.

Notice & Note: Mark the foreign phrase the author uses in the second sentence of paragraph 12.

Infer: What clues in the sentence help you figure out the meaning of the phrase? Explain.

---

[8] ***casus belli*** (kā´səs bĕl´ī): Latin: cause for war.

© Houghton Mifflin Harcourt Publishing Company • Image Credits: ©dani3315/Getty Images

stoically

(stō´ ĭk-lē) *adv.* without showing emotion or feeling.

ANALYZE LANGUAGE

Annotate: Mark words in paragraph 13 that describe the contrast between life inside and outside the settlement.

Predict: Given this contrast, what is suggested by the final sentence of the selection?

were rarely killed, though they were sometimes abducted and forced to join the winning group. Captured men were often tortured (they were admired, though not necessarily spared, if they endured the pain **stoically**). Now and then, as a sign of victory, slain foes were scalped, much as British skirmishes with the Irish sometimes finished with a parade of Irish heads on pikes. In especially large clashes, adversaries might meet in the open, as in European battlefields, though the results, Roger Williams noted, were "farre less bloudy, and devouring then the cruell Warres of Europe." Nevertheless, by Tisquantum's time defensive palisades[9] were increasingly common, especially in the river valleys.

13   Inside the settlement was a world of warmth, family, and familiar custom. But the world outside, as Thomas put it, was "a maze of confusing actions and individuals fighting to maintain an existence in the shadow of change."

14   And that was before the Europeans showed up.

---

[9] **defensive palisades:** fortified walls of tall stakes.

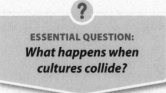

ESSENTIAL QUESTION:
What happens when cultures collide?

Review your notes and add your thoughts to your Response Log.

COLLABORATIVE DISCUSSION

With a partner, discuss what impressed you most about life in Patuxet, and why.

Assessment Practice

Answer these questions before moving on to the **Analyze the Text** section on the following page.

1. Why does Mann begin the selection with a discussion of Tisquantum?

   (A) It serves to introduce the topic of Wampanoag culture at Patuxet.

   (B) It gives important details about the way the Wampanoag lived at Patuxet.

   (C) It suggests a reason that the Pilgrims continually failed to understand Wampanoag culture.

   (D) It provides background information on why the Pilgrims traveled from Europe and encountered Wampanoag culture.

2. Why was Patuxet called the Dawnland?

   (A) The Pilgrims called the New England shoreline the Dawnland.

   (B) The Pilgrims called their own settlement in New England the Dawnland.

   (C) In the language of the Wampanoag, the New England shoreline was called the Dawnland.

   (D) In the language of the Wampanoag, the Pilgrim settlement in New England was called the Dawnland.

3. How does Mann characterize life at Patuxet?

   (A) difficult and harsh

   (B) peaceful and civilized

   (C) unorganized and chaotic

   (D) primitive and violent

☺Ed
Test-Taking Strategy

Analyze the Text

Support your responses with evidence from the text.

NOTICE & NOTE

Review what you **noticed and noted** as you read the text. Your annotations can help you answer these questions.

1. **ANALYZE** Note sensory details Mann uses in paragraph 4 to describe life in Patuxet at the end of the 16th century. What is the purpose of these details? What impression of the community does this use of imagery create?

2. **SYNTHESIZE** Review instances in which Mann cites evidence from European primary sources from the 17th century. How does Mann's use of the primary texts convey his view of Patuxet society? Cite text evidence in your response.

Synthesis		
Source Quotes	**My Analysis of the Quotes**	**Overall View of Patuxet Society**
	+	=

3. **DRAW CONCLUSIONS** What central idea about Native American societies in the Dawnland is communicated in this excerpt? Explain.

4. **EVALUATE** What do you think was Mann's overall purpose for writing this text? Cite reasons and evidence in your answer.

5. **ANALYZE** In paragraph 6, Mann creates a **Word Gap** by describing *nokake* as "a flour-like powder." What purpose might he want to achieve by comparing a Native American food with one that is commonly known today?

6. **ANALYZE** What details support the idea that Native Americans in 16th-century New England lived in a world that was "a maze of confusing actions and individuals fighting to maintain an existence in the shadow of change?"

Choices

Here are some other ways to demonstrate your understanding of the ideas in this lesson.

As you write and discuss, be sure to use the Academic Vocabulary words.

adapt

coherent

device

displace

dynamic

Writing
↳ Letter to the Author

Write a letter to Charles C. Mann and let him know what you thought of this excerpt from his book. Comment on what you found particularly interesting or memorable. Did he succeed in making his subject engaging or relevant to you? If not, what could he have done differently? As you write, think about the following aspects of his writing:

- the descriptive language and vocabulary
- the details and examples he included
- the structure of his chapter
- the conclusions he drew about Wampanoag life

Research
↳ Historical Foods

In a small group, find recipes for both a meal that a Pilgrim might have cooked and one that a Native American might have prepared. Compare ingredients and calorie counts—which one appeals to you more? If you need help finding recipes, use the following keywords:

Smithsonian Magazine, Smithsonian National Museum of the American Indian, North American indigenous cooking, the Sioux Chef, Plimoth Patuxet, 17th-century English recipes

Media
↳ Social Media Posts

Tisquantum has begun his training to become a *pniese*. Create a series of social media posts that he would make as he goes through the rigorous training regimen to become a counselor and bodyguard to his sachem. Use details from Mann's account to form the basis of the posts.

Expand Your Vocabulary

PRACTICE AND APPLY

Use complete sentences to answer each question, showing that you understand the meaning of each vocabulary word.

1. When Native Americans remained unphased by torture, what did they hope to **project?**

2. Why would a sachem worry about the **defection** of a small **settlement?**

3. Why did young Wampanoags have to endure their training **regimen stoically?**

Vocabulary Strategy:
↳ **Specialized Vocabulary**

Mann's writing cites a variety of sources. For example, he quotes an archaeologist and ethnohistorian, recounts observations from Pilgrim writers, and uses words and phrases from other languages. Many terms he uses are words specific to a particular topic, or **specialized vocabulary.** The word *settlement,* for example, is a word you may know, but here it's used in a specialized sense: "a small community in a sparsely populated area."

The following strategies can help you understand specialized vocabulary:

- Use a dictionary. If a text is about a topic with which you are unfamiliar (for example, *volcanology*, the study of volcanoes), expect to encounter specialized vocabulary that you will need to look up.

- Try to guess the meaning. Use context clues, including the word's part of speech and its use in the sentence, to help determine the meaning. Very often, specialized vocabulary will be defined in the text for readers.

- For technical words, get more specific information in a specialized reference, such as an atlas or the glossary in a book on a specialized topic.

☺Ed
Interactive Vocabulary Lesson: Specialized Vocabulary

PRACTICE AND APPLY

Review "Coming of Age in the Dawnland" to find the following terms. Identify context clues for each term's meaning. Then complete the chart.

Word	Context Clues	Meaning
tripartite alliance		
sachem		
ad hoc		

Watch Your Language!

Dependent Clauses

All **clauses** contain a subject and a verb. A **dependent** or **subordinate clause** depends on, or is subordinate to, an independent clause and cannot stand alone. Using dependent clauses skillfully allows Charles C. Mann to vary the **syntax,** or arrangement of words, of his sentences.

Consider these examples from "Coming of Age in the Dawnland."

> **And it is true that I refer to him as an Indian, <u>because the label is useful shorthand</u> . . . .**
> **<u>Although Europeans bemoaned the lack of salt in Indian cuisine,</u> they thought it nourishing.**

In each of these complex sentences, the dependent clause begins with a **subordinating conjunction** (*because* and *although*). The conjunction reveals a relationship between the two clauses. The word *because* indicates a cause-and-effect relationship between two factors. *Although* indicates a concession or exception to the point that Mann makes. Using subordinating conjunctions allows Mann to make nuanced and detailed arguments appropriate to his topic. It also allows him to create a varied rhythm in his prose, making his text more engaging and easier to read.

😊 **Ed**

**Interactive Grammar Lesson:
Kinds of Clauses**

This chart shows some common subordinating conjunctions and the relationships they signal.

Type of Relationship	Subordinating Conjunctions
Causal (i.e., making something happen)	because, since
Concession/Contrast	although, as, as much as, than, though, while
Place	where, wherever
Purpose	in order that, so that, that
Time	after, as, as long as, as soon as, before, since, until, when, whenever, while

PRACTICE AND APPLY

Find five sentences in the reading that have dependent clauses and write them down. Mark the subordinating conjunction, if there is one, and label the type of relationship between the two clauses.

© Houghton Mifflin Harcourt Publishing Company

from **Of Plymouth Plantation**

Historical Narrative by **William Bradford**

Engage Your Brain

Choose one or more of these activities to start connecting with the historical narrative you're about to read.

Merry Happy Whatever!

With your classmates, share the words and ideas you associate with celebrations and marking special occasions. Find images to represent those words and ideas and use them to make a collage. Display your finished art in the classroom.

Pilgrim v. Puritan

You might think the terms are synonymous, but Pilgrims and Puritans had rather different beliefs. Do some research and write down five differences between the two groups.

First Impressions

Look at the image below and write down details that grab your attention. Does anything strike you as odd or compelling? What overall impression are you left with?

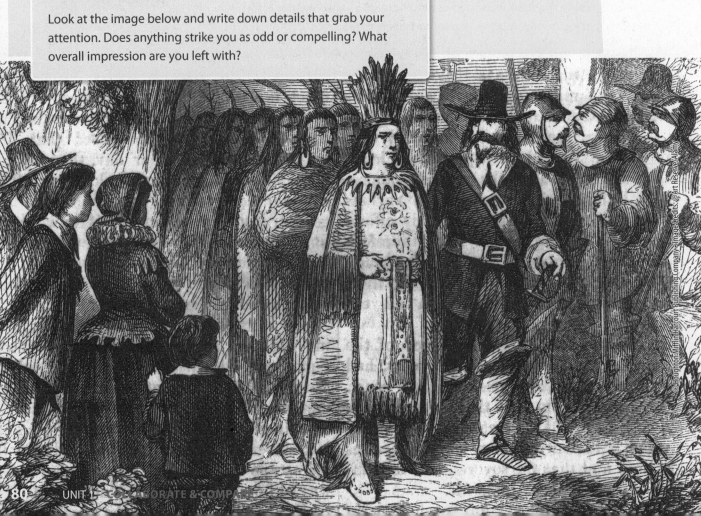

Analyze Primary Sources

Anyone interested in the past will look to **primary sources,** or letters, diaries, or other written accounts from people who either participated in or witnessed certain events. To better understand these sources, it helps to determine why the author wrote about the events in the first place.

If an author writes to inform, entertain, express beliefs or feelings, or persuade, that is the **author's purpose**. To analyze an author's purpose, consider

- a text's **genre,** which may provide clues to the author's overall purpose. *Of Plymouth Plantation* is a historical narrative—a text about real past events.

- a text's intended **audience,** or the people who will read it, which suggests the author's reason for writing. *Of Plymouth Plantation* includes the Mayflower Compact and was probably intended for future generations as a document of historical significance.

- the author's attitude toward the topic, or **tone.** Note Bradford's feelings about people and events to determine the tone.

Focus on Genre
↳ **Historical Narrative**

- tells a true story about events that happened in the past

- is a narrative text that relates events in chronological order, or the order in which they happened

- may be considered a **primary source** if the author observed the events personally

Determine Central Idea

Central ideas are sometimes stated directly in an introduction or conclusion, but more often are implied. The reader has to look at the details and logically conclude what the central idea is. Effective supporting details explain the central idea and clarify it. Depending on the type of text you're reading, you may find

- detailed descriptions that appeal to the senses

- domain-specific vocabulary that precisely names objects or phenomena

- data, statistics, or other facts; expert quotes

- personal observations and experiences; different perspectives

- explanations that clarify or emphasize significance

- transition words and phrases, such as *for example*, *in addition*, *first*, *next*, *as a result*

As you read *Of Plymouth Plantation*, use the chart to keep track of the details you think support Bradford's main ideas.

Details in the Text	Types of Detail	Ideas They Support

Annotation in Action

Here are the notes a student took on the types of detail in *Of Plymouth Plantation*.

. . . but Squanto continued with them and was their interpreter and was a special instrument sent of God for their good beyond their expectation. He directed them how to set their corn, where to take fish, and to procure other commodities, and was also their pilot to bring them to unknown places for their profit, and never left them till he died.

These details explain how Squanto was really helpful to the colonists. The main idea could be that Squanto was the most valuable ally they had.

Expand Your Vocabulary

Put a check mark next to the vocabulary words that you feel comfortable using when speaking or writing.

patent	☐
clave	☐
calamity	☐
sundry	☐
divers	☐

Then, use the words to talk about the different types of experiences you think the Pilgrims had. As you read *Of Plymouth Plantation*, use the definitions in the side column to learn the vocabulary words you don't already know.

Background

Born in England, **William Bradford** (1590–1657) became involved in the Protestant Reformation while still a boy. He joined the Puritans, reformers who wanted to purify the Church of England and eventually separated from it. With other Puritans, he migrated to Holland in search of religious freedom. He helped organize the journey on the *Mayflower* in 1620 that brought about 100 people—half of them his fellow "Pilgrims"—to the New World. His *History of Plymouth Plantation, 1620–1647* describes this journey and provides a glimpse of the settlers' life in what became New England.

from

Of Plymouth Plantation

Historical Narrative by **William Bradford**

NOTICE & NOTE
As you read, use the side margin to make notes about the text.

The first colonists and Native Americans negotiate a peaceful relationship over time.

The Second Book

1   The rest of this history (if God give me life and opportunity) I shall, for brevity's sake, handle by way of annals, noting only the heads of principal things, and passages as they fell in order of time, and may seem to be profitable to know or to make use of. And this may be as the Second Book.

Chapter XI

The Remainder of Anno 1620
[The Mayflower Compact]

2   I shall a little return back, and begin with a combination made by them before they came ashore; being the first foundation of their government in this place. Occasioned partly by the discontented and

☺Ed
Close Read Screencast
Listen to a modeled close read of this text.

mutinous[1] speeches that some of the strangers amongst them had let fall from them in the ship: That when they came ashore they would use their own liberty, for none had power to command them, the **patent** they had being for Virginia and not for New England, which belonged to another government, with which the Virginia Company had nothing to do. And partly that such an act by them done, this their condition considered, might be as firm as any patent, and in some respects more sure.

The form was as followeth:
In the Name of God, Amen.

3   We whose names are underwritten, the loyal subjects of our dread Sovereign Lord King James, by the Grace of God of Great Britain, France, and Ireland King, Defender of the Faith, etc.

4   Having undertaken, for the Glory of God and advancement of the Christian Faith and Honour of our King and Country, a Voyage to plant the First Colony in the Northern Parts of Virginia, do by these presents solemnly and mutually in the presence of God and one of another, Covenant and Combine ourselves together into a Civil Body Politic, for our better ordering and preservation and furtherance of the ends aforesaid; and by virtue hereof to enact, constitute and frame such just and equal Laws, Ordinances, Acts, Constitutions and Offices, from time to time, as shall be thought most meet and convenient for the general good of the Colony, unto which we promise all due submission and obedience. In witness whereof we have hereunder subscribed our names at Cape Cod, the 11th of November, in the year of the reign of our Sovereign Lord King James, of England, France, and Ireland the eighteenth, and of Scotland the fifty-fourth. Anno Domini 1620.

5   After this they chose, or rather confirmed, Mr. John Carver (a man godly and well approved amongst them) their Governor for that year. And after they had provided a place for their goods, or common store (which were long in unlading for want of boats, foulness of the winter weather and sickness of **divers**) and begun some small cottages for their habitation; as time would admit, they met and consulted of laws and orders, both for their civil and military government as the necessity of their condition did require, still adding thereunto as urgent occasion in several times, and as cases did require.

6   In these hard and difficult beginnings they found some discontents and murmurings arise amongst some, and mutinous speeches and carriages in other; but they were soon quelled and

---

patent
(păt´nt) *n.* an official document granting ownership.

ANALYZE PRIMARY SOURCES

Annotate: Mark three phrases in paragraph 4 that suggest a formal tone.

Infer: What can you infer about the author's purpose based on his tone thus far? Cite text evidence in your response.

divers
(dī´vərz) *adj.* various; several.

VOCABULARY

Archaic Vocabulary: Out-of-date language is a characteristic of historical narrative. Words and word usage change over time, so that what people said in the 1600s may not be what people say today. If you suspect a word or phrase is archaic, use context to infer what it means, and look it up to be sure.

Summarize: How would you rewrite the sentence fragment in paragraph 5 that starts "they met and consulted ... did require" to better understand the word *thereunto*?

---

[1] **mutinous:** rebellious.

overcome by the wisdom, patience, and just and equal carriage of things, by the Governor and better part, which **clave** faithfully together in the main.

clave

(klāv) *v.* past tense of *cleave:* to cling; to adhere.

[The Starving Time]

7   But that which was most sad and lamentable was, that in two or three months' time half of their company died, especially in January and February, being the depth of winter, and wanting houses and other comforts; being infected with the scurvy[2] and other diseases which this long voyage and their inaccommodate condition had brought upon them. So as there died some times two or three of a day in the foresaid time, that of 100 and odd persons, scarce fifty remained. And of these, in the time of most distress, there was but six or seven sound persons who to their great commendations, be it spoken, spared no pains night nor day, but with abundance of toil and hazard of their own health, fetched them wood, made them fires, dressed them meat, made their beds, washed their loathsome[3] clothes, clothed and unclothed them. In a word, did all the homely and necessary offices for them which dainty and queasy stomachs cannot endure to hear named; and all this willingly and cheerfully, without any grudging in the least, showing herein their true love unto their friends and brethren; a rare example and worthy to be remembered. Two of these seven were Mr. William Brewster, their reverend Elder, and Myles Standish, their Captain and military commander, unto whom myself and many others were much beholden in our low and sick condition. And yet the Lord so upheld these persons as in this general **calamity** they were not at all infected either with sickness or lameness. . . .

DETERMINE CENTRAL IDEA

Annotate: Mark words that describe the events that occurred in January and February.

Analyze: What do the details here say about the colonists' experience in their new surroundings? What central idea do they suggest?

calamity

(kə-lăm′ĭ-tē) *n.* an event that brings terrible loss or lasting distress.

[Indian Relations]

8   All this while the Indians came skulking about them, and would sometimes show themselves aloof off, but when any approached near them, they would run away; and once they stole away their tools where they had been at work and were gone to dinner. But about the 16th of March, a certain Indian came boldly amongst them and spoke to them in broken English, which they could well understand but marveled at it. At length they understood by discourse with him, that he was not of these parts, but belonged to the eastern parts where some English ships came to fish, with whom he was acquainted and could name **sundry** of them by their names, amongst whom he had got his language. He became profitable to them in acquainting them with many things concerning the state of the country in the east parts where he lived, which was afterwards profitable unto them; as also of the people here, of their names, number and strength, of their

ANALYZE PRIMARY SOURCES

Annotate: Mark words in paragraph 8 that show how Bradford feels about the Native Americans.

Evaluate: Is the tone the same throughout, or does it change? If so, why?

sundry

(sŭn′drē) *adj.* various or assorted.

---

[2] **scurvy:** a disease caused by a lack of vitamin C in the diet.
[3] **loathsome:** offensive or disgusting.

situation and distance from this place, and who was chief amongst them. His name was Samoset. He told them also of another Indian whose name was Squanto, a native of this place, who had been in England and could speak better English than himself.

Being, after some time of entertainment and gifts dismissed, a while after he came again, and five more with him, and they brought again all the tools that were stolen away before, and made way for the coming of their great Sachem,[4] called Massasoit. Who, about four or five days after, came with the chief of his friends and other attendance, with the aforesaid Squanto. With whom, after friendly entertainment and some gifts given him, they made a peace with him (which hath now continued this 24 years) in these terms:

1. That neither he nor any of his should injure or do hurt to any of their people.
2. That if any of his did hurt to any of theirs, he should send the offender, that they might punish him.
3. That if anything were taken away from any of theirs, he should cause it to be restored; and they should do the like to his.
4. If any did unjustly war against him, they would aid him; if any did war against them, he should aid them.

---

[4] **Sachem:** chief.

5. He should send to his neighbours confederates[5] to certify them of this, that they might not wrong them, but might be likewise comprised in the conditions of peace.

6. That when their men came to them, they should leave their bows and arrows behind them.

10   After these things he returned to his place called Sowams, some 40 miles from this place, but Squanto continued with them and was their interpreter and was a special instrument sent of God for their good beyond their expectation. He directed them how to set their corn, where to take fish, and to procure other commodities, and was also their pilot to bring them to unknown places for their profit, and never left them till he died. He was a native of this place, and scarce any left alive besides himself. He was carried away with divers others by one Hunt, a master of a ship, who thought to sell them for slaves in Spain. But he got away for England and was entertained by a merchant in London, and employed to Newfoundland and other parts, and lastly brought hither into these parts by one Mr. Dermer, a gentleman employed by Sir Ferdinando Gorges and others for discovery and other designs in these parts. . . .

© Houghton Mifflin Harcourt Publishing Company • Image Credits: ©The Granger Collection, NYC

DETERMINE CENTRAL IDEA

Annotate: In paragraphs 9 and 10, mark words that describe relations between the colonists and the Native Americans.

Summarize: How can you summarize these details to briefly describe the interactions between the two groups?

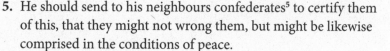

[5] **confederates:** allies; persons who share a common purpose.

[First Thanksgiving]

ANALYZE PRIMARY SOURCES

Annotate: In paragraph 11, mark the activities the colonists engage in to prepare for winter.

Analyze: Why would Bradford's audience be interested in knowing these details?

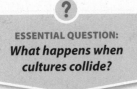

ESSENTIAL QUESTION:
What happens when cultures collide?

Review your notes and add your thoughts to your Response Log.

11 They began now to gather in the small harvest they had, and to fit up their houses and dwellings against winter, being all well recovered in health and strength and had all things in good plenty. For as some were thus employed in affairs abroad, others were exercised in fishing, about cod and bass and other fish, of which they took good store, of which every family had their portion. All the summer there was no want; and now began to come in store of fowl, as winter approached, of which this place did abound when they came first (but afterward decreased by degrees). And besides waterfowl there was great store of wild turkeys, of which they took many, besides venison, etc. Besides they had about a peck a meal a week to a person, or now since harvest, Indian corn to that proportion. Which made many afterwards write so largely of their plenty here to their friends in England, which were not feigned but true reports.[6]

---

[6] **reports:** Although the specific day of the Plymouth colonists' first Thanksgiving is not known, it occurred in the fall of 1621. For three days, Massasoit and almost a hundred of his men joined the Pilgrims for feasts and games.

COLLABORATIVE DISCUSSION

With a partner, discuss how someone in 1651 would have reacted after reading Bradford's accounts. How different might that reaction be from yours?

Assessment Practice

Answer these questions before moving on to the **Analyze the Text** section on the following page.

1. Why did the colonists decide to create the Mayflower Compact?

   (A) King James required them to sign such a document.

   (B) Some of them were speaking out against King James.

   (C) Their original patent did not extend to establishing a colony in New England.

   (D) They were facing extreme hardship and starvation and wanted to elect a new leader.

2. Why were Squanto and Samoset able to help make peace between the colonists and the Native Americans?

   (A) They spoke English and could help the two groups communicate.

   (B) They showed the colonists what foods to eat to avoid scurvy.

   (C) They brought the colonists food during the winter so they would not starve.

   (D) They planned a three-day festival where both groups could share abundant food.

3. How did Squanto help the colonists prepare for the winter?

   (A) He showed them how to build fires and cook food.

   (B) He showed them how to sew warmer clothing.

   (C) He showed them how to make their homes sturdier.

   (D) He showed them how to grow and find food to store.

☺Ed
Test-Taking Strategies

Analyze the Text

Support your responses with evidence from the text.

NOTICE & NOTE

Review what you **noticed and noted** as you read the text. Your annotations can help you answer these questions.

(1) **SUMMARIZE** Look back at the chart on p. 81 that you filled in as you read. What types of details does Bradford include? What about these types of details makes them important in a primary source?

(2) **ANALYZE** What does the Mayflower Compact say explicitly? What does it suggest through its careful word choice and tone?

(3) **EVALUATE** Summarize the terms of the treaty between Massasoit and the Pilgrims (paragraph 9). Then, evaluate the treaty. Is it equally fair to both sides? Explain.

(4) **ANALYZE** Which beliefs most contributed to the colonists' willingness to face hardships together? What passages best reveal those beliefs?

(5) **DRAW CONCLUSIONS** Complete the following chart with examples from the text. Based on the information, what do you think Bradford's purpose was in writing *Of Plymouth Plantation*?

Genre	Audience	Tone
Examples:	Examples:	Examples::
What These Examples Suggest About the Author's Purpose		

(6) **SYNTHESIZE** What is the central idea of the excerpt from *Of Plymouth Plantation*? How does this reflect Bradford's purpose in writing it?

Choices

Here are some other ways to demonstrate your understanding of the ideas in this lesson.

Writing
↳ **Compare-and-Contrast Essay**

Write an essay in which you compare how present-day immigrants are similar to and different from the Pilgrims. State your topic and identify the organizational structure in the opening of your essay. Make sure your ideas and supporting details flow logically from one paragraph to the next. Use examples from the reading to support your thesis statement. To make your comparison, think about

- reasons people have for leaving their homeland
- the hardships they face
- the resources they have or don't have
- the points of contact they have with an unknown culture

As you write and discuss, be sure to use the **Academic Vocabulary** words.

> **adapt**
> **coherent**
> **device**
> **displace**
> **dynamic**

Social & Emotional Learning
↳ **Proposal**

In many Native American communities, the Thanksgiving holiday is a day of mourning. For example, the United American Indians of New England describe it this way:

> Thanksgiving day is a reminder of the genocide of millions of Native people, the theft of Native lands, and the relentless assault on Native culture. . . .

They invite the wider community to join them in remembering their ancestors and protesting injustices. Use the following questions to draft a proposal to school administrators to allow students to participate in the Day of Mourning.

- How will the experience help students question the stereotypes they know?
- How will the event help students understand and build empathy for this different point of view?

Speaking & Listening
↳ **Interview**

You have an opportunity to tell the story of the first encounter from Samoset and Squanto's perspective. Work with two partners to interview them and have them recount their experiences with the Pilgrims. Refer to paragraphs 8-10 in Bradford's account, if you need to refresh your memory on what Bradford said happened.

1. Create an interview script with questions you'd like answered.

2. With two classmates, role-play the interview. Decide who will be the interviewer and who will be the two Native Americans.

3. Record the interview to share with the class.

Expand Your Vocabulary

PRACTICE AND APPLY

Mark the italicized alternative that best relates to the vocabulary word in each sentence. Then explain your choice.

patent	clave	calamity	sundry	divers

1. You and your friends have **divers** opinions about food. Is it *easy* or *difficult* to eat out?

2. Did the *Mayflower* passengers' **patent** *officially* or *unofficially* say they would live in Virginia?

3. Would **sundry** pairs of shoes be *identical* to or *different* from each other?

4. If you experienced a **calamity,** would the result be *good* or *bad*?

5. If you **clave** to someone's principles, did you *support* or *oppose* them?

Vocabulary Strategy
↳ **Archaic Vocabulary**

Of Plymouth Plantation contains many examples of **archaic vocabulary**— words that are no longer commonly used. The word *divers,* for example, was common until the end of the 17th century but has now been replaced by *diverse.* Use these strategies to understand archaic vocabulary:

- Notice whether the word is similar to a current, familiar word, and try substituting the current word to make a meaningful sentence.

- Use context clues when you come across archaic vocabulary. Read the text around the unknown word for hints about its meaning.

- Use a dictionary's notes on archaic words and meanings, which are found at the end of an entry, labeled *archaic* or *obsolete.*

PRACTICE AND APPLY

Use the strategies and the chart to determine the meaning of the following archaic vocabulary from *Of Plymouth Plantation.*

Word	Meaning	Effective Strategy
aforesaid (paragraph 4)		
thereunto (paragraph 5)		
inaccommodate (paragraph 7)		

Watch Your Language!

Active and Passive Voice

The **voice** of a verb tells whether its subject performs or receives the verb's action. If the subject *performs* the action, the verb is in the **active voice.** If the subject *receives* the action, the verb is in the **passive voice.** In Bradford's writing, the colonists or the Native Americans are most often subjects who perform the action. Sometimes, however, the subject of a sentence or clause receives the action.

Interactive Grammar Lesson: Active Voice and Passive Voice

This example uses active voice to show how six or seven colonists helped the others when illness struck:

> . . . there was but six or seven sound persons who to their great commendations, be it spoken, <u>spared</u> no pains night nor day, but with abundance of toil and hazard of their own health, <u>fetched</u> them wood, <u>made</u> them fires, <u>dressed</u> them meat, <u>made</u> their beds, <u>washed</u> their loathsome clothes, <u>clothed</u> and <u>unclothed</u> them.

Now consider this example, which contains both active voice and passive voice:

> He <u>was carried</u> away with divers others by one Hunt, a master of a ship, who thought to sell them for slaves in Spain. But he <u>got away</u> for England and <u>was entertained</u> by a merchant in London. . . .

Squanto managed to learn English through a sequence of events in which he sometimes takes action (*got away*) and sometimes has actions done to or for him (*was carried, was entertained*). Note how the sentence shows a contrast between the way the slaver and the merchant treated Squanto—he was carried away by one but entertained by the other.

PRACTICE AND APPLY

Read the following sentences and determine whether they are in active or passive voice. Then rewrite them, using the opposite voice.

1. The Pilgrims crafted their own patent since the one that was granted to them by the king was not for New England, but Virginia.

2. The Native Americans approached the European settlers in an effort to find out who they were.

3. Negotiations were carried out between the two groups so they could agree on how to share the land.

4. Native Americans showed the Pilgrims how to plant and where to hunt and fish, so that they wouldn't starve come winter.

Synthesize Information

As you've read the excerpts from "Coming of Age in the Dawnland" and *Of Plymouth Plantation*, you've seen how authors use many details to express and support a central idea. By analyzing the information from each source, and then combining it, you can understand a topic more broadly and make new connections. For example, you may notice similar details between the two texts, or connect ideas that the authors express differently. Use the graphic below to organize your thoughts as you synthesize information about the Native American and European encounters.

A Information from "Coming of Age in the Dawnland"	**B** Information from *Of Plymouth Plantation*

What I Understand About How Europeans Viewed Native Americans
Central idea:
Strongest supporting details from both texts:

Analyze the Texts

Discuss these questions in your group.

1. **CONTRAST** How is the historical figure Tisquantum, or Squanto, portrayed in each text?

2. **COMPARE** How were the European colonists surprised by the Native Americans they encountered in each text?

3. **EVALUATE** How well do the details of each account support the ideas that the authors want to communicate? Is there one source that was better at using supporting details than the other?

4. **ANALYZE** What types of details do primary and secondary accounts rely on? Because of these details when is it appropriate to use a primary source over a secondary source, or vice versa?

Collaborate and Present

Your group can continue exploring the ideas in these texts by collaborating on a media presentation about European perceptions of Native Americans. Follow these steps:

1. **PICK YOUR TALKING POINTS** With your group, decide which ideas and details you want to present. Think about ways your group can combine the sources to interpret the information in authentic ways.

2. **FILL IN THE GAPS** Do additional research where necessary. Look at the ideas and details you have, and ask yourselves if there is missing information that would make your presentation stronger.

3. **ORGANIZE YOUR SOURCES** Analyze any additional source materials you found, then quote, summarize, or paraphrase them to fit your presentation.

4. **CHOOSE A MEDIUM** Decide which medium or media would be best to use, based on the sources you have. Outline the content and organize the elements of the presentation.

5. **COMPOSE** Work together to write the narration and design the content. Review and revise each other's work.

6. **POLISH AND PRESENT** Practice your presentation and revise and refine it as needed. Then share it with the class.

Collaborate & Compare

Compare Poems

You are about to read two poems about the treasures of this world and what brings lasting happiness. As you read, notice the style and themes of the poems. Then, think about the differences in their styles, and the themes they express.

A

Here Follow Some Verses Upon the Burning of Our House, July 10th, 1666

Poem by Anne Bradstreet
pages 100–103

B

World, in hounding me . . .

Poem
by **Sor Juana Inés de la Cruz**
Translation by **Alan S. Trueblood**
pages 104–107

After you have read the poems, you will explore ideas in both by having a group discussion where you analyze the literary elements in the two poems. You will follow these steps:

- Set ground rules
- Prepare for the discussion
- Draft your script
- Hold a panel discussion
- Wrap up the discussion

Here Follow Some Verses Upon the Burning of Our House, July 10th, 1666

Poem by **Anne Bradstreet**

World, in hounding me . . .

Poem by **Sor Juana Inés de la Cruz**

Engage Your Brain

Choose one or more of these activities to start connecting with the poems you're about to read.

A Day in the Life

Do some research on or recall what you know about life in the 1600s. Then, think about these questions:

- What would a woman in Puritan society or a woman in a convent have experienced at this time?

- What would their daily routines have been like?

- What structures would have governed their lives?

Discuss your ideas with a partner.

Your Most Prized Possession

What do you consider to be the best thing you own? It can be a tangible object or an intangible idea, value, or personality trait. Take five minutes to write down your ideas and reasons for believing what you do.

Vanity, All Is Vanity

In the 1600s and 1700s, the *vanitas* was a genre of painting that depicted worldly pursuits and pleasures. Look at this *vanitas* painting and think about the message the artist is trying to convey. What do you think he or she is saying? Compare your answers with those of a classmate.

Paraphrase

Paraphrasing can help you understand difficult sections of a poem. Bradstreet and Sor Juana, for example, both use inverted syntax, or sentence structure in which the expected order of words is reversed. Paraphrasing the passage can ensure that you understand it. To paraphrase:

- Look up any words you don't know.

- Note the words and phrases that suggest and support a key idea.

- Cover the poem and rewrite it in your own words. Reorder the verses so the syntax sounds like normal speech.

- Compare your version to the original and edit out words and phrases that are too similar.

- Check that your version doesn't change the meaning of the original.

> **Focus on Genre**
> ↳ **Poetry**
>
> - uses word choice, structure, and tone to convey ideas
> - often includes figurative language and poetic devices to deepen meaning
> - may be written to express a writer's feelings or beliefs

Here is a sample paraphrase of the first stanza of Bradstreet's poem.

Poem	Paraphrase
In silent night when rest I took For sorrow near I did not look I wakened was with thund'ring noise And piteous shrieks of dreadful voice. That fearful sound of "Fire!" and "Fire!" Let no man know is my desire.	In the silence of night, I was sleeping and did not expect something bad to happen. I awoke to a loud noise and a voice pitifully shrieking "Fire!" I pray that no person ever hears such a frightening sound.

Analyze Theme

Themes are the ideas or truths about life a writer wants to convey. Though Bradstreet and Sor Juana lived in different places, both of these poems focus on the topics of *vanity* and *treasure*. In the chart, indicate when these words are positive or negative and how they contribute to the poem's themes. Notice whether any themes may be universal, meaning they apply to anyone regardless of time or place.

	Vanity	Treasure
Bradstreet		
Sor Juana		

Analyze Style

Style is the distinctive way a text is written. Both of these poems are about worldly pleasures, but their styles are different. As you read, think about these elements and how they contribute to each text.

- **Word choice:** What words and images stand out?

- **Sentence structure:** Does the poet use standard sentence structure? Is the word order of sentences inverted?

- **Tone:** What is the poet's attitude toward the subject?

- **Speaker:** What is the personality of the speaker?

Annotation in Action

Here are notes one student made about Bradstreet's poem. As you read the poems, mark words and phrases that define each poet's style.

> In silent night when rest I took
> For sorrow near I did not look
> I wakened was with thund'ring noise
> And piteous shrieks of dreadful voice.
> That fearful sound of "Fire!" and "Fire!"
> Let no man know is my desire.

The word "sorrow" suggests something sad might happen.

This image makes me think the speaker is terrified.

Background

Anne Bradstreet (1612–1672) was one of the first poets in the American colonies. Married at 16 she gave up a life of wealth in England to follow her father and husband to the wild, unsettled colonies of New England. Much of her poetry focuses on her internal struggle between desiring the pleasures of the world and focusing on the promise of heaven. On the date referenced in the title of this poem, Bradstreet's home was destroyed by a fire.

Sor Juana Inés de la Cruz (1651–1695) began her life in a poor Mexican village, but at age sixteen she was presented as a lady-in-waiting to the Spanish court. She gave up this sophisticated life four years later to enter a convent. As a Catholic nun, she devoted herself to books, learning, and writing poetry, plays, songs, and essays on the rights of women. She became famous for her works and keen intellect. Under criticism for her outspoken views of women, she abruptly gave up her studies and her vast library. She dedicated the rest of her life to convent duties. When an epidemic struck the convent, she nursed sick nuns until falling ill herself and dying.

Here Follow Some Verses Upon the Burning of Our House, July 10th, 1666

Poem by **Anne Bradstreet**

Human beings often love material things. But do those things bring true happiness?

© Houghton Mifflin Harcourt Publishing Company • Image Credits: ©DEA/S. DA RE/Getty Images

ANALYZE STYLE

Annotate: Mark words that suggest a contrast in lines 1–6.

Analyze: What is happening in these lines? How does the word choice convey the urgency of the situation?

In silent night when rest I took
For sorrow near I did not look
I wakened was with thund'ring noise
And piteous shrieks of dreadful voice.
5 That fearful sound of "Fire!" and "Fire!"
Let no man know is my desire.

I, starting up, the light did spy,
And to my God my heart did cry
To strengthen me in my distress
10 And not to leave me succorless.¹
Then, coming out, beheld a space
The flame consume my dwelling place.

---

¹ **succorless** (sŭk´ər-lĭs): without help or relief.

And when I could no longer look,
I blest His name that gave and took,[2]
15 That laid my goods now in the dust:
Yea, so it was, and so 'twas just.
It was His own, it was not mine,
Far be it that I should repine;[3]

He might of all justly bereft,
20 But yet sufficient for us left.
When by the ruins oft I past,
My sorrowing eyes aside did cast,
And here and there the places spy
Where oft I sat and long did lie:

25 Here stood that trunk and there that chest,
There lay that store I counted best.
My pleasant things in ashes lie,
And them behold no more shall I.
Under thy roof no guest shall sit,
30 Nor at thy table eat a bit.

No pleasant tale shall e'er be told,
Nor things recounted done of old.
No candle e'er shall shine in thee,
Nor bridegroom's voice e'er heard shall be.
35 In silence ever shalt thou lie;
Adieu, Adieu, all's vanity.[4]

Then straight I 'gin my heart to chide,[5]
And did thy wealth on earth abide?
Didst fix thy hope on mold'ring[6] dust?
40 The arm of flesh didst make thy trust?
Raise up thy thoughts above the sky
That dunghill mists away may fly.

PARAPHRASE

Annotate: **Inverted syntax** refers to sentence structure in which the expected order of words is reversed. Mark an example of inverted syntax in lines 25–30.

Paraphrase: Create a paraphrase of the example of inverted syntax you marked.

---

[2] **I . . . took:** an allusion to Job 1:21 in the Bible—"The Lord gave, and the Lord hath taken away; blessed be the name of the Lord."
[3] **repine:** to complain or fret; to long for something.
[4] **all's vanity:** an allusion to Ecclesiastes 1:2 in the Bible—"All is vanity," meaning that all is temporary and meaningless.
[5] **chide:** to scold mildly so as to correct or improve.
[6] **mold'ring:** crumbling, disintegrating, decaying.

Annotate: Mark words in the final stanzas that suggest the poet's attitude about wealth and treasures.

Compare: How does the poet's choice of words differ at the end of the poem from that of the beginning? How does this affect the poem's theme?

Thou hast an house on high erect,
Framed by that mighty Architect,
45 With glory richly furnishéd,[7]
Stands permanent though this be fled.
It's purchaséd and paid for too
By Him who hath enough to do.

A price so vast as is unknown
50 Yet by His gift is made thine own;
There's wealth enough, I need no more,
Farewell, my pelf,[8] farewell my store.
The world no longer let me love,
My hope and treasure lies above.[9]

[7] **Thou . . . furnishéd:** an allusion to John 14:2–3 in the Bible, where Jesus assures his disciples that, even if they have nothing in this life, there are mansions prepared for them in heaven.
[8] **pelf:** wealth or riches, especially when dishonestly acquired.
[9] **treasure . . . above:** an allusion to Matthew 13:44–46, which relates how heavenly treasures are safe from thieves and destruction.

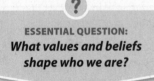

ESSENTIAL QUESTION:
What values and beliefs shape who we are?

Review your notes and add your thoughts to your Response Log.

COLLABORATIVE DISCUSSION

Get together with a partner and talk about things the fire destroyed and what the speaker is likely to miss the most.

Assessment Practice

Answer these questions before moving on to the next poem.

1. What is the speaker's first response to hearing the "fearful sound" of fire?

   (A) She looked for water.

   (B) She prayed for strength

   (C) She gathered her belongings.

   (D) She started to scream.

2. The lines *When by the ruins oft I past, / My sorrowing eyes aside did cast* emphasize that the speaker

   (A) is struggling to let go of her home

   (B) is glad her house burned down

   (C) is watching the house be rebuilt

   (D) no longer wants to have a house

3. What conclusion helps the poet overcome her sorrow?

   (A) Her family is still around her.

   (B) She has started to build anew.

   (C) She knows heaven will be her home.

   (D) She replaces sorrow with anger.

Test-Taking Strategies

World, in hounding me . . .

Poem by **Sor Juana Inés de la Cruz**

translated by **Alan S. Trueblood**

NOTICE & NOTE

As you read, use the side margins to make notes about the text.

Can earthly treasures bring real happiness? Or are they worthless?

PARAPHRASE

Annotate: Mark the words in lines 1-4 that show to whom the two questions are directed.

Paraphrase: Paraphrase the questions.

> World, in hounding me, what do you gain?
> How can it harm you if I choose, astutely,
> rather to stock my mind with things of beauty,
> than waste its stock on every beauty's claim?
> 5   Costliness and wealth bring me no pleasure;
> the only happiness I care to find
> derives from setting treasure in my mind,
> and not from mind that's set on winning treasure.

I prize no comeliness. All fair things pay
10 to time, the victor, their appointed fee
and treasure cheats even the practiced eye.
    Mine is the better and the truer way:
to leave the vanities of life aside,
not throw my life away on vanity.

9 **comeliness:** beauty.

ANALYZE THEME

Annotate: Mark the words that show the speaker's attitude about beauty and fair things.

Analyze: How do these lines develop the poet's ideas on treasure?

Sor Juana Inés de la Cruz (1750) by Miguel Cabrera (1695–1768). Oil on canvas.

En perseguirme, mundo . . .

Poema de **Sor Juana Inés de la Cruz**

**¿Se puede llegar a ser feliz por medio de las vanidades?
¿O son de poco valor?**

> En perseguirme, mundo, ¿qué interesas?
> ¿En qué te ofendo, cuando sólo intento
> poner bellezas en mi entendimiento
> y no mi entendimiento en las bellezas?
> 5   Yo no estimo tesoros ni riquezas;
> y así, siempre me causa más contento
> poner riquezas en mi pensamiento
> que no mi pensamiento en las riquezas.
>   Y no estimo hermosura que, vencida,
> 10 es despojo civil de las edades,
> ni riqueza me agrada fementida,
>   teniendo por mejor, en mis verdades,
> consumir vanidades de la vida
> que consumir la vida en vanidades.

ANALIZAR EL ESTILO

Anotar: Indica las palabras en los versos 5–9 que riman y se repiten.

Analizar: ¿Qué efecto tienen la rima y la repetición?

?

ESSENTIAL QUESTION:
What values and beliefs shape who we are?

Review your notes and add your thoughts to your Response Log.

COLLABORATIVE DISCUSSION

Get together with a partner and talk about why the poet might feel "hounded" by the world.

Assessment Practice

Answer these questions before moving on to the **Analyze the Texts** section on the following page.

1. What is the speaker choosing to emphasize?

   (A) every pretty thing

   (B) talents and accomplishments

   (C) money and wealth

   (D) knowledge and wisdom

2. What does not bring the speaker happiness?

   (A) choosing a better way

   (B) putting aside vanity

   (C) seeking earthly treasures

   (D) developing her intellect

3. What happens to "all fair things"?

   (A) They grow sweeter with time.

   (B) They become more valuable.

   (C) They decay or decline with time.

   (D) They triumph over time.

☺Ed
Test-Taking Strategies

Analyze the Texts

Support your responses with evidence from the texts.

NOTICE & NOTE

Review what you **noticed and noted** as you read the text. Your annotations can help you answer these questions.

1. **DRAW CONCLUSIONS** Use details from "Here Follow Some Verses Upon the Burning of Our House" to explain what you learn about the speaker's feelings and beliefs. How does your impression of the speaker change over the course of the poem?

2. **INTERPRET** A **metaphor** is a direct comparison of two unlike things that does not use the word *like* or *as*. In lines 43–48, Bradstreet uses a metaphor to make a comparison to something she holds dear. What two things does she compare, and what do they stand for?

3. **PARAPHRASE** How would you paraphrase lines 19–20 of Bradstreet's poem: "He might of all justly bereft, / But yet sufficient for us left"?

4. **ANALYZE** Use the graphic organizer to list the things from Bradstreet's poem that the speaker mourns. Then list the things she values. How does this comparison contribute to the poem's theme?

Things She Mourns	Things She Values
Contribution to theme:	

5. **SYNTHESIZE** Sor Juana uses the word *treasure* in different ways. How do the different meanings of the same word develop the poem's theme?

6. **INTERPRET** **Personification** gives human traits and emotions to nonhuman things. In lines 9–11, what three things does Sor Juana personify? What human qualities does she give them?

7. **CRITIQUE** How does Sor Juana summarize her beliefs in lines 12–14? How effective is her argument? Explain.

Choices

Here are some other ways to demonstrate your understanding of the ideas in this lesson.

Writing
↳ Poem

In both Anne Bradstreet and Sor Juana's poems, *vanity* is defined as something that is empty of value. How do you define it, and what does it look like? Once you've answered those questions, write your own poem about vanity. You can use rhyming couplets like Anne Bradstreet or a sonnet like Sor Juana. Not feelin' it? Pick your own verse form. To help you brainstorm, think about

- what makes something empty of value
- whether vanity is good or bad
- what should go in its place, if vanity is something to be avoided
- what benefits come from indulging in vanity

As you write and discuss, be sure to use the **Academic Vocabulary** words.

adapt
coherent
device
displace
dynamic

Media
↳ Mixed-Media Collage

In art, you can mix media to break the boundary of a particular form and get wildly creative. For example, you can draw over photographs or add pressed flowers to an oil painting. With your classmates, think about the themes of treasure and vanity that Bradstreet and Sor Juana write about in their poems. Then, create a class collage that combines several different media to represent these themes. Explore creative ways to mix the printed word with paints, pastels, or needlework. Want a digital collage? Try to incorporate eye-catching images, special effects, and music.

Speaking & Listening
↳ Role-play

With a partner, role-play a conversation between Anne Bradstreet and Sor Juana Inés de la Cruz. As women who lived in the 1600s, how would their lives and experiences be similar or different? You may want to include the following in your conversation:

- the role of religion in their lives
- the role of women in the 17th century
- how their experience shapes their writing

Compare Poems

Both Bradstreet and Sor Juana's poems develop similar themes, but their poems have very different styles. Some of those elements of style include imagery, tone, diction and syntax, structure, and poetic devices, such as extended metaphors, similes, symbols, paradox, rhetorical questions, and rhyme. Which poem's style is more appealing and communicates its theme more convincingly?

In a small group, complete the chart below to examine the two poems. Be sure to support your ideas with text evidence.

	A Here Follow Some Verses Upon the Burning of Our House, July 10th, 1666	**B** World, in hounding me . . .
Tone: attitude toward the topic		
Imagery: language that appeals to the five senses		
Diction and syntax: word choice and word order		
Poetic devices: paradox, symbol, personification, etc.		
Structure: rhyming couplets, sonnet form		

Analyze the Texts

Discuss these questions in your group.

1. **COMPARE** Both poems consider the appeal and limits of worldly pleasures. Compare the **tone,** or attitude, each writer takes toward worldly pleasures. In what ways are they similar or different?

2. **ANALYZE** Think about how each poet uses different forms of verse to develop themes. Is one structure more appealing? If so, why? Is one speaker more relatable? What elements contribute to the appeal?

3. **CRITIQUE** Critique each poet's use of poetic devices. Which poet uses figurative language more effectively? Use examples from the poems to support your opinions.

4. **EVALUATE** Does one poem make a better case for the vanity of earthly things? Use examples from the poems, as well as what you have observed or read, to state what brings lasting happiness.

Collaborate and Present

Your group can continue exploring the style and effectiveness of these poems by collaborating on a panel discussion. Follow these steps:

1. **SET GROUND RULES** As a group, you will decide if one poem's style is more effective than the other, or if both poems are equally effective. Determine if you need a leader, note taker, etc., and how much time each person will have to talk. Aim to represent the opinions of everyone in the group. Then decide how to best synthesize the group's ideas when you are done with your discussion.

2. **PREPARE FOR THE DISCUSSION** To get ready for the discussion, reread each poem and take notes. Individually decide which elements make each poem appealing and distinctive. Determine which elements are not as powerful and lessen the poem's appeal. These will be your talking points.

3. **DRAFT YOUR SCRIPT** Create a rough draft of the points you will make and the stylistic elements you will address. Remember to define each element you are describing. Use specific lines from the poem to illustrate the elements you're calling out, as well as to support your opinions.

4. **HOLD A PANEL DISCUSSION** Reconvene as a group and listen as others present their ideas. Ask the speaker to clarify if you have questions. Encourage the members who may not be speaking as much to voice their ideas and opinions. Respond politely to each other's ideas and make sure each person has a chance to participate.

5. **WRAP UP THE DISCUSSION** Synthesize all the information presented, then try to summarize the group opinion. Did you come to an agreement or did you agree to disagree? Is there a poem the group liked better?

© Houghton Mifflin Harcourt Publishing Company

Reader's Choice

Continue your exploration of the Essential Questions for this unit by doing some independent reading. Read the titles and descriptions shown. Then mark the texts that interest you.

ESSENTIAL QUESTION:
Review the four Essential Questions for this unit on page 1.

Short Reads   Available on ☺Ed

These texts are available in your ebook. Choose one to read and rate. Then defend your rating to the class.

from **The Way to Rainy Mountain**

Memoir by **N. Scott Momaday**

A man visits his grandmother's grave to reflect on his Native American heritage and connect to his homeland.

Rate It

Mother Tongue

Essay by **Amy Tan**

Discover how a best-selling novelist learned to appreciate the expressiveness of her mother's imperfect English.

Rate It

from **La relación**

Historical Narrative by **Álvar Núñez Cabeza de Vaca**

How do Native Americans respond to shipwrecked Spanish explorers who are starving and near death?

Rate It

from **The General History of Virginia**

Historical Narrative by **John Smith**

What is the fate of Jamestown when colonist John Smith is taken prisoner by the Powhatan people?

Rate It

Voyage

Poem by **Carmen Tafolla**

If a fourth ship had sailed with Christopher Columbus, imagine what its claim to fame would be.

Rate It

Long Reads

Here are three recommended books that connect to this unit. For additional options, ask your teacher, school librarian, or peers. Which titles spark your interest?

The Namesake

Novel by **Jhumpa Lahiri**

Ashoke and Ashima leave India to start new lives in America. Ashima resists assimilation and gives her firstborn son a name rich with heritage that burdens him.

An Indigenous People's History of the United States

Nonfiction by **Roxanne Dunbar-Ortiz**

Told from the perspective of Native Americans, this work challenges understandings of American history.

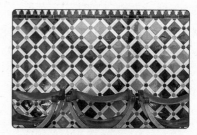

The Moor's Account

Novel by **Laila Lalami**

Estebanico, the enslaved man who served a Spanish conquistador, recounts his experiences as one of four survivors on Álvar Núñez Cabeza de Vaca's expedition.

Extension

↳ Connect & Compare

TO FACE THE UNKNOWN A strong theme within this unit is how humans try to maintain their sense of self when forced into unfamiliar circumstances. Is this true for the text you chose? If so, what values and beliefs did the protagonist try to maintain? How did circumstances affect his or her ability to do so? Discuss your ideas with others who read the same text you did, or create an online chat to share your thoughts.

DEEP IN THE HEART OF . . . Several texts in this unit deal with people who have strong connections to certain places. In the texts you read independently, what places matter to the central characters? Why do they try to maintain ties to this place? Do you have similar ties to a particular place?

NOTICE & NOTE

- Pick one of the texts and annotate the Notice & Note signposts you find.

- Then use the **Notice & Note Writing Frames** to help you write about the significance of the signposts.

- Compare your findings with those of other students who read the same text.

Notice & Note Writing Frames

Write an Informative Essay

Writing Prompt

Using ideas, information, or examples from selections in this unit, write an informative essay for your school newspaper in which you examine what it means to be a stranger in a strange land.

Manage your time carefully so that you can

- come up with ideas to include in your essay;
- plan your essay;
- write a complete first draft; and
- revise and edit your essay.

Be sure to

- clearly state the main idea of your essay;
- provide clear examples to support your ideas;
- use precise language in your descriptions; and
- check that your essay flows logically from one idea to the next.

> ### Review the
> ### Mentor Text
>
> For an example of a well-written piece you can use as a mentor text and inspiration for your essay, review
>
> - **"A Desperate Trek Across America"** (pages 43–49)
>
> Review your notes and annotations about this text. Think about how the author describes the situations and brings them to life.

Consider Your Sources

Review the list of texts in the unit and choose at least three that you may want to use as support for your informative essay.

As you review the potential sources, consult the notes you made in your **Response Log** and make additional notes about ideas that might be useful as you write. Consider how a combination of descriptive language and concrete evidence can help you create an engaging informative essay.

UNIT 1 SOURCES

- [ ] **The World on the Turtle's Back**
- [ ] **Balboa**
- [ ] **A Desperate Trek Across America**
- [ ] **New Orleans**
- [ ] **Coming of Age in the Dawnland**
- [ ] *from* **Of Plymouth Plantation**
- [ ] **Here Follow Some Verses Upon the Burning of Our House**
- [ ] **World, in hounding me . . .**

Analyze the Prompt

Review the prompt to make sure you understand the assignment.

- Mark the sentence in the prompt that identifies the topic of your informative essay. Rephrase the sentence in your own words.

- Look for words that indicate the purpose and audience of your essay. Write a sentence describing each.

© Houghton Mifflin Harcourt Publishing Company

Consider Your Audience

As you respond, ask yourself these questions about your audience:

- Who will read my essay?

- What information will my readers need to understand what I'm describing?

- How can I connect my subject to my readers' lives?

What is my topic? What is my writing task?

What is my purpose for writing the informative essay?

Who is my audience?

Review the Rubric

Your informative essay will be scored using a rubric. As you write, focus on the characteristics of a high-scoring essay as described in the chart. You will learn more about these characteristics as you work through the lesson.

Purpose, Focus, and Organization	Evidence and Elaboration	Conventions of Standard English
The response includes: - A strongly maintained controlling idea - Use of transitions to connect ideas - Logical progression of ideas - Appropriate style and tone	The response includes: - Effective use of evidence and sources - Effective use of elaboration - Clear and effective expression of ideas - Appropriate vocabulary - Varied sentence structure	The response may include: - Some minor errors in usage but no patterns of errors - Correct punctuation, capitalization, sentence formation, and spelling - Command of basic conventions

1 PLAN YOUR INFORMATIVE ESSAY

Develop Your Topic

What does it mean to be a stranger in a strange land? Brainstorm some ideas that show a reader what it means to feel out of place or completely new to an unfamiliar environment. Use the chart to jot down ideas.

What does it mean to be a stranger in a strange land?	Reasons for Feeling Out of Place

Identify Your Main Idea and Support

Choose one of your ideas and think about the following:

- What could be the **main idea,** or **thesis,** for my essay?
- What **evidence** can I find to support my idea?
- Is there **information** from the texts I could use?
- What **experiences** have I had that connect to my main idea?

Main Idea/Thesis

The **main idea**, or **thesis**, of an essay should be a clearly stated single sentence that tells the reader what you are going to be writing about. It usually appears near the end of the first paragraph.

Use the chart to outline your informative essay.

Informative Essay Planning	
Main Idea/Thesis	
Evidence from Texts and Background Reading	1. 2. 3.
Experiences	
Ideas to Research	

Use Text Features

Some texts in this unit use features to help readers understand what is being described. Text features include:

- photos
- graphs and charts
- sidebars
- maps
- illustrations
- text headings and subheadings

⏀ **Ed**

Help with Planning

Consult **Interactive Writing Lesson: Writing Informative Texts**

Review your sources and make notes of the ways authors use text features to aid comprehension. Consider whether you can use text features to help readers understand your essay.

Sources	Text Features	Helps Comprehension by . . .
1. "A Desperate Trek Across America"	• subheading with date and location	Identifies the time and place
2.		
3.		

Organize Ideas

Now organize your notes in a way that will help you draft your informative essay. Keep in mind that a well-written essay presents events in a logical, coherent order. Use the table below to organize your ideas and create coherence.

Structure

- Try to make your first paragraph engaging to your readers.
- Present the information in an order that makes logical sense.
- Use text features to help organize your essay.

INTRODUCTION AND MAIN IDEA/ THESIS	• Begin with an attention-grabbing description, anecdote, or quotation. • Introduce your topic and clearly state your main idea.
BODY PARAGRAPHS	• Use facts, details, and other evidence to support your main idea. • Connect your ideas with transitional words and phrases. • Use text features to help transition between ideas or to provide additional support for your main idea.
CONCLUSION	• Restate your main idea in a different way. • Include an idea or a question that may give readers something new to think about.

2 DEVELOP A DRAFT

Now it is time to draft your essay. Look at how professional writers craft their essays—you can use similar techniques in your own writing.

Use Precise Language

EXAMINE THE MENTOR TEXT

Writers use precise language to ensure that their ideas are clear. The author of "A Desperate Trek Across America" uses precise language to show that the conquistadors were exposed to danger in the New World.

A Desperate Trek Across America

The author lists **specific** tools the conquistadors used.

> Like past conquistadors, Cabeza de Vaca and his men had relied on their breastplates, horses, and lethal weapons to keep the Indians at bay. Such overwhelming technological advances meant they often did not even bother to negotiate, instead simply imposing their will. By sacrificing the very tools of their supremacy, they would now have to face the New World fully exposed to its perils and hold on only by their wits.

The writer **clarifies** why the conquistadors are in danger.

APPLY TO YOUR DRAFT

Rewrite the sentences with more precise language.
Refer to your sources to help you.

Someone was a stranger in a strange land.	**Who was it? Where were they?**
They faced an obstacle in an unfamiliar place.	**What was the obstacle? Where were they?**
These surroundings gave them a new feeling.	**What was the feeling? Why did they feel this way?**

© Houghton Mifflin Harcourt Publishing Company • Image Credits: ©Cabeza de Vaca, 1994 (w/c on paper), Harlin, Greg (b.1957)/Private Collection/Wood Ronsaville Harlin, Inc. USA/Bridgeman Images

Include Concrete Details & Evidence

EXAMINE THE MENTOR TEXT

Support the ideas in your informative essay with concrete details and evidence. Notice how Reséndez uses a quote from Cabeza de Vaca's diary to draw conclusions about the Spanish conquistadors' journey across the Gulf of Mexico and into Texas.

Drafting Online

Check your assignment list for a writing task from your teacher.

The author **specifies** exactly how many men were onboard.

> Fifty men crowded aboard each craft, the fifth commanded by Cabeza de Vaca. "And so greatly can necessity prevail," he observed, "that it made us risk going in this manner and placing ourselves in a sea so treacherous, and without any one of us who went having any knowledge of the art of navigation."

The author uses a **direct quote** as evidence that the Spaniards had to use their wits to survive in this new land.

APPLY TO YOUR DRAFT

Review your notes and make a list of the specific details and evidence you want to be sure to include in your essay. Cite each source and page number so you can find it easily. Jot a quick note or two about why you want to use that specific detail and how it will help convey your ideas to your readers. You may not use all of these, but this will keep them in mind as you draft.

Try These Suggestions

Vary the ways you integrate information from sources into your writing:

- In [Title of Source], the author states . . .
- According to [Author]'s [Title of Source], . . .
- This is an example of . . .

Detail & Evidence	Source	Why Use It? How Will It Help Readers?

3 REVISE YOUR INFORMATIVE ESSAY

Even experienced writers know how important revising is—it's where the real work of writing happens. Use this guide to help you revise your informative essay.

Help with Revision

Find a **Peer Review Guide** and **Student Models** online.

REVISION GUIDE		
Ask Yourself	**Prove It**	**Revise It**
Introduction Does my introduction engage the reader? Does my thesis statement clearly explain my purpose?	**Highlight** the sentences that grab the reader's attention. **Underline** your thesis statement.	**Add** vivid language to engage the reader. **Reword** your thesis statement to clarify the topic.
Evidence Do I provide enough evidence for my claims? Is it clear how the evidence supports the main idea?	**Highlight** the evidence you used. **Check** that it clearly connects to and supports your main idea.	**Add** additional evidence where needed. **Elaborate** on how your evidence supports your main idea to make the connection clear.
Organization Are my ideas and paragraphs organized logically? Do my transitions clearly connect each new idea?	Read each paragraph and **note** the order in which your ideas are presented. **Circle** transitional words and phrases.	**Reorder** the sentences in your paragraphs for logical flow. **Add** or **reword** transitional language for clarity.
Language Are my word choices precise and clear?	**Cross out** (X) unclear words or phrases. **Underline** any informal language.	**Reword** instances of unclear and informal language.
Conclusion Does my conclusion logically wrap up the ideas I presented?	**Put a star** (★) next to parts of your conclusion that connect back to your main idea or thesis.	**Revise** your conclusion to make the connection to your main idea clearer.

APPLY TO YOUR DRAFT

Consider the following as you look for opportunities to improve your writing:

- Make sure your thesis statement is a clearly stated and well supported.
- Don't assume what your readers know—provide the details and background they need to follow your essay.
- Use precise language and concrete details to convey your ideas.
- Correct any errors in grammar and punctuation.

Peer Review in Action

Once you have finished revising your informative essay, you will exchange papers with a partner in a **peer review** during which you will give suggestions to improve your partner's draft.

Read the introduction from a student's draft and examine the comments made by her peer reviewer to see how it's done.

First Draft

"In Desperate Situations and Dire Straits"
By Maria Cruz, Island High School

Cabeza de Vaca and his fellow Spaniards are the first example of the fate of strangers in a strange land.
They found themselves in a situation that seemed past all hope. Now they just wanted to survive.

Maybe open with a more dramatic description that grabs the reader.

A line from the diary to show how desperate they felt.

Read the revised introduction below. Notice how the writer has improved her draft by making revisions based on her peer reviewer's comments.

Revision

"In Desperate Situations and Dire Straits"
By Maria Cruz, Island High School

Planting the flag on the coast of southwestern Florida, Cabeza de Vaca, the expedition's royal treasurer, must have been figuring out how much treasure he would reap from the bold actions of his country to claim the New World for "His Most Catholic Majesty" (Reséndez, "A Desperate Trek Across America," paragraphs 2, 5). Yet a short time later, he squatted in a low-riding raft in the treacherous tides of the Gulf of Mexico, desperately hoping to survive. "We were in such straits that anything that had some semblance of a solution seemed good to us . . . one can imagine for himself what could happen in a land so strange" (Reséndez, "A Desperate Trek Across America," paragraph 2). They might as well have landed on Mars. At that point in his life, Cabeza de Vaca stood as only the first stranger to arrive in the New World and to fall victim to its strangeness. Others would follow with stories perhaps equally as harrowing.

Interesting opening—it kind of puts the reader in the situation.

Good use of a source quote here. It gets across how out of place they felt.

APPLY TO YOUR DRAFT

During your peer review, give specific suggestions for how to make your partner's essay more effective. Use the revision guide to help you.

When receiving feedback from your partner, listen attentively and ask questions to make sure you fully understand the revision suggestions.

4 EDIT YOUR INFORMATIVE ESSAY

Edit your draft to check for proper use of standard English conventions and to correct any misspellings or grammatical errors.

Watch Your Language!

Interactive Grammar Lesson: Active Voice and Passive Voice

USE THE ACTIVE VOICE

The subject of a sentence in the active voice performs the action. The subject receives the action in a passive sentence. Although passive voice has a place in writing, most authors choose the active voice because the passive is less direct, less forceful, and sometimes awkward and dull.

Read the following sentence from "In Desperate Situations and Dire Straits":

> Yet a short time later, he <u>squatted</u> in a low-riding raft in the treacherous tides of the Gulf of Mexico, desperately hoping to survive.

Note what happens to the drama and life of the prose when the verb is changed to the passive voice:

> He <u>was being carried</u> aboard a raft. . . .

The passive voice deadens the prose and flattens out the drama.

APPLY TO YOUR DRAFT

Now apply what you have learned to your own work.

1. **Read your paper aloud.** Listen to your word choices and the rhythm of your sentences.

2. **Check your verb choices.** Change any use of passive voice to active where it can enliven your writing.

3. **Exchange drafts** with a peer and review the writing, checking the conventions and grammar.

5 PUBLISH YOUR INFORMATIVE ESSAY

Share It!

Finalize your informative essay for your school newspaper. You may also use your essay as the basis for other projects.

Verb Voice

Active voice uses present and past tenses of the verb. In writing, the active voice is dramatic and energizing.

Lightning struck the barn.

Passive voice includes a form of the verb *to be* and the past participle of the verb. In writing, the passive voice can lead to wordiness and clunky sentences.

The barn was struck by lightning.

Ways to Share

- **Present your essay for discussion,** focusing on its main idea—the feeling of being in a strange place or feeling out of place.

- **Create a social media story** using images that reflect the main ideas in your essay.

- **Record a podcast** using voice and sound to bring your essay to life, and share it with the class.

Present an Informative Essay

Your informative essay may explore historical figures or people starting a new life, but the topic is one that most people can relate to. Work with a group to broaden the discussion into a **panel presentation.** Use media for your presentation and plan to host a class discussion on the topic.

Plan Your Presentation

With your group, review your essays and decide which ideas you will present to the class. Divide up the ideas so every group member can contribute. Consider the following for your presentation:

- What is the best order to present the main ideas to the class?
- How can the group bring specific events or details to life for the class?
- Are there visual and audio media you could use to enhance the presentation?
- What can you do to get the audience thinking about how the ideas apply to their lives?

Use the planning chart to help you with your group's panel presentation.

Be an Effective Group

Here are ways your group can make the best use of your planning time:

- Come to all group meetings prepared.
- Set clear goals and deadlines to complete each step.
- Ask each other questions to make sure you're all on the same page.

PRESENTATION PLANNING CHART	
Introduce the Topic	• Have a moderator introduce the topic and explain the format. • State how the panel is going to address the question: "What does it mean to be a stranger in a strange land?"
Present	• Create and follow an organizational plan. • Speak clearly and try not to rush through your material.
Audio/Visuals	• Be sure to have double-checked your media before starting. • Allow time for the audience to view any visuals you present.
Discussion	• Allow 10–15 minutes after the presentation for questions and comments from the audience. • Prompt discussion with a question, such as "What does this topic mean to us today?" • Have the moderators sum up the comments and discussion.

Practice with Your Group

Once you have made your group assignments and agreed on the format of the presentation, it is time to practice. It is important that everyone feels comfortable with the material they're presenting.

As you practice, give each other constructive feedback or suggestions. Use the guide to think about ways to help your group members. Make notes on the feedback your group gives you.

Presentation Elements	Notes for Improvement
Content Am I familiar enough with the text I'm presenting? Are there any sentences I need to tweak to be easier to read?	
Delivery Am I loud enough to be heard? Am I speaking at an even rate? Am I making eye contact with the audience?	
Media Do the media I'm using help people understand my points? Is my delivery coordinated properly with my media?	

MODERATING A DISCUSSION

Here are some things to keep in mind for the discussion portion of your presentation:

- **Prepare** a few prompt questions to keep the discussion going.

- **Listen** closely to questions and comments from the audience.

- **Acknowledge** what was said or asked.

- **Make sure** different people get a chance to talk.

Record Your Presentation

With your teacher, plan to record your presentation and discussion. Review it as a group and make any edits needed (such as cutting out dead air or interruptive noises) so that the recording sounds smooth and professional.

Share It!

- **Post it online** so other students, friends, or family members can listen to it.

- **Make it a mini-documentary** by editing in music, adding images or video, and reordering the content.

- **Host a discussion** about the issues in your presentation with other students outside of class (at lunch or after school).

 Ed

Interactive Speaking & Listening Lesson: Giving a Presentation

Reflect & Extend

Here are some other ways to show your understanding of the ideas in Unit 1.

Reflect on the Essential Questions

Think about the Essential Question you identified as most intriguing on page 2. Has your answer to the question changed after reading the texts in the unit? Discuss your ideas. You can use these sentence starters to help you reflect on your learning:

- **I want to learn more about . . .**
- **The selection affected my thinking about . . .**
- **I still don't understand . . .**

Project-Based Learning
↳ Create a Sketchnote

With a group of classmates, create a sketchnote about a person, event, or idea presented in this unit. Here are some questions to get you started:

- What topic would you like to understand more deeply by making a sketchnote?
- What structure for your sketchnote would make sense for your topic: a timeline, a flowchart, a web diagram, or something else?
- What combination of visual and textual elements would best convey your topic in a sketchnote format?
- Will you use a drawing application on a computer or tablet, or physical materials such as poster board and markers?
- How will you divide the work among the members of your group?

Media Projects

To find help with this task online, access **Create a Sketchnote.**

Writing
↳ Write a Short Story

. . . about being a stranger in a strange land. Your setting could be another country, another time period, or even an alien world. Have a theme in mind—an idea about life that you want to convey. Use the chart to record notes and ideas. Then write your story.

Ask Yourself	My Notes
What is the **setting**? Is it unfamiliar to the character, to the reader, or both?	
Who is the main character? What other **characters** will there be? What is the main **conflict**?	
What are the key developments I want to present in the **plot**? How do these plot points support the **theme** I want to express?	

"A nation is formed by the willingness of each of us to share the responsibility for upholding the common good."

—Barbara Jordan

The Revolutionary Period

Building a Democracy

? As you read the texts in this unit, think about how they explore these **Essential Questions.**

What does oppression look like?
The men who founded the United States fought some forms of oppression, but many of them held individuals in slavery and denied rights to women.

How do we gain our freedom?
The struggle for freedom is embedded in the founding of the United States and continues for some people today.

How can we share power and build alliances?
After gaining independence from England, the 13 former colonies had to work together to build a better future.

How do we reach our goals?
From the Founding Fathers to people arriving in the United States today, Americans have reinvented themselves as they confronted new opportunities and challenges.

ANALYZE THE IMAGE
How does this image reflect the idea that building a democracy is a shared responsibility?

 Ed

Explore unit themes and build background.

Stream to Start Video

Spark Your Learning

Here are some opportunities to think about issues related to **Unit 2: Building a Democracy.**

As you read, you can use the **Response Log** (page R2) to track your thinking about the Essential Questions.

Make the Connection

Think about the title of this unit, Building a Democracy. Then discuss the following questions with a partner:

- What are the characteristics of a democracy?

- What actions can people take to help build a democracy?

Think About the Essential Questions

Review the Essential Questions on page 127. Which question is most intriguing to you? Perhaps it relates to something you have read or reminds you of a personal experience. Write down your thoughts.

Prove It!

Use one of the Academic Vocabulary words in a sentence in which you share something you know about the American Revolution and the founding of the United States.

Build Academic Vocabulary

You can use these Academic Vocabulary words to write and talk about the topics and themes in the unit. Which of these words do you already feel comfortable using when speaking or writing?

	I can use it!	I understand it.	I'll look it up.
contrary	☐	☐	☐
founder	☐	☐	☐
ideological	☐	☐	☐
publication	☐	☐	☐
revolution	☐	☐	☐

Preview the Texts

Review the images, titles, and descriptions of the texts in the unit.
Mark the title of the text that interests you most.

The Declaration of Independence

Public Document by Thomas Jefferson

This document declared the 13 colonies were free from British rule.

One Today

Poem by Richard Blanco

This poem presents a sweeping view of life across America.

American Experience: Alexander Hamilton

Video by PBS

Discover Hamilton's influence on America in this video.

Thomas Jefferson: The Best of Enemies

History Writing by Ron Chernow

Thomas Jefferson and Alexander Hamilton disagreed on how America should be governed.

A Soldier for the Crown

Short Story by Charles Johnson

This story tells about one person's pursuit of freedom from racial enslavement during the American Revolution.

from The Autobiography

Autobiography by Benjamin Franklin

Join this unique American founder on his quest for moral perfection.

On Being Brought from Africa to America

Poem by Phillis Wheatley

The speaker, a person who is enslaved, shares her experience.

Sympathy

Poem by Paul Laurence Dunbar

The poem describes the pain one feels when freedom is denied.

from Lean In

Essay by Sheryl Sandberg

The executive and thought leader shares her philosophy on life.

Letter to John Adams

Letter by Abigail Adams

Abigail Adams speaks out as her husband drafts a set of laws for the United States.

Building a Democracy

The road to the American Revolution began in the early 1760s, when tensions built up between Britain's thirteen North American colonies and Britain's government and king, George III, who ruled over them. The British protected the colonies from Native American and European threats. After American colonial forces under George Washington failed to drive the French from the Ohio River valley, Britain sent reinforcements. When the French and Indian War ended in 1763, Britain controlled all the land east of the Mississippi River. But when the British tried to recover the costs of the war by taxing the colonists, rebellion against Britain began.

Thomas Paine

The Rise of Rationalism

In Europe, the political and social turmoil of the 17th century caused many people to question the divine right of monarchs and traditional authority. A new movement called the Enlightenment began to spread. Supporters of the Enlightenment believed in a philosophy called rationalism, the belief that human beings can arrive at truth by using reason. American colonial writers such as Benjamin Franklin, Thomas Paine, and Thomas Jefferson adapted the ideals of the

1730s
Great Awakening begins.

1754
French and Indian War begins.

1700

1733
Georgia becomes the
13th British colony.

Enlightenment to their own circumstances. This new philosophy combined with a wave of religious enthusiasm called the Great Awakening, in which preachers such as Jonathan Edwards called upon colonists to rededicate themselves to the Puritan ideals of sinless living, hard work, thrift, and responsibility.

Politics, Pamphlets, and Propaganda

As the colonists began to question their relationship with Britain, many gifted minds turned to political writing. Between 1763 and 1783, about 2,000 pamphlets were published, reaching thousands of people and stirring debate and action. *Common Sense* by Thomas Paine was a key pamphlet that helped move the colonists to revolution. Paine's Enlightenment ideas were combined with the Puritan belief that America was destined to be a model of freedom to the world. Thomas Jefferson also wrote pamphlets, but his great contribution to American government, literature, and the cause of freedom throughout the world is the Declaration of Independence, in which he eloquently articulated

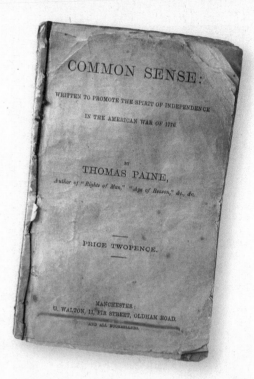

EXTEND

Think of a question you have about a topic, an event, or a person from the historical period. Then, research the answer and add it as an entry to the timeline.

1776
Declaration of Independence is adopted.

1803
U.S. purchases the Louisiana Territory from France.

1810

1765
Colonists rebel against the Stamp Act.

1783
American Revolution ends.

1788
U.S. Constitution is adopted.

Patrick Henry delivering his "Speech to the Virginia Convention" in 1775, which includes the famous line, "Give me liberty, or give me death!"

the natural law that would govern America. This natural law is the idea that people are born with rights and freedoms and that it is the function of government to protect those freedoms in a democratic society.

Jefferson's Declaration marked the beginning of the colonies' independence, but it was the adoption of the Constitution of the United States of America in 1788 that created the lasting framework for an independent government. Ideological debates over the scope and nature of federal power raged throughout the republic's early years. For example, in 1803, President Thomas Jefferson stirred controversy by purchasing the vast Louisiana Territory west of the Mississippi River from France, thus doubling the size of the United States. Jefferson, who normally favored a limited federal government, took this bold step even though the Constitution gave him no explicit authority to do so.

Voices of the People

Statesmen were not the only people who contributed to the political writing of the day. Even poetry sometimes examined political and social themes. Among the finest is the work of Phillis Wheatley, a poet who was formerly enslaved. In her poems and letters, Wheatley wrote of the "natural rights" of African Americans and pointed out the discrepancy between the colonists' "cry for freedom" and their enslavement of fellow human beings.

© Houghton Mifflin Harcourt Publishing Company • Image Credits: ©Artokoloro Quint Lox Limited/Alamy

Another voice calling for the rights of all citizens was that of Abigail Adams, whose husband, John, became the nation's second president. In letters written while the couple was apart, Adams encouraged her husband to include the rights of women in the nation's founding documents. Wheatley, Adams, and other women writers joined the Puritans and patriots who came before them to give us an understanding of the dreams and values that shaped our nation. All contributed their voices and ideals to building the metaphorical "city upon a hill" that Puritan preacher John Winthrop first envisioned as a beacon to all in 1630.

COLLABORATIVE DISCUSSION

In a small group, discuss events from the historical essay that you believe had a lasting effect on American life and literature. Why do you think this is so?

Assessment Practice

Choose the best answer to each question.

1. Why did the American colonists rebel against Britain?
   - (A) They didn't want to defend territory Britain had captured from the French.
   - (B) They didn't want to pay the costs of the French and Indian War.
   - (C) Britain tried to outlaw slavery in the colonies.
   - (D) Britain tried to keep Jefferson from buying the Louisiana Territory.

2. What type of publication was especially useful in spreading revolutionary ideas?
   - (A) books
   - (B) almanacs
   - (C) pamphlets
   - (D) newspapers

3. In what kind of writing did Abigail Adams express her political views?
   - (A) drama
   - (B) poetry
   - (C) sermons
   - (D) letters

Test-Taking Strategies

The Declaration of Independence

Public Document by **Thomas Jefferson**

Engage Your Brain

Choose one or more of these activities to start connecting with the public document you're about to read.

Influence Is No Government

What makes a government oppressive or representative? How should a government go about representing the will of the people? Why would a government choose not to do so? Free write for five minutes to answer.

Student Council

Think about student government at your school. With a partner, discuss how involved the student council is in shaping policies for students. How do their actions and decisions directly affect student life?

Declaration v. Constitution v. Bill of Rights

The three most important public documents in the United States are the Declaration of Independence, the Constitution, and the Bill of Rights. How well do you know what's in them? Look at the following statements and identify which of the three documents they come from. Next to each statement, write *DI* for Declaration of Independence, *C* for Constitution, or *BR* for Bill of Rights.

- "Congress shall make no law respecting an establishment of religion, or prohibiting the free exercise thereof."

- "All legislative Powers herein granted shall be vested in a Congress of the United States, which shall consist of a Senate and House of Representatives."

- "The powers not delegated to the United States by the Constitution, nor prohibited by it to the States, are reserved to the States respectively, or to the people."

- "[A]s free and independent states, they have full power to levy war, conclude peace, contract alliances, establish commerce, and to do all other acts and things which independent states may of right do."

- "[T]o secure these rights, governments are instituted among men, deriving their just powers from the consent of the governed."

- "Treason against the United States, shall consist only in levying War against them, or in adhering to their Enemies, giving them Aid and Comfort."

Determine Central Idea

The Declaration of Independence is a public document focused on a **central idea,** or an overall message in the text. Like any other well-written text, a public document may contain more than one idea. To recognize a central idea, ask yourself:

- What is the most important thing the author is saying?
- What details support the author's ideas?
- What words and phrases are repeated or emphasized?

For example, Jefferson repeats the words *tyranny* and *tyrant* to justify the colonies' move to independence. As you read the Declaration of Independence, notice the ways Jefferson conveys central ideas.

Focus on Genre
↳ **Public Document**

- establishes a legal and/or philosophical framework for structuring society and civic life
- has great historical or social significance
- includes a clear purpose and a strong theme
- uses repetition of words and phrases to reinforce meaning and create rhythm
- uses parallelism, or similar grammatical structures, to express ideas that are related or equal in importance

Analyze Argument

The power of the Declaration of Independence comes not just from *what* it says but *how* Jefferson says it. Jefferson combines rhetoric and structure to create a compelling argument. The structural features of Jefferson's argument include

- a clear, arguable **central idea**
- **reasons** and **evidence** that support the central idea
- logical and emotional **appeals** to the audience
- a convincing **conclusion** that sums up the important ideas
- a **call to action** that encourages the audience to do something

As you read, use the structure of the text to follow Jefferson's reasoning. Use the chart to analyze the structural elements of Jefferson's argument.

Central Ideas	Logical and Emotional Appeals	Conclusion	Call to Action

Annotation in Action

Here are one student's comments on the features of an argument.
As you read, mark words or phrases that move the argument forward.

> When, in the course of human events, it becomes necessary for one people to dissolve the political bands which have connected them with another, and to assume, among the powers of the earth, the separate and equal station to which the laws of nature and of nature's God entitle them, a decent respect to the opinions of mankind requires that they should declare the causes which impel them to the separation.

Jefferson will offer reasons for the action he proposes.

Expand Your Vocabulary

Put a check mark next to the vocabulary words that you feel comfortable using when speaking or writing.

establish	
affect	
invest	
abdicate	

Turn to a partner and discuss what you know about the Declaration of Independence. As you read, use the definitions in the side column to learn the vocabulary words you don't already know.

Background

Thomas Jefferson (1743–1826) was one of the most accomplished of our nation's founders. He was minister to France after the American Revolution and the third president of the United States. However, more important than his titles was his vision of liberty and self-government, eloquently expressed in the Declaration of Independence. Drafted by Jefferson, the Declaration was debated by the Second Continental Congress and adopted on July 4, 1776. The Declaration begins with an assertion of the Enlightenment ideas of "self-evident" truths of liberty and human rights.

The Declaration of Independence

Public Document by **Thomas Jefferson**

Pay attention to the evidence Jefferson uses to support the idea of American independence.

1   When, in the course of human events, it becomes necessary for one people to dissolve the political bands which have connected them with another, and to assume, among the powers of the earth, the separate and equal station to which the laws of nature and of nature's God entitle them, a decent respect to the opinions of mankind requires that they should declare the causes which impel them to the separation.

2   We hold these truths to be self-evident:—That all men are created equal; that they are endowed by their Creator with certain unalienable rights; that among these are life, liberty, and the pursuit of happiness. That, to secure these rights, governments are instituted among men, deriving their just powers from the consent of the governed; that, whenever any form of government becomes destructive of these ends, it is the right of the people to alter or to abolish it, and to institute a new government, laying its foundation on such principles, and organizing its powers in such form, as to them shall seem most likely to effect their safety and happiness. Prudence, indeed, will dictate that governments long **established** should not

DETERMINE CENTRAL IDEA

Annotate: Mark words in paragraph 2 that state Jefferson's central idea.

Cite Evidence: What details in paragraph 2 present justification for his central idea? Explain.

establish
(ĭ-stăb′lĭsh) *v.* to formally set up; institute.

be changed for light and transient causes; and, accordingly, all experience hath shown that mankind are more disposed to suffer, while evils are sufferable, than to right themselves by abolishing the forms to which they are accustomed. But, when a long train of abuses and usurpations, pursuing invariably the same object, evinces a design to reduce them under absolute despotism,[1] it is their right, it is their duty, to throw off such government, and to provide new guards for their future security. Such has been the patient sufferance of these colonies; and such is now the necessity that constrains them to alter their former systems of government. The history of the present King of Great Britain[2] is a history of repeated injuries and usurpations, all having, in direct object, the establishment of an absolute tyranny over these States. To prove this, let facts be submitted to a candid world.

3   He has refused his assent to laws[3] the most wholesome and necessary for the public good.

4   He has forbidden his Governors to pass laws of immediate and pressing importance, unless suspended in their operation till his assent should be obtained; and, when so suspended, he has utterly neglected to attend to them.

5   He has refused to pass other laws for the accommodation of large districts of people, unless these people would relinquish the right of representation in the legislature—a right inestimable to them, and formidable to tyrants only.

6   He has called together legislative bodies at places unusual, uncomfortable, and distant from the depository of their public records, for the sole purpose of fatiguing them into compliance with his measure.

7   He has dissolved representative houses repeatedly, for opposing, with manly firmness, his invasions on the rights of the people.

8   He has refused, for a long time after such dissolutions, to cause others to be elected; whereby the legislative powers, incapable of annihilation, have returned to the people at large for their exercise; the State remaining, in the meantime, exposed to all dangers of invasion from without, and convulsions within.

9   He has endeavored to prevent the population[4] of these States; for that purpose obstructing the laws for the naturalization of foreigners; refusing to pass others to encourage their migration hither, and raising the conditions of new appropriations of lands.

10   He has obstructed the administration of justice, by refusing his assent to laws for establishing judiciary powers.

11   He has made judges dependent on his will alone for the tenure of their offices,[5] and the amount and payment of their salaries.

© Houghton Mifflin Harcourt Publishing Company

[1] **despotism** (dĕs′pə-tĭz-əm): government by a ruler with unlimited power.
[2] **the present King of Great Britain:** George III, who reigned from 1760 to 1820.
[3] **refused his assent to laws:** Laws passed in the colonial legislative assemblies needed the king's approval; sometimes it took years for laws to be approved or rejected.
[4] **to prevent the population:** to keep the population from growing.
[5] **the tenure of their offices:** their job security.

Close Read Screencast

Listen to a modeled close read of this text.

ANALYZE ARGUMENT

Annotate: Circle the repeated phrase in paragraphs 3–10. Underline the phrases in paragraphs 6 and 7 that give reasons for the king's behavior.

Draw Conclusions: How does the structure of Jefferson's complaints strengthen his argument?

12   He has erected a multitude of new offices, and sent hither swarms of officers to harass our people and eat out their substance.[6]

13   He has kept among us, in times of peace, standing armies, without the consent of our legislatures.

14   He has **affected** to render the military independent of, and superior to, the civil power.

15   He has combined with others to subject us to a jurisdiction foreign to our constitutions,[7] and unacknowledged by our laws; giving his assent to their acts of pretended legislation:

16   For quartering large bodies of armed troops among us;

17   For protecting them, by a mock trial, from punishment for any murders which they should commit on the inhabitants of these States;

18   For cutting off our trade with all parts of the world;

19   For imposing taxes on us without our consent;

20   For depriving us, in many cases, of the benefits of trial by jury;

21   For transporting us beyond the seas, to be tried for pretended offenses;

22   For abolishing the free system of English laws in a neighboring province,[8] establishing there an arbitrary government, and enlarging its boundaries, so as to render it at once an example and fit instrument for introducing the same absolute rule into these colonies;

23   For taking away our charters, abolishing our most valuable laws, and altering, fundamentally, the forms of our governments;

24   For suspending our own legislatures, and declaring themselves **invested** with power to legislate for us in all cases whatsoever.

25   He has **abdicated** government here, by declaring us out of his protection, and waging war against us.

26   He has plundered our seas, ravaged our coasts, burnt our towns,[9] and destroyed the lives of our people.

27   He is at this time transporting large armies of foreign mercenaries to complete the works of death, desolation, and tyranny, already begun with circumstances of cruelty and perfidy scarcely paralleled in the most barbarous ages, and totally unworthy the head of a civilized nation.

28   He has constrained our fellow citizens, taken captive on the high seas, to bear arms against their country, to become the executioners of their friends and brethren, or to fall themselves by their hands.

29   He has excited domestic insurrection amongst us,[10] and has endeavored to bring on the inhabitants of our frontiers the merciless Indian savages, whose known rule of warfare is an undistinguished destruction of all ages, sexes, and conditions.

affect
(ə-fĕkt´) *v.* to cause or influence.

ANALYZE ARGUMENT

Annotate: The repetition of grammatical constructions to express ideas that are related is called **parallelism**. Mark examples of parallelism that Jefferson uses in paragraphs 16–24.

Analyze: How does the use of parallelism strengthen Jefferson's argument?

invest
(ĭn-vĕst´) *v.* to grant or endow.

abdicate
(ăb´dĭ-kāt) *v.* to relinquish or cede responsibility for.

---

[6] **eat out their substance:** use up their resources.

[7] **subject us . . . our constitutions:** Parliament had passed the Declaratory Act in 1766, stating that the king and Parliament could make laws for the colonies.

[8] **a neighboring province:** the province of Quebec, which at the time extended south to the Ohio River and west to the Mississippi.

[9] **plundered . . . our towns:** American seaports such as Norfolk, Virginia, had already been shelled.

[10] **excited . . . amongst us:** Lord Dunmore, the royal governor of Virginia, had encouraged slaves to rise up and rebel against their masters.

NOTICE & NOTE
EXTREME OR ABSOLUTE LANGUAGE

When you notice language that leaves no doubt about a situation or an event, or allows no compromise, you've found an **Extreme or Absolute Language** signpost.

Notice & Note: Mark examples of extreme or absolute language in paragraph 30.

Interpret: How does the author use this language to support the idea of declaring independence?

30   In every stage of these oppressions we have petitioned for redress,[11] in the most humble terms; our repeated petitions have been answered only by repeated injury. A prince whose character is thus marked by every act which may define a tyrant is unfit to be the ruler of a free people.

31   Nor have we been wanting in our attentions to our British brethren. We have warned them, from time to time, of attempts by their legislature to extend an unwarrantable jurisdiction over us. We have reminded them of the circumstances of our emigration and settlement here. We have appealed to their native justice and magnanimity; and we have conjured them, by the ties of our common kindred, to disavow these usurpations, which would inevitably interrupt our connections and correspondence.

32   They, too, have been deaf to the voice of justice and of consanguinity.[12] We must, therefore, acquiesce in the necessity which denounces our separation; and hold them, as we hold the rest of mankind, enemies in war, in peace friends.

33   We, Therefore, the Representatives of the United States of America, in General Congress assembled, appealing to the Supreme Judge of the world for the rectitude[13] of our intentions, do, in the name and by the authority of the good people of these colonies, solemnly publish and declare, that these United Colonies are, and of right ought to be, Free and Independent States; that they are absolved from all allegiance to the British crown, and that all political connection between them and the state of Great Britain is,

---

[11] **redress:** the correction of a wrong; compensation.
[12] **deaf to . . . consanguinity:** The British have ignored pleas based on their common ancestry with the colonists.
[13] **rectitude:** morally correct behavior or thinking.

and ought to be, totally dissolved; and that, as free and independent states, they have full power to levy war, conclude peace, contract alliances, establish commerce, and to do all other acts and things which independent states may of right do. And, for the support of this declaration, with a firm reliance on the protection of Divine Providence, we mutually pledge to each other our lives, our fortunes, and our sacred honor.

?

ESSENTIAL QUESTION:
How do we gain our freedom?

Review your notes and add your thoughts to your **Response Log.**

COLLABORATIVE DISCUSSION

According to Jefferson, what are the characteristics of a good government? Discuss your ideas with a partner.

Assessment Practice

Answer these questions before moving on to the **Analyze the Text** section on the following page.

1. On what did Jefferson base his belief that all men are created equal?

   (A) their rights as British citizens

   (B) the will of the British king

   (C) the laws of nature and God

   (D) traditions of the colonies

2. What is Jefferson's main argument against remaining connected to Britain?

   (A) The colonies are ready to be on their own.

   (B) The British king has been an unjust tyrant.

   (C) The colonists no longer wish to obey British law.

   (D) Other countries expect this of the colonists.

3. What is the conclusion of Jefferson's argument?

   (A) The colonists must separate from Britain.

   (B) The colonists should give Britain another chance.

   (C) Britain had always been good to the colonists.

   (D) Britain should overthrow its king.

Test-Taking Strategies

© Houghton Mifflin Harcourt Publishing Company

Analyze the Text

Support your responses with evidence from the text.

NOTICE & NOTE

Review what you **noticed and noted** as you read the text. Your annotations can help you answer these questions.

1. **EVALUATE** When you read paragraph 2, you identified Jefferson's central idea. How does Jefferson use **Extreme or Absolute Language** to support his central idea? Explain whether you find the use of this language effective.

2. **ANALYZE** A **logical appeal** is a method of argument based on evidence and reasons. Choose an example of a logical appeal in the Declaration and explain how it supports the thesis.

3. **EVALUATE** Jefferson's list of complaints against the king makes up a large part of the text. How do these complaints fit into Jefferson's argument and support his central idea? Use the chart to help you answer.

Complaint	How it Supports the Argument

4. **EVALUATE** Examine Jefferson's repetition of the words *tyrant* and *tyranny* throughout the text. How do these words help support his argument?

5. **ANALYZE** **Tone** is the author's attitude toward the subject. What tone does Jefferson create in the final paragraph? Consider his diction in your response, including

   - the repetition of the word *all*
   - the phrase *totally dissolved*
   - the use of the word *independent*

6. **INTERPRET** What is Jefferson's call to action? How does this call to action relate to his central idea?

Choices

Here are some other ways to demonstrate your understanding of the ideas in this lesson.

Writing
↳ **Evaluating Equality**

"All men are created equal" are perhaps the most famous words of the Declaration of Independence or of any document in American history. What do you think the statement really meant to Jefferson and the men who revised his draft—considering that they went on to form a government in which slavery was legal, women could not vote, and Native Americans were called "merciless Indian savages"? Write an essay in which you assess the Declaration of Independence in light of these facts. Consider the following in your essay:

- Does this knowledge change the way you perceive Jefferson's ideas?

- What is Jefferson's idea of equality and freedom?

- How has the passage of time altered the perception of his ideas?

As you write and discuss, be sure to use the **Academic Vocabulary** words.

| contrary |
| founder |
| ideological |
| publication |
| revolution |

Speaking & Listening
↳ **Recite the Text**

At the time of its publication, many colonists heard the Declaration of Independence read aloud in public places. Evaluate the effectiveness of the document as a persuasive speech.

1. Work with a partner and take turns presenting part of the text as a speech. For example, you might recite the opening and closing paragraphs and your partner may recite the list of complaints.

2. As a speaker, use tone of voice and pacing to communicate meaning.

3. As a listener, pay attention to how well you can follow the line of reasoning.

4. Present to the class. Be sure to use appropriate eye contact, volume, and pronunciation.

Social & Emotional Learning
↳ **Finding Freedom**

The Declaration of Independence is responsible for the idea that America is "a free country." However, you or someone you know may feel that your freedom is limited. In a class discussion, address the following questions.

- Is freedom an important ideal to you?

- Why might people's freedom be limited today?

- Can some people's freedom cause others to have less freedom?

- What responsibility do you have to others who may not have the same freedoms as you do?

- How can you support freedom for yourself and for others?

Expand Your Vocabulary

To explore a new word, like *institute,* use a semantic map, which defines a
term, provides synonyms and related words, and shows the word in use.

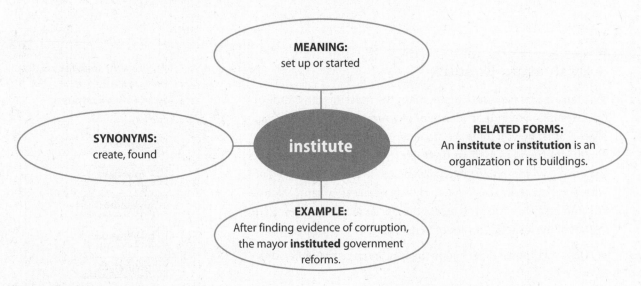

PRACTICE AND APPLY

Create a semantic map for each vocabulary word. Use print or online references
to check your work.

1. **establish**
   meaning:
   synonyms:
   related forms:
   example:

2. **affect**
   meaning:
   synonyms:
   related forms:
   example:

3. **invest**
   meaning:
   synonyms:
   related forms:
   example:

4. **abdicate**
   meaning:
   synonyms:
   related forms:
   example:

Vocabulary Strategy
↳ Domain-Specific Words

In the Declaration of Independence, Jefferson uses the vocabulary word *abdicate.* This word is more common in works of political science than in other writing. Political science, or the study of government, has **domain-specific words** that identify types of government or describe the way a government acts. Context clues, knowledge of Greek and Latin roots, and a dictionary can help establish the meaning of a word. Dictionaries also show related forms of a word, such as *legislative, legislature,* and *legislate.*

Ed

Interactive Vocabulary Lesson: Specialized Vocabulary

PRACTICE AND APPLY

Work with a partner and use a dictionary to find the meaning, **etymology** (word origin), and related forms of these domain-specific words.

1. sovereign
2. despotism
3. tyranny
4. govern

5. oligarchy
6. republic
7. democracy
8. legislative

9. executive
10. judicial

Watch Your Language!

Parallel Structure

Jefferson frequently uses the rhetorical device of parallelism in the Declaration of Independence. **Parallelism** is the use of similar grammatical constructions to express ideas that are closely related or equal in importance. It helps emphasize important ideas.

The chart shows examples of parallel structure from the Declaration of Independence. Read each passage aloud. Note how the parallelism creates rhythm and helps emphasize similarities among related ideas.

Structure	Example
Parallel phrases	He has plundered our seas, ravaged our coasts, burnt our towns, and destroyed the lives of our people.
Parallel clauses or sentences	We have warned them, from time to time, of attempts by their legislature to extend an unwarrantable jurisdiction over us. We have reminded them of the circumstances of our emigration and settlement here. We have appealed to their native justice and magnanimity; and we have conjured them, by the ties of our common kindred, to disavow these usurpations . . .

PRACTICE AND APPLY

Review a piece you have recently written. Try to incorporate parallel structure by grouping related ideas together.

One Today

Poem by Richard Blanco

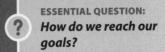

Engage Your Brain

Choose one or more of the following activities to start connecting with the poem you're about to read.

Not Your Typical Poetry Slam

Those few poets who have read poems at a presidential inauguration have been in the enviable position of sharing their poems with millions of people. Research which poets have written and read inaugural poems. For which presidents did they do so? What poems did they read?

Something in Common

In a small group, talk about what you have in common. Is it a shared routine, shared opinions, or shared experiences? Even when you have differences, is there something that still links you in some way?

Shared Values

Rate the following from most to least important, giving 6 points to the most important, and 1 point to the least. If you have a class polling app available to you, use it to tally the results. If not, tally the results with a spreadsheet or by hand. After the poll, have a class discussion about the results.

- respecting everyone's contributions equally
- showing common courtesy to everyone
- respecting life in all its forms
- being thankful for small things
- acknowledging the sacrifices of others
- building community

Analyze Structure

One building block of poetry is the **stanza,** a group of lines that forms a unit in a poem. Some poets use stanzas to develop different ideas that contribute to the poem's overall themes. As you read "One Today," consider these questions:

- What is the focus of each stanza?

- How does each stanza contribute to the theme?

- What words, phrases, and images are repeated across the stanzas? What effect does the repetition have?

Focus on Genre
↳ **Poetry**

- is arranged in lines and stanzas
- relies on figurative language and imagery to convey ideas
- may be commissioned for special occasions, such as an inauguration

Analyze Imagery

Imagery is the use of words and phrases that appeal to the reader's five senses. Poets use imagery to create a more vivid experience for the reader and to convey the poem's themes, mood, and tone. Images full of color and light, for example, create positive feelings or vibrant pictures for the reader and contribute to a positive theme. Use the chart below to identify images in each stanza of "One Today" and to indicate what feelings they evoke.

Stanza	Images	Feelings and Connotations

Determine Themes

A **theme** is a central idea about life or human nature. Richard Blanco's poem "One Today" was written for the second inauguration of President Barack Obama in 2013. The occasion for the poem, the imagery, and the main ideas in each stanza are clues to the poem's themes. As you read, consider how these elements contribute to the poem's themes.

Element	Contribution to Themes
Main idea of each stanza	Consider the main focus of each stanza. Taken together, what themes or aspects of the theme do the stanzas suggest?
Imagery	Are the images positive, negative, or neutral? What feelings do the images evoke for the reader?
Occasion	What does the poem's occasion suggest about themes? What does the writer want the reader to know or grasp?

Annotation in Action

Here is an example of notes a student made about images from "One Today." As you read, mark words that appeal to the senses.

> One sun rose on us today, kindled over our shores,
> peeking over the Smokies, greeting the faces
> of the Great Lakes, spreading a simple truth
> across the Great Plains, then charging across the Rockies.

Nice and warm

Sun seems friendly

High energy!

Background

Richard Blanco (b. 1968) is part of a Cuban family who immigrated to the United States from Spain in 1968. He grew up in Miami and earned a degree in civil engineering. He began writing poetry while working as an engineer and was selected as an inaugural poet for President Barack Obama's 2013 inauguration. Blanco was the youngest person to become an inaugural poet, as well as the first immigrant, the first Latino, and the first openly gay person to receive this honor. He has written several books of poetry, two memoirs, and numerous essays. He enjoys inspiring students to love and write poetry, and he teaches diverse audiences in colleges, schools, prisons, and nursing homes.

One Today

Poem by **Richard Blanco**

When you have one chance to say anything to the entire country, what do you say?

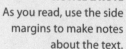

NOTICE & NOTE
As you read, use the side margins to make notes about the text.

One sun rose on us today, kindled over our shores,
peeking over the Smokies, greeting the faces
of the Great Lakes, spreading a simple truth
across the Great Plains, then charging across the Rockies.
5   One light, waking up rooftops, under each one, a story
told by our silent gestures moving behind windows.

My face, your face, millions of faces in morning's mirrors,
each one yawning to life, crescendoing into our day:
pencil-yellow school buses, the rhythm of traffic lights,
10   fruit stands: apples, limes, and oranges arrayed like rainbows
begging our praise. Silver trucks heavy with oil or paper—
bricks or milk, teeming over highways alongside us,
on our way to clean tables, read ledgers, or save lives—
to teach geometry, or ring-up groceries as my mother did
15   for twenty years, so I could write this poem for us today.

All of us as vital as the one light we move through,
the same light on blackboards with lessons for the day:
equations to solve, history to question, or atoms imagined,
the "I have a dream" we keep dreaming,
20   or the impossible vocabulary of sorrow that won't explain
the empty desks of twenty children marked absent
today, and forever. Many prayers, but one light
breathing color into stained glass windows,
life into the faces of bronze statues, warmth
25   onto the steps of our museums and park benches
as mothers watch children slide into the day.

One ground. Our ground, rooting us to every stalk
of corn, every head of wheat sown by sweat
and hands, hands gleaning coal or planting windmills
30   in deserts and hilltops that keep us warm, hands
digging trenches, routing pipes and cables, hands
as worn as my father's cutting sugarcane
so my brother and I could have books and shoes.

The dust of farms and deserts, cities and plains
35   mingled by one wind—our breath. Breathe. Hear it
through the day's gorgeous din of honking cabs,
buses launching down avenues, the symphony
of footsteps, guitars, and screeching subways,
the unexpected song bird on your clothes line.

40   Hear: squeaky playground swings, trains whistling,
or whispers across café tables, Hear: the doors we open
for each other all day, saying: *hello / shalom /
boun giorno / howdy / namaste /* or *buenos días*
in the language my mother taught me—in every language
45   spoken into one wind carrying our lives
without prejudice, as these words break from my lips.

ANALYZE STRUCTURE

Annotate: In lines 16–26, mark the word or phrase that suggests the central focus of the stanza.

Analyze: How does the stanza develop this image?

ANALYZE IMAGERY

Annotate: In lines 40–46, mark the greetings that appeal to the sense of sound.

Analyze: What feelings do these greetings convey to the reader? How do they help develop the poem's theme?

Annotate: Review the last three stanzas. Mark the recurring image that appears in all three stanzas.

Analyze: How does this image develop the theme of the poem?

One sky: since the Appalachians and *Sierras* claimed
their majesty, and the Mississippi and *Colorado* worked
their way to the sea. Thank the work of our hands:
50 weaving steel into bridges, finishing one more report
for the boss on time, stitching another wound
or uniform, the first brush stroke on a portrait,
or the last floor on the Freedom Tower
jutting into a sky that yields to our resilience.

55 One sky, toward which we sometimes lift our eyes
tired from work: some days guessing at the weather
of our lives, some days giving thanks for a love
that loves you back, sometimes praising a mother
who knew how to give, or forgiving a father
60 who couldn't give what you wanted.

We head home: through the gloss of rain or weight
of snow, or the plum blush of dusk, but always, always
home, always under one sky, our sky. And always
one moon like a silent drum tapping on every rooftop
65 and every window, of one country—all of us—
facing the stars. *Hope*—a new constellation waiting
for us to map it, waiting for us to name it—together.

ESSENTIAL QUESTION:
*How do we reach
our goals?*

Review your notes and
add your thoughts to your
Response Log.

COLLABORATIVE DISCUSSION

Why would President Obama select this poem to be read at his inauguration? Discuss your ideas in a small group.

Assessment Practice

Answer these questions before moving on to the **Analyze the Text**
section on the following page.

1. The literary device used to describe the sun in the first stanza is

   (A) simile

   (B) metaphor

   (C) personification

   (D) allusion

2. The overall structure of the poem moves from the

   (A) winter to spring

   (B) morning to night

   (C) personal to universal

   (D) mountains to sea

3. Which view best describes the speaker's attitude toward his parents?

   (A) He dislikes how hard they had to work.

   (B) He wishes they had more money.

   (C) He appreciates their commitment to the community.

   (D) He appreciates their hard work and sacrifices.

☺Ed
Test-Taking Strategies

Analyze the Text

Support your responses with evidence from the text.

NOTICE & NOTE

Review what you **noticed and noted** as you read the text. Your annotations can help you answer these questions.

1. **COMPARE** Reread the first and second stanzas. What shift in focus does the speaker make from the first to the second stanzas? What is the effect of the shift?

2. **INTERPRET** An **allusion** is a direct or indirect reference to a person, place, event, or literary work that the poet believes the reader will know. What is the allusion in line 19? How is that allusion appropriate for a poem read at a presidential inauguration? How does the allusion help to develop the poem's theme? Explain.

3. **ANALYZE** **Synecdoche** is a literary device that uses one part of something to represent the whole. What synecdoche is used in lines 29–31? What does the synecdoche represent? What effects does the synecdoche create?

4. **CITE EVIDENCE** What is the speaker's attitude about work and working people? What specific images convey this attitude in the lines listed below?

Lines	Images of Working People and Work	Attitudes/Feelings
10–15		
28–33		
49–54		

5. **CRITIQUE** Reread the first and last stanzas. How does the poet connect the beginning and ending of the poem? How do these stanzas relate to the poem's title? How effective is the ending for an inaugural poem? Explain.

6. **EVALUATE** What is the theme of this poem? What central images develop the theme?

Choices

Here are some other ways to demonstrate your understanding of the ideas in this lesson.

Writing
↳ Compare Inaugural Poems

In addition to Richard Blanco's presentation in 2013, poets were asked to read an original work at the inaugurations of 1961, 1993, 1997, and 2009. Find one of the poems, read it, and note similarities and differences with Blanco's poem. Then write a compare-and-contrast essay that examines the following points:

- stanza structure
- themes
- imagery
- tone

Follow these steps for writing:

1. Outline your essay to keep the compare-and-contrast focus on your topic.
2. Cite examples from the text to support your analysis.
3. Maintain an objective and formal tone throughout.
4. Proofread your essay for correct spelling, punctuation, grammar, and usage.
5. Ask a classmate to be your peer reviewer.

As you write and discuss, be sure to use the **Academic Vocabulary** words.

- contrary
- founder
- ideological
- publication
- revolution

Media
↳ Illustrate "One Today"

You've analyzed Blanco's poem for its use of rich imagery. How would you represent it visually? Using examples from the poem, create a collage, a painting, or a slideshow of images that helps capture its message. Share your final images with your classmates.

Speaking & Listening
↳ Poetry Reading

You have the honor of writing and delivering a poem for the next presidential inauguration.

What do you say and how do you say it? Craft a message appropriate to the occasion and then present the poem to your classmates. Keep in mind

- message and tone, given the occasion and audience
- a theme that resonates with the audience
- imagery and sound devices that will make your poem memorable
- a poetic form or structure that focuses your ideas and delivery

When your poem is done, record your presentation as you deliver it to the class. If possible, post the recordings to a class website.

ESSENTIAL QUESTION:

How can we share power and build alliances?

MEDIA

American Experience: Alexander Hamilton

Video by **PBS**

Engage Your Brain

The Quotable Alexander Hamilton

You're about to watch a video about one of the Founding Fathers of the United States. Alexander Hamilton was a passionate speaker and writer and had much to say about nation building. With a partner, read the following quotation and discuss why you think it's significant. Based on what Hamilton says, what system of government do you think he'd try to set up?

"Constitutions should consist only of general provisions; the reason is that they must necessarily be permanent, and that they cannot calculate for the possible change of things."

Background

The PBS *American Experience* documentary "Alexander Hamilton" traces Hamilton's life from his tragic childhood to his rise to prominence in the American Revolution and in the founding of the United States. It focuses on Hamilton's unique perspective, intellectual genius, and strong personality. It connects these characteristics to both his remarkable achievements and his demise. The segment of the documentary that you are about to watch explains the influence of Hamilton on the establishment of the central government in the challenging aftermath of the Revolution.

Alexander Hamilton

Determine Author's Purpose

The **purpose,** or intent, of informational videos is often to explain a topic. To achieve the purpose, the video's creator uses words as well as graphic features and sound elements. In a documentary about a historical person, the purpose is often to explain that person's achievements to an audience.

Evaluate Information in Media

Digital texts like videos convey ideas through visual and graphic features and sound elements. You must determine if they are effective. **Graphic features** help viewers clarify their understanding of complex events.

Focus on Genre
↳ Video

- is created for a specific purpose, to convey a message
- targets a particular audience
- includes visual and graphic features, as well as sound elements to convey ideas

Stills	Motionless images, such as illustrations, maps, or photographs
Animation	Drawings, computer graphics, photographs, or images that move
Actor portrayals	Actors playing the roles of historical or fictional people

Sound elements are what viewers hear in a video or embedded sound file.

Music	Songs, orchestration, or computer-generated tones to create mood
Narration	Narrator voice-overs that clarify a script or bridge between sections
Sound effects	Background sounds that add realism to reenactments or animations

To evaluate the information, check the reliability and accuracy of the sources, then look at how the information is **synthesized,** or combined, to support the author's purpose.

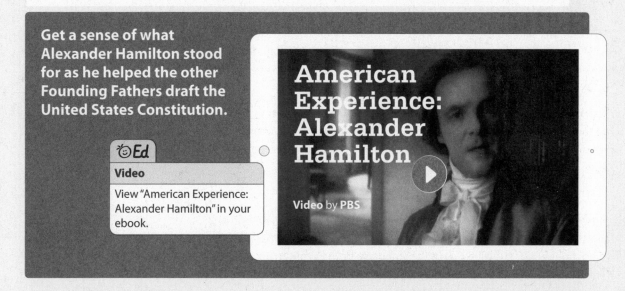

Get a sense of what Alexander Hamilton stood for as he helped the other Founding Fathers draft the United States Constitution.

☺**Ed**

Video

View "American Experience: Alexander Hamilton" in your ebook.

American Experience: Alexander Hamilton

Video by **PBS**

Analyze Media

Support your responses with evidence from the video.

1. **ANALYZE** The video states that Hamilton was "almost alone in his determination to change the direction of the country." Explain whether the various audiovisual elements effectively reflect this statement.

2. **SUMMARIZE** In two or three sentences, summarize what the video excerpt is about.

3. **INFER** According to the video, how did Hamilton's childhood in the Caribbean affect his approach to solving the nation's problems?

4. **EVALUATE** What is the overall purpose of the video segment? How well does the author achieve the purpose? In your response consider the sources of information that are cited in the video. Also consider graphic features and sound elements that convey information. Use the chart to help you.

Types of Graphic Features and Sound Elements in Video	Accuracy and Credibility of Information in Graphic and Sound Features	How Well Information in Graphic and Sound Features Supports Author's Purpose

5. **ANALYZE** How does the video characterize the Confederation Congress in the narrator's voice-over? How does the actor speaking Hamilton's own words show a contrast between the government's present state and Hamilton's dreams for a better government?

6. **EVALUATE** According to the historians in the video, what is Hamilton's strategy for putting his ideas forward? How does Hamilton himself portray his actions? How effectively does the video use both Hamilton's own ideas and the ideas of others to create a full picture of a complex person?

Choices

Here are some other ways to demonstrate your understanding of the ideas in this lesson.

Writing
↳ **Art Comparison**

There are a number of paintings that depict the Constitutional Convention. Find two of them to compare. Consider

- similarities between the two
- differences
- how the artists present the elements they think are important

Write a response in which you compare and contrast the two paintings. Then conclude with an answer to the following question: If you had to use one of the paintings as a still for a documentary, which one would you choose and why?

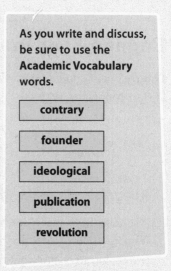

As you write and discuss, be sure to use the **Academic Vocabulary** words.

contrary

founder

ideological

publication

revolution

Research
↳ **Summary of the Constitutional Convention**

Hamilton was a delegate to the Constitutional Convention. Research this important meeting to answer the following questions. Then write a summary about the Convention and its significance.

- Which state did Alexander Hamilton represent at the Convention, and who were the other delegates from that state?
- Which state did not send delegates to the Convention? Why not?
- Of the 55 men who went to the Convention, how many did not sign the Constitution? What were their reasons?

Media
↳ **Multimedia Presentation**

Alexander Hamilton's contributions to the founding of the United States are numerous. Create a multimedia presentation that describes two or three of them.

1. Conduct research to fill in any gaps of knowledge you have about Hamilton's contributions. Use credible sources to get accurate information, and don't forget to cite them at the end of your presentation.

2. Choose a presentation format: you can use slides with embedded photo stills, audio, and video, or you can create a podcast or video presentation.

3. Keep your presentation organized. Open with a clear thesis statement, use examples to support your explanation, and conclude with a summarizing statement.

MENTOR TEXT

Thomas Jefferson: The Best of Enemies

History Writing by **Ron Chernow**

ESSENTIAL QUESTION:
How can we share power and build alliances?

Engage Your Brain

Choose one or more of these activities to start connecting with the historical account you're about to read.

Keep Your Enemies Closer

It is well known that Alexander Hamilton and Thomas Jefferson were not friends. At one point, Hamilton purportedly said he wanted to hit Jefferson with a chair. What would make him say something so harsh? How might Jefferson have responded? As you answer the questions, describe what it must have been like to be a member of George Washington's Cabinet when these two fought.

Picture This!

In groups of four, take turns drawing the following terms and concepts from the reading. If you aren't drawing, see if you can be the first to guess the art on the page.

Jefferson and Hamilton—Who Knew?

While neither was perfect, both Hamilton and Jefferson had lasting impacts on American politics and life. Research their lives and list three positive contributions they each made.

states' rights	national bank
national debt	yeoman farmer
central government	trade

Analyze Ideas and Events

Authors use organizational patterns to help convey information and ideas. For example, a writer might organize a text around comparison/contrast, problem/solution, or cause-and-effect relationships. Sometimes writers use multiple organizational patterns to explain their ideas clearly. In this article, one organizational pattern that Chernow uses is **chronological order,** which presents events in the order in which they happened. Through this structure, Chernow follows the sequence of events important to the relationship between Jefferson and Hamilton and explores how their ideas about government developed.

Use these strategies to analyze the sequence of events in informational text:

- Look for dates or words and phrases that identify time, such as *in a year, the following summer,* and *the next day.*

- Look for words that signal order, such as *first, afterward, then, during,* and *finally* to see how events or ideas are related.

As you read the text, trace both the order of external events that occur and also the changing relationship between Jefferson and Hamilton.

Focus on Genre

↳ **History Writing**

- presents information about historical events or persons
- includes facts, dates, and information presented in chronological order
- may employ narrative elements to emphasize details and increase readers' interest

Analyze Structure

The second organizational structure of Chernow's article is a point-by-point **comparison and contrast** of Jefferson and Hamilton that shows how and why they became "the best of enemies." In such a structure, a writer discusses a particular point of comparison about both subjects and then moves on to the next point. Chernow uses this structure to make his exposition of complex ideas clear, weaving in narrative elements to make the text more engaging.

	Events in Chronological Order	Evolution of Ideas	Comparisons
Thomas Jefferson			
Alexander Hamilton			

As you read, notice how Chernow uses structure to achieve his purpose.

Annotation in Action

Here are one student's notes on the structure of Chernow's essay. As you read, note how the author compares Hamilton and Jefferson and uses time-order words to tell you the sequence of events.

On March 21, 1790, Thomas Jefferson belatedly arrived in New York City to assume his duties as the first Secretary of State after a five-year ministerial stint in Paris. Tall and lanky, with a freckled complexion and auburn hair, Jefferson, 46, was taken aback by the adulation being heaped upon the new Treasury Secretary, Alexander Hamilton, who had streaked to prominence in his absence. Few people knew that Jefferson had authored the Declaration of Independence. . . . Instead, the Virginian was eclipsed by the 35-year-old wunderkind from the Caribbean.

The author includes time references to events he will describe.

Expand Your Vocabulary

Put a check mark next to the vocabulary words that you feel comfortable using when speaking or writing.

tepid	☐
copious	☐
cardinal	☐
rudiment	☐
façade	☐
anomalous	☐

With a partner, write a few sentences about someone planning something, using as many of the words as you can. As you read "Jefferson and Hamilton: The Best of Enemies," use the definitions in the side column to learn the vocabulary words you don't already know.

Background

Ron Chernow (b. 1949) is an award-winning author of several biographies, including *Alexander Hamilton* (2004) and *Washington: A Life* (2010). In this magazine article from 2004, he explores the ideological differences that brought Thomas Jefferson (1743–1826) and Alexander Hamilton (1755/57–1804) into conflict when both served in President George Washington's first Cabinet.

Thomas Jefferson: The Best of Enemies

History Writing by **Ron Chernow**

The Founding Fathers wanted to form a democracy. They just didn't agree on what it should look like.

NOTICE & NOTE

As you read, use the side margins to make notes about the text.

1   On March 21, 1790, Thomas Jefferson belatedly arrived in New York City to assume his duties as the first Secretary of State after a five-year ministerial stint in Paris. Tall and lanky, with a freckled complexion and auburn hair, Jefferson, 46, was taken aback by the adulation being heaped upon the new Treasury Secretary, Alexander Hamilton, who had streaked to prominence in his absence. Few people knew that Jefferson had authored the Declaration of Independence, which had yet to become holy writ for Americans. Instead, the Virginian was eclipsed by the 35-year-old wunderkind from the Caribbean, who was a lowly artillery captain in New York

ANALYZE IDEAS AND EVENTS

Annotate: Mark chronological information that is given in paragraph 1, such as dates and ages.

Infer: Why does the author begin the essay with the developing professional relationship between Jefferson and Hamilton?

when Jefferson composed the famous document. Despite his murky background as an illegitimate orphan, the self-invented Hamilton was trim and elegant, carried himself with an erect military bearing and had a mind that worked with dazzling speed. At first, Hamilton and Jefferson socialized on easy terms, with little inkling that they were destined to become mortal foes. But their clash inside George Washington's first Cabinet proved so fierce that it would spawn the two-party system in America. It also produced two divergent visions of the country's future that divide Americans to the present day.

2   For Hamilton, the first Treasury Secretary, the supreme threat to liberty arose from insufficient government power. To avert that, he advocated a vigorous central government marked by a strong President, an independent judiciary and a liberal reading of the Constitution. As the first Secretary of State, Jefferson believed that liberty was jeopardized by concentrated federal power, which he tried to restrict through a narrow construction of the Constitution. He favored states' rights, a central role for Congress and a comparatively weak judiciary.

3   At first glance, Hamilton might seem the more formidable figure in that classic matchup. He took office with an ardent faith in the new national government. He had attended the Constitutional Convention, penned the bulk of the Federalist papers to secure

passage of the new charter and spearheaded ratification efforts in New York State. He therefore set to work at Treasury with more unrestrained gusto than Jefferson—who had monitored the Constitutional Convention from his post in Paris—did at State. Jefferson's enthusiasm for the new political order was **tepid** at best, and when Washington crafted the first government in 1789, Jefferson didn't grasp the levers of power with quite the same glee as Hamilton, who had no ideological inhibitions about shoring up federal power.

4   Hamilton—brilliant, brash and charming—had the self-reliant reflexes of someone who had always had to live by his wits. His overwhelming intelligence petrified Jefferson and his followers. As an orator, Hamilton could speak extemporaneously for hours on end. As a writer, he could crank out 5,000- or 10,000-word memos overnight. Jefferson never underrated his foe's **copious** talents. At one point, a worried Jefferson confided to his comrade James Madison that Hamilton was a one-man army, "a host[1] within himself."

5   Whether in person or on paper, Hamilton served up his opinions promiscuously. He had a true zest for debate and never left anyone guessing where he stood. Jefferson, more than a decade older, had the quiet, courtly manner of a Virginia planter. He was emphatic in his views—Hamilton labeled him "an atheist in religion and a fanatic in politics"—but shrank from open conflict. Jefferson, a diffident speaker, mumbled his way through his rare speeches in a soft, almost inaudible voice and reserved his most scathing strictures for private correspondence.

6   The epic battle between these two Olympian[2] figures began not long after Jefferson came to New York City to assume his State Department duties in March 1790. By then Hamilton was in the thick of a contentious campaign to retire massive debt inherited from the Revolution. America had suspended principal and interest payments[3] on its obligations, which had traded as low as 15¢ on the dollar. In an audacious scheme to restore public credit, Hamilton planned to pay off that debt at face value, causing the securities to soar from depressed levels. Jefferson and Madison thought the original holders of those securities—many of them war veterans—should profit from that appreciation even if they had already sold their paper to traders at depressed prices. Hamilton thought it would be impractical to track them down. With an eye on future U.S. capital markets, he wanted to enshrine the **cardinal** principle that current owners of securities incurred all profits and losses, even if that meant windfall gains for rapacious speculators who had only recently bought the securities.

tepid
(tĕp´ĭd) *adj.* lukewarm; indifferent.

copious
(kō´pē-əs) *adj.* extensive.

ANALYZE IDEAS AND EVENTS

Annotate: Mark words in paragraph 6 that show the sequence of events.

Infer: How do the events described in paragraph 6 affect the relationship between Jefferson and Hamilton?

cardinal
(kär´dn-əl) *adj.* most important; prime.

---

[1] **host:** an army or large group of troops.
[2] **Olympian:** like a god; one from Mount Olympus.
[3] **principal and interest payments:** the amount borrowed and the fees charged by the lender.

7　　That skirmish over Hamilton's public credit plan was part of a broader tussle over the U.S.'s economic future. Jefferson was fond of summoning up idyllic scenes of an agrarian America peopled by sturdy yeoman farmers.[4] That poetic vision neglected the underlying reality of large slave plantations in the South. Jefferson was a fine populist on paper but not in everyday life, and his defense of Virginia interests was inextricably bound up with slavery. Hamilton—derided as a pseudo aristocrat, an elitist, a crypto-monarchist[5]—was a passionate abolitionist with a far more expansive economic vision. He conceded that agriculture would persist for decades as an essential component of the economy. But at the same time he wanted to foster the **rudiments** of a modern economy—trade, commerce, banks, stock exchanges, factories and corporations—to enlarge economic opportunity.

8　　Hamilton dreamed of a meritocracy, not an aristocracy, while Jefferson retained the landed gentry's disdain for the vulgar realities of trade, commerce and finance. And he was determined to undermine Hamilton's juggernaut.[6]

9　　Because we celebrate Jefferson for his sonorous words in the Declaration of Independence—Hamilton never matched Jefferson's gift for writing ringing passages that were at once poetic and inspirational—we sometimes overlook Jefferson's consummate skills as a practicing politician. A master of subtle, artful indirection, he was able to marshal his forces without divulging his generalship. After Hamilton persuaded President Washington to create the Bank of the United States, the country's first central bank, Jefferson was aghast

rudiment
(rōō′də-mənt) *n.* basic form.

---

[4] **yeoman farmers:** owners of small independent farms.
[5] **crypto-monarchist:** one who secretly supports government rule by a king.
[6] **juggernaut:** an extremely powerful force.

at what he construed[7] as a breach of the Constitution and a perilous expansion of federal power. Along with Madison, he recruited the poet Philip Freneau to launch an opposition paper called the National Gazette. To subsidize the paper covertly, he hired Freneau as a State Department translator. Hamilton was shocked by such flagrant disloyalty from a member of Washington's Cabinet, especially when Freneau began to mount withering assaults on Hamilton and even Washington. Never one to suffer in silence, Hamilton retaliated in a blizzard of newspaper articles published under Roman pseudonyms. The backbiting between Hamilton and Jefferson grew so acrimonious that Washington had to exhort both men to desist.

10   Instead, the feud worsened. In early 1793, a Virginia Congressman named William Branch Giles began to harry Hamilton with resolutions ordering him to produce, on short deadlines, stupendous amounts of Treasury data. With prodigious bursts of energy, Hamilton complied with those inhuman demands, foiling his opponents. Jefferson then committed an unthinkable act. He secretly drafted a series of anti-Hamilton resolutions for Giles, including one that read, "Resolved, That the Secretary of the Treasury has been guilty of maladministration in the duties of his office and should, in the opinion of Congress, be removed from his office by the President of the United States." The resolution was voted down, and the effort to oust Hamilton stalled. Jefferson left the Cabinet in defeat later that year.

11   Throughout the 1790s, the Hamilton-Jefferson feud continued to fester in both domestic and foreign affairs. Jefferson thought Hamilton was "bewitched" by the British model of governance,

© Houghton Mifflin Harcourt Publishing Company

---

[7] **construed:** interpreted.

NOTICE & NOTE
QUESTIONING STANCE

When you read informational texts, you should take a **Questioning Stance,** which means that you engage with the information the author provides rather than accept it without thinking.

Notice & Note: Mark details in paragraphs 9 and 10 that help you answer this **Big Question**: What surprised you about Jefferson and Hamilton's relationship when they served on Washington's Cabinet and why?

Annotate: Mark the references to time in paragraph 11.

Analyze: How did the men's view of the French Revolution change over time? Cite text evidence in your response.

while Hamilton considered Jefferson a credulous apologist for the gory excesses of the French Revolution. Descended from French Huguenots[8] on his mother's side, Hamilton was fluent in French and had served as Washington's liaison with the Marquis de Lafayette and other French aristocrats who had rallied to the Continental Army. The French Revolution immediately struck him as a bloody affair, governed by rigid, Utopian thinking. On Oct. 6, 1789, he wrote a remarkable letter to Lafayette, explaining his "foreboding of ill" about the future course of events in Paris. He cited the "vehement character" of the French people and the "reveries" of their "philosophic politicians," who wished to transform human nature. Hamilton believed that Jefferson while in Paris "drank deeply of the French philosophy in religion, in science, in politics." Indeed, more than a decade passed before Jefferson fully realized that the French Revolution wasn't a worthy sequel to the American one so much as a grotesque travesty.[9]

12   If Jefferson and Hamilton define opposite ends of the political spectrum in U.S. history and seem to exist in perpetual conflict, the two men shared certain traits, feeding a mutual cynicism. Each scorned the other as excessively ambitious. In his secret diary, or Anas, Jefferson recorded a story of Hamilton praising Julius Caesar as the greatest man in history. (The tale sounds dubious, as Hamilton invariably used Caesar as shorthand for "an evil tyrant.") Hamilton repaid the favor. In one essay he likened Jefferson to "Caesar coyly refusing the proffered diadem"[10] and rejecting the trappings, but "tenaciously grasping the substance of imperial domination."

13   Similarly, both men hid a potent hedonism[11] behind an intellectual **façade**. For all their outward differences, the two politicians stumbled into the two great sex scandals of the early Republic. In 1797 a journalist named James T. Callender exposed that Hamilton, while Treasury Secretary and a married man with four children, had entered into a yearlong affair with grifter Maria Reynolds, who was 23 when it began. In a 95-page pamphlet, Hamilton confessed to the affair at what many regarded as inordinate length. He wished to show that the money he had paid to Reynolds' husband James had been for the favor of her company and not for illicit speculation in Treasury securities, as the Jeffersonians had alleged. Forever after, the Jeffersonians tagged Hamilton as "the amorous Treasury Secretary" and mocked his pretensions to superior morality.

façade
(fə-säd´) *n.* false or misleading appearance.

---

[8] **French Huguenots:** a group of Protestants who were persecuted in Catholic France; many fled to North America.
[9] **travesty:** an unreasonable distortion or parody.
[10] **Caesar . . . diadem":** In Shakespeare's *Julius Caesar*, the Roman general refuses a crown three times, but his critics believe he really wanted to be named king.
[11] **hedonism:** the belief that personal pleasure is the primary goal in life.

Thomas Jefferson

14 By an extraordinary coincidence, during Jefferson's first term as President, Callender also exposed Jefferson's relationship with Sally Hemings. Callender claimed that "Dusky Sally," a.k.a. the "African Venus," was the President's slave concubine, who had borne him five children. "There is not an individual in the neighborhood of Charlottesville who does not believe the story," Callender wrote, "and not a few who know it." Jefferson never confirmed or denied Callender's story. But the likely truth of the Hemings affair was dramatically bolstered by DNA tests published in 1998, which indicated that a Jefferson male had sired at least one of Hemings' children.

15 The crowning irony of the stormy relations between Hamilton and Jefferson is that Hamilton helped install his longtime foe as President in 1801. Under constitutional rules then in force, the candidate with the majority of electoral votes became President; the runner-up became Vice President. That created an **anomalous** situation in which Jefferson, his party's presumed presidential nominee, tied with Aaron Burr, its presumed vice presidential nominee. It took 36 rounds of voting in the House to decide the election in Jefferson's favor. Faced with the prospect of Burr as President, a man he considered unscrupulous, Hamilton not only

NOTICE & NOTE
CONTRASTS AND CONTRADICTIONS

When you notice a sharp contrast between what you would expect and what you observe happening, you've found a **Contrasts and Contradictions** signpost.

Notice & Note: Mark a surprising fact that Chernow includes in the paragraph 15 of the article.

Analyze: What contradiction does this fact reveal? Explain.

anomalous
(ə-nŏm´ə-ləs) *adj.* unusual.

opted for Jefferson as the lesser of two evils but also was forced into his most measured assessment of the man. Hamilton said he had long suspected that as President, Jefferson would develop a keen taste for the federal power he had deplored in opposition. He recalled that a decade earlier, in Washington's Cabinet, Jefferson had seemed like a man who knew he was destined to inherit an estate—in this case, the presidency—and didn't wish to deplete it. In fact, Jefferson, the strict constructionist, freely exercised the most sweeping powers as President. Nothing in the Constitution, for instance, permitted the Louisiana Purchase.[12] Hamilton noted that with rueful mirth.

---

[12] **Louisiana Purchase:** France's 1803 sale of its territory west of the Mississippi River to the United States.

COLLABORATIVE DISCUSSION

With a partner, discuss how modern politics reflect some of Jefferson's and Hamilton's ideas. Think of the ideas each man proposed, and then compare how those ideas influence modern-day politicians and legislation.

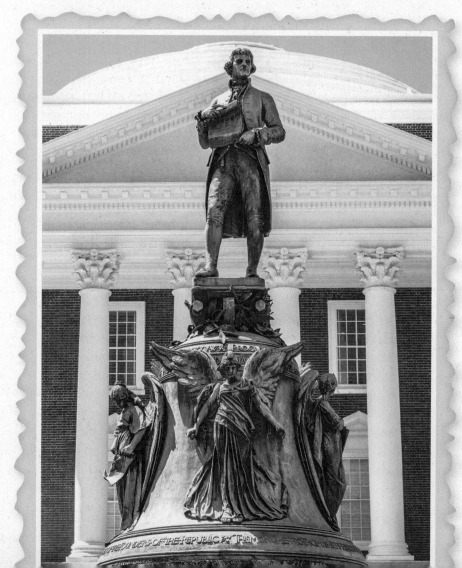

Assessment Practice

Answer these questions before moving on to the **Analyze the Text** section on the following page.

1. What event sparked the beginning of the conflict between Hamilton and Jefferson?

   (A) Jefferson came back from France.

   (B) Hamilton arrived from the Caribbean.

   (C) Jefferson wrote the Declaration of Independence.

   (D) Hamilton attended the Constitutional Convention.

2. What is a main difference between the economic visions of America held by Jefferson and Hamilton?

   (A) Jefferson's vision was urban, while Hamilton's was rural.

   (B) Jefferson's vision was modern, while Hamilton's was traditional.

   (C) Jefferson's vision included slavery, while Hamilton's was abolitionist.

   (D) Jefferson's vision included government controls, while Hamilton favored the aristocracy.

3. How did Hamilton respond to the accusations of illicit speculation?

   (A) He confessed to illegally investing in Treasury securities.

   (B) He confessed at length to having an extramarital affair.

   (C) He accused Jefferson of having an affair with Sally Hemings.

   (D) He accused the Jeffersonians of lying about his financial dealings.

Test-Taking Strategies

Analyze the Text

Support your responses with evidence from the text.

NOTICE & NOTE

Review what you **noticed and noted** as you read the text. Your annotations can help you answer these questions.

1. **ANALYZE** What event sparked the conflict between Hamilton and Jefferson? What sequence of events caused the feud to worsen?

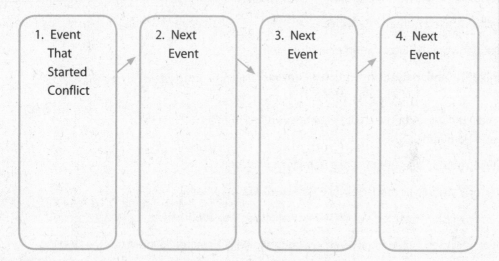

1. Event That Started Conflict

2. Next Event

3. Next Event

4. Next Event

2. **EVALUATE** How did Jefferson's election as president change the relationship between the two men?

3. **CITE EVIDENCE** How did Hamilton's and Jefferson's different personal styles affect the ways they carried out their feud?

4. **ANALYZE** How does Chernow's point-by-point comparison of these two rivals add to the strength of his concluding paragraph?

5. **COMPARE** Chernow points out that despite the two leaders' conflicts, they shared some common traits. In what ways were Jefferson and Hamilton similar, according to Chernow? How does describing their **Contrasts and Contradictions** strengthen the article?

6. **EVALUATE** How effectively did Chernow combine chronological order and compare-and-contrast structures to portray the idea that Hamilton and Jefferson were "destined to become mortal foes"?

7. **CONNECT** Think about what you knew about Jefferson and Hamilton prior to reading this text. Take a **Questioning Stance** and identify what information challenged, changed, or confirmed what you already knew about these two Founding Fathers.

Choices

Here are some other ways to demonstrate your understanding of the ideas in this lesson.

Writing
↳ Social Media Profile

Thomas Jefferson and Alexander Hamilton find themselves in the 21st century and need to come up to speed. Help them write their social media profiles.

1. Decide which type of platform they should use to create a profile: personal or professional.

2. Write the profiles following format guidelines posted in the app.

3. Use details from Chernow's article to make sure your profiles accurately represent their interests, likes and dislikes, and ideals.

4. Have a classmate read the profiles and make comments and editorial suggestions.

5. Revise your profiles, add images if you like, and then share them with the class, or post your profiles to a website or LAN.

As you write and discuss, be sure to use the **Academic Vocabulary** words.

> contrary
>
> founder
>
> ideological
>
> publication
>
> revolution

Media
↳ Cabinet Battles

Lin-Manuel Miranda based *Hamilton the Musical* on Ron Chernow's book, *Hamilton*. In a stroke of genius, he turned the Jefferson-Hamilton philosophical clashes into rap battles. Find the original cast recording of the musical and listen to Cabinet Battle #1 and Cabinet Battle #2. Use the songs to evaluate how well Miranda captured Chernow's description of both men and what they stood for.

Speaking & Listening
↳ Debate

Chernow mentions Hamilton's contributions to the *Federalist Papers*. Perhaps his most famous is Federalist 84, in which he airs his views on the Bill of Rights. In groups of four, research the essay and James Madison's reaction to it.

1. Use reliable sources. Look for URLs with .edu or .gov. Congress.gov has links to many resources concerning the *Federalist Papers*.

2. When you've finished researching, summarize Hamilton's position and Madison's reaction.

3. Divide into two teams, one debating the merits of Hamilton's position and the other the merits of Madison's. Prepare rebuttals and counterarguments to possible claims your opponents could make.

4. After you've prepared, hold the debate. Record it to share with the class.

Expand Your Vocabulary

PRACTICE AND APPLY

Choose the letter of the answer to the questions and explain your responses.

1. Which of these responses is **tepid**?

   a. a shrug   **b.** a shout

2. An **anomalous** answer to a question is most likely to provoke

   a. satisfaction   **b.** confusion

3. Which type of print material has a **copious** number of pages?

   a. pamphlet   **b.** encyclopedia

4. A **façade** is most similar to which of the following?

   a. a mask   **b.** a hat

5. How does a musician learn the **rudiments** of playing an instrument?

   a. practicing   **b.** humming

6. Which of the following is a **cardinal** principle of American democracy?

   a. free markets   **b.** individual rights

Vocabulary Strategy

↳ **Use Reference Materials**

Interactive Vocabulary Lesson: Using Reference Sources

Consulting **reference materials,** such as dictionaries and thesauruses, helps you learn more than just a word's meaning. A dictionary entry includes the word's pronunciation, part of speech, definitions, word derivation, and related words.

PRACTICE AND APPLY

Consult references to find additional information about each word below. Take notes in the chart. Then, discuss with a partner how this knowledge helps you understand Ron Chernow's article better.

Word	Additional Information
copious	
cardinal	
rudiments	
façade	
anomalous	

Watch Your Language!

Hyphenation

"Thomas Jefferson: The Best of Enemies" uses hyphenated words in a variety of ways. Hyphens join words into compounds so that their meaning is clear. Using hyphenated words can also be a simple way of expressing an idea. Compare the phrase from the article to its nonhyphenated alternative.

Phrase from the article:

> after a <u>five-year</u> ministerial stint in Paris

Nonhyphenated alternative:

> after a ministerial stint of <u>five years</u> in Paris

The hyphenated adjective creates a succinct text and contributes to a straightforward style. The chart below shows other uses of hyphens.

Uses of Hyphens	
Purpose	**Examples**
join parts of a compound with *all-, ex-, self-,* or *-elect*	*the self-invented Hamilton, the self-reliant reflexes*
join numbers to a noun to make an adjective	*35-year-old wunderkind, a 95-page pamphlet*
join a prefix to a proper noun	*anti-Hamilton resolutions*
join two or more compounds to a single base	*5,000- or 10,000-word memos*
join a prefix or suffix to a noun	*crypto-monarchist, runner-up*

Some compounds do not use hyphens. They may be open, as in *stock exchange* or closed, as in *courthouse*. When in doubt, consult a dictionary.

PRACTICE AND APPLY

In each sentence, write hyphens where they are needed.

1. A group of ten and eleven year olds played softball in the park.

2. Ahmed was excited when he got a five dollar raise at work.

3. We know several people who are mountain climbing enthusiasts.

4. Pratichi's mother is president elect of the PTA.

ⓒEd
Interactive Grammar Lesson: Hyphens

A Soldier for the Crown

Short Story by **Charles Johnson**

ESSENTIAL QUESTION:
How do we gain our freedom?

Engage Your Brain

Choose one or more of these activities to start connecting with the short story you're about to read.

Risk-Taker or Risk Averse?

List four reasons you would take a risk. Think about what circumstances might prompt the need to do so. What's an acceptable risk and what's not? Compared to others, are you comfortable with taking risks? Write your ideas in a paragraph.

No, No, No, Don't Spoil It!

What are really effective ways that TV shows, books, and movies maintain that balance between leaving the audience guessing and not spoiling the end? How do authors and directors keep from giving away too much information? In a small group, talk about examples of shows or books that have done a good job of this. How did they do it?

Soldiers for Both Sides

During the American Revolution, African Americans fought for both the Patriots and the Loyalists. Do some research so that you can create a two-minute video about their participation in the Revolutionary War. Include:

- the approximate number of soldiers who fought on each side

- the reasons they fought

- what happened to them when the war was over

Analyze Point of View

Point of view refers to the perspective an author uses to narrate a story. There are three main points of view in literature:

- **first-person point of view,** in which the narrator is a character in the story and events are told in his or her own words, using the pronouns *I, me,* and *my*

- **third-person point of view,** where the narrator is not a character, but an outside observer telling the story as it happened to someone else, using the pronouns *he, she, they, it,* etc. An **omniscient narrator** reports on all events and all the characters' thoughts. A **limited third-person narrator** focuses on one character's thoughts and feelings.

- **second-person point of view,** in which the narrator addresses someone using the pronoun *you*

With the second-person point of view, the reader may not know if the author is addressing a character, the reader, or the author's own self. In "A Soldier for the Crown," the narrator addresses the main character, Alexander Freeman, but often reveals the character's feelings, similar to third-person narration. To understand the point of view, the reader must distinguish between what is directly stated, by whom, and what is really meant in order to understand events and determine the story's underlying message.

Analyze Plot

Plot is the sequence of events in a literary work. Charles Johnson deliberately structures the plot of "A Soldier for the Crown" to achieve certain effects and develop his central character, Alexander Freeman.

- **Suspense** is the excitement or tension that readers feel as they wait to find out how a story ends. The author builds suspense when he introduces the main character as a risk-taker and builds interest in the story's outcome with statements such as "But did you win *this* time?"

- **Ambiguity** is the uncertainty created when readers can interpret words, phrases, or events in more than one way. The author builds the story by forcing the reader to put together clues about Freeman. As you read, your understanding of these clues may change.

As you read, note details that build suspense or create ambiguity.

Suspense	Ambiguity

Annotation in Action

Here are one student's comments about point of view in "A Soldier for the Crown." As you read, note how the use of second-person point of view reveals details about character and events.

> Before the war broke out, when you were still a servant in Master William Selby's house, you'd bet on anything—how early spring thaw might come, or if your older brother Titus would beat your cousin Caesar in a wrestling match—and most of the time you won.

Second-person point of view reveals character traits, such as a love of betting.

Expand Your Vocabulary

Put a check mark next to the vocabulary words that you feel comfortable using when speaking or writing.

capacity	☐
belatedly	☐
unalienable	☐
elusive	☐

With a partner, write a few sentences about a risky situation, using as many of the words as you can. As you read "A Soldier for the Crown," use the definitions in the side column to learn the vocabulary words you don't already know.

Background

Charles Johnson (b.1948), a writer, philosopher, artist, and educator, has often confronted the effects of race and racism. "Racism is based on our belief in a division between Self and Other, and our tendency to measure ourselves against others," he says. "Sad to say, it is also based on fear." Johnson's work has earned a MacArthur fellowship, the National Book Award for *Middle Passage* (1990), and the American Academy of Arts and Letters Award.

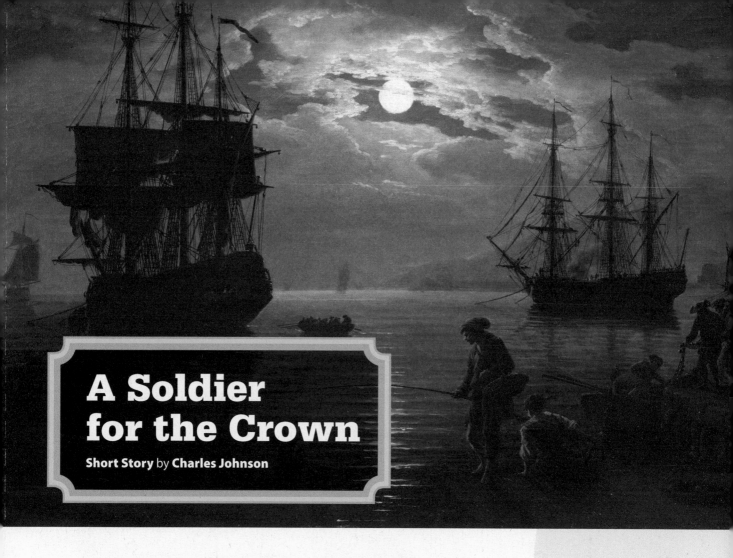

A Soldier for the Crown

Short Story by **Charles Johnson**

Some people are born risk-takers. Find out just how much one soldier will risk for a new life.

NOTICE & NOTE

As you read, use the side margins to make notes about the text.

1 YOU ALWAYS WERE a gambler.

2 Before the war broke out, when you were still a servant in Master William Selby's house, you'd bet on anything—how early spring thaw might come, or if your older brother Titus would beat your cousin Caesar in a wrestling match—and most of the time you won. There was something about gambling that you could not resist. There was suspense, the feeling that the future was not already written by white hands. Or finished. There was chance, the luck of the draw. In the roll of dice or a card game, there was always—what to call it?—an *openness*, a chance that the outcome would go this way or that. For or against you. Of course, in bondage to Master Selby there were no odds. Whichever way the dice fell or the cards came up, you began and ended your day a slave.

ANALYZE PLOT

Annotate: Identify statements in paragraph 2 that create suspense.

Infer: What do these statements make you wonder about what will happen next?

© Houghton Mifflin Harcourt Publishing Company • Image Credits: ©Photo Josse/Leemage/Getty Images

TOUGH QUESTIONS

When you notice characters asking questions that reveal their internal struggles, you've found a **Tough Questions** signpost.

Notice & Note: In paragraph 3, mark the question the narrator asks.

Analyze: What does this question make you wonder?

3
4

But did you win *this* time?

Standing by the wooden rail on a ship bound for Nova Scotia, crammed with strangers fleeing the collapse of their colonial world— women and children, whites and blacks, whose names appear in Brigadier General Samuel Birch's *Book of Negroes*—you pull a long-shanked pipe from your red-tinted coat, pack the bowl with tobacco, and strike a friction match against a nail in your bootheel. You know you are fortunate to be on board. Now that the Continental Army is victorious, blacks who fought for the crown are struggling desperately to leave on His Majesty's ships departing from New York harbor. Even as your boat eased away from the harbor, some leaped from the docks into the water, swimming toward the ship for this last chance to escape slavery. Seeing them, you'd thought, *That might have been me.* But it wasn't; you've always been lucky that way, at taking risks. Running away from bondage. Taking on new identities. Yet you wonder what to call yourself now. A loyalist? A traitor? A man without a country? As the harbor shrinks, growing fainter in the distance, severing you forever from this strange, newly formed nation called the United States, you haven't the slightest idea after years of war which of these names fits, or what the future holds, though on one matter you *are* clear:

Ships in the New York Harbor—1776

Portrait of British General
Sir Henry Clinton

5   From the start, you were fighting for no one but yourself.

6   The day after Lieutenant General Sir Henry Clinton promised liberty to all blacks deserting the rebel standard and willing to fight on the side of the British, you learned that Titus and Caesar were planning to flee. In the evening, on your way to the quarters after finishing your duties in the house, Titus stopped you outside the barn, and asked, "Can you go back to the kitchen and sneak out some provisions for us?" Naturally, you'd asked him what for, and he put his fingers to his lips, shushing you. They planned to steal two horses, he said. Then ride to safety behind British lines. "You're leaving?" You were almost speechless with anger. "And you're not taking *me*?"

7   "How can I?" he asked. "You're only fifteen."

8   "What's that got to do with anything? I can fight!"

9   "You ever fired a gun?"

10   "No, but I can learn!"

11   "Once I'm free, and got the papers to prove it, I'll come back."

12   "Titus, if you don't take me, I'll *tell*."

13

For a heartbeat or two, Titus looked as if he might hit you. Grudgingly, he agreed to bring you along, despite your age and his declaration after your parents' deaths that he'd keep you from harm. You did as he requested, returning to the house and filling a sack with food, Master Selby's clothing, even some of the mistress's jewelry that the three of you might barter, then delivered all this to your brother and Caesar in the barn. The three of you left that night on two of the master's best horses, you riding behind Titus, your arms tightly circling his waist until you stopped to make camp in the woods. There, Caesar suggested that it would help if you all changed your names and appearances as much as possible since Master Selby was sure to post your descriptions. Titus said fine, he'd grow a beard and call himself John Free. Caesar liked that, said, "Then I'll be George Liberty." They waited for you to pick a name, poking sticks at the campfire, sending up sparks into the starless sky. "Give me time," you'd said, changing into buckskin breeches, blue stockings, and a checkered, woolen shirt. "I'll shave my hair off, and I'll think of *some*thing before we get there. I don't want to rush." What you didn't tell them that night was how thrilling, how sweet this business of renaming oneself felt, and that you wanted to toy with a thousand possibilities—each name promising a new nature—turning them over on your tongue, and creating whole histories for each before settling, as you finally did, on "Alexander Freeman" as your new identity.

14

Thus, it was Alexander Freeman, George Liberty, and John Free who rode a few days later, bone weary from travel, into the British camp. You will never forget this sight: scores of black men in British uniforms, with the inscription LIBERTY TO SLAVES on their breasts, bearing arms so naturally one would have thought they were born with a rifle in their hands. Some were cleaning their weapons. Others marched. Still others were relaxing or stabbing their bayonets at sacks suspended from trees or performing any of the thousand chores that kept a regiment well-oiled and ready. When you signed on, the black soldier who wrote down your names didn't question you, though he remarked he thought you didn't look very strong. The three of you were put immediately to work. Harder work, you recall, than anything you'd known working in Master Selby's house, but for the first time in fifteen years you fell to each task eagerly, gambling that the labor purchased a new lease on life.

15

Over the first months, then years of the seesawing war, you, Titus, and Caesar served His Majesty's army in more **capacities** than you had fingers on the hand: as orderlies[1] to the white officers, laborers, cooks, foragers, and as foot soldiers who descended upon

---

[1] **orderlies:** soldiers who provide assistance to and perform tasks for an officer.

ANALYZE PLOT

Annotate: Mark the phrase in paragraph 13 that tells what Titus decided.

Infer: What questions from the beginning of this story are answered by his decision? What new question arises?

capacity
(kə-păs´ĭ-tē) *n.* ability to hold or have something; function or role.

Don't forget to
Notice & Note as you
read the text.

farms abandoned by their white owners, burning the enemy's fortifications and plundering plantations for much-needed provisions; as spies slipping in and out of southern towns to gather information; and as caretakers to the dying when smallpox swept through your regiment, weakening and killing hundreds of men. Your brother among them. And it was then you nearly gave up the gamble. You wondered if it might not be best to take your chips off the table. And pray the promise of the Virginia Convention that black runaways to the British side would be pardoned was genuine. And slink back home, your hat in your hand, to Master Selby's farm—if it was still there. Or perhaps you and Caesar might switch sides, deserting to the ranks of General Washington who, pressured for manpower, **belatedly** reversed his opposition to Negroes fighting in the Continental Army. And then there was that magnificent Declaration penned by Jefferson, proclaiming that "We hold these truths to be self-evident, that all men are created equal, that they are endowed by their Creator with certain **unalienable** Rights, that among these are Life, Liberty and the pursuit of Happiness," words you'd memorized after hearing them. If the Continentals won, would this brave, new republic be so bad?

16   "Alex, those are just *words*," said Caesar. "White folks' words for other white folks."

17   "But without us, the rebels would lose—"

18   "So would the redcoats. Both sides need us, but I don't trust neither one to play fair when this thing is over. They can do that Declaration over. Naw, the words I want to see are on a British pass with my name on it. I'm stayin' put 'til I *see that*."

19   Caesar never did. A month later your regiment was routed by the Continental Army. The rebels fired cannons for six hours, shelling the village your side occupied two days before. You found pieces of your cousin strewn everywhere. And you ran. Ran. You lived by your wits in the countryside, stealing what you needed to survive until you reached territory still in British hands, and again found yourself a pawn in the middle of other men's battles— Camden, where your side scattered poorly trained regulars led by General Gates, then liberated slaves who donned their masters' fancy clothing and powdered wigs and followed along behind Gates as his men pressed on; and the disastrous encounter at Guilford Court House, where six hundred redcoats died and Cornwallis was forced to fall back to Wilmington for supplies, then later abandon North Carolina altogether, moving on to Virginia. During your time as a soldier, you saw thousands sacrifice their

belatedly
(bĭ-lā´tĭd-lē) *adv.* done too late or overdue.

unalienable
(ŭn-āl´yə-nə-bəl) *adj.* impossible to be taken away.

ANALYZE POINT OF VIEW

Annotate: Mark details in paragraph 19 that refer to Freeman's feelings.

Interpret: What is the effect of the second-person point of view on your understanding of Freeman?

Battle of Camden—
Death of DeKalb by
Alonzo Chappel

lives, and no, it wasn't as if you came through with only a scratch. At Camden you took a ball in your right shoulder. Fragments remain there still, making it a little hard for you to sleep on that side or withstand the dull ache in your shoulder on days when the weather is damp. But, miraculously, as the war began to wind down, you were given the **elusive**, long-coveted British pass.

elusive
(ĭ-lōō´sĭv) *adj.* difficult to obtain or define.

20   On the ship, now traveling north past Augusta, you knock your cold pipe against the railing, shaking dottle from its bowl, then reach into your coat for the scrap of paper that was so difficult to earn. Behind you, other refugees are bedding down for the night, covering themselves and their children with blankets. You wait until one of the hands on deck passes a few feet beyond where you stand, then you unfold the paper with fingers stiffened by the cold. In the yellowish glow of the ship's lantern, tracing the words with your forefinger, shaping your lips silently to form each syllable, you read:

> This is to certify to whomfoever[2] it may concern, that the Bearer hereof . . . Alexander Freeman . . . a Negro, reforted to the Britifh Lines, in confequence of the Proclamations of Sir William Howe, and Sir Henry Clinton, late Commanders in Chief in America; and that the faid Negro has hereby his Excellency Sir Benjamin Hampton's Permiffion to go to Nova-Scotia, or wherever elfe he may think proper . . . By Order of Brigadier General Ruttledge

ANALYZE PLOT

Annotate: Mark the sentence in paragraph 21 that reveals a surprising truth about the main character.

Infer: Why doesn't the narrator name the main character until the end? What ambiguity about the situation remains?

21   The document, dated April 1783, brings a broad smile to your lips. Once your ship lands, and you find a home, you will frame this precious deed of manumission.[3] At least in this sense, your gamble paid off. And for now you still prefer the adopted name Alexander Freeman to the one given you at birth—Dorothy.

---

[2] **whomfoever . . . :** In the 1800s, handwritten and printed documents sometimes used the "long s," which looked like an *f* without the crossbar, in place of a lowercase *s*.

[3] **deed of manumission:** a document confirming a person's release from slavery.

22   Maybe you'll be Dorothy again, later in Nova Scotia. Of course, you'll keep the surname Freeman. And, Lord willing, when it's safe you will let your hair grow out again to its full length, wear dresses, and perhaps start a new family to replace the loved ones you lost during the war.

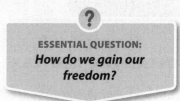

ESSENTIAL QUESTION:
How do we gain our freedom?

Review your notes and add your thoughts to your **Response Log.**

COLLABORATIVE DISCUSSION

With a partner, say whether you were surprised by the twist at the end of the story. What events appear in a new light? Include examples from the story in your response.

Assessment Practice

Answer these questions before moving on to the **Analyze the Text** section on the following page.

1. What is Dorothy doing when the story begins?

    (A) sailing away from New York to freedom

    (B) fleeing from Master Selby's farm

    (C) running away from the army after a battle

    (D) sailing with British troops for a new military campaign

2. Which most likely explains why Titus resists taking Dorothy with him?

    (A) He does not take his promise to protect her seriously.

    (B) He does not want her to slow down their escape.

    (C) He does not think she will be safe because she is young and female.

    (D) He thinks she would be happier staying on Master Selby's farm.

3. How does Dorothy gain the pass granting her freedom?

    (A) She takes Caesar's pass after he was killed in battle.

    (B) She earns it through her service in the British army.

    (C) She has to buy the pass from a British soldier.

    (D) The British give passes to all African Americans.

Test-Taking Strategies

Analyze the Text

Support your responses with evidence from the text.

1 **INTERPRET** What events in the story can be interpreted in more than one way? Was the ambiguity of these episodes due more to the story's point of view or to the plot structure?

Event	Possible Interpretations	Point of View or Plot?
	1. 2.	
	1. 2.	
	1. 2.	
	1. 2.	

2 **ANALYZE** Why does the conversation between Caesar and Dorothy about the Declaration of Independence hold greater significance once Dorothy's identity is revealed?

3 **ANALYZE** Why does the writer include Dorothy's reaction to Titus's death? How does it build suspense in the story?

4 **INTERPRET** What effect does the use of the second-person point of view have on the scene in paragraph 13? What idea is the author able to communicate by using this point of view?

5 **ANALYZE** Why is it **ironic,** or contrary to what you might have expected, that Dorothy considers the deed of manumission to be so precious?

6 **DRAW CONCLUSIONS** The **theme** is the truth about life that the writer conveys. Theme can be suggested by what happens to the main character and how that character changes over the course of the story. When Dorothy reflects on **Tough Questions**, what theme is suggested?

Choices

Here are some other ways to demonstrate your understanding of the ideas in this lesson.

Writing
↳ A Different Point of View

"A Soldier for the Crown" is narrated in the second person, which is a fairly rare narrative style. How does the story change if you write it from a different point of view? Give it a try! Your choices are first-person, third-person limited, or third-person omniscient. There's also first-person plural narration, in which multiple people tell the story collectively, using the pronouns *we, our,* and *ours*. As you write, consider

- what insights your narrator has into the thoughts and feelings of the characters

- what events your narrator would have enough knowledge of to describe to readers

- what limitations your style of narration brings to your storytelling

- what story aspects your narrative style lets you explore

As you write and discuss, be sure to use the **Academic Vocabulary** words.

> contrary

> founder

> ideological

> publication

> revolution

Social & Emotional Learning
↳ Diary Entry

Dorothy seems to have a fair amount of self-awareness. Find examples in the story where she recognizes her own strengths and limitations or shows confidence and an ability to act independently. How does she grow through her experience? Write a diary entry for Dorothy after she arrives in Nova Scotia. Include moments of reflection in which she looks back on all the events and takes stock of what she has learned.

Speaking & Listening
↳ Debate

In a small group, debate whether Dorothy's "gamble" paid off. Divide into teams based on who believes the gamble did pay off and who believes it didn't. Find details in the text to support your group's opinion, then draft your arguments. Try to anticipate any opposing views and have a rebuttal on hand to affirm your case.

1. Present your claim, reasons, and supporting evidence.

2. Listen to your opponents' claims and note any weaknesses in their arguments.

3. Present supporting evidence that reveals the weaknesses in your opponents' stance.

4. Present your rebuttal to any opposing views your opponents raised to your first claim.

Expand Your Vocabulary

PRACTICE AND APPLY

Show your understanding of the vocabulary words by answering these questions.

| capacity | belatedly | unalienable | elusive |

1. What do you possess as an individual with **unalienable** qualities? Explain.

2. Describe a circumstance in which you receive something **belatedly**.

3. When have you tried to grasp something that proved **elusive**? Explain.

4. In what **capacity** might you help out at a local animal shelter?

Vocabulary Strategy
↳ **Prefixes and Suffixes**

Adding a **prefix** to a word changes the word's meaning. Adding a **suffix** changes the word's part of speech. The vocabulary word *unalienable* is an example of a word built by adding the prefix *un-* and the suffix *-able* to the base word *alien*. As the word web shows, other prefixes and suffixes can be added to the base word *alien* with a variety of meanings and parts of speech.

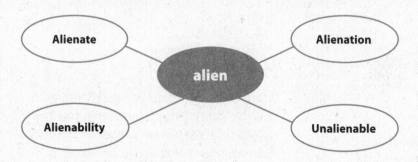

⊙Ed

Interactive Vocabulary Lesson: Understanding Word Origins

PRACTICE AND APPLY

Each of the following words appears in the selection. For each one, identify the base word and at least three other words that can be formed by adding other prefixes or suffixes. For each word you list, identify its part of speech. If you need help, use a print or online dictionary to identify forms of the word.

1. **colonial**

2. **wooden**

3. **liberty**

4. **inscription**

Watch Your Language!

Subject-Verb Agreement

The rules for **subject-verb agreement** are relatively simple—subjects and verbs should agree in number (singular or plural). When the subject is a pronoun, the verb must also agree in person—first person, second person, or third person.

First-Person Singular	I *ride* a bike to school every day.
Third-Person Singular	She *rides* a bike to school every day.
First-Person Plural	We *ride* our bikes to school together every day.

Compound subjects make subject-verb agreement more complicated. If two single subjects are joined by *and,* the subjects become a plural compound subject and need a plural verb, since both subjects are doing the action. If two singular subjects are joined by the words *or* or *nor,* they function in the sentence as a singular subject because *either one* is doing the action, but not both.

Plural Compound Subject	Terry **and** Raja *ride* their bikes to school every day.
Singular Compound Subject	Either Terry **or** Raja *rides* a bike to school every day.

If the subject is a **collective noun**—one that refers to several individuals—the verb may be singular or plural, depending on how the noun is used. The subject takes a singular verb if the subject is being viewed as a unit. It takes a plural verb if the focus is on the individual members of the collective group.

Interactive Grammar Lesson: Subject-Verb Agreement

As a Unit	The **team** *takes* the bus to the game.
As Individuals	The **team** *take* turns at practice.

PRACTICE AND APPLY

Read the passage from the story that includes the escape from the Selby farm. Write a third-person narrative of what the three characters did to prepare and to flee. Use a mix of singular and compound subjects and choose the correct verb form to show subject-verb agreement.

from
The Autobiography

Autobiography by **Benjamin Franklin**

Engage Your Brain

Choose one or more of these activities to start connecting with the autobiography you're about to read.

By Virtue of . . .

Here are three excerpts from the passage you are about to read. Based on the excerpts, what is the passage about? How do you think the ideas are linked? Discuss your ideas with a partner.

- "While my care was employed in guarding against one fault, I was often surprised by another."

- "I determined to give a week's strict attention to each of the virtues successively."

- ". . . that a perfect character might be attended with the inconvenience of being envied and hated; and that a benevolent man should allow a few faults in himself, to keep his friends in countenance."

Life, in Five Sentences or Fewer

You want to post your life story in a social media profile and have five sentences in which to do it. What will you write to sum up your life and still have it fit in a phone screen?

Self-Improvement Everywhere

Today a walk through a bookstore or a glance at popular web pages can show that self-improvement is a hot topic. Jot down the titles of any self-help books, videos, or podcasts that you have seen. Why do you think content about self-improvement is so popular? Discuss your ideas with a partner.

Make Inferences

One of the pleasures of reading an autobiography is getting to know the writer's personality, as well as his or her philosophical beliefs and attitudes—in other words, what makes the writer "tick." In many cases, though, writers don't directly reveal this information. Readers need to look beneath the surface of the text to **infer**, or make an educated guess about, the writer's beliefs.

- First, note what the author is telling you directly.

- Then, think about what you already know about the topic.

- Make an inference based on details in the text and your prior knowledge.

As you read, make inferences on Franklin's attitudes and beliefs. For example, how do you think Franklin felt about being self-reliant and practical?

> **Focus on Genre**
> ↳ Autobiography
>
> - uses the first-person point of view
> - focuses on significant events in the author's life
> - often includes thoughts about or interpretations of what is happening

Analyze and Evaluate Structure

In this excerpt from his autobiography, Benjamin Franklin describes his quest for moral perfection. A quest is a search for something, which often includes a journey. In this case, Franklin's quest is a moral journey to improve himself. He uses the structure of the quest to make his moral transformation clear.

Franklin includes graphic features to help the reader track his progress. By including these structural elements in his autobiography, Franklin builds interest in his quest and helps the reader understand his challenges. Use a chart like the one below to evaluate whether these graphic features build your interest and understanding in Franklin's journey.

Graphic Feature	Effectiveness

Annotation in Action

Here is one student's attempt to make an inference about Ben Franklin. As you read, mark details that support your inferences.

> As I knew, or thought I knew, what was right and wrong, I did not see why I might not always do the one and avoid the other. But I soon found I had undertaken a task of more difficulty than I had imagined.

Franklin seems to believe his assumption was wrong. Why was it more difficult than he thought?

Expand Your Vocabulary

Put a check mark next to the vocabulary words that you feel comfortable using when speaking or writing.

contrive	☐
trifling	☐
unremitting	☐
affluence	☐
eradicate	☐
incorrigible	☐
artifice	☐
felicity	☐

Turn to a partner and discuss a time when you tried to improve yourself. Use as many of the vocabulary words as you can. As you read, use the definitions in the side column to learn the vocabulary words you don't already know.

Background

Benjamin Franklin (1706–1790) was the oldest of the founders. He was 69 when he was sent as a delegate to the Second Continental Congress, where he assisted Thomas Jefferson in drafting the Declaration of Independence. But by that time, he'd already had a remarkable life, finding success as a printer, publisher, scientist, inventor, businessman, philosopher, postmaster, and statesman. He was also a prolific writer, producing volumes of essays, travel journals, newspaper articles, almanacs, speeches, and more. His autobiography, however, was his masterpiece, and it is still popular today.

from
The Autobiography

Autobiography by **Benjamin Franklin**

Look for details that reveal Franklin's belief in the possibility of human perfectibility.

NOTICE & NOTE
As you read, use the side margins to make notes about the text.

1   It was about this time I conceived the bold and arduous project of arriving at moral perfection. I wished to live without committing any fault at any time; I would conquer all that either natural inclination, custom, or company might lead me into. As I knew, or thought I knew, what was right and wrong, I did not see why I might not always do the one and avoid the other. But I soon found I had undertaken a task of more difficulty than I had imagined. While my care was employed in guarding against one fault, I was often surprised by another; habit took the advantage of inattention; inclination was sometimes too strong for reason. I concluded, at length, that the mere speculative conviction that it was our interest to be completely virtuous, was not sufficient to prevent our slipping; and that the contrary habits must be broken, and good ones acquired and established, before we can have any dependence on a steady, uniform rectitude of conduct. For this purpose I therefore **contrived** the following method.

MAKE INFERENCES

Annotate: Mark the words in the first paragraph that Franklin uses to describe the project.

Analyze: What do Franklin's words and his plan tell you about his character?

contrive
(kən-trīv´) *v.* to plan skillfully; to design.

from The Autobiography   **193**

Annotate: Mark where Franklin's list of virtues begins.

Analyze: What does this list tell you about the choices Franklin makes in presenting information?

trifling
(trī′flĭng) *adj.* frivolous; inconsequential.

VOCABULARY

Latin Roots: Mark the word *Industry* in Franklin's list. *Industry* is derived from the Latin word *industria*, meaning "diligence, hard work."

Analyze: How does the meaning of the Latin root relate to Franklin's description?

2   In the various enumerations of the moral virtues I had met with in my reading, I found the catalogue more or less numerous, as different writers included more or fewer ideas under the same name. Temperance, for example, was by some confined to eating and drinking, while by others it was extended to mean the moderating every other pleasure, appetite, inclination, or passion, bodily or mental, even to our avarice and ambition. I proposed to myself, for the sake of clearness, to use rather more names, with fewer ideas annexed to each, than a few names with more ideas; and I included under thirteen names of virtues all that at that time occurred to me as necessary or desirable, and annexed to each a short precept, which fully expressed the extent I gave to its meaning.

3   These names of virtues, with their precepts were:

1. **Temperance.** Eat not to dullness; drink not to elevation.

2. **Silence.** Speak not but what may benefit others or yourself; avoid **trifling** conversation.

3. **Order.** Let all your things have their places; let each part of your business have its time.

4. **Resolution.** Resolve to perform what you ought; perform without fail what you resolve.

5. **Frugality.** Make no expense but to do good to others or yourself; *i.e.,* waste nothing.

6. **Industry.** Lose no time; be always employed in something useful; cut off all unnecessary actions.

7. **Sincerity.** Use no hurtful deceit; think innocently and justly; and, if you speak, speak accordingly.

8. **Justice.** Wrong none by doing injuries, or omitting the benefits that are your duty.

9. **Moderation.** Avoid extremes; forbear resenting injuries so much as you think they deserve.

10. **Cleanliness.** Tolerate no uncleanliness in body, clothes, or habitation.

11. **Tranquillity.** Be not disturbed at trifles, or at accidents common or unavoidable.

12. **Chastity.** Rarely use venery but for health or offspring, never to dullness, weakness, or the injury of your own or another's peace or reputation.

13. **Humility.** Imitate Jesus and Socrates.[1]

4   My intention being to acquire the *habitude* of all these virtues, I judged it would be well not to distract my attention by attempting

---

[1] **Socrates** (sŏk′rə-tēz): Greek philosopher (470?–399 BC) who believed that true knowledge comes through dialogue and systematic questioning of ideas.

Don't forget to
Notice & Note as you
read the text.

the whole at once, but to fix it on one of them at a time; and, when I should be master of that, then to proceed to another, and so on, till I should have gone through the thirteen; and, as the previous acquisition of some might facilitate the acquisition of certain others, I arranged them with that view, as they stand above. Temperance first, as it tends to procure that coolness and clearness of head, which is so necessary where constant vigilance was to be kept up, and guard maintained against the **unremitting** attraction of ancient habits, and the force of perpetual temptations. This being acquired and established, Silence would be more easy; and my desire being to gain knowledge at the same time that I improved in virtue, and considering that in conversation it was obtained rather by the use of the ears than of the tongue, and therefore wishing to break a habit I was getting into of prattling, punning, and joking, which only made me acceptable to trifling company, I gave *Silence* the second place. This and the next, *Order,* I expected would allow me more time for attending to my project and my studies. *Resolution,* once become habitual, would keep me firm in my endeavors to obtain all the subsequent virtues; *Frugality* and Industry freeing me from my remaining debt, and producing **affluence** and independence, would make more easy the practice of Sincerity and Justice, etc., etc.

unremitting
(ŭn rĭ-mĭt´ĭng) *adj.* constant; never stopping.

affluence
(ăf´lōō-əns) *n.* wealth.

Form of the pages.

TEMPERANCE							
eat not to dullness; drink not to elevation.							
	S.	M.	T.	W.	T.	F.	S.
T.							
S.	•	•		•		•	
O.	••	•	•		•	•	•
R.			•			•	
F.		•			•		
I.			•	•			
S.							
J.							
M.							
C.							
T.							
C.							
H.							

ANALYZE AND EVALUATE STRUCTURE

Annotate: Mark the area of the chart that shows that Franklin succeeded in being temperate for most of the week.

Analyze: How does this chart help the reader understand Franklin's ideas?

Conceiving then, that, agreeably to the advice of Pythagoras in his Golden Verses,[2] daily examination would be necessary, I contrived the following method for conducting that examination.

5 I made a little book, in which I allotted a page for each of the virtues. I ruled each page with red ink, so as to have seven columns, one for each day of the week, marking each column with a letter for the day. I crossed these columns with thirteen red lines, marking the beginning of each line with the first letter of one of the virtues, on which line, and in its proper column, I might mark, by a little black spot, every fault I found upon examination to have been committed respecting that virtue upon that day.

6 I determined to give a week's strict attention to each of the virtues successively. Thus, in the first week, my great guard was to avoid every[3] the least offense against *Temperance,* leaving the other virtues to their ordinary chance, only marking every evening the faults of the day. Thus, if in the first week I could keep my first line, marked T, clear of spots, I supposed the habit of that virtue so much strengthened, and its opposite weakened, that I might venture extending my attention to include the next, and for the following week keep both lines clear of spots. Proceeding thus to the last, I could go through a course complete in thirteen weeks, and four courses in a year. And like him who, having a garden to weed, does not attempt to **eradicate** all the bad herbs at once, which would exceed his reach and his strength, but works on one of the beds at a time, and, having accomplished the first, proceeds to a second, so I should have, I hoped, the encouraging pleasure of seeing on my pages the progress I made in virtue, by clearing successively my lines of their spots, till in the end, by a number of courses, I should be happy in viewing a clean book, after thirteen weeks' daily examination. . . .

7 The precept of *Order* requiring that *every part of my business should have its allotted time,* one page in my little book contained the following scheme of employment for the twenty-four hours of a natural day.

8 I entered upon the execution of this plan for self-examination, and continued it with occasional intermissions for some time. I was surprised to find myself so much fuller of faults than I had imagined; but I had the satisfaction of seeing them diminish. To avoid the trouble of renewing now and then my little book, which, by scraping out the marks on the paper of old faults to make room for new ones in a new course, became full of holes, I transferred my tables and precepts to the ivory leaves of a memorandum book, on which the lines were drawn with red ink, that made a durable stain, and on those lines I marked my faults with a black-lead pencil, which marks I could easily wipe out with a wet sponge. After a while I went through one course only in a year, and afterward only one in several years,

NOTICE & NOTE
EXTREME OR ABSOLUTE LANGUAGE

When you notice language that allows no compromise or seems to exaggerate or overstate a case, you've found an **Extreme or Absolute Language** signpost.

Notice & Note: Mark the statement in paragraph 6 that contains extreme or absolute language.

Interpret: Explain whether Franklin is stating an uncompromising position or an exaggeration.

eradicate
(ĭ-răd′ĭ-kāt) *v.* tear up by the roots; eliminate.

---

[2] **Pythagoras**(pĭ-thăg′ər-əs)**. . . Golden Verses:** Pythagoras was a Greek philosopher.
[3] **every:** even.

The Morning. *Question.* What good shall I do this day?	5 6 7	Rise, wash, and address *Powerful Goodness!* Contrive day's business, and take the resolution of the day; prosecute the present study, and breakfast.
	8 9 10 11	Work.
Noon.	12 1	Read, or overlook my accounts, and dine.
	2 3 4 5	Work.
Evening. *Question.* What good have I done today?	6 7 8 9	Put things in their places. Supper. Music or diversion, or conversation. Conversation. Examination of the day.
	10 11 **Night.** 12 1 2 3 4	Sleep.

ANALYZE AND EVALUATE STRUCTURE

Annotate: Underline the areas of Franklin's schedule in which he tries to monitor his progress toward moral perfection.

Analyze: How does this chart help the reader understand Franklin's ideas?

till at length I omitted them entirely, being employed in voyages and business abroad, with a multiplicity of affairs that interfered; but I always carried my little book with me.

9 My scheme of *Order* gave me the most trouble; and I found that, though it might be practicable where a man's business was such as to leave him the disposition of his time, that of a journeyman printer, for instance, it was not possible to be exactly observed by a master, who must mix with the world, and often receive people of business at their own hours. *Order,* too, with regard to places for things, papers, etc., I found extremely difficult to acquire. I had not been early accustomed to it, and, having an exceeding good memory, I was not so sensible of the inconvenience attending want of method. This article, therefore, cost me so much painful attention, and my faults in it vexed me so much, and I made so little progress in amendment, and had such frequent relapses, that I was almost ready to give up the attempt, and content myself with a faulty character in that respect, like the man who, in buying an ax of a smith, my neighbor, desired to have the whole of its surface as bright as the edge. The smith consented to grind it bright for him if he would turn the wheel; he turned, while the smith pressed the broad face of the ax hard and heavily on the

Annotate: Mark the phrase in paragraph 9 that tells the kind of ax the man decided was best.

Analyze: Why does the man in the story decide that he likes "a speckled ax best"? What information from the text helps you make this inference?

incorrigible
(ĭn-kôr´ĭ-jə-bəl) *adj.* incapable of being reformed or corrected.

artifice
(är´tə-fĭs) *n.* a clever means to an end.

felicity
(fĭ-lĭs´ĭ-tē) *n.* great happiness.

stone, which made the turning of it very fatiguing. The man came every now and then from the wheel to see how the work went on, and at length would take his ax as it was, without farther grinding. "No," said the smith, "turn on, turn on; we shall have it bright by-and-by; as yet, it is only speckled." "Yes," says the man, *"but I think I like a speckled ax best."* And I believe this may have been the case with many, who, having, for want of some such means as I employed, found the difficulty of obtaining good and breaking bad habits in other points of vice and virtue, have given up the struggle, and concluded that *"a speckled ax was best;"* for something, that pretended to be reason, was every now and then suggesting to me that such extreme nicety as I exacted of myself might be a kind of foppery in morals,[4] which, if it were known, would make me ridiculous; that a perfect character might be attended with the inconvenience of being envied and hated; and that a benevolent man should allow a few faults in himself, to keep his friends in countenance.

10   In truth, I found myself **incorrigible** with respect to Order; and now I am grown old, and my memory bad, I feel very sensibly the want of it. But, on the whole, though I never arrived at the perfection I had been so ambitious of obtaining, but fell short of it, yet I was, by the endeavor, a better and a happier man than I otherwise should have been if I had not attempted it; as those who aim at perfect writing by imitating the engraved copies, though they never reach the wished-for excellence of those copies, their hand is mended by the endeavor, and is tolerable while it continues fair and legible.

11   It may well be my posterity should be informed that to this little **artifice,** with the blessing of God, their ancestor owed the constant **felicity** of his life, down to his 79th year, in which this is written. What reverses may attend the reminder is in the hand of Providence; but, if they arrive, the reflection on past happiness enjoyed ought to help his bearing them with more resignation. To Temperance he ascribes his long-continued health, and what is still left to him of a good constitution; to Industry and Frugality, the early easiness of his circumstances and acquisition of his fortune, with all that knowledge that enabled him to be a useful citizen, and obtained for him some degree of reputation among the learned; to Sincerity and Justice, the confidence of his country, and the honorable employs it conferred upon him; and to the joint influence of the whole mass of the virtues, even in the imperfect state he was able to acquire them, all that evenness of temper, and that cheerfulness in conversation, which makes his company still sought for, and agreeable even to his younger acquaintance. I hope, therefore, that some of my descendants may follow the example and reap the benefit.

---

[4] **foppery in morals:** excessive regard for and concern about one's moral appearance.

COLLABORATIVE DISCUSSION

Which of Franklin's virtues seem most important? Which do not seem important? Discuss your ideas with a partner.

? ESSENTIAL QUESTION:
How do we reach our goals?

Review your notes and add your thoughts to your **Response Log**.

Assessment Practice

Answer these questions before moving on to the **Analyze the Text** section on the following page.

1. What reason did Franklin have for listing *Temperance* first?

(A) He hoped to achieve the most difficult goal first.

(B) Mastering it would make the others easier to achieve.

(C) Since it was mentioned by other writers, it must be most important.

(D) Temperance was the virtue he valued most.

2. Why did Franklin make a book with a chart for each of the virtues?

(A) to keep track of how well he was doing

(B) to share the information with the people he knew

(C) because his employer told him to do it

(D) because he preferred thinking in visual terms

3. What did Franklin think of the endeavor, once he realized he would not achieve his original goals?

(A) He believed the endeavor had been a waste of time and nothing had been gained.

(B) He decided that his ideas about reason and order were probably wrong.

(C) He was better and happier than he would have been if he hadn't tried.

(D) He believed he was a worse man than he had been when he started out.

Test-Taking Strategies

Analyze the Text

Support your responses with evidence from the text.

NOTICE & NOTE

Review what you **noticed and noted** as you read the text. Your annotations can help you answer these questions.

1 **EVALUATE** Why did Franklin believe that temperance should go first on his list of virtues? Do you agree with his reasoning? Explain.

2 **EVALUATE** How did the print and graphic features Franklin included help you understand his progress on his project? Include your answers in the chart.

Print Features	Graphic Features

3 **INFER** In his later life, do you think Franklin still believed that people could achieve moral perfection? Explain.

4 **INFER** Do you think Franklin's descendants would have benefited from his example, as he hoped they would? Why or why not?

5 **EVALUATE** Some critics consider Franklin to be self-righteous and materialistic; others have ridiculed his plan for moral perfection as regimented and superficial. Do you find any evidence for these charges in the excerpt? Explain.

6 **EVALUATE** Franklin's stated goal is "to live without committing any fault at any time." Does Franklin's **Extreme Language** convince you that this goal is important? Is this a reasonable expectation? Explain, citing evidence from the text.

Choices

Here are some other ways to demonstrate your understanding of the ideas in this lesson.

Writing
↳ Essay

Write an essay in which you evaluate Franklin's scheme for moral perfection.

- Begin with your overall impression of Franklin's plan.

- Discuss parts of Franklin's approach that seem useful as well as those that might not be practical.

- Consider how his plan compares with the self-improvement books or videos that you know. What are the advantages and disadvantages of each?

- Draw a conclusion about whether Franklin's goals are achievable today.

As you write and discuss, be sure to use the **Academic Vocabulary** words.

| contrary |
| founder |
| ideological |
| publication |
| revolution |

Speaking & Listening
↳ Elevator Pitch

Imagine you get on an elevator with the CEO of a world-famous publisher of self-help books. In the few minutes you'd have to get from the ground floor to the top, you have a chance to pitch your idea—some seriously awesome advice—for a best-selling self-help book. What ideas do you pitch? What virtue might you focus on? Write a draft of what you'd say, then make your pitch to a partner.

Research
↳ Find Out About Franklin

Benjamin Franklin was a remarkable, brilliant, and accomplished person. Do some research about his life and accomplishments and answer the following questions:

- What are two things Benjamin Franklin invented?

- What was Franklin's association with the postal service?

- In what foreign country did Franklin work during the American Revolution, and what job did he have there?

Expand Your Vocabulary

PRACTICE AND APPLY

Show your understanding of the vocabulary words by answering these questions.

1. What is a project that requires **unremitting** attention?

2. What news might give you a feeling of **felicity**?

3. What would people wear to display their **affluence**?

4. How would you **eradicate** weeds from a field of grass?

5. Is a **trifling** issue something you should spend much time on?

6. Would you describe a hero or a villain as **incorrigible**?

7. Would someone use **artifice** to perform a magic trick?

8. Why might you **contrive** a way to get the day off?

Vocabulary Strategy

↳ **Latin Roots**

⊙Ed

Interactive Vocabulary Lesson: Understanding Word Origins

A **root** is a word part that carries the core meaning of a word. In most cases, roots combine with other word parts to form whole words. Often, these word parts are prefixes or suffixes, but sometimes they are additional roots. Groups of words with the same root are called **word families**.

English has collected words and roots from around the world. Thousands of those roots came into English from Latin. Knowing some of the roots can help you figure out other words in the family. For example, the words *number, numerous,* and *enumeration* are all in one word family with the Latin root *numerus,* meaning "a number or quantity."

PRACTICE AND APPLY

Use a dictionary to identify the root or roots of each of these words from the text. Then, name at least one other word in the same word family.

1. **acquisition**

2. **circumstances**

3. **conduct**

4. **judge**

Watch Your Language!

Standard English

Standard English requires a writer to follow the conventions of sentence structure, usage, and punctuation. While most people agree on these conventions, they may change over time. Some conventions, like that of ending sentences with prepositions, are **contested,** meaning there is widespread disagreement about whether the usage is acceptable.

Writers can use resources called **style guides** to identify departures from conventions and suggest ways to improve their writing. Style guides explain the rules of Standard English and show examples of correct and incorrect usage to help illustrate those rules. Writers may also use grammar and style checker to check for possible errors.

A style guide can also provide suggestions on how to undertake such tasks as varying sentence structure. It can provide examples of various sentence types, such as these examples from the selection:

Simple sentence: *It was about this time I conceived the bold and arduous project of arriving at moral perfection.*

Compound sentence: *I entered upon the execution of this plan for self-examination, and continued it with occasional intermissions for some time.*

Complex sentence: *As I knew, or thought I knew, what was right and wrong, I did not see why I might not always do the one and avoid the other.*

PRACTICE AND APPLY

Write four or five sentences stating your opinion of Franklin's character and judgment based on the excerpt from *The Autobiography*. Be sure to include a mix of sentence structures to give variety to your writing. Then, check your sentences against a style guide to ensure that you have structured sentences and used punctuation correctly.

Collaborate & Compare

Compare Themes

As you read, note sound devices, voice, and key details in each poem to help you identify the poem's **theme,** or message about life, society, or human nature. Then, think about how the themes of the two poems relate to each other. After you read the poems, you will collaborate with a small group on a final project.

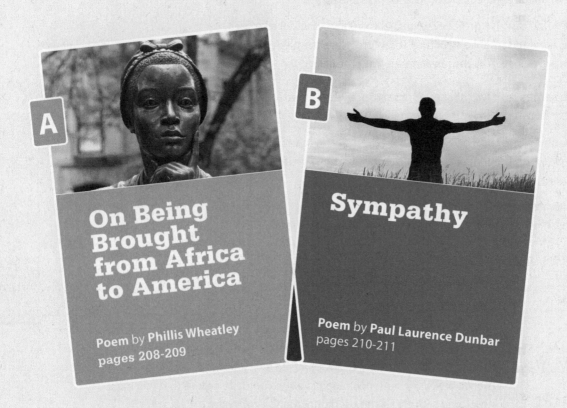

A

On Being Brought from Africa to America

Poem by **Phillis Wheatley**
pages 208-209

B

Sympathy

Poem by **Paul Laurence Dunbar**
pages 210-211

After you read, you will explore ideas in the poems by collaborating with a small group on a presentation. You will follow these steps:

- Determine the most important details
- Determine the theme of each poem
- Compare themes
- Present to the class

On Being Brought from Africa to America

Poem by **Phillis Wheatley**

Sympathy

Poem by **Paul Laurence Dunbar**

Engage Your Brain

Choose one or more of these activities to start connecting with the poems you're about to read.

"It Is a Truth Universally Acknowledged . . ."

Are there themes or ideas that are universal? What does that even mean? Think about myths, fairy tales, stories, or songs that have been around for a very long time. Do they mention ideas or situations that you can relate to? If so, what are they? Make a list with the title of the story, the song, the idea or situation, and how they all relate to your experience.

From "The Star Spangled Banner" to George Michael to Beyoncé

The topic is freedom. Your task, should you accept it, is to come up with a list of songs that deal with freedom—however you want to define the term. Just be prepared to defend your definition and choices to a partner.

Trailblazing

What is it like to be the first to do something? With a classmate, make a minute-long video or a podcast about someone who is considered a "trailblazer." Consider the following questions:

- What did this person do that was so special?
- How does this person view his or her accomplishments?
- How did other people benefit from this person's contributions?

Analyze Themes

The **theme** of a work is its message about life or human nature. There is usually one central theme, but a work may have additional themes. This message may be stated directly, but readers often must infer what it is. To **infer** a poem's theme, note details about its speaker, its key ideas, the feelings it expresses, and the poet's use of language and sound devices.

Some themes are **universal,** meaning they are found in literature across all time periods. These poems were written during two different literary periods. However, they both express important ideas, such as freedom. As you read, note the themes that each poem suggests and consider whether these themes are universal.

Focus on Genre
↳ **Poetry**

- develops a theme (or multiple themes) in the work
- may express a universal theme
- is more condensed and suggestive than prose
- uses a variety of sound devices to add emphasis and convey meaning

"On Being Brought from Africa to America"	"Sympathy"
Details and Suggested Themes	Details and Suggested Themes

Analyze Sound Devices

Poets use a number of sound devices to emphasize ideas, add a musical quality, create mood, and reinforce meaning.

- **Rhyme** is the occurrence of similar or identical sounds at the end of two or more words. Rhyme that occurs within a single line of poetry is called **internal rhyme.** Rhyme that appears at the end of a set of lines is called **end rhyme.**

- **Rhythm** refers to the "beat" of a poem and is created by the pattern of stressed and unstressed syllables.

- **Meter** is the repetition of a regular rhythmic unit in a line.

- **Repetition** is a poetic device in which a sound, word, phrase, or line is repeated to emphasize the importance of an idea, as well as to create an appealing rhythm.

- **Alliteration** is the repetition of consonant sounds at the beginnings of words, placing emphasis on those words, their sounds, and their meanings.

As you read, notice the way that the two poets use sound devices to create unique voices, draw attention to important ideas, convey meaning, and suggest themes.

Annotation in Action

Here are one student's notes about the poet's use of repetition and other sound devices in "Sympathy." As you read, notice the use of repetition and other sound devices in each poem.

I know what the caged bird feels, alas!
  When the sun is bright on the upland slopes;
When the wind stirs soft through the springing grass,
And the river flows like a stream of glass;
  When the first bird sings and the first bud opes,

Repetition of "When the" emphasizes the bird's longing.

Background

Born in West Africa, probably in 1753, **Phillis Wheatley** would become the first African American to publish a book of poetry. She was enslaved in 1761 and brought to Boston, where she was purchased by a local merchant, John Wheatley. She learned to read and write and was recognized as a prodigy. She published her first poem at age 13 in 1767.

Wheatley went on to publish a number of other poems and by 1770 her work was known throughout the colonies. In 1773, Wheatley published her first and only book of verse, *Poems on Various Subjects, Religious and Moral*, the publication of which is considered a landmark achievement in U.S. history. Wheatley became the first African American and first person held in slavery in the U.S. to publish a book of poems. Phillis was given her freedom after Susannah Wheatley's death in 1774.

Paul Laurence Dunbar was born in Ohio in 1872. He was the only African American student in his high school class, and he published poems in the school newspaper, eventually becoming the editor. He self-published his first collection of poems, titled *Oak and Ivy,* in 1893. Dunbar was one of the premier poets in the United States. Dunbar continued publishing poetry and other writing until his death at age 33 in 1906.

On Being Brought from Africa to America

by **Phillis Wheatley**

Notice details that tell you about the speaker's attitude towards America.

NOTICE & NOTE

As you read, use the side margins to make notes about the text.

'Twas mercy brought me from my *Pagan* land,
Taught my benighted[1] soul to understand
That there's a God, that there's a *Saviour* too:
Once I redemption neither sought nor knew.
5 Some view our sable[2] race with scornful eye,
"Their colour is a diabolic die."[3]
Remember, *Christians*, *Negroes*, black as *Cain*,
May be refin'd, and join th' angelic train.

ANALYZE THEME

Annotate: In lines 7 and 8, mark the advice the speaker gives.

Analyze: What is the message in this advice?

---

[1] **benighted:** ignorant.
[2] **sable:** dark brown or black.
[3] **diabolic die:** an evil or devilish coloring agent (dye).

© Houghton Mifflin Harcourt Publishing Company • Image Credits: ©Randy Duchaine/Alamy

ESSENTIAL QUESTION:
What does oppression look like?

Review your notes and
add your thoughts to your
Response Log.

Assessment Practice

Answer these questions about "On Being Brought to America" before
moving on to the next selection.

1. A theme of "On Being Brought from Africa to America" is

(A) freedom rests on the ability to read

(B) all people need understanding

(C) bigotry toward African Americans is morally wrong

(D) being brought to America from Africa was an act of oppression

2. Who is the speaker in the poem?

(A) an enslaved person in America

(B) a preacher at a church

(C) a Christian slaveholder in Africa

(D) a sailor on a voyage

3. Which phrase reveals the speaker's attitude about being taken from Africa to
America?

(A) *'Twas mercy brought me*

(B) *redemption neither sought nor knew*

(C) *our sable race*

(D) *May be refin'd*

Test-Taking Strategies

Sympathy

by **Paul Laurence Dunbar**

Notice the way the writer uses word choice and sound devices to convey themes.

NOTICE & NOTE

As you read, use the side margins to make notes about the text.

ANALYZE SOUND DEVICES

Annotate: In the first and second stanzas, mark the phrase that is repeated.

Analyze: What idea does the writer emphasize through the use of repetition?

ANALYZE THEMES

Annotate: In lines 18–20, mark the words and phrases that refer to the bird's song.

Contrast: What two ways of interpreting the bird's song are noted by the speaker? How does the difference between these two ways help develop the theme?

I know what the caged bird feels, alas!
   When the sun is bright on the upland slopes;
When the wind stirs soft through the springing grass,
And the river flows like a stream of glass;
5   When the first bird sings and the first bud opes[1],
And the faint perfume from its chalice steals—
I know what the caged bird feels!

I know why the caged bird beats his wing
   Till its blood is red on the cruel bars;
10 For he must fly back to his perch and cling
When he fain[2] would be on the bough a-swing;
   And a pain still throbs in the old, old scars
And they pulse again with a keener sting—
I know why he beats his wing!

15 I know why the caged bird sings, ah me,
   When his wing is bruised and his bosom sore,—
When he beats his bars and he would be free;
It is not a carol of joy or glee,
   But a prayer that he sends from his heart's deep core,
20 But a plea, that upward to Heaven he flings—
I know why the caged bird sings!

---

[1] **opes:** *v.* opens.
[2] **fain:** *adv.* happily, gladly.

COLLABORATIVE DISCUSSION

How would you describe the speaker's attitude about freedom in each poem? Share your ideas with a partner.

Review your notes and add your thoughts to your **Response Log.**

Assessment Practice

Answer these questions before moving on to the **Analyze the Texts** section on the following page.

1. Which action stirs feelings in the caged bird?

- (A) when it is caged
- (B) when it hears the first bird sing
- (C) when it feels pain from old scars
- (D) when it prays

2. Which line in "Sympathy" describes what the bird wants to do?

- (A) *When the sun is bright on the upland slopes;*
- (B) *For he must fly back to his perch and cling*
- (C) *When he fain would be on the bough a-swing;*
- (D) *But a plea, that upward to Heaven he flings—*

3. Which line in the poem most directly refers to the conditions of slavery?

- (A) *When the wind stirs soft through the springing grass,*
- (B) *For he must fly back to his perch and cling*
- (C) *It is not a carol of joy or glee,*
- (D) *And a pain still throbs in the old, old scars*

Test-Taking Strategies

Analyze the Texts

Support your responses with evidence from the texts.

NOTICE & NOTE

Review what you **noticed and noted** as you read the text. Your annotations can help you answer these questions.

1 **INTERPRET** Reread "On Being Brought from Africa to America." Note the rhyming words at the ends of the lines. How do these rhyming words emphasize contrasts between ideas?

2 **INTERPRET** Reread lines 1–7 of "Sympathy." How would you describe the language that expresses the speaker's feelings in this stanza?

3 **ANALYZE** How would you describe the **rhyme** scheme of the stanzas in the poem "Sympathy"? Which words are emphasized through Dunbar's use of **alliteration**? What is the effect of each sound device?

4 **CONTRAST** What effect does the contrast between the imagery in the first stanza and the second stanza of "Sympathy" have? How does this contrast help develop the poem's themes?

5 **CONNECT** Think about the themes expressed in each poem. Which theme resonates with you the most? Consider the following in your response:

- word choice
- imagery
- sound devices

6 **EVALUATE** Explain whether the two poems have a theme in common and whether this theme is universal. Does it seem to be true across time periods and cultures? Explain, using examples from the texts to support your answer.

Choices

Here are some other ways to demonstrate your understanding of the ideas in this lesson.

Writing
↳ **Compare the Poems**

Write a brief essay in which you compare and contrast the use of literary elements in "On Being Brought from Africa to America" and "Sympathy." Choose from the list of elements below:

- images
- sound devices
- tone
- word choice

Cite specific examples from the poems. To conclude, note which writer used literary elements most effectively.

As you write and discuss, be sure to use the **Academic Vocabulary** words.

- contrary
- founder
- ideological
- publication
- revolution

Speaking & Listening
↳ **Connect to the Modern Day**

Even though these poems were written long ago, they discuss ideas about freedom and justice that are still relevant today. Did the ideas in either of these poems remind you of anything you have read, seen, or listened to recently? Work with a partner, discuss a connection you can make between these poems and stories you have read, shows you have watched, or songs you have listened to.

Media
↳ **Present a Poem About Freedom**

Use the poems you just read as an inspiration for a modern-day poem about freedom that you will present to your class.

- Determine the theme about freedom you want to convey.
- Choose an image in the spirit of Dunbar's "caged bird" that conveys the theme.
- Include details and language that make your poem uniquely modern.
- Consider visual support to highlight the theme or clarify your central image.
- Use technology to produce, edit, and present or publish your version of the poem.

Compare Themes

Both "On Being Brought from Africa to America" and "Sympathy" deal with the issues of slavery and oppression, although they address the topics in very different ways. Each has a specific **theme,** or message about life, society, and human nature, that the poet develops over the course of the poem.

You can infer a theme based on the speaker's voice and point of view. You can also identify and evaluate important details to determine the theme, or listen to see how sound devices emphasize parts of the text. As you examine the poems to determine theme(s), consider:

- **Speaker and point of view**—Who is speaking? What does the speaker feel, want, or believe?

- **Important details**—What information is provided by each poem's speaker?

- **Sound devices**—Does the poet use rhyme, repetition, or other sound devices to highlight or convey important information? What do the devices suggest?

With your group, complete the chart with details from both poems.

	A "On Being Brought from Africa to America"	**B** "Sympathy"
Important Details		
Speaker and Point of View		
Sound Devices		

Analyze the Texts

Discuss these questions in your group.

1. **CONTRAST** Review the notes you made on the speakers in the chart. How do the speaker or the point of view differ between the two poems? Explain.

2. **MAKE INFERENCES** What inference(s) can you make about the attitude toward slavery and oppression expressed by each poem?

3. **EVALUATE** Both poems rhyme. Which poem's rhyme scheme did you find to be the most engaging? Explain why.

4. **INTERPRET** What role does religion or religious faith play in each poem? Cite evidence from the poems in your discussion.

Collaborate and Present

Now create and present a theme board listing the major themes of the two poems. Follow these steps:

1. **DETERMINE THE IMPORTANT DETAILS** With your group, review your chart and determine which details are most important. Decide how you want to present your analysis of the poems' themes using text evidence.

2. **CREATE THEME STATEMENTS** Decide as a group what the theme or themes are in each poem. You can use a chart to organize your ideas.

Details from "On Being Brought from Africa to America"	Details from "Sympathy"	Theme(s)

3. **COMPARE THEMES** Discuss with your group similarities and differences in the themes of the poems. Listen actively, and ask others to explain any points that are not clear. Summarize common or universal themes you found in the two poems.

4. **PRESENT TO THE CLASS** Clearly state and outline the thematic similarities and differences between the two poems. At the end, ask for and answer questions from the class. If others disagree with your interpretation, be polite as you justify your response.

Collaborate & Compare

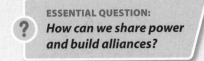
Compare Tone

You're about to read two women's efforts to address important issues at different times in history. As you read, pay attention to the **tone,** or the attitude of each author toward the subject she's addressing. Think about the similarities and differences in both the content and tone of their concerns.

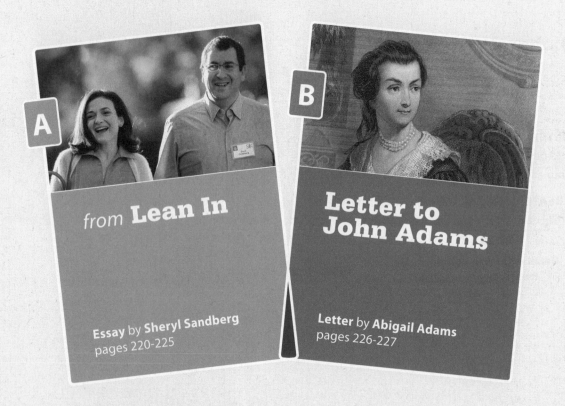

A

from **Lean In**

Essay by **Sheryl Sandberg**
pages 220-225

B

Letter to John Adams

Letter by **Abigail Adams**
pages 226-227

After you read the essay and the letter, you will collaborate with a small group on an analysis of both texts. You will follow these steps:

- Examine a topic
- Conduct research
- Develop a plan
- Create and present a presentation

from **Lean In**

Essay by **Sheryl Sandberg**

Letter to John Adams

Letter by **Abigail Adams**

Engage Your Brain

Choose one or more of these activities to start connecting with the essay and letter you're about to read.

A Delicate Balance

Sometimes it's hard to ask for help. Other times it's tempting to have someone else do what we know we ought to take care of ourselves. When is it better for you to be responsible for your life and do what needs doing, as opposed to relying on others? When is it appropriate to have someone help on your behalf? Write your response to those questions in your class journal.

Advocacy

An advocate is someone who publicly supports and recommends a cause or policy. If you could be an advocate for any one thing, what would it be and why? Discuss your answer with a small group of classmates.

Second First Lady Trivia

What do you know about Abigail Adams, the second First Lady of the United States? Do some research to answer the following questions:

1. How many presidents was she related to?

2. Where was she on the night of March 4, 1797, and where should she have been?

3. Which of the Founding Fathers made her angry?

4. What were two or three causes she was passionate about?

5. As a wife, what was different about her role, compared to that of her contemporaries?

Analyze Tone

Think about the different ways someone could ask you, "Are you ready?" Even if the words do not change, the tone of voice lets you know if the speaker is annoyed, neutral, or surprised.

When we read, we don't hear an actual voice, so we have to look for other clues to tell us the author's tone.

- One clue is the vocabulary an author chooses, or **diction**. For example, an author could use one of the words, *mean, nasty,* or *vile,* to describe someone; the word he or she picks helps you guess the degree of that author's feelings.

- Another clue is **syntax,** or how the author arranges words and forms sentences. Compare: "It appeared he had a rather mean streak." to "That's just one mean man!" The first is a neutral observation while the second is an opinionated exclamation.

Diction and syntax can tell you if a text is formal, informal, explanatory, sarcastic, or humorous. As you read, note words or phrases that might reveal how Sandberg and Adams feel about their topic.

Focus on Genre
↳ **Essay**

- is a short work of nonfiction on a single subject
- may use informal language
- can be autobiographical

Analyze Author's Purpose

Authors can have more than one reason to write a text: they might want to persuade, explain, express thoughts or feelings, or entertain. The **purpose** of the text is often related to the text's **message,** or the main idea an author wants to convey, and the intended **audience,** or the people an author wants to influence or affect.

You can determine an author's purpose by making inferences, or logical guesses, based on the use of key details, word choice, and tone. As you read each text, use the chart to help you infer what the author's purpose is.

Focus on Genre
↳ **Letter**

- is addressed to a specific person or group
- may have a formal or informal tone, depending on writer's purpose
- may convey personal information, share opinions, or make requests

	Message	Audience	Purpose
from *Lean In*			
Letter to John Adams			

Annotation in Action

These are one student's notes on Sheryl Sandberg's tone. As you read, note how Sandberg and Adams use word choice and word order to convey tone.

...I headed to my first day of work as chief operating officer of a small company called Facebook. As I pulled out of my driveway, I remember feeling **excited**. I also felt a little **nervous** . . . a little **anxious** . . . okay, maybe even a little **scared** about this new challenge.

The choice of words "excited," "nervous," "anxious," and "scared" makes the tone edgy—energy mixed with fear.

Expand Your Vocabulary

Put a check mark next to the vocabulary words that you feel comfortable using when speaking or writing.

demurred	☐	**parity**	☐
watershed	☐	**deprive**	☐
internalize	☐	**impunity**	☐

With a partner, write a few sentences about equality, using as many of the words as you can.

As you read the excerpt from *Lean In*, as well as Abigail Adams's letter to her husband, use the definitions in the side column to learn the vocabulary words you don't already know.

Background

With degrees in economics and business from Harvard, **Sheryl Sandberg** (b. 1969) became chief of staff in the U.S. Treasury Department, then vice president at Google, and in 2008, chief operating officer at Facebook. *Lean In*, the title of her book, also became the name of an organization that she founded. By 2014, she was a billionaire. In 2015, Sandberg's husband died suddenly, and Sandberg began to rethink some of her goals. Today, she is still with Facebook, but also helps women dealing with grief.

Abigail Adams was educated by her parents and grandparents because public education for women was limited. Access to her family's library grounded her in the classics, history, government, law, and philosophy. Married in 1764 to future U.S. President John Adams, Abigail had four children by the time John was sent to the Second Continental Congress in 1774. After that, John was absent more than he was at home. Abigail cared for the farm and the children, and she began the correspondence that would continue for the rest of her life. Her letters reflect life at the time but are also filled with her passion for politics and her intense patriotism.

"Remember the Ladies"

from

Lean In

Essay by **Sheryl Sandberg**

Note details that tell you what a highly successful career woman says about her work-life balance.

ANALYZE TONE

Annotate: Mark elements in paragraph 1 that help establish Sandberg's tone.

Analyze: What is the author's attitude toward her new job?

1 On March 24, 2008, I headed to my first day of work as chief operating officer of a small company called Facebook. As I pulled out of my driveway, I remember feeling excited. I also felt a little nervous . . . a little anxious . . . okay, maybe even a little scared about this new challenge. It wasn't anything specific that concerned me. I knew the tech business well after spending more than six years at Google. I had shared many dinners with CEO[1] Mark Zuckerberg before he offered me the job, and I knew we were in sync about the importance of Facebook's mission. My fear was more the general anxiety you feel over the risks associated with a new job and the worry that you won't succeed.

---

[1] **CEO:** chief executive officer, the highest-ranking executive at a company.

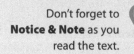
2   I parked my car and went up to an industrial, open-plan office space. My desk faced Mark's and was near the very popular Rainbow Room, which was crammed with couches and video games. At the time, the office walls were bare. Today, those walls are filled with posters that reflect the company's philosophy and encourage employees to take risks. "Proceed and be bold," declares one. "Move fast and break things," advises another. But the one that would have helped me on that first morning doesn't make a statement; it asks a question: "What would you do if you weren't afraid?"

3   This question speaks to everyone, but I think it has special significance for women. Fear is at the root of so many of the barriers that women face. Fear of not being liked. Fear of making the wrong decision. Fear of drawing negative attention. Fear of overreaching. Fear of being judged. Fear of failure. And for those who want to have children, the fear that we can't be both good employees and good mothers.

4   I know it's pointless to tell someone to be fearless. I regularly fail to convince even myself. But it does help to tell ourselves to fight our fears at every stage of our lives. In school, don't be afraid to raise your hand. When you are attending a meeting, don't be afraid to sit at the table. Don't be afraid to offer your opinion. Don't be afraid of waiting to find a life partner who will support you in achieving your dreams. And don't be afraid to be fully engaged in your career, even as you plan to have a family. By fighting these fears, women can pursue professional success and personal fulfillment—and freely choose one or the other . . . or both.

5   Five years ago, I dove into my new Facebook job as fearlessly as I could. And although at the time a lot of people questioned why I would want to go to work for a 23-year-old, no one asks me that question anymore.

6   It's your turn now. Please ask yourself: *What would I do if I weren't afraid?* And then go do it.

Success Secret 1: Sit at the Table

7   A few years ago, I hosted a meeting for Treasury Secretary Tim Geithner at Facebook. We invited 15 executives from across Silicon Valley[2] for breakfast and a discussion about the economy. Secretary Geithner arrived with four members of his staff, two senior and two more junior, and we all gathered in our one nice conference room. After the usual milling around, I encouraged everyone to take a seat. Our invited guests, mostly men, sat down at the large conference table. Secretary Geithner's team, all women, took their food last and sat in chairs off to the side of the room. I motioned

ANALYZE AUTHOR'S PURPOSE

Annotate: In paragraph 2, mark the question that Sandberg refers to in paragraph 3.

Predict: Why do you think she says it has "special significance for women"? What does this suggest about her purpose?

VOCABULARY

Analyze Idioms: Idioms are expressions that don't literally mean what the words say. For example, a person who is all "sweetness and light" is someone who is extremely pleasant, maybe even overly so. In paragraph 4, mark the expression "sit at the table."

Analyze: What context clues lead you to think that Sandberg may not mean this literally? What does using this idiom suggest about her tone?

[2] **Silicon Valley:** the location in California of many of the large tech companies, so named because silicon is the element from which computer chips are made.

© Houghton Mifflin Harcourt Publishing Company

demurred

(dĭ-mûrd´) v. disagreed or refused to accept a request or suggestion.

watershed

(wô´tər-shĕd) n. a turning point, a crucial dividing line.

internalize

(ĭn-tûr´nə-līz) v. to make something, such as an idea or a value, an important part of the kind of person you are.

for the women to come sit at the table, waving them over publicly so they would feel welcomed. They **demurred** and remained in their seats.

8   The four women had every right to be at this meeting, but because of their seating choice, they seemed like spectators rather than participants. I knew I had to say something. So after the meeting, I pulled them aside to talk. I pointed out that they should have sat at the table even without an invitation, but when publicly welcomed, they most certainly should have joined. At first, they seemed surprised, then they agreed.

9   It was a **watershed** moment for me. A moment when I witnessed an internal barrier altering women's behavior. A moment when I realized that in addition to facing institutional obstacles, women face a battle from within. We consistently underestimate ourselves. Multiple studies in multiple industries show that women often judge their own performance as worse than it actually is, while men judge their own performance as better than it actually is.

10   We hold ourselves back in ways both big and small, by lacking self-confidence, by not raising our hands, and by pulling back when we should be leaning in. We **internalize** the negative messages we get throughout our lives—the messages that say it's wrong to be outspoken, aggressive, or more powerful than men. We lower our own expectations of what we can achieve. We continue to do the

majority of the housework and childcare. We compromise our career goals to make room for partners and children who may not even exist yet. Compared to our male colleagues, fewer of us aspire to senior positions.

11   Internal obstacles are rarely discussed and often underplayed. Throughout my life, I was told over and over about inequalities in the workplace and how hard it would be to have a career and a family. I rarely, however, heard anything about the ways I might hold myself back. These internal obstacles deserve a lot more attention because they are under our control. We cannot change what we are unaware of, and once we are aware, we cannot help but change.

12   I know that in order to continue to grow and challenge myself, I have to believe in my own abilities. I still face situations that I fear are beyond my qualifications. And I still sometimes find myself spoken over and discounted while men sitting next to me are not. But now I know how to take a deep breath and keep my hand up. I have learned to sit at the table.

Success Secret 2: Make Your Partner a Real Partner

13   I truly believe that the single most important career decision that a woman makes is whether she will have a life partner and who that partner is. A woman who can find someone who is willing to share the burdens—and joys—of home life will go further in her work life. I don't know of a single woman in a leadership position whose life partner is not fully—and I mean fully—supportive of her career. No exceptions. And contrary to the popular notion that only unmarried women can make it to the top, the majority of the most successful female business leaders have partners.

14   In the last thirty years, women have made more progress in the workforce than in the home. When a husband and wife both work full-time, the mother does 40 percent more childcare and about 30 percent more housework than the father. So while men are taking on more household responsibilities, this increase is happening very slowly, and we are still far from **parity**. . . .

15   This has to change. Just as we need to encourage women to lean in to their careers, we need to encourage men to lean in to their families. If we expect and allow them to do more, they will do more. And everyone will benefit.

16   When husbands do more housework, wives are less depressed, marital conflicts decrease, and satisfaction rises. When women work outside the home and share breadwinning duties, couples are more likely to stay together. In fact, the risk of divorce reduces by about half when a wife earns half the income and a husband does half the housework. For men, participating in child rearing

ANALYZE TONE

Annotate: Mark in paragraph 11 the two examples of "internal obstacles."

Infer: The essay starts out bright and breezy, but the tone changes here. What is the relationship between the topic and the tone?

parity
(păr´ĭ-tē) *n.* equality, being equivalent.

fosters the development of patience, empathy, and adaptability, characteristics that benefit them in all their relationships. For women, earning money increases their decision-making ability in the home, protects them in case of divorce, and can be important security in later years, as women often outlive their husbands. . . .

17   I could not do what I do without my husband, Dave. Still, like all marriages, ours is a work in progress. Dave and I have had our share of bumps on our path to achieving a roughly 50/50 split. After a lot of effort and seemingly endless discussion, we are truly partners.

18   The good news is that men in younger generations appear more eager to be real partners than previous generations did. A survey that asked participants to rate the importance of various job characteristics found that men in their 40s most frequently selected "work that challenges me" as very important, while men in their 20s and 30s most frequently selected having a job with a schedule that "allows me to spend time with my family." If these trends hold as this group ages, this could signal a promising shift toward greater equality.

19   Wonderful, sensitive men of all ages are out there. And the more that women value kindness and support in their boyfriends, the more men will demonstrate it.

20   So, when looking for a life partner, my advice to women is date all of them: the bad boys, the cool boys, the commitment-phobic boys, the crazy boys. But do not marry them. . . . When it comes time to settle down, find someone who wants an equal partner. Someone who thinks women should be smart, opinionated, and ambitious. Someone who values fairness and expects or, even better, wants to do his share in the home. And at the start of a romance, even though it may be tempting for you to show a more classic girlfriend-y side by cooking meals and taking care of errands, hold yourself back from doing this too much. If a relationship begins in an unequal place, it is likely to get more unbalanced if and when children are added to the equation. Instead, use the beginning of a relationship to establish the bar for the division of labor.

ANALYZE AUTHOR'S PURPOSE

Annotate: Mark Sheryl Sandberg's advice in paragraph 20.

Infer: Why do you think she gives this advice? How does it support her overall purpose?

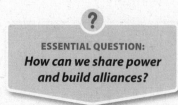

ESSENTIAL QUESTION:
How can we share power and build alliances?

Review your notes and add your thoughts to your **Response Log.**

COLLABORATIVE DISCUSSION

With a partner, talk about how you think Sandberg's advice applies to both young women and men who live at home and attend high school, rather than women and men in the workplace or in a dating relationship.

Assessment Practice

Answer these questions before moving on to the next selection.

1. Why was Sandberg nervous when she started at Facebook?
   - (A) It was such a small company at the time.
   - (B) She worried that she might not succeed.
   - (C) She didn't know anything about technology.
   - (D) She had never met Mark Zuckerberg before.

2. Sandberg thinks women could do better in business
   - (A) if they had more education
   - (B) if they attended more meetings
   - (C) if they didn't give in to fear
   - (D) if they didn't work at tech companies

3. For Sandberg, relationships are an important part of success
   - (A) because the right partner will be fully supportive
   - (B) because the wrong partner will lead to divorce
   - (C) because you can't get ahead if you're not married
   - (D) because you can't get ahead if you are married

Test-Taking Strategies

Letter to John Adams

Letter by **Abigail Adams**

Find out what Abigail Adams tells her husband as he works to promote freedom for the American colonies.

Braintree, March 31, 1776

1 I wish you would ever write me a Letter half as long as I write you; and tell me if you may where your Fleet are gone? What sort of Defence Virginia can make against our common Enemy?[1] Whether it is so situated as to make an able Defence? Are not the Gentery Lords and the common people vassals,[2] are they not like the uncivilized Natives Brittain represents us to be? I hope their Riffel Men who have shewen themselves very savage and even Blood thirsty; are not a specimen of the Generality of the people. I am willing to allow the Colony great merrit for having produced a Washington but they have been shamefully duped by a Dunmore.[3] I have sometimes been ready to think that the passion for Liberty cannot be Eaquelly Strong in the Breasts of those who have been accustomed to **deprive** their fellow Creatures of theirs.[4] Of this I am certain that it is not founded upon that generous and christian principal of doing to others as we would that others should do unto us. . . .

2 I long to hear that you have declared an independancy—and by the way in the new Code of Laws which I suppose it will be necessary for you to make I desire you would Remember the Ladies, and be more generous and favourable to them than your ancestors. Do not put such unlimited power into the hands of the Husbands. Remember all Men would be tyrants if they could. If perticuliar care and attention is not paid to the Ladies we are determined to foment[5] a Rebelion, and will not hold ourselves bound by any Laws in which we have no voice, or Representation.

---

[1] **common Enemy:** Great Britain; Virginia and Massachusetts were the oldest colonies, and both were influential, but their cultures were very different. Adams is wondering here if Virginia will be helpful if the colonies break with Britain.

[2] **vassal** (vă´səl)**:** a subordinate or dependent.

[3] **Dunmore:** Lord Dunmore was the last British governor of Virginia. In April 1775, in reaction to events in Boston, Dunmore had all the gunpowder in Williamsburg confiscated. Then, in November 1775, he offered freedom to any slaves or indentured servants who would leave and join the British to fight the colonists.

[4] **I have sometimes . . . of theirs:** Adams is referring to slavery, which was common in Virginia. She questioned whether those who denied slaves freedom would not really have a passion for freedom.

[5] **foment** (fō-mĕnt´)**:** to arouse or incite.

3   That your Sex are Naturally Tyrannical is a Truth so thoroughly established as to admit of no dispute, but such of you as wish to be happy willingly give up the harsh title of Master for the more tender and endearing one of Friend. Why then, not put it out of the power of the vicious and the Lawless to use us with cruelty and indignity with **impunity**. Men of Sense in all Ages abhor those customs which treat us only as the vassals of your Sex. Regard us then as Beings placed by providence under your protection and in immitation of the Supreme Being make use of that power only for our happiness.

ANALYZE AUTHOR'S PURPOSE

Annotate: In paragraph 3, mark phrases describing the nature of men, according to Adams.

Draw Conclusions: What might her purpose for using these phrases be?

impunity

(ĭm-pyo͞o′nĭ-tē): *n.* exemption from punishment, penalty, or harm.

COLLABORATIVE DISCUSSION

Pair up with a partner to discuss how John Adams might have reacted when he received this letter.

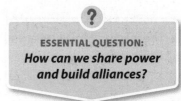

ESSENTIAL QUESTION:
How can we share power and build alliances?

Review your notes and add your thoughts to your **Response Log.**

Assessment Practice

Answer these questions before moving on to the **Analyze the Texts** section on the following page.

1. What is the complaint with which Abigail Adams begins the letter?

- (A) Her husband's letters are too short.
- (B) Her husband is in Philadelphia.
- (C) Her husband is going to Virginia.
- (D) Her husband is with his Fleet.

2. Why does Abigail Adams think Virginia might not be passionate about liberty?

- (A) It is a new colony.
- (B) It allows slavery.
- (C) It is Washington's home.
- (D) It won't defend itself.

3. What does Abigail Adams predict will happen if no laws protect women?

- (A) Men will naturally become tyrannical.
- (B) Men will imitate the supreme being.
- (C) Men will give up the title of master.
- (D) Women will incite a revolt of their own.

Test-Taking Strategies

Analyze the Texts

Support your responses with evidence from the texts.

NOTICE & NOTE

Review what you **noticed and noted** as you read the text. Your annotations can help you answer these questions.

(1) **SUMMARIZE** In two or three sentences apiece, summarize Sandberg's essay and Adams's letter. Then look back to the chart on page 218 that you've been filling in as you read. How does summarizing their main ideas help you confirm the message, audience, and author's purpose?

(2) **INTERPRET** In paragraph 4, Sandberg writes that it is pointless to tell someone to be fearless. Explain what you think she means by this. How does this belief reveal her tone?

(3) **EXPLAIN** In paragraph 9, why does Sandberg describe the events from paragraph 8 as a "watershed moment"? How does this reveal her purpose?

(4) **EVALUATE** Do you think Sandberg makes a good case for a life partner being the biggest decision for a woman's career? Is it really bigger than education, interests, talent, or career choice? Explain.

(5) **DRAW CONCLUSIONS** What can you determine about the relationship between John and Abigail Adams based on what she writes about men? Why do you think she includes this information?

(6) **EVALUATE** Do you think Abigail Adams does a good job of presenting her case for the need to pass laws that protect women? Support your response with evidence from the text.

(7) **ANALYZE** Use the chart below to list the words and phrases you think help you determine each author's tone. How does the tone reflect the purpose of the essay and the letter?

	Words and Phrases	**Overall Tone**	**Purpose**
from *Lean In*			
Letter to John Adams			

Choices

Here are some other ways to demonstrate your understanding of the ideas in this lesson.

Writing
↳ Argument

In an article for *The Atlantic,* Anne-Marie Slaughter, former Director of Policy Planning at the State Department, criticized Sheryl Sandberg's stance that "women do not dream big enough," and that they should "lean in" to their careers rather than "lean back" once they consider raising a family. Slaughter's counterargument was that plenty of career-minded women balancing work and family are not hampered by lack of ambition, but rather by "societal and business structures" that make it impossible to "have it all." Which viewpoint do you think reflects current reality? Write an argument that considers the following:

- attitudes people have about men and women who prioritize family over career

- the role of men in creating a work-life balance for all

- income and resources needed to raise a family

- children's school and activity schedules and parental work schedules

> As you write and discuss, be sure to use the **Academic Vocabulary** words.
>
> | contrary |
> | founder |
> | ideological |
> | publication |
> | revolution |

Media
↳ Sketchnote

Create a sketchnote for one of the texts you just read.

- Capture the most important ideas and use text features to make certain ideas stand out.

- Use illustrations and other graphic elements to make your sketchnote engaging.

- Share you sketchnote with a group or display it in class.

Social & Emotional Learning
↳ Social Media Message

Advocates work on behalf of vulnerable people to give them access to information and services, protect their rights, and give them a voice in the decisions and policies that affect their lives.

In a small group, discuss how Sheryl Sandberg or Abigail Adams could turn her argument into advocacy. Reread the texts, then create a media message from one of them that supports a cause. Think about

- problems they would address and solutions they might propose

- skills they would need to find resources to help solve the problem

- how they could communicate their message to a larger public

- what success would look like

Expand Your Vocabulary

PRACTICE AND APPLY

Mark the letter of the best answer to each question. Then, explain your response.

1. A **watershed** event is more likely to be
   a. boring
   b. life-changing

2. Criminals who break laws with **impunity**
   a. are punished
   b. are not punished

3. People who achieve **parity** could be said to be
   a. subordinate
   b. equal

4. Someone who **demurred** when given a suggestion will have said
   a. yes
   b. no

5. If a person **internalizes** certain ideals, those ideals
   a. become part of the person
   b. are rejected by the person

6. People **deprived** of sunlight
   a. may be unusually pale
   b. may be sunburned

Vocabulary Strategy
↳ **Analyze Meanings of Idioms**

An **idiom** is a common figure of speech whose meaning is different from the literal meaning of its words. For example, *throw in the towel* comes from boxing, but it can be used in any situation in which someone wants to quit. Idioms are more likely to appear in informal writing, and they often have nuanced meanings. In the example above, *throw in the towel* means "quit," but the connotation is quitting during a fight that cannot be won.

PRACTICE AND APPLY

The following idioms can be found in one of the texts you just read. For each word or phrase, write the non-idiomatic definition of each word in the idiom. Then, write what the idiom means. Finally, explain any nuanced meanings or connotations of the idiom.

1. watershed moment

2. in sync

3. milling around

4. bloodthirsty

© Houghton Mifflin Harcourt Publishing Company

Watch Your Language!

Formal English and Contested Usage

Formal English follows the established rules of grammar and usage. It is required for legal and business documents, as well as research papers or college essays. Texts from the past sound more formal than modern-day texts because formality levels have relaxed. For example, Abigail Adams' letter is personal, but her diction and syntax are formal by today's standards:

> **That your Sex are Naturally Tyrannical is a Truth so thoroughly established as to admit of no dispute, but such of you as wish to be happy willingly give up the harsh title of Master for the more tender and endearing one of Friend.**

Today we'd write: "Everyone knows men want to control their wives, but if you want a happy marriage, treat women as equals."

Some grammar and usage rules have been contested, or deliberately broken, for decades. Contested usage is common in informal writing but rarely accepted in formal writing. When breaking the rules, the writer still needs to be clear and understandable, and should skirt convention only to create an effect or make a point.

For example, Sheryl Sandberg chooses to begin sentences with the conjunctions *And* and *But*. Doing so makes her writing sound personable and her advice more compelling.

"Some say I shouldn't be so picky, which is why I'm not going to stop seeing you for ending a sentence with a preposition."

> **And don't be afraid to be fully engaged in your career, even as you plan to have a family.**

Sandberg also deliberately uses sentence fragments. Complete sentences have a subject and verb, but she drops the verbs to create a rhythm that emphasizes what people fear.

> **Fear of making the wrong decision. Fear of drawing negative attention. Fear of overreaching. Fear of being judged. Fear of failure.**

The practice of ending sentences with prepositions is also contested, but abiding by this rule can create awkward sentences. "That is something I will not put up with" sounds much less awkward than "That is something up with which I will not put." As always, consult a usage manual or style guide to be sure what the correct rules are.

PRACTICE AND APPLY

Write three sentences that employ contested usage. Then rewrite them, using formal English. With a partner, discuss where it would be appropriate to use each type.

Compare Tone

Lean In and "Letter to John Adams" were written two centuries apart and under very different circumstances. You may have noticed similarities and differences in the tone of each selection.

In a small group, discuss how tone in these two works compare. Then, work together to complete the chart with examples from each text that reveal tone. In the second column, note the tone that these details reveal and if you think the examples are similar or different.

	Tone	Comments
A *Lean In*		
B Letter to John Adams		

Analyze the Texts

Discuss these questions in your group.

(1) **INFER** Do you think the two women would agree on what makes an ideal marriage? Explain, using examples from each text.

(2) **SYNTHESIZE** How do Adams's comments about the approaching revolution suggest that she would have appreciated Sandberg's advice on pursuing success?

(3) **COMPARE** Though the two writers have different styles, they have energy and passion in common. Use evidence from the texts—such as details related to style or tone—that demonstrate their energy and passion.

(4) **EVALUATE** What do these two works suggest about how involved the writers want to be in the world around them?

Collaborate and Present

Your group can continue exploring the ideas in these texts by collaborating on a multimedia presentation.

(1) **EXAMINE THE TOPIC** Discuss what each writer thought about the role of women, marriage, and contributions to the world outside the home.

(2) **CONDUCT RESEARCH** Find out more about each woman and the people in her life. Gather images, video, and sound files to illustrate their passions, beliefs, and ideas.

(3) **DEVELOP A PLAN** Synthesize the information you found in your research. Draft an outline that compares and contrasts the views of the two women. Refine your outline as you go, adding details to support your main ideas.

(4) **CREATE A PRESENTATION** Decide on the types of media you want to include and create your presentation. Make sure your organization is clear and that your audience will be engaged.

(5) **POLISH AND PRESENT** Do a trial run of your presentation and refine either the content or the delivery as necessary.

Reader's Choice

Continue your exploration of the Essential Questions for this unit by doing some independent reading. Read the titles and descriptions shown. Then mark the texts that interest you.

? **ESSENTIAL QUESTIONS:** *Review the four Essential Questions for this unit on page 127.*

Short Reads Available on Ed

These texts are available in your ebook. Choose one to read and rate. Then defend your rating to the class.

Speech to the Virginia Convention
Speech by **Patrick Henry**

It was in this speech that Henry passionately declared, "Give me liberty or give me death!" Why would he say that?

Rate It

from
The U.S. Constitution: The Bill of Rights
Public Document

What rights did the founders believe were essential for the protection of citizens?

Rate It

from
Poor Richard's Almanack
Aphorisms by **Benjamin Franklin**

Benjamin Franklin was a keen observer of human behavior. This book shares some of his wittier sayings.

Rate It

Abigail Adams' Last Act of Defiance
History Writing by **Woody Holton**

Never one to blindly follow the status quo, Abigail Adams defied the patriarchal property laws of her time.

Rate It

Democracy
Poem by **Langston Hughes**

How does a 20th-century poet express his desire to be free?

Rate It

Long Reads

Here are three recommended books that connect to this unit. For additional options, ask your teacher, school librarian, or peers. Which titles spark your interest?

1776

Nonfiction by **David McCullough**

The true story of the brave boys and men—turned soldiers—who marched with General George Washington in the year the colonies declared independence from England.

What the Constitution Means to Me

Drama by **Heidi Schreck**

After defending the merits of the U.S. Constitution in numerous high school debates, Heidi Schreck examines how this seminal document affected four generations of women in her family, and how the laws it enshrines still affect the American people.

For All of Us, One Today

Memoir by **Richard Blanco**

In 2013, Richard Blanco was chosen to be the United States's fifth inaugural poet. In this book, he shares his experiences as a Latino immigrant, an openly gay man, and a proud American.

Extension
↳ **Connect & Create**

HUDDLED MASSES YEARNING TO BREATHE FREE An overarching theme in this unit is the desire to fight oppression. Was this theme reflected in the text you chose? If so, did the subject of this text have anything in common with other works you read in this unit? With someone else who read the same text, compare the ways in which people in the various texts resisted oppression. Then come up with a list of best practices for (lawfully) recognizing and fighting oppression.

ON THE STAGE TODAY Several texts in this unit examine the ways that people work together—or don't. In the texts you read independently, was there a balance of power or evidence of people partnering for a common goal? Imagine that a character or subject were giving a presentation about sharing power. What would he or she say? Include the following:

- a brief description of the situation and the potential conflicts

- how everyone managed to compromise and work together

- lessons learned

NOTICE AND NOTE

- Pick one of the texts and annotate the Notice & Note signposts you find.

- Then use the **Notice & Note Writing Frames** to help you write about the significance of the signposts.

- Compare your findings with those of other students who read the same text.

Notice & Note Writing Frames

Write a Research Report

Writing Prompt

Using information from texts in this unit and other print and digital sources, write a report for a class collection on the foundations of democracy. Explain how America's founding documents, government structure, or fundamental principles facilitated a system of shared power and alliances.

Manage your time carefully so that you can

- conduct short and sustained research;
- plan your report;
- write your report; and
- revise and edit your report.

Be sure to

- clearly state your thesis;
- cite evidence from multiple sources; and
- avoid plagiarism and relying too much on one source.

> ### Review the
> ### Mentor Text
>
> For an example of a well-written article that you can use as a mentor text and source for your research report, review:
>
> - **"Thomas Jefferson: The Best of Enemies"** (pages 163–171)
>
> Consult your notes and annotations about this text. Think about how the evidence supports the author's points.

Consider Your Sources

Review the list of texts in the unit and choose at least three that you may want to use as support for your research report.

As you review potential sources, consult the notes you made in your **Response Log** and make additional notes about ideas that might help direct your research. Make sure your notes include titles and page numbers so that you can easily find and cite the information later.

UNIT 2 SOURCES

- [ ] **The Declaration of Independence**
- [ ] **One Today**
- [ ] **American Experience: Alexander Hamilton** `MEDIA`
- [ ] **Thomas Jefferson: The Best of Enemies**
- [ ] **A Soldier for the Crown**
- [ ] *from* **The Autobiography**
- [ ] **On Being Brought from Africa to America**
- [ ] **Sympathy**
- [ ] *from* **Lean In**
- [ ] **Letter to John Adams**

Analyze the Prompt

Review the prompt to make sure you understand the assignment.

1. Mark the sentence in the prompt that identifies your research task. List types of information you will gather.

2. Mark the sentence that identifies the topic of your research report. Rephrase the sentence in your own words.

3. Then, look for words that indicate the purpose and audience of your research report. Write a sentence describing each.

Find a Purpose

Two common purposes of a research report are:

- to **inform** and **educate**
- to **demonstrate** the writer's **knowledge**

What is my research task? What kind of information do I gather?

What is my writing task? What am I explaining?

What is my purpose for writing?

Who will read my report? What do they already know about my topic?

Review the Rubric

Your research report will be scored using a rubric. As you write, focus on the characteristics of a high-scoring essay as described in the chart. You will learn more about these characteristics as you work through the lesson.

Purpose, Focus, and Organization	Evidence and Elaboration	Conventions of Standard English
The response includes: • A clear thesis • A strongly maintained controlling idea • A logical structure • Transitions to connect ideas	The response includes: • Effective evidence and sources • Effective use of elaboration • Clear expression of ideas • Appropriate vocabulary • Varied sentence structure	The response may include: • Some minor errors in usage but no pattern of errors • Correct punctuation, capitalization, sentence formation, and spelling • Command of basic conventions

1 PLAN YOUR RESEARCH REPORT

Develop a Thesis

A research report depends on a good **thesis**. A good thesis

- is a clear and concise sentence
- states the **controlling idea**
- informs the reader of exactly what you will explain

To develop your preliminary thesis,

- review the prompt and **narrow** the topic
- formulate your **research question** about the topic

Refine Your Thesis

As your research your topic, you may choose to narrow or broaden your thesis based on what you learn from your sources.

Research Question	Preliminary Thesis

Identify Research Sources

Finding quality research sources is an important step in refining your thesis and supporting your ideas. Your sources should

- be both primary and secondary sources
- contain authoritative and reliable information
- come from a variety of print and digital formats

Use the table below to record your sources.

Choose Primary and Secondary Sources

- Examples of **primary sources** include diaries, autobiographies, interviews, and speeches.
- Newspaper or magazine articles, biographies, and documentaries are all **secondary sources**.

Primary Sources	Title: Author: Page Number or URL:
	Title: Author: Page Number or URL:
Secondary Sources	Title: Author: Page Number or URL:
	Title: Author: Page Number or URL:

Take Notes

As you research, keep complete notes on all your primary and secondary sources. Make sure you

- evaluate the sources for their relevance to your thesis;
- understand the purpose, main ideas, and arguments in the source materials.

Use the following chart to take notes.

Help with Planning

Consult **Interactive Writing Lesson: Conducting Research**

Primary/Secondary Source Citations	Main Ideas	Develops Thesis by . . .
1.		
2.		
3.		

Organize Your Ideas

Based on your research, background reading, and note-taking, refine your thesis and decide on supporting details and text evidence. Use the chart below to map out an organizational structure.

INTRODUCTION	• Clearly introduce your thesis. • Include an interesting anecdote or fact to grab your reader's attention.
BODY PARAGRAPHS	• Support your thesis with information from your research. • Cite evidence from your sources. • Link your ideas with transitional phrases, such as *first of all, another example,* or *similarly.*
CONCLUSION	• Restate your thesis in different words. • Include an idea for your readers to think about.

BUILD YOUR STRUCTURE

Consider these options as you plan a structure for your report:

- Use **chronological order** to describe events as they occurred.
- Present evidence in their **order of importance**.
- Use a **compare-and-contrast** structure to compare events, people, or ideas.

2 DEVELOP A DRAFT

Now it is time to draft your report. To develop your writing skill, analyze what the experts do. Read about the techniques professional writers use to craft their informative articles.

Use Quotations and Paraphrases

EXAMINE THE MENTOR TEXT

Notice how the author of "Thomas Jefferson: The Best of Enemies" uses sources to support the idea that Jefferson and Hamilton were both cynical.

The author **paraphrases** ideas from Jefferson's diary.

> If Jefferson and Hamilton define opposite ends of the political spectrum in U.S. history and seem to exist in perpetual conflict, the two men shared certain traits. . . . Each scorned the other as excessively ambitious. In his secret diary, or Anas, Jefferson recorded a story of Hamilton praising Julius Caesar as the greatest man in history. . . . Hamilton repaid the favor. In one essay he likened Jefferson to "Caesar coyly refusing the proffered diadem" and rejecting the trappings, but "tenaciously grasping the substance of imperial domination."

The author **directly quotes** from an essay by Hamilton.

Avoid Plagiarism

Even when you cite your sources, use your own words to paraphrase those ideas that you do not quote directly.

APPLY TO YOUR DRAFT

Use a variety of signal phrases to integrate sources into your writing. Then, cite the title and author's name in parentheses. Use this frame to practice citing sources for your draft.

Signal Phrase	Textual Evidence (paraphrase or quote)	Citation (in parentheses)
Chernow states that . . .	Hamilton had "an ardent faith in the new national government."	(Ron Chernow, "Thomas Jefferson: The Best of Enemies," paragraph 3)
According to . . .		
The study suggests that . . .		

Use Transitions

EXAMINE THE MENTOR TEXT

Historical texts often use a combination of structures. The author of "Thomas Jefferson: The Best of Enemies" uses transitions to signal comparison-and-contrast and chronological order in this passage.

Drafting Online

Check your assignment list for a writing task from your teacher.

The writer used the word *Instead* to signal a **contrast**.

> The backbiting between Hamilton and Jefferson grew so acrimonious that Washington had to exhort both men to desist.
>   Instead, the feud worsened. In early 1793, a Virginia Congressman named William Branch Giles began to harry Hamilton. . . . With prodigious bursts of energy, Hamilton complied with those inhuman demands, foiling his opponents. Jefferson then committed an unthinkable act.

The author uses transitional phrases such as *In early 1793* and *then* to signal **chronological order**.

APPLY TO YOUR DRAFT

Consult the chart for transitional words and phrases you can use for different organizational structures. Mark the words or phrases you would like to use. Then, practice using them in the chart.

1 2 3 Chronological Order		A B C Order of Importance		Comparison-and-Contrast	
initially	subsequently	of primary significance	foremost	similar to	as opposed to
prior to	soon thereafter	most noteworthy	primarily	likewise	conversely
earlier	eventually	an equally significant		in common	on the contrary
		increasingly important			

3 REVISE YOUR RESEARCH REPORT

Even the best writers revise their work to ensure they are communicating their ideas effectively. Use the guide to help you revise your research report.

Help with Revision

Find a **Peer Review Guide** and **Student Models** online.

REVISION GUIDE		
Ask Yourself	**Prove It**	**Revise It**
Introduction Does my introduction contain a clear thesis statement?	Circle your thesis.	**Reword** your thesis.
Support Do I present relevant evidence to support my thesis and ideas?	**Highlight** each central idea. **Underline** evidence that supports each idea.	**Add** evidence for any idea that is not supported.
Citations Do I cite sources correctly?	**Put a star** (★) next to citation information.	**Revise** citations to match content from sources.
Elaboration Do I elaborate on the meaning of each source?	**Cross out** (X) evidence that seems weak or unexplained.	**Add** elaboration to clarify the meaning of each source.
Organization Is my report logically organized with transitions linking ideas?	**Bracket** [ ] major sections that reflect your organizational structure. Circle transitions.	**Reorder** paragraphs as needed. **Add** transitions to clarify relationships between ideas.
Language Do I use formal, precise language to maintain an objective tone?	**Cross out** (X) informal language. **Highlight** instances of a biased perspective.	**Reword** text to increase its formality. **Replace** sentences that express an opinion.
Conclusion Does my conclusion follow logically from the ideas I present?	**Underline** the summary of your ideas in the conclusion.	**Add** a closing statement to sum up the information that your report presents.

APPLY TO YOUR DRAFT

Consider the following as you look to improve your writing:

- Make sure your introduction grabs your reader's attention.
- Use elaboration to connect evidence back to the idea it supports.
- Correct any errors in grammar or punctuation.

Peer Review in Action

ANALYZE A STUDENT MODEL

Now that you have finished revising your research report, exchange papers with a partner for a **peer review.** During your peer review, give suggestions for how to improve your partner's draft.

Read the introduction from a student's draft and examine his peer reviewer's comments.

First Draft

"We Mutually Pledge to Each Other . . ."
By Roman Hernandez, Coastal Bend High School

The words from the Declaration of Independence established the importance of working together for the good of the United States. Even though Jefferson and Hamilton held opposite values and worked vigorously to have their views dominate Washington's first Cabinet, their disagreements managed to bring out the best in each other.

I think you need to cite a source for this information.

Try a more dramatic opening to grab your reader's attention.

You could strengthen your thesis by elaborating on the last part.

Now read the revised introduction. Notice how the writer has improved his draft by revising based on his peer reviewer's comments.

Revision

"We Mutually Pledge to Each Other . . ."
By Roman Hernandez, Coastal Bend High School

Once Thomas Jefferson encountered the fiercely ambitious Alexander Hamilton, he must have gritted his teeth over writing that the new Americans pledged to each other "our lives, our fortunes, and our sacred honor" (Thomas Jefferson, Declaration of Independence, paragraph 33). The young lion Hamilton roared about the importance of the federal government, while Jefferson languidly took the side of states' rights. (Ron Chernow, "Jefferson and Hamilton: The Best of Enemies," paragraphs 6–7). Yet, here they were—facing off against one another in Washington's first Cabinet. Their battles of principles and politics proved that the best of enemies did indeed find ways to work together for the good of the country. They embodied the spirit of the founding documents that powers must be shared and alliances must be constructive for the democracy to flourish.

Good job citing sources!

Nice first sentence. This characterization of Jefferson grabs the reader's attention.

I like how you elaborate on your thesis here and set up the following paragraphs.

APPLY TO YOUR DRAFT

During your peer review, give each other suggestions for how you could express your ideas more effectively. Use your revision guide to help you.

When facing feedback from a partner, listen attentively and ask questions to make sure that you fully understand your reviewer's suggestions.

4 EDIT YOUR RESEARCH REPORT

Edit your final draft for proper use of Standard English conventions and to correct any misspellings or grammatical errors.

Watch Your Language!

USE EM DASHES

An em dash allows writers to quickly clarify ideas. An occasional use of a well-placed em dash can add variety to your sentence structure and create emphasis.

- Em dashes may be used in pairs, similar to the use of parentheses.
- A single em dash may also be used at the end of a sentence to emphasize a word or phrase.

Read the following sentence from the revised introduction of "We Mutually Pledge to Each Other . . ." on page 243.

> **Yet, here they were—facing off against one another in Washington's first Cabinet.**

The dash before the final phrase of the sentence calls attention to the drama of the conflict between Jefferson and Hamilton. The dash breaks up an ordinary sentence and creates interest and variety.

APPLY TO YOUR DRAFT

Now apply what you have learned to your own work.

1. **Read your paper aloud.** Listen to your word choices and the rhythm of your sentences.
2. Look for a sentence or two in which you may **add em dashes** to signal an abrupt break or explain an idea.
3. **Exchange drafts** with a peer and review your writing, checking the conventions and grammar.

Interactive Grammar Lesson: Dashes, Parentheses, and Brackets

EM DASHES

- Use an em dash to signal **an abrupt break** in thought or speech.
- Use an em dash to mean *namely,* or *that is,* before an explanation.

Ways to Share

- **Record a podcast** to educate your audience about founding documents and principles.
- **Create a blog post** and invite your classmates to comment on your ideas.
- **Deliver a class presentation** and respond to your classmates' questions. See the next task for tips.

5 PUBLISH YOUR RESEARCH REPORT

Share It!

Finalize your research report for your class collection about the foundations of democracy.

You may also use your report as inspiration for other projects.

Present a Research Report

Your research report provides interesting information, so why keep it to yourself? Adapt your research report for a presentation so that your classmates can learn from your ideas.

Plan Your Presentation

Read through your research report and think about how to present your information and supporting evidence in an engaging way. Look for ways to integrate one or more of the following:

- graphics or representations of the founding documents
- audio or video clips of readings of any founding documents or dramatic presentations of important moments in history
- music that represents patriotic themes

Use the following planning document to help you with your presentation:

Search for an Engaging Hook

You'll want to capture your audience's attention from the beginning. Start your presentation with

- a surprising statistic
- a powerful quote
- an interesting anecdote
- a question or poll of your audience

PRESENTATION PLANNING CHART		
Title and Introduction	How can you capture an audience's attention? Is there a way to use graphics to state your title and thesis?	
Audience	What will your audience already know? What information should you include or exclude? How could digital media assist you?	
Effective Language and Organization	Will the structure you used to organize your report work well for an oral presentation? How can you present your support clearly?	
Visuals or Audio	What part of your presentation would benefit from audio or video clips? What images or sounds should you choose?	

© Houghton Mifflin Harcourt Publishing Company

Practice with a Partner or a Group

Once you have planned and drafted your presentation, practice your presentation with a partner or a small group.

PRACTICE EFFECTIVE PRESENTATION TECHNIQUES

- **Enunciation** Practice speaking aloud to avoid stumbling over words. Rearrange sentences so that your delivery is smooth.
- **Eye Contact** Look at the audience as you present your material. Avoid looking at just one person.
- **Media Use** Make sure that your supplemental media is ready so that you do not fumble with any equipment.

> ### Speak Effectively
>
> Your audience will respond positively to effective use of your voice.
>
> Be sure to
>
> - **speak loudly** so that everyone in the room can hear you
> - **speak slowly** and use pauses for dramatic effect
> - **emphasize important information** and show enthusiasm where appropriate

Use the chart to plan for your polished delivery. Ask yourself:

Which sentences should I rearrange?	
Which words or ideas should I emphasize?	
How can I introduce and use media seamlessly?	
Where should I pause for dramatic effect?	

Record Your Presentation

After you and your partner or group have practiced your presentation, record it.

Use these tips:

- Record your presentation in a quiet place without visual distractions.
- Review your video, looking for places to add graphics, text, or sound effects.
- Use free editing software to edit your presentation.

> ### Share It!
>
> - **Post your presentation to the Internet** and invite others to comment on it.
> - **Present the video to your class** rather than doing an in-person presentation.
>
> **Ed**
> **Interactive Speaking & Listening Lesson: Giving a Presentation**

Reflect & Extend

Here are some other ways to show your understanding of the ideas in Unit 2.

Reflect on the Essential Questions

Think about the Essential Question you identified as most intriguing on page 128. Has your answer to the question changed after reading the texts in the unit? Discuss your ideas.

You can use these sentence starters to help you reflect on your learning:

- **The text that most influenced my thinking was. . . .**
- **I feel different about democracy because. . . .**
- **The selection that meant the most to me was. . . .**

Project-Based Learning
↳ Create an Edutainment Video

You've read about many historical figures in this unit. Choose one and create a "History in a Minute (or Two)" edutainment video. Use an entertaining style to chronicle the person's life and accomplishments.

Here are some questions to ask yourself as you get started:

- What information about the person will interest my audience?
- Do I want to record interviews or dramatizations for my video?
- What graphics, online text, animations, or sound effects will engage my audience?
- Who will I present the video to?

Media Project

To find help with this task online, access **Create an Edutainment Video.**

Writing
↳ Write an Argument

Write a persuasive letter to your representative in Congress, expressing your concern regarding polarization on an issue that is divisive today. Use ideas from sources in this unit to convince your congressperson to address your concern.

Use these steps to plan your letter:

- State your concern in the first paragraph.
- Provide two or three reasons for your concern.
- Support each reason with evidence, pulling from sources in this unit, as needed.
- Offer up an opposing claim, but counter it with a strong rebuttal.
- Request action, using an appropriate tone.
- Conclude by thanking your congressperson and signing your letter.

"*Trust thyself: every heart vibrates to the iron string.*"
—Ralph Waldo Emerson

Literature of the American Renaissance

The Individual and Society

? As you read the texts in this unit, think about how they explore these **Essential Questions.**

How can we be true to ourselves?
Transcendentalism exalted the dignity of the individual, an idea that remains part of American consciousness today. This desire to be our authentic selves guides us in all we do.

How do we relate to the world around us?
In the early 19th century, Romantics reacted to industrialization by turning to nature and to the self for simplicity and beauty. Today, technological advances are constantly changing our lives.

What do we secretly fear?
Edgar Allan Poe and other Gothic writers were able to make fear exciting, and modern masters of horror continue to use fear to entertain us.

When should we stop and reflect on our lives?
Reflecting on your life can help you learn from your mistakes, give you great ideas, and help you put things in perspective.

ANALYZE THE IMAGE
What message does the image convey about the individual's place in society? Why might one person have gone a different way?

Explore unit themes and build background.

Stream to Start Video

Spark Your Learning

Here are some opportunities to think about issues related to **Unit 3: The Individual and Society.**

As you read, you can use the **Response Log** (page R3) to track your thinking about the Essential Questions.

Make the Connection

For each bulleted item, choose the boldfaced term that best reflects your thoughts as they relate to the unit topic, The Individual and Society. Then discuss your ideas with a partner, using specific examples if you can.

- The interests of the individual and society are usually (**aligned/ opposed**).

- The (**individual/society**) should take priority in most situations.

Think About the Essential Questions

Review the Essential Questions on page 249. Which question is most intriguing to you? Perhaps it relates to something you have read or reminds you of a personal experience. Write down your thoughts.

Prove It!

Use one of the Academic Vocabulary words in a sentence where you discuss what actions you can take to pause and reflect.

Build Academic Vocabulary

You can use these Academic Vocabulary words to write and talk about the topics and themes in the unit. Which of these words do you already feel comfortable using when speaking or writing?

	I can use it!	I understand it.	I'll look it up.
analogy			
denote			
quote			
topic			
unique			

Preview the Texts

Review the images, titles, and descriptions of the texts in the unit. Mark the title of the text that interests you most.

from **Song of Myself**
Poem by **Walt Whitman**

The great American poet celebrates aspects of American life, himself included.

My Friend Walt Whitman
Essay by **Mary Oliver**

In the absence of friends at school, the writer finds "shadow companions" in books.

Poems by Emily Dickinson

This unique American poet is known as the "Belle of Amherst."

In the Season of Change
Poem by **Teresa Palomo Acosta**

The speaker imagines she meets Emily Dickinson in a café.

from **Last Child in the Woods**
Essay by **Richard Louv**

The writer relates the way he connected to nature as a child.

from **Walden**
Essay by **Henry David Thoreau**

The well-known transcendentalist yearns for a simpler life.

The Minister's Black Veil
Short Story by **Nathaniel Hawthorne**

A new accessory alarms the people in a New England town.

The Fall of the House of Usher
Short Story by **Edgar Allan Poe**

A family's decline is reflected by their home in a rather horrifying fashion.

The Individual and Society

America's victory in the War of 1812 with Great Britain cemented the reality of independence and brought great changes to the nation, including a new spirit of nationalism. Because the war interrupted trade, Americans had to produce many of the goods that they had previously imported. This period marked the beginning of the Industrial Revolution in the United States, which transformed the country from a largely agricultural economy to an industrial powerhouse. The growth of the factory system brought many people from farms into cities, where they worked long hours for low wages, often under harsh conditions.

America On the Move

American settlers in search of new farmland and opportunities had been moving west since the late 1700s. This often led to direct conflict with Native American groups living on these lands. In 1830, the United States Congress passed the Indian Removal Act, forcing Native Americans to relocate west of the Mississippi River. Those who resisted were often brutally pushed off their lands.

1810

1812–15
War of 1812 reaffirms U.S. independence from Great Britain.

1822
Factories built in Lowell, Massachusetts, make it one of the country's largest industrial cities.

1825
Erie Canal links the Great Lakes with the Hudson River.

1830
Congress passes the Indian Removal Act.

By the mid-1800s, many Americans embraced the idea of "manifest destiny"—the belief that the United States was destined to expand westward. The United States gained Texas after a war with Mexico, and used treaties, land purchases, and force to annex territory all the way to the Pacific Ocean, which devastated Native American communities.

Pioneers Crossing the Plains of Nebraska by Carl Christian Anton Christensen (1831–1912)

Nationalism vs. Sectionalism

In the early 1800s, the issue of slavery increasingly divided North and South. As new territories achieved statehood, the northern and southern states wrangled over the balance between free and slave states. Economic interests also threatened American unity. Tariffs on manufactured goods from Britain forced southerners to buy more expensive goods manufactured in the North. From the South's point of view, the North was getting rich at the South's expense. Sectionalism, or the placing of the interests of one's own region ahead of the nation as a whole, began to take hold.

EXTEND

Think of a question you have about a topic, an event, or a person from the historical period. Then, research the answer and add it as an entry to the timeline.

1837
John Deere develops a steel plow for the western prairies.

1846–48
Mexican-American War expands the western territory of the United States.

1844
Samuel B. Morse transmits the first successful telegraph message.

1848
Discovery of gold in California leads to a gold rush.

1850

California gold diggers

Mount Starr King, Yosemite
(1866) by Albert Bierstadt
(1830–1902)

In Search of Transcendental Truth

American writers of this period were influenced by European Romanticism but soon adapted it to their own culture. Ralph Waldo Emerson, a New England writer, led a group focused on transcendentalism. The term *transcendentalism* came from Immanuel Kant, a German philosopher who wrote about "transcendent forms" of knowledge that exist beyond reason and experience. Emerson gave this European philosophy a uniquely American spin, saying that all individuals are capable of discovering higher truth through their own intuition.

The transcendentalists disliked the commercial side of American life and the hectic pace of the Industrial Revolution. Instead, they stressed spiritual well-being, achieved through intellectual activity and a close relationship to nature. Emerson's friend Henry David Thoreau put his beliefs into practice by building a small cabin on Walden Pond in Massachusetts and living there for two years, writing and studying nature.

In 1842, Emerson called for the emergence of a poet worthy of the new America—a fresh voice with limitless passion and originality. Two such poets were Walt Whitman and Emily Dickinson. Both wrote poetry that broke with the traditional conventions of poetic form and content. In this way, they followed the transcendentalist ideals of individuals discovering the truth through intuition and following their own beliefs.

Romanticism on the Dark Side

Not all American Romantics were optimistic or had faith in the innate goodness of humankind. Edgar Allan Poe and Nathaniel Hawthorne have been called "dark" or "brooding" Romantics or "antitranscendentalists." Their stories are characterized by a probing of the inner lives of their characters—an examination of the complex and often mysterious forces that motivate human behavior. Their stories are Romantic, however, in their emphasis on emotion, nature, the individual, and the unusual. Both Poe and Hawthorne used elements that are common in Gothic fiction, such as grotesque characters, bizarre situations, and violent events, in order to explore the unknown.

COLLABORATIVE DISCUSSION

How did the events in this historical period contribute to the new spirit of nationalism in the United States? Discuss with a partner.

Assessment Practice

Choose the best answer to each question.

1. Which of the following was a threat to nationalism in the United States?

   (A) the War of 1812

   (B) the Indian Removal Act

   (C) the Mexican-American War

   (D) sectionalism

2. What is "manifest destiny"?

   (A) the shift from an agricultural to an industrial economy

   (B) the official act of removing Native Americans from their homelands

   (C) the belief that the United States was meant to expand to the Pacific Ocean

   (D) the balance of power between free and slave states

3. Which of the following is a characteristic of transcendentalism?

   (A) an emphasis on material prosperity

   (B) the rigid obedience to the laws of society

   (C) the belief that individuals can discover higher truths through intuition

   (D) an examination of the complex forces that motivate human behavior

Test-Taking Strategies

from

Song of Myself

Poem by **Walt Whitman**

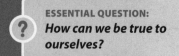

ESSENTIAL QUESTION:
How can we be true to ourselves?

Engage Your Brain

Choose one or more of these activities to start connecting with the poem you're about to read.

You Say "Unconventional," I Say "Unique!"

Conventions are the norms that most people tacitly agree to follow. However, for some, it's really hard to follow convention. What do you think it means to be unconventional? What advantages and disadvantages are there to defying convention? When is it okay to break away from what's expected? Freewrite your ideas.

Connections in Common

How do we feel a connection with others, especially people we don't know or aren't very familiar with? Choose a partner you don't normally work with and ask each other the following questions. See if you can find a shared interest.

- What's a food you've never eaten, but would like to try?

- If you could travel anywhere for free, where would you go?

- When you become famous, what will it be for?

- If you could have any animal as a pet, what would you choose and why?

- If you could paint your room any color, what would it be and why?

Your Song of Yourself

If you were to write a song about yourself, what kind of music would you set it to? How many verses would it have? What would the **refrain** (repeated lines that hook the listener) be? Write your song and share it with a classmate. If you want to, you can set it to music and then share the recording.

Analyze Free Verse

"Song of Myself" is written in **free verse.** Poems written in free verse do not have regular patterns of rhyme and rhythm and may not have conventional stanzas. Because it uses varied line lengths and does not rhyme, free verse poetry often has a **rhythm,** or pattern of stressed and unstressed sounds, that is closer to that of everyday speech.

Free verse poetry also uses cataloging and repetition, which are elements that impose rhythm, heighten emotion, and convey meaning.

- **Cataloging** is the frequent listing of people, things, and attributes.

- **Repetition** is the repeated use of words or phrases.

As you read "Song of Myself," use the chart to list examples of cataloging and repetition in the poem. One example has been filled in for you.

Focus on Genre
↳ Free Verse

- uses uneven, unrhymed lines and stanzas that sound like everyday speech
- uses elements such as cataloging and repetition to convey meaning and emotion
- includes elements of traditional poetry like imagery and sound devices

Examples of Cataloging	Examples of Repetition
"The whizz of limbs, heads, stone, wood, iron, high in the air." (from "I understand the large hearts of heroes" line 47)	

Analyze Themes

The **theme** or themes of a poem are the underlying message or messages that a poet wants to convey. The poet will not state a theme directly. It is up to you to infer it based on details in the text.

In the selections from "Song of Myself" that you are about to read, Whitman uses the poetic elements listed in the chart below to communicate several themes. As you read, consider how these elements affect your understanding of the poems and the themes they express.

Elements	How They Reveal Themes
Free verse	Look for words that stand out because the poet has manipulated lines, or repeated words and phrases in order to create rhythm and heighten emotion in key places. Also note lists of people, things, or attributes that create rhythm and evoke imagery.
Imagery	Think about how the poet uses language that appeals to the five senses and why the poet wants readers to get caught up in these details.
Figures of speech	Note how the poet uses comparisons in the form of similes and metaphors to make readers see connections between unrelated objects or ideas.
Symbols	Pay attention to how a person, place, or thing can have meaning beyond itself and be central to the poem's meaning.
Direct statements	Note when the poet expresses ideas directly.

Annotation in Action

This model shows one student's notes about repetition at the beginning of "Song of Myself." As you read, note how Whitman uses repetition and other elements of free verse to convey meaning and heighten emotion.

I celebrate myself, and sing myself,
And what I assume you shall assume,
For every atom belonging to me as good
    belongs to you.

Repetition creates urgency. It also sets up a rhythmic speech pattern.

from

Song of Myself

Poem by **Walt Whitman**

Walt Whitman (1819–1892)

One of nine children born to a house builder, Walt Whitman grew up in rural Long Island and Brooklyn, New York. Although he was a voracious reader, he did not have much formal education and showed little literary promise. At age twelve, he began work as a printer, but switched jobs often, taking positions as an office boy, a typesetter, a schoolteacher, and a carpenter.

In the 1840s, Whitman published some fairly conventional poems, short stories, and even a novel, none of which stood out from the literature of the day. He had yet to unlock his voice as a writer. He soon found inspiration in the writings of poet and philosopher Ralph Waldo Emerson. After reading Emerson's work, Whitman realized that he could celebrate nature and humanity by using spiritual language.

In the early 1850s, Whitman devoted himself to writing his collection of poems entitled *Leaves of Grass*. He printed the volume in 1855 and endured scathing critiques from readers who did not appreciate his revolutionary content and form. Undeterred, Whitman spent the rest of his life revising and rearranging the existing poems, as well as adding new ones. The ninth and final edition, published in 1892, contained nearly 400 poems.

Whitman celebrated all aspects of American life—the commonplace and the unique, the ugly and the beautiful. Rejecting rigid poetic conventions, Whitman's poetry captures the vitality, optimism, and voice of America in a style that reflects the freedom and vastness of his beloved country. Today, *Leaves of Grass* is widely regarded as some of the most influential poetry in American literature.

"**I find** [*Leaves of Grass*] **the most extraordinary piece of wit and wisdom that America has yet contributed.**"

—**Ralph Waldo Emerson**

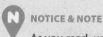

NOTICE & NOTE

As you read, use the side margins to make notes about the text.

Pay attention to Whitman's unique style and how he uses poetic elements to develop a theme.

1 I celebrate myself, and sing myself

I celebrate myself, and sing myself,
And what I assume you shall assume,[1]
For every atom belonging to me as good belongs to you.

I loaf and invite my soul,
5   I lean and loaf at my ease observing a spear of summer grass.

My tongue, every atom of my blood, form'd from this soil, this air,
Born here of parents born here from parents the same, and their
    parents the same,
I, now thirty-seven years old in perfect health begin,
Hoping to cease not till death.

10 Creeds and schools in abeyance,[2]
Retiring back a while suffced at what they are, but never forgotten,
I harbor for good or bad, I permit to speak at every hazard,
Nature without check with original energy.

ANALYZE FREE VERSE

Annotate: Mark words and phrases that are repeated in line 7.

Analyze: What is the effect of this repetition?

Ed

Close Read Screencast

Listen to a modeled close read of this text.

---

[1] **assume:** Here, the word *assume* means "take on."
[2] **abeyance:** temporary suspension; inactivity.

6 A child said *What is the grass?*

A child said *What is the grass?* fetching it to me with full hands;
How could I answer the child? I do not know what it is any more
    than he.

I guess it must be the flag of my disposition, out of hopeful green
    stuff woven.

Or I guess it is the handkerchief of the Lord,
5   A scented gift and remembrancer designedly dropt,
Bearing the owner's name someway in the corners, that we may see
    and remark, and say *Whose?*

Or I guess the grass is itself a child, the produced babe of the
    vegetation.

Or I guess it is a uniform hieroglyphic,[1]
And it means, Sprouting alike in broad zones and narrow zones,
10 Growing among black folks as among white,
Kanuck, Tuckahoe, Congressman, Cuff,[2] I give them the same,
    I receive them the same.

And now it seems to me the beautiful uncut hair of graves.

Tenderly will I use you curling grass,
It may be you transpire from the breasts of young men,
15 It may be if I had known them I would have loved them,
It may be you are from old people, or from offspring taken soon out
    of their mothers' laps,
And here you are the mothers' laps.

The grass is very dark to be from the white heads of old mothers,
Darker than the colorless beards of old men,
20 Dark to come from under the faint red roofs of mouths.

O I perceive after all so many uttering tongues,
And I perceive they do not come from the roofs of mouths for
    nothing.

I wish I could translate the hints about the dead young men and
    women,
And the hints about old men and mothers, and the offspring taken
    soon out of their laps.

25 What do you think has become of the young and old men?
And what do you think has become of the women and children?

ANALYZE THEMES

Annotate: Mark examples of metaphor in lines 3–11.

Analyze: How do these metaphors give structure to the poem? What theme do they suggest?

☺ *Ed*

Close Read Screencast

Listen to a modeled close read of this text.

---

[1] **hieroglyphic:** picture symbol used in a writing system to represent sounds or words.
[2] **Kanuck, Tuckahoe, . . . Cuff:** *Kanuck, Tuckahoe,* and *Cuff* are slang terms, now considered offensive, for a French Canadian, an inhabitant of the Virginia lowlands, and an African American, respectively.

Annotate: In lines 27–32, mark places where the poet expresses his thoughts directly.

Cite Evidence: How do these ideas relate to each other and to Whitman's theme(s)?

They are alive and well somewhere,
The smallest sprout shows there is really no death,
And if ever there was it led forward life, and does not wait at the
    end to arrest it,
30 And ceas'd the moment life appear'd.

All goes onward and outward, nothing collapses,
And to die is different from what any one supposed, and luckier.

from 33 I understand the large hearts of heroes

I understand the large hearts of heroes,
The courage of present times and all times,
How the skipper saw the crowded and rudderless wreck of the
    steam-ship, and Death chasing it up and down the storm,
How he knuckled tight and gave not back an inch, and was faithful
    of days and faithful of nights,

5 And chalk'd in large letters on a board, *Be of good cheer,*
    we will not desert you;
How he follow'd with them and tack'd with them three days and
    would not give it up,
How he saved the drifting company at last,
How the lank loose-gown'd women look'd when boated from the
    side of their prepared graves,
How the silent old-faced infants and the lifted sick, and the
    sharp-lipp'd unshaved men;
10 All this I swallow, it tastes good, I like it well, it becomes mine,
I am the man, I suffer'd, I was there.

The disdain and calmness of martyrs,
The mother of old, condemn'd for a witch, burnt with dry wood,

her children gazing on,
The hounded slave that flags in the race, leans by the fence,
    blowing, cover'd with sweat,
15 The twinges that sting like needles his legs and neck, the
    murderous buckshot and the bullets,
All these I feel or am.

I am the hounded slave, I wince at the bite of the dogs,
Hell and despair are upon me, crack and again crack the
    marksmen,
I clutch the rails of the fence, my gore dribs, thinn'd with the ooze
    of my skin,
20 I fall on the weeds and stones,
The riders spur their unwilling horses, haul close,
Taunt my dizzy ears and beat me violently over the head with
    whip-stocks.

Agonies are one of my changes of garments,
I do not ask the wounded person how he feels, I myself become the
    wounded person,
25 My hurts turn livid upon me as I lean on a cane and observe.
I am the mash'd fireman with breast-bone broken,
Tumbling walls buried me in their debris,
Heat and smoke I inspired,[1] I heard the yelling shouts of my
    comrades,
I heard the distant click of their picks and shovels,
30 They have clear'd the beams away, they tenderly lift me forth.

I lie in the night air in my red shirt, the pervading hush is for
    my sake,
Painless after all I lie exhausted but not so unhappy,
White and beautiful are the faces around me, the heads are bared
    of their fire-caps,
The kneeling crowd fades with the light of the torches.

35 Distant and dead resuscitate,
They show as the dial or move as the hands of me, I am the clock
    myself.

I am an old artillerist, I tell of my fort's bombardment,
I am there again.

Again the long roll of the drummers,
40 Again the attacking cannon, mortars,
Again to my listening ears the cannon responsive.

I take part, I see and hear the whole,
The cries, curses, roar, the plaudits for well-aim'd shots,
The ambulanza slowly passing trailing its red drip,

ANALYZE FREE VERSE

Annotate: Mark the examples of cataloging you see in lines 42–48.

Analyze: How does the cataloging Whitman uses help you understand the poem?

---

[1] **inspired:** breathed in.

45   Workmen searching after damages, making indispensable repairs,
The fall of grenades through the rent roof, the fan-shaped
     explosion,
The whizz of limbs, heads, stone, wood, iron, high in the air.

Again gurgles the mouth of my dying general, he furiously waves
     with his hand,
He gasps through the clot *Mind not me—mind—the entrenchments.*

52 The spotted hawk swoops by

The spotted hawk swoops by and accuses me, he complains
     of my gab and my loitering.

I too am not a bit tamed, I too am untranslatable,
I sound my barbaric yawp[1] over the roofs of the world.

The last scud[2] of day holds back for me,
5   It flings my likeness after the rest and true as any on the
     shadow'd wilds,
It coaxes me to the vapor and the dusk.

I depart as air, I shake my white locks at the runaway sun,
I effuse[3] my flesh in eddies,[4] and drift it in lacy jags.

I bequeath myself to the dirt to grow from the grass I love,
10   If you want me again look for me under your boot-soles.

You will hardly know who I am or what I mean,
But I shall be good health to you nevertheless,
And filter and fiber your blood.

Failing to fetch me at first keep encouraged,
15   Missing me one place search another,
I stop somewhere waiting for you.

---

[1] **yawp:** a loud, harsh cry.
[2] **scud:** windblown mist and low clouds.
[3] **effuse:** spread out.
[4] **eddies:** small whirlwinds.

© Houghton Mifflin Harcourt Publishing Company

ANALYZE THEMES

Annotate: In lines 1–3, mark descriptive or action words associated with the spotted hawk. Then mark descriptive or action words associated with the speaker.

Draw Conclusions: Why does the speaker compare himself to the hawk?

?

ESSENTIAL QUESTION:
How can we be true to ourselves?

Review your notes and add your thoughts to your **Response Log.**

COLLABORATIVE DISCUSSION

With a partner, discuss what makes Whitman's poetry unique. How is Whitman's poetry different from the style and subjects of other poems you have read?

Assessment Practice

Answer these questions before moving on to the **Analyze the Text**
section on the following page.

1. Which line best supports the idea that the speaker feels connected and relates to
    all of humankind?

    (A) *My tongue, every atom of my blood, form'd from this soil, this air*
    (from "I celebrate myself . . . " line 6)

    (B) *I do not ask the wounded person how he feels, I myself become
    the wounded person* (from "I understand . . . " line 24)

    (C) *I sound my barbaric yawp over the roofs of the world*
    (from "The spotted hawk . . ." line 3)

    (D) *I stop somewhere waiting for you* (from "The spotted hawk . . . " line 16)

2. According to the speaker in "I understand the large hearts of heroes," what is the
    common characteristic shared by all heroes?

    (A) Heroes show deep love for all of humanity.

    (B) Heroes are willing to die for their cause.

    (C) Heroes are able to act despite pain.

    (D) Heroes demonstrate courage.

3. Which symbol does the speaker most closely associate with his own spirit?

    (A) the grass (from "A child said . . . ")

    (B) the child (from "A child said . . . ")

    (C) the slave (from "I understand . . . ")

    (D) the hawk (from "The spotted hawk . . . ")

Test-Taking Strategies

Analyze the Text

Support your responses with evidence from the text.

NOTICE & NOTE

Review what you **noticed and noted** as you read the text. Your annotations can help you answer these questions.

1 **ANALYZE** "I celebrate myself . . ." is the first section of Whitman's poem "Song of Myself." In what ways does this section serve as an introduction to the themes and poetic vision described in these excerpts?

2 **COMPARE** How do the sections "I celebrate myself . . ." and "I understand the large hearts . . ." communicate Whitman's vision of a bond that unites all humanity?

3 **INFER** What does the grass symbolize in the section "A child said . . ."? How does this symbol relate to the deeper meaning of the poem?

4 **INTERPRET** Compare the themes of "A child said . . ." and "The spotted hawk swoops by." What insight do they share?

5 **ANALYZE** In "I understand the large hearts . . . ," what details appeal to readers' senses? In the chart, note details revealed by sensory language, the senses they appeal to, and the effect these details have on readers.

Detail	Sense	Effect

6 **ANALYZE** Think of Whitman's topics and the ideas he expresses in his poetry. Why is free verse the best form of poetry for him to use? Explain.

Choices

Here are some other ways to demonstrate your understanding of the ideas in this lesson.

Writing
↳ What If Whitman Wrote Today?

Whitman's America is different from the country you know. Reflect upon your experience, and then create a poem in the style of Whitman that describes America as you see it today.

- Decide on what aspects of American life you will focus. You may choose a topic that Whitman wrote about, like nature or heroism, or decide on some other aspect.

- List people, things, and attributes related to your topic that you want to include in your poem.

- Write a free verse poem in the style of Whitman. Mimic the patterns of everyday speech, and incorporate techniques such as cataloging, repetition, and figures of speech.

- Share your poem with the class.

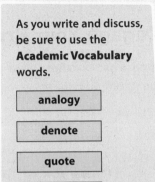

As you write and discuss, be sure to use the **Academic Vocabulary** words.

analogy

denote

quote

topic

unique

Media
↳ A Short Film

With a group, create a short film based on one of the poem's sections.

- Discuss what your short film will be like. Will you read the poem and show related images? Will you create a dramatization?

- Decide on roles within your group. Who will be onscreen? Who will do the filming?

- Create your film and share at a Whitman Film Festival.

Speaking & Listening
↳ Roundtable Discussion

In the preface to *Leaves of Grass,* Whitman describes the American poet: "His spirit responds to his country's spirit. . . . he incarnates its geography and natural life. . . . For such the expression of the American poet is to be transcendent and new. . . . He is the equalizer of his age and land." With this quote in mind, discuss the following questions:

- How well does Whitman live up to his own description?

- Who fits this description in the present day? (You may cite someone other than a poet, such as a singer or an actor.)

- Does Whitman's description reflect the role of a writer or an artist?

My Friend Walt Whitman

Essay by **Mary Oliver**

Engage Your Brain

Choose one or more of these activities to start connecting with the essay you're about to read.

I'd Like You to Meet My Friend

If you had to imagine an ideal friend, what would this friend be like? Write a description of this person and answer the following questions:

- What values would this person have?
- What interests would you have in common?
- What would you tell this person that you wouldn't tell other people?
- What advice would your friend give you?

Words to Live By

Is there a quote or saying you find inspirational? Share it with your classmates and say why you think it's inspirational. As a class, use your quotes to create a "Words to Live By" board in the classroom or online.

Dead Poet Pals

When the poet Mary Oliver died, one obituary quoted her as saying: "The two things I loved from a very early age were the natural world and dead poets, [who] were my pals when I was a kid." Why might a young child be fascinated with dead poets? How might this fascination shape their future?

© Houghton Mifflin Harcourt Publishing Company • Image Credits: (t) ©Brand X Pictures/Getty Images; (b) ©Jennifer Bosvert/Alamy

Analyze Structure and Purpose

Essays can be written for many purposes: to inform, persuade, express an idea or feelings, or entertain. An essay can be formal or informal. This essay is informal—it is conversational, personal, and engaging.

Writers often use structures to support their purpose. Oliver incorporates two structures into her writing:

- **Description** is writing that helps a reader picture scenes, events, and characters. Effective description usually relies on imagery and precise word choice.

- **Cause and effect** shows the relationships between actions and events. A **cause** is an action or event that results in another event or action. An **effect** is the outcome or result of an action.

As you read, note the structural elements that Oliver uses and how they convey ideas and support her purpose.

Focus on Genre
↳ **Essay**

- includes a central idea related to the writer's argument or purpose
- offers details or evidence to develop the central idea
- has a conclusion that summarizes the writer's view

Analyze Development of Ideas

Authors **develop ideas** by including a variety of evidence—such as facts, quotations, examples, statistics, or personal experiences. To analyze important ideas, think about how the details support the author's ideas and purpose.

Oliver supports her ideas by citing quotations from Walt Whitman's work and relating her experiences with Whitman's poetry over time. Take notes to keep track of the significant details and how they support your understanding of Oliver's important ideas. As you list the details, you can determine the evidence that supports Oliver's key ideas.

Type of Evidence	Details from Text	How It Supports Oliver's Ideas
Quotations by Whitman		
Personal experiences		

Annotation in Action

Here are one student's notes about Mary Oliver's ideas in "My Friend Walt Whitman." As you read, notice how Oliver develops ideas throughout her essay.

My town was no more or less congenial to the fact of poetry than any other small town in America—I make no special case of a solitary childhood. Estrangement from the mainstream of that time and place was an unavoidable precondition, no doubt, to the life I was choosing from among all the lives possible to me.

She had other options; what influenced her to make this choice?

Expand Your Vocabulary

Put a check mark next to the vocabulary words that you feel comfortable using when speaking or writing.

inclination	☐
estrangement	☐
delinquent	☐
bravado	☐
metaphysical	☐

Turn to a partner and talk about the vocabulary words you already know. Then, talk about a work of literature that is meaningful to you, using as many of the vocabulary words as you can. As you read, use the definitions in the side column to help you learn the vocabulary words you don't already know.

Background

Mary Oliver (1935–2019) was born in Maple Heights, Ohio. Her first book of poetry, *No Voyage and Other Poems*, was published in the United Kingdom in 1963, when Oliver was 28. Oliver went on to become a prolific poet and won numerous honors, including the Pulitzer Prize and the National Book Award. Her poetry is known for its focus on the natural world and her effort to explore both the beauty and difficulty of nature. Oliver rarely granted interviews, saying she wanted people to discover her through her writing.

My Friend Walt Whitman

Essay by **Mary Oliver**

Notice details that tell you who Oliver's friends are and why they are important to her.

NOTICE & NOTE

As you read, use the side margins to make notes about the text.

1   In Ohio, in the 1950s, I had a few friends who kept me sane, alert, and loyal to my own best and wildest **inclinations**. My town was no more or less congenial to the fact of poetry than any other small town in America—I make no special case of a solitary childhood. **Estrangement** from the mainstream of that time and place was an unavoidable precondition, no doubt, to the life I was choosing from among all the lives possible to me.

2   I never met any of my friends, of course, in a usual way—they were strangers, and lived only in their writings. But if they were only shadow-companions, still they were constant, and powerful, and amazing. That is, they said amazing things, and for me it changed the world.

> *This hour I tell things in confidence,*
> *I might not tell everybody but I will tell you.*[1]

inclination

(ĭn-klə-nā´shən) *n.* a characteristic disposition or tendency to act in a certain way; a propensity.

estrangement

(ĭ-strānj´mənt) *n.* the condition of being detached or withdrawn; alienation.

ANALYZE STRUCTURE AND PURPOSE

Annotate: In paragraph 2, mark words that describe Oliver's friends.

Analyze: How does Oliver's word choice convey how important these friends are?

---

[1] All text in italics, including italic text that is not set apart from the main text, is from Walt Whitman's poem "Song of Myself."

Notice & Note: Mark the Walt Whitman quotes on this page.

Analyze: What is unique about the way Oliver organizes her essay?

delinquent

(dĭ-lĭng´kwənt) *adj.* failing to do what law or duty requires.

ANALYZE DEVELOPMENT OF IDEAS

Annotate: Mark details that describe Oliver's behavior in paragraph 4.

Infer: How do these details relate to the quotation from Whitman that concludes this paragraph?

bravado

(brə-vä´dō) *n.* a show of bravery or defiance, often in order to make a false impression or mislead someone.

metaphysical

(mĕt-ə-fĭz´ĭ-kəl) *adj.* based on speculative or abstract reasoning.

3   Whitman was the brother I did not have. I did have an uncle, whom I loved, but he killed himself one rainy fall day; Whitman remained, perhaps more avuncular[2] for the loss of the other. He was the gypsy boy my sister and I went off with into the far fields beyond the town, with our pony, to gather strawberries. The boy from Romania[3] moved away; Whitman shone on in the twilight of my room, which was growing busy with books, and notebooks, and muddy boots, and my grandfather's old Underwood typewriter.

> *My voice goes after what my eyes cannot reach,*
> *With the twirl of my tongue I encompass worlds and volumes*
> *of worlds.*

4   When the high school I went to experienced a crisis of **delinquent** student behavior, my response was to start out for school every morning but to turn most mornings into the woods instead, with a knapsack of books. Always Whitman's was among them. My truancy was extreme, and my parents were warned that I might not graduate. For whatever reason, they let me continue to go my own way. It was an odd blessing, but a blessing all the same. Down by the creek, or in the wide pastures I could still find on the other side of the deep woods, I spent my time with my friend: my brother, my uncle, my best teacher.

> *The moth and the fisheggs are in their place,*
> *The suns I see and the suns I cannot see are in their place,*
> *The palpable is in its place and the impalpable is in its place.*

5   Thus Whitman's poems stood before me like a model of delivery when I began to write poems myself: I mean the oceanic power and rumble that travels through a Whitman poem—the incantatory[4] syntax, the boundless affirmation. In those years, truth was elusive—as was my own faith that I could recognize and contain it. Whitman kept me from the swamps of a worse uncertainty, and I lived many hours within the lit circle of his certainty, and his **bravado**. *Unscrew the locks from the doors! Unscrew the doors themselves from their jambs!* And there was the passion which he invested in the poems. The **metaphysical** curiosity! The oracular[5] tenderness with which he viewed the world—its roughness, its differences, the stars, the spider—nothing was outside the range of his interest. I reveled in the specificity of his words. And his faith—that kept my spirit buoyant surely, though his faith was without a name that I ever heard of.

---

[2] **avuncular:** of or having to do with an uncle.
[3] **boy from Romania:** This phrase refers to the gypsy in the previous sentence. The gypsies, also called Romani, are one of the largest minority groups in Romania.
[4] **incantatory:** in the manner of a verbal charm or spell.
[5] **oracular:** resembling or characteristic of an oracle; solemnly prophetic.

Do you guess I have some intricate purpose? Well I have . . . for the April rain has, and the mica on the side of a rock has.

6   But first and foremost, I learned from Whitman that the poem is a temple—or a green field—a place to enter, and in which to feel. Only in a secondary way is it an intellectual thing—an artifact, a moment of seemly and robust wordiness—wonderful as that part of it is. I learned that the poem was made not just to exist, but to speak—to be company. It was everything that was needed, when everything was needed. I remember the delicate, rumpled way into the woods, and the weight of the books in my pack. I remember the rambling, and the loafing—the wonderful days when, with Whitman, *I tucked my trowser-ends in my boots and went and had a good time.*

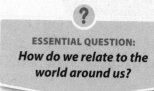

ESSENTIAL QUESTION:
How do we relate to the world around us?

Review your notes and add your thoughts to your **Response Log.**

COLLABORATIVE DISCUSSION

What do you think of Oliver's ideas about poetry that conclude the essay? Discuss your ideas with a partner.

Assessment Practice

Answer these questions before moving on to the **Analyze the Text** section on the following page.

1. How did Oliver think of Whitman?

   (A) as her uncle or Romanian cousin

   (B) as the brother she didn't have

   (C) as a somewhat interesting poet

   (D) as a poet she was forced to read

2. What triggered Oliver's truancy?

   (A) Students in her class displayed delinquent behavior.

   (B) Her parents did not believe in the school.

   (C) The school stopped teaching writing.

   (D) She was meeting her friend and goofing off.

3. What does Oliver mean when she writes that "the poem is a temple"?

   (A) Writing is a religious experience for her.

   (B) Whitman wrote religious poetry.

   (C) It allows her to explore her emotions.

   (D) She prefers traditional forms of poetry.

Test-Taking Strategies

Analyze the Text

Support your responses with evidence from the text.

NOTICE & NOTE

Review what you **noticed and noted** as you read the text. Your annotations can help you answer these questions.

(1) **INTERPRET** In the first paragraph, Oliver writes that she makes "no special case of a solitary childhood." What do you think she means by this? Why do you think she includes this information?

(2) **ANALYZE** What are the causes of Oliver's "friendship" with Whitman? What are the effects of this friendship? Add your ideas to the cause-and-effect chain.

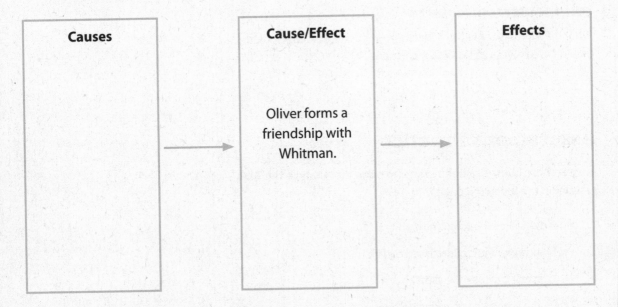

Causes	Cause/Effect	Effects
	Oliver forms a friendship with Whitman.	

(3) **INFER** Oliver does not directly state her purpose for writing. It is up to you to infer it based on details in the text. What is Oliver's main purpose for writing? Cite text evidence in your response.

(4) **EVALUATE** How do the **Quoted Words** from Whitman create a structure for the essay? How does this structure support Oliver's ideas?

(5) **DRAW CONCLUSIONS** What has Oliver learned from Whitman? How has this idea been developed throughout the essay?

(6) **INFER** The poem quoted throughout the essay is Walt Whitman's "Song of Myself." How does the title of this poem and the use of **Quoted Words** support the main idea of Oliver's essay?

Choices

Here are some other ways to demonstrate your understanding of the ideas in this lesson.

Writing
↳ Essay

Write an essay about an author whom you admire or whose work you enjoy. Focus on why you think the author's work is important and/or influential.

1. Decide on your central idea—what you are going to claim about the author.

2. Express why the author is important to you. You might focus on details from your own experience, as Oliver does.

3. Include direct quotations from the author's work that relate to your central idea and lend structure to your essay.

4. Include a conclusion that summarizes your central idea.

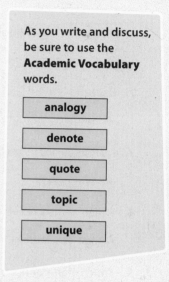

As you write and discuss, be sure to use the **Academic Vocabulary** words.

- analogy
- denote
- quote
- topic
- unique

Research
↳ My Friend Mary Oliver

Mary Oliver is famous for poetry that focuses on nature. Create a presentation on Oliver's view of nature.

- Review "My Friend Walt Whitman" and take notes on the ideas about nature in the essay.

- Find and read poems about nature by Oliver, such as "Sleeping in the Forest," "Why I Wake Early," and "Song of the Builders." What view about nature does she express in her poetry?

- Conduct research to find some literary criticism or commentary on Oliver's work.

- Synthesize the information from the essay, at least one of the poems, and an example of criticism or commentary to summarize Oliver's view of nature.

- Present an oral or multimedia presentation on Oliver's view of the natural world. Include specific details from your research.

Speaking & Listening
↳ Respond to a Quote

While Oliver describes her own loneliness, her obituary in *The New Yorker* stated her poems "were not poems about isolation, though, but about pushing beyond your own sense of emotional quarantine, even when you feel fear. Everywhere you look, in Oliver's verse, you find threads of connectivity." With a small group, discuss the following questions as they relate to "My Friend Walt Whitman."

- What ideas about isolation does Oliver express?

- Does she push beyond her "emotional quarantine"?

- Do you find "threads of connectivity" in the essay?

Expand Your Vocabulary

PRACTICE AND APPLY

Show your knowledge of the vocabulary words by choosing the letter of the best answer to each question. Then, explain your response.

1. An example of **delinquent** behavior is —

   a. doing homework   **b.** not doing chores

2. **Bravado** is more likely to result in —

   a. standing your ground   **b.** running away

3. An interest in the **metaphysical** might draw one to —

   a. philosophy   **b.** engineering

4. Which of the following might lead to **estrangement**?

   a. working with someone   **b.** arguing with someone

5. Which is an example of an **inclination** of an organized person?

   a. being on time   **b.** being spontaneous

Vocabulary Strategy
↳ Use Print and Digital Reference Materials

Digital and print reference materials, such as online and print dictionaries, can give more information about unfamiliar words and help you verify the meaning of a word. Using these materials helps when context is unclear, when a word has multiple meanings, or when the word is archaic, or no longer used.

Find the entry for the vocabulary word *inclination* in a dictionary. You may notice that a number of definitions are given. Sentences using the word may also be included to help the user understand the word in context. In many entries, the word's etymology or word derivation is shown in brackets. Related words are also shown.

Interactive Vocabulary Lesson: Using Reference Sources

PRACTICE AND APPLY

Look up the remaining vocabulary words in a dictionary. With a partner, discuss how the information in each entry, such as the word's etymology or related words, adds to your understanding of each word.

Watch Your Language!

Informal Style

Authors choose what style they will use based on their purpose for writing. **Formal language** is used for academic or business settings. **Informal language** is often used in personal essays, so it sounds more conversational, as if the author is talking to the reader. Informal language often includes slang, idioms, or colloquial phrases. Oliver uses many aspects of informal style.

- Her sentences are long and sound as if they are part of a conversation.

> The boy from Romania moved away; Whitman shone on in the twilight of my room, which was growing busy with books, and notebooks, and muddy boots, and my grandfather's old Underwood typewriter.

- Here, Oliver interjects information in the middle of the sentence.

> Only in a secondary way is it an intellectual thing—an artifact, a moment of seemly and robust wordiness—wonderful as that part of it is.

- She begins a sentence with a conjunction. Note that beginning a sentence with a conjunction is an example of contested usage—a way of using words that some people approve of and some do not.

> And there was the passion which he invested in the poems.

- She shows empathy for the reader and adds clarification in a relatable way.

> That is, they said amazing things, and for me it changed the world.

PRACTICE AND APPLY

Write a paragraph about Mary Oliver, Walt Whitman, or any other writer you admire, using an informal style. As you write, think about how you would talk to someone about the subject you've chosen. Remember that the writing still has to be clear, but it can be friendly and conversational.

Poems by
Emily Dickinson

Engage Your Brain

Choose one or more of these activities to start connecting with the poems you're about to read.

Mythbusters

Even in her lifetime, Emily Dickinson was known in Amherst as "the Myth." Her unconventional behavior, and later her poems, sparked all manner of speculation and rumor. Do some research to either confirm or "bust" the following claims. (Keep in mind answers may be somewhere in between.)

- Emily Dickinson was an atheist.

- Emily Dickinson was antisocial.

- Although not close to people outside her family circle, Emily Dickinson had a good relationship with her immediate family.

- Emily Dickinson never fell in love.

- She only ever wore white dresses.

- After the 1860s, Emily Dickinson had no contact with the outside world.

She's Popular, Our Emily

The public fascination with Emily Dickinson is stronger than ever. Go online to find titles of books, TV series, or movies about Emily Dickinson's life and family. Read the descriptions of the ones you find and see if you can figure out what the author or director's take on her life is. Share your findings with a classmate, then say which one you'd most like to read or watch and why.

Lifetime Achievement Award

Everyone is looking for the proverbial "fifteen minutes of fame." Or are they? Why might some people choose leading a private life over public acclaim? With a partner, list as many famous people as you can who have purposefully avoided the public eye. Then choose one and discuss why they may have chosen to avoid the spotlight.

Analyze Theme

The **theme** of a poem is its underlying message—the point the poet wants to make about life. In a complex poem, poets may develop two or more themes that build on one another to produce a more sophisticated message. Remember that a theme is different from a subject. A poem's subject might be "death" or "love," but the theme is a statement a poet expresses about the subject.

In her nearly 1,800 poems, Emily Dickinson deals with an abundance of themes, many of which she returns to again and again. Some of these themes center on death, madness or insanity, truth as the poet sees it, the beauty of nature, friendship and love, and God and religion. Readers can infer the theme by analyzing the images that Dickinson creates with words, the speaker's point of view, and the tone.

Focus on Genre
↳ **Poetry**

- is arranged in verse, or lines, and stanzas
- uses figurative language to convey ideas
- often has patterns of meter and rhyme

Analyze Figurative Language

Figurative language conveys meaning beyond the basic definitions of words and is meant to make unfamiliar or abstract ideas easier to understand. The chart contains some different types of figurative language Dickinson uses in her poems. As you read, look for examples of each type and record them in the chart.

Type of Figurative Language	Examples
Metaphor: a comparison of two unlike things that have something in common	
Extended metaphor: an idea developed over a number of lines, or through multiple examples	
Simile: a comparison using *like* or *as* of two unlike things that have something in common	
Personification: the giving of human qualities to an object, animal, idea, or abstract concept	
Paradox: a statement that seems to contradict itself but that suggests an important truth	

Analyze Structure

Dickinson carefully structures her poems to express her ideas and themes.
As you read, look for the following structural elements:

Structural Elements	Examples in Dickinson's Poems
Stanzas: lines grouped together to form "paragraphs" within a poem. A stanza often expresses a key idea.	
Line breaks: a visual pause within a stanza that can signify an interruption in thought or a shift in thinking. An unnatural break or pause draws attention to a particular line.	
Em dashes (—): punctuation used to show an interruption or abrupt shift in thought; used to give emphasis or express uncertainty or indecision	
Meter: the repetition of a regular rhythmic unit. The unit, or **foot**, has at least one stressed and one unstressed syllable. Poems in English favor the **iamb**, which is one unstressed syllable followed by a stressed syllable.	
Rhythm: the repeated pattern formed by the **meter** that brings out a musical quality in the poem; can also emphasize ideas and reinforce the subject matter	
Rhyme scheme: occurrence of identical or similar sounds at the ends of words; can emphasize important ideas	
Repetition: the use of sound, word, phrase, or line over and over again for emphasis or unity; can reinforce meaning	

Annotation in Action

One student made this comment about Emily Dickinson's use of em dashes. As you read, note the structural elements of her poems.

> The Soul selects her own Society—
> Then—shuts the Door—
> To her divine Majority—
> Present no more—

These dashes are jarring. They stop the flow of every line.

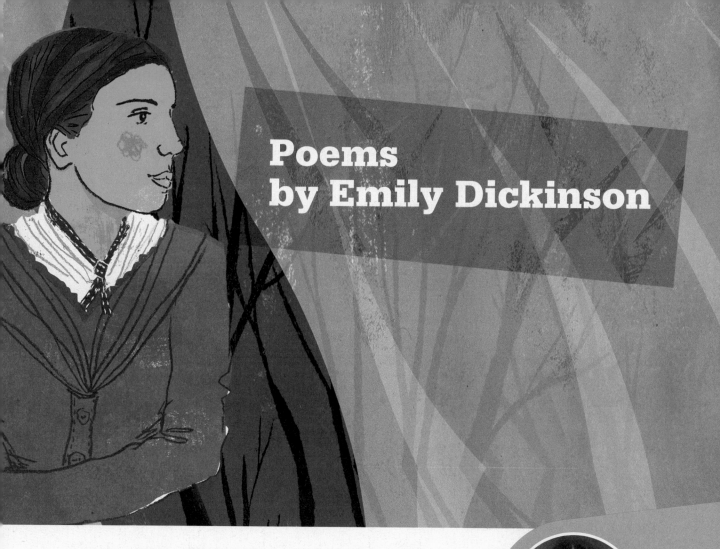

Poems by Emily Dickinson

Emily Dickinson (1830–1886)

Emily Dickinson was not known as a poet during her lifetime. After her death, her sister discovered some 1,800 poems in her home, written mostly between 1858 and 1865. Dickinson spent her entire life in and around Amherst, Massachusetts. Although formal schooling was unusual for girls at the time, Dickinson attended school, including Amherst Academy and Mount Holyoke Female Seminary. She occupied her time reading and writing letters as well as singing, gardening, and taking walks in nature. In her youth, she was very social, attending numerous church activities and cultivating a number of close friendships.

As she grew older, Dickinson retreated from public life. In her later years, she mostly interacted with the outside world through writing, corresponding through letters with a few close friends. During her most productive years, she occupied a bedroom in the family home in Amherst. Letters from this time suggest a troubled romantic attachment that was the source of her creative drive.

Dickinson took an interest in writing poetry in her teens, and by the time she was 35 she had composed more than 1,100 poems in her concise lyrical style, capturing her astute observations on love, nature, art, pain, and joy. She did share a small portion of these poems with friends and family. A few of her poems were published in newspapers, but anonymously and apparently without her consent.

Emily Dickinson died at age 55. When the first volume of her poems was published in 1890, it won great critical and public acclaim, and she is now considered one of the greatest American poets.

"Saying nothing . . . sometimes says the most."

—Emily Dickinson

© Houghton Mifflin Harcourt Publishing Company • Image Credits: (r) ©Three Lions/Stringer/Hulton Archive/Getty Images

NOTICE & NOTE

As you read, use the side margins to make notes about the text.

Ideas and images come in starts and stops from one of America's most original poets.

The Soul selects her own Society

The Soul selects her own Society—
Then—shuts the Door—
To her divine Majority—
Present no more—

5 Unmoved—she notes the Chariots—pausing—
At her low Gate—
Unmoved—an Emperor be kneeling
Upon her Mat—

I've known her—from an ample nation—
10 Choose One—
Then—close the Valves of her attention—
Like Stone—

ANALYZE FIGURATIVE LANGUAGE

Annotate: Mark the simile in lines 11–12.

Analyze: What two things are being compared? What theme about the soul does this image suggest?

Because I could not stop for Death

Because I could not stop for Death—
He kindly stopped for me—
The Carriage held but just Ourselves—
And Immortality.

5   We slowly drove—He knew no haste
And I had put away
My labor and my leisure too,
For His Civility—

We passed the School, where Children strove
10 At Recess—in the Ring—
We passed the Fields of Gazing Grain—
We passed the Setting Sun—

Or rather—He passed Us—
The Dews drew quivering and chill—
15 For only Gossamer,[1] my Gown—
My Tippet—only Tulle[2]—

We paused before a House that seemed
A Swelling of the Ground—
The Roof was scarcely visible—
20 The Cornice[3]—in the Ground—

Since then—'tis Centuries—and yet
Feels shorter than the Day
I first surmised the Horses' Heads
Were toward Eternity—

---

[1] **Gossamer:** thin, soft material.
[2] **Tippet . . . Tulle:** shawl made of fine netting.
[3] **Cornice:** molding at the top of a building.

ANALYZE FIGURATIVE LANGUAGE

Annotate: In the first three stanzas, mark examples of personification.

Analyze: How does the personification of death affect the meaning of the poem?

ANALYZE STRUCTURE

Annotate: Mark the word in the fourth stanza that signifies a shift in thinking.

Analyze: How does the speaker's perception of what is happening change in this stanza? Explain.

Illustration of Emily Dickinson's home

Much Madness is divinest Sense

Much Madness is divinest Sense—
To a discerning Eye—
Much Sense—the starkest Madness—
'Tis the Majority
In this, as All, prevail—
Assent—and you are sane—
Demur—you're straightway dangerous—
And handled with a Chain—

5

ANALYZE STRUCTURE

Annotate: In line 3, mark the words between dashes.

Interpret: What is the function of the dashes in line 3? Does putting the words between dashes suggest a theme? If so, what?

ANALYZE THEME

Annotate: Mark the uses of the word *Truth* in this poem.

Analyze: What themes does the use of this repetition suggest?

Tell all the Truth but tell it slant

Tell all the Truth but tell it slant—
Success in Circuit[4] lies
Too bright for our infirm Delight
The Truth's superb surprise
As Lightning to the Children eased
With explanation kind
The Truth must dazzle gradually
Or every man be blind—

---

[4] **Circuit:** indirect path.

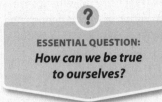

?

ESSENTIAL QUESTION:
How can we be true to ourselves?

Review your notes and add your thoughts to your **Response Log**.

COLLABORATIVE DISCUSSION

With a partner, discuss the themes that Dickinson explores in her poetry. Do you think the themes are unique to her experience or are they universal?

Assessment Practice

Answer these questions before moving on to the **Analyze the Text** section on the following page.

1. What is the theme of "The Soul selects her own Society"?

   (A) It's wrong not to be open to making new friends.

   (B) You shouldn't give up if someone refuses to talk to you.

   (C) The speaker blames herself for her loneliness.

   (D) People reveal their feelings to very few friends.

2. In the fifth stanza of "Because I could not stop for Death," what is the speaker describing?

   (A) an underground chapel

   (B) her own grave

   (C) her own fallen-down house

   (D) the house of the person they are visiting

3. Which of the following is an example of personification?

   (A) *I've known her—from an ample nation—*

   (B) *In this, as All, prevail—*

   (C) *The Truth must dazzle gradually*

   (D) *The Roof was scarcely visible—*

Test-Taking Strategies

Analyze the Text

Support your responses with evidence from the text

NOTICE & NOTE

Review what you **noticed and noted** as you read the text. Your annotations can help you answer these questions.

1 INFER Themes often must be inferred from clues in the text. Look at the different types of figurative language Dickinson uses in each poem. What themes does this language suggest? Use the chart to help you answer.

Title of Poem	Type of Figurative Language	Theme(s)
The Soul selects her own Society		
Because I could not stop for Death		
Much Madness is divinest Sense		
Tell all the Truth but tell it slant		

2 INFER In both "Much Madness is divinest Sense" and "The Soul selects her own Society," the speaker mentions the Majority. To what or to whom does the Majority refer? What does the speaker think of the Majority?

3 ANALYZE A common foot in English verse is the **iamb**, which is an unstressed syllable followed by a stressed syllable. If a line has three feet, then the verse is iambic trimeter; four, and it's iambic tetrameter. One of the most common meters is iambic pentameter, or five iambs in a single line. What meter do these poems use? How does the meter affect your understanding of the poem?

4 INTERPRET In the second stanza of "The Soul selects her own Society," which word does the speaker repeat? What is the effect of the repeated word?

5 ANALYZE Identify the paradoxes you find in "Tell all the Truth but tell it slant" and "Much Madness is divinest Sense." What truth does each paradox reveal?

6 INTERPRET Dickinson uses dashes freely in her poems. How do the dashes affect the way you read the poems? How do they help clarify the meaning that she conveys?

Choices

Here are some other ways to demonstrate your understanding of the ideas in this lesson.

Writing
↳ Micro-story

Select one of Dickinson's poems and rewrite it as a micro-story—a very brief work of fiction. Limit yourself to 300 words or less. As you write, remember that every word counts, so choose them all carefully.

Ideas to consider:

- Micro-stories still rely on plot, setting, point of view, and characterization, so think about how to convey those elements in a few words.

- Imagery is important—remember, "a picture is worth a thousand words."

- Hook your readers from the start and then make them do the work. Use your limited word count to imply actions, events, and character motivations, but let the reader fill in the gaps.

As you write and discuss, be sure to use the **Academic Vocabulary** words.

analogy

denote

quote

topic

unique

Media
↳ Collage

In the four Dickinson poems you read, pick three lines that stuck with you the most. Use a computer to print the lines in an eye-catching font, then select images that best represent them. Create a collage, mixing the words and images together to present Dickinson's ideas. If you prefer, you can draw, paint, or use other media to come up with the images.

Speaking & Listening
↳ Video Presentation

With a small group, prepare a script for a panel discussion called *An Evening with Emily Dickinson*. You will ask Dickinson questions on any or all of the following:

- her life
- her views of poetry and language
- her feelings about nature, faith, and eternity

When the script is done, have one person role-play Emily while the other group members play the panelists. Engage in a Q & A, asking questions and following up on "Emily's" answers. You can have her read selected poems, as well. Film your discussion to share with the class.

In the Season of Change

Poem by **Teresa Palomo Acosta**

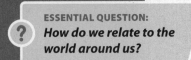

ESSENTIAL QUESTION:
How do we relate to the world around us?

Engage Your Brain

Choose one or more of these activities to start connecting with the poem you're about to read.

Coffee Talk

You have the unheard-of opportunity to interview anyone you want—dead or alive—over coffee (or tea or hot chocolate). Whom do you choose and what do you talk about? Write down a list of questions. Then share them with a partner and explain what you hope to learn by asking them.

Getting to Know You

Freewrite your ideas in response to these questions.

- How do you get to know someone and find out what you have in common?
- Is it possible to connect with someone you will never meet or see?
- How can you discover connections if a person is no longer living?

Song of the Day

Emily Dickinson wrote over 1,800 poems about love, nature, grief, pain, isolation, individuality, family, death and immortality, and religion, just to name a few. Pick one of those topics and create a list of five or six songs you think relate.

Analyze Sound Devices

"In the Season of Change" is an example of **free verse.** Free verse is poetry that does not have the regular meter or rhyming patterns of traditional poetry. Instead, free verse uses the natural rhythm of everyday speech. This poem also includes **sound devices** to contribute to the structure, rhythm, and meaning of the work. You will find the following sound devices in the poem:

- **Alliteration:** repetition of consonant sounds at the beginning of words

- **Assonance:** repetition of vowel sounds in nearby words

- **Consonance**: repetition of consonants within or at the end of a word

As you read, note examples of alliteration, assonance, and consonance in the poem. Think about the effect these sound devices have on the poem.

Focus on Genre
↳ **Free Verse**

- does not have regular meter or rhyme patterns
- flows like natural speech
- lines can break within or flow across stanzas
- uses imagery and sound devices to evoke emotions or draw connections

Analyze Imagery

All poets use language to help them convey **themes,** or messages about life. Many poems convey themes through **imagery,** or vivid language that appeals to the senses. Imagery infuses a poem with meaning and allows readers to connect with similar emotions or experiences they've had.

In "In the Season of Change," Teresa Palomo Acosta uses imagery to create a link with Emily Dickinson across time and cultures. In addition, she pairs Spanish terms with English terms—great-grandmothers and *bisabuelas,* rhubarb pie and *cafecito,* chatting and *chismeando.* Using Spanish terms emphasizes Acosta's heritage and sets up a comparison between her world and Dickinson's.

As you read "In the Season of Change," write down examples of imagery you find and note the senses they appeal to.

Sense	Imagery
Sight	
Sound	
Smell	
Touch	
Taste	

Analyze Structure

All poems contain structural elements that affect meaning. **Lines** are the core unit of a poem. **Line breaks** occur where a line of poetry ends. A line break can come at the end of a thought or sentence, but sometimes poets choose to break in the middle of a thought for effect. **Stanzas** are the groups of lines that form a unit of thought in a poem. When determining the meaning of a poem, consider the key ideas contained in each stanza.

As you read, think about the effect line breaks have on the meaning of poem and consider the impact each stanza has on the ideas the writer expresses.

Annotation in Action

Here are one student's notes on the imagery in the first stanza of "In the Season of Change." As you read the poem, note the writer's use of imagery.

> If E. Dickinson and I had been friends,
> we would have each owned a treasure chest
> filled with doilies for laying under our silverware,
> for showing off atop our china cabinets.
> For softening the scars in the 300-year-old dining room tables
> we would have inherited
> from our great-grandmothers.

The poet's descriptions help me picture the furniture.

Background

Teresa Palomo Acosta (b. 1949) was born in McGregor, Texas, to Mexican parents who had migrated to Texas during the Great Depression. Acosta earned a degree in ethnic studies at the University of Texas and then a master's degree at the Columbia University School of Journalism. She went on to become a leading voice of multiculturalism in the United States. She says her writing helps her retell stories about herself and about the Chicana experience. Acosta is also the coauthor of *Las Tejanas: 300 Years of History*, a history of women of Spanish and/or Mexican origin in Texas.

In the Season of Change

Poem by **Teresa Palomo Acosta**

Note the details that suggest a sense of longing, and think about what the poet longs for.

NOTICE & NOTE
As you read, use the side margins to make notes about the text.

If E. Dickinson and I had been friends,
we would have each owned a treasure chest
filled with doilies for laying under our silverware,
for showing off atop our china cabinets.
5   For softening the scars in the 300-year-old dining room tables
we would have inherited
from our great-grandmothers.

But our bisabuelas[1] never met,
exchanged glances or
10 sat next to each other in church.
And I only discovered E. Dickinson
in the few pages she was allowed
to enter in my high school literature texts.

ANALYZE IMAGERY

Annotate: In the first and second stanzas, mark images that appeal to the senses.

Analyze: How does the poet use the images to describe her relationship to Emily Dickinson?

---

[1] **bisabuelas** (bēs-ä-bwä´läs): great-grandmothers.

Annotate: Use brackets to mark each sentence in lines 14–21.

Infer: How does the line length reflect the ideas expressed in the stanza?

15　Only years later did
　　I finally pore over her words,
　　believing that
　　her songs held
　　my name inscribed within.
　　And that they might fill the air
20　with the ancient signs of kinship
　　that women can choose to pass along.

　　And thus left on our own,
　　E. Dickinson and I
　　sat down at the same table,
25　savoring her rhubarb pie and my cafecito[2]
　　chatting and chismeando[3]
　　and trading secrets
　　despite decrees demanding silence between us:

　　women from separate corners of the room.

ANALYZE SOUND DEVICES

Annotate: Mark the alliteration in lines 22–28.

Analyze: How does the alliteration serve to unify the lines in the stanza? What is the connection between the stanza and line 29?

---

[2] **cafecito** (kä-fä-sē´tô): little cup of coffee.
[3] **chismeando** (chēs-mä-än´dô): gossiping.

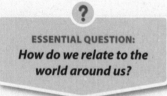

ESSENTIAL QUESTION:
How do we relate to the world around us?

Review your notes and add your thoughts to your **Response Log.**

COLLABORATIVE DISCUSSION

With a partner, discuss what the title of the poem might mean, and what message it implies. Consider what might be changing for the poet and which seasons signify change in our world.

Assessment Practice

Answer these questions before moving on to the **Analyze the Text**
section on the following page.

1. Which of the following phrases from the poem is an example of assonance?

（A）*a treasure chest* (line 2)

（A）*high school literature texts* (line 13)

（A）*they might fill the air* (line 19)

（B）*despite decrees demanding* (line 28)

2. How does the poet discover Dickinson?

（A）The poet's great-grandmother introduces her.

（B）She finds a few Dickinson poems in her literature book.

（C）Her high school teacher spends a lot of time teaching Dickinson.

（D）She finds a book of Dickinson's poems in a china cabinet.

3. What do the lines *her songs held / my name inscribed within* (lines 17–18) mean?

（A）Dickinson had known someone with the poet's name.

（B）Someone had written in the poet's literature book.

（C）The poet felt a strong kinship with Dickinson.

（D）The poet put her name in the book to show it was hers.

Ed
Test-Taking Strategies

Analyze the Text

Support your responses with evidence from the text.

NOTICE & NOTE

Review what you **noticed and noted** as you read the text. Your annotations can help you answer these questions.

1. **INFER** Why does the poet think that she and Dickinson could become friends?

2. **ANALYZE** How do the poem's stanzas give a structure to the poem? How does the structure support the poem's message?

Purpose of Stanza	Effect on Message
1.	
2.	
3.	
4.	

3. **EVALUATE** Think about the Spanish terms Acosta includes. What is the effect of using this imagery in the poem?

4. **INTERPRET** Poets may use sound devices to emphasize important ideas. What idea does Acosta emphasize by saying that she and Dickinson are sharing secrets "despite decrees demanding silence between [them]"?

5. **ANALYZE** What examples of consonance do you find in the first two stanzas of the poem? What is the effect of this consonance?

6. **CONNECT** How do the lines *And thus left on our own, / E. Dickinson and I / sat down at the same table* help communicate the poem's theme?

Choices

Here are some other ways to demonstrate your understanding of the ideas in this lesson.

Writing
↳ Poem

Write a poem about a person you admire. Follow the steps below.

1. After you choose your subject, outline your poem stanza by stanza.

2. Think carefully about the imagery you want to include.

3. Think about sound devices you can use to keep your poem interesting and create rhythm.

4. As you draft your poem, think about the theme, or message, you want to convey.

5. Work with a classmate to edit your draft. Give your partner feedback about language and style.

6. Revise your poem as necessary, based on your partner's feedback.

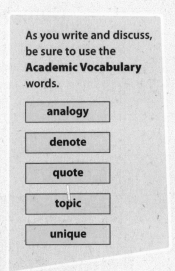

As you write and discuss, be sure to use the **Academic Vocabulary** words.

- analogy
- denote
- quote
- topic
- unique

Media
↳ Java Jive Playlist

The speaker in the poem has gotten her wish and will meet up with Emily Dickinson in real time. Create a list of four to five songs that can serve as background music. Compare your list of songs with that of a partner and say why you chose what you did.

Speaking & Listening
↳ Role-play

With a partner, talk about a well-known person you admire and would like to know better. Imagine that you have the chance to go out for coffee with this person. Take turns playing the interviewer and the celebrity.

1. Before you start, write three questions you'd like to ask. Share them with your partner.

2. If you are the celebrity, be prepared to do a little research to be able to answer your partner's questions.

3. Conduct the interviews. If you'd like, you can film them and post to a school website.

Collaborate & Compare

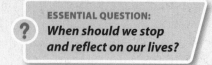
Compare Main Ideas

In the 19th century, Henry David Thoreau espoused the view that divinity was found in nature. The contemporary writer Richard Louv believes that humanity's essential connection to nature has been lost. As you read, consider what each author believes people gain from interacting with nature.

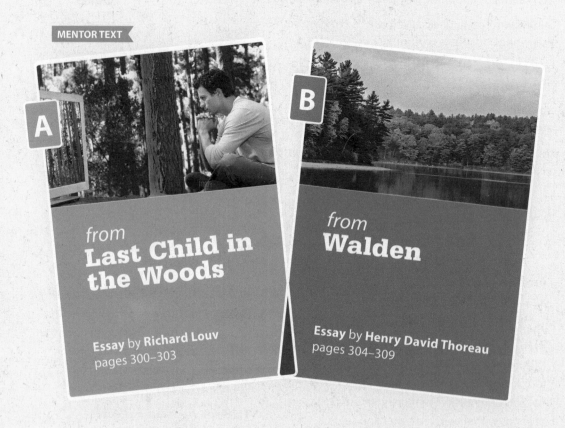

MENTOR TEXT

A

from
Last Child in the Woods

Essay by **Richard Louv**
pages 300–303

B

from
Walden

Essay by **Henry David Thoreau**
pages 304–309

After you read, you will explore ideas in the poems by collaborating with a small group on a presentation. You will follow these steps:

- Decide on the most important ideas
- Compare main ideas
- Synthesize information
- Present to the class

from **Last Child in the Woods**

Essay by **Richard Louv**

from **Walden**

Essay by **Henry David Thoreau**

Engage Your Brain

Choose one or more of these activities to start connecting with the essays you're about to read.

A Walk in the Woods

Create a flyer for a walk in the woods. What aspects of nature would you emphasize? What benefits would you highlight? Follow the instructions.

1. Make sure the key details are included.

2. Keep the words to a minimum.

3. Use text features like headings, bullet points, and photographs, illustrations, or graphics.

4. Revise and proofread before publishing.

Suck the Marrow out of Life. Huh?

In one of the essays you're about to read, Henry David Thoreau says: "I wanted to live deep and suck out all the marrow of life, to live so sturdily and Spartan-like as to put to rout all that was not life, to cut a broad swath and shave close, to drive life into a corner, and reduce it to its lowest terms." Sounds awesome, but what the heck does he mean? Get with a partner and see if you can guess what the essay will be about, based on that quote.

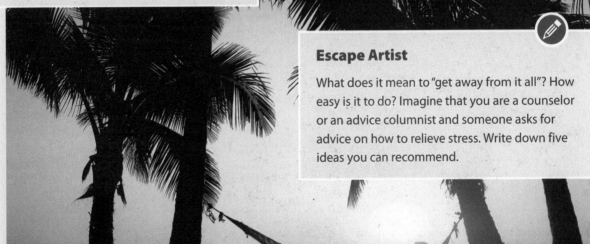

Escape Artist

What does it mean to "get away from it all"? How easy is it to do? Imagine that you are a counselor or an advice columnist and someone asks for advice on how to relieve stress. Write down five ideas you can recommend.

Summarize

When you **summarize**, you restate a text's central ideas in your own words. A summary is much shorter than the original text and includes only the most important supporting details. To be objective, a summary cannot include your own thoughts or opinions. Use these strategies to summarize the texts:

- Skim **text features** such as titles, headings, and photographs to predict what the text will be about.

- See if a topic sentence, usually at the beginning or end of a paragraph, explicitly states the paragraph's central idea.

- Infer a central idea from the details contained in a paragraph.

- If you are struggling, summarize individual paragraphs or sections first.

Focus on Genre
↳ **Essays**

- **clearly convey central ideas**
- **contain details that support key ideas**
- **use elements of style, including rhetorical devices and figures of speech**

Analyze Style

Style refers to how an author expresses his or her ideas. Authors use elements of style to make ideas more compelling and make a text more engaging. Two aspects of style are rhetorical devices and figures of speech.

Elements of Style	
Rhetorical Devices: Language structures that produce a special effect or convey additional meaning to a text	**Rhetorical question** A question that requires no reply **Repetition** To repeat a sound, word, or phrase for emphasis or unity **Irony** A contrast between appearances and reality **Verbal irony** A contrast between what is said and what is meant
Figures of Speech: Language that communicates ideas beyond the literal meaning of the words used	**Simile** A comparison between two things, using *like* or *as* **Metaphor** A direct comparison that does not use *like* or *as* **Hyperbole** An exaggeration of the truth for emphasis or humorous effect **Personification** To give human traits to objects, animals, or ideas

As you read the texts, notice how each writer employs elements of style to help readers understand the ideas he wants to communicate.

Annotation in Action

In the model, you can see one student's notes about Thoreau's distinctive style. As you read, make notes on what you notice about each author's style.

I wanted to live deep and suck out all the marrow of life, to live so sturdily and Spartan-like as to put to rout all that was not life, to cut a broad swath and shave close, to drive life into a corner, and reduce it to its lowest terms, and, if it proved to be mean, why then to get the whole and genuine meanness of it, and publish its meanness to the world; or if it were sublime, to know it by experience, and be able to give a true account of it in my next excursion.

This is a strong image and conveys an important idea: enthusiasm for life!

Expand Your Vocabulary

Put a check mark next to the vocabulary words that you feel comfortable using when speaking or writing.

remunerative	
superfluous	
unfathomed	
perturbation	

Then, write a paragraph about a time you felt a connection to nature, using as many of the vocabulary words as you can. As you read the texts, use the definitions in the side column to help you learn the vocabulary words you don't already know.

Background

Journalist **Richard Louv** (b. 1949) is an active writer and speaker about the importance of reconnecting children to nature. He cofounded the Children & Nature Network, an organization whose vision is a "world in which all children play, learn and grow with nature in their everyday lives."

Henry David Thoreau (1817–1862) of Concord, Massachusetts, was a transcendentalist like his friend and mentor Ralph Waldo Emerson. In 1845, he began his two-year experiment living in a cabin that he built in the woods near Walden Pond on property owned by Emerson. *Walden* (1854) is a collection of 18 essays based on his experiences.

NOTICE & NOTE

As you read, use the side margins to make notes about the text.

from

Last Child in the Woods

Essay by **Richard Louv**

As you read, note how Louv supports his ideas about how people's relationship to nature has changed.

SUMMARIZE

Annotate: Mark sentences and phrases in paragraph 4 that contrast the author's childhood and the lives of children today.

Compare: What main idea does this comparison communicate?

1   One evening when my boys were younger, Matthew, then ten, looked at me from across a restaurant table and said quite seriously, "Dad, how come it was more fun when you were a kid?"

2   I asked what he meant.

3   "Well, you're always talking about your woods and tree houses, and how you used to ride that horse down near the swamp." At first, I thought he was irritated with me. I had, in fact, been telling him what it was like to use string and pieces of liver to catch crawdads in a creek, something I'd be hard-pressed to find a child doing these days. Like many parents, I do tend to romanticize my own childhood— and, I fear, too readily discount my children's experiences of play and adventure. But my son was serious; he felt he had missed out on something important.

4   He was right. Americans around my age, baby boomers or older, enjoyed a kind of free, natural play that seems, in the era of kid pagers, instant messaging, and video games, like a quaint artifact. Within the space of a few decades, the way children understand and experience nature has changed radically. The polarity of the relationship has reversed. Today, kids are aware of the global threats to the environment—but their physical contact, their intimacy with

nature, is fading. That's exactly the opposite of how it was when I was a child.

5   As a boy, I was unaware that my woods were ecologically connected with any other forests. Nobody in the 1950s talked about acid rain or holes in the ozone layer or global warming. But I knew my woods and my fields; I knew every bend in the creek and dip in the beaten dirt paths. I wandered those woods even in my dreams. A kid today can likely tell you about the Amazon rain forest—but not about the last time he or she explored the woods in solitude, or lay in a field listening to the wind and watching the clouds move.

6   The shift in our relationship to the natural world is startling, even in settings that one would assume are devoted to nature. Not that long ago, summer camp was a place where you camped, hiked in the woods, learned about plants and animals, or told firelight stories about ghosts or mountain lions. As likely as not today, "summer camp" is a weight-loss camp, or a computer camp. For a new generation, nature is more abstraction than reality. Increasingly, nature is something to watch, to consume, to wear—to ignore. A recent television ad depicts a four-wheel-drive SUV racing along a breathtakingly beautiful mountain stream—while in the backseat two children watch a movie on a flip-down video screen, oblivious to the landscape and water beyond the windows.

7   A century ago, the historian Frederick Jackson Turner announced that the American frontier had ended. His thesis has been discussed and debated ever since. Today, a similar and more important line is being crossed.

8   Our society is teaching young people to avoid direct experience in nature. That lesson is delivered in schools, families, even organizations devoted to the outdoors, and codified into the legal and regulatory structures of many of our communities. Our institutions, urban/suburban design, and cultural attitudes unconsciously associate nature with doom—while disassociating[1] the outdoors from joy and solitude. Well-meaning public-school systems, media, and parents are effectively scaring children straight out of the woods and fields. In the patent-or-perish environment of higher education, we see the death of natural history as the more hands-on disciplines, such as zoology, give way to more theoretical and **remunerative** microbiology and genetic engineering. Rapidly advancing technologies are blurring the lines between humans, other animals, and machines. The postmodern notion that reality is only a construct—that we are what we program—suggests limitless human possibilities; but as the young spend less and less of their lives in natural surroundings, their senses narrow, physiologically and psychologically, and this reduces the richness of human experience.

9   Yet, at the very moment that the bond is breaking between the young and the natural world, a growing body of research links our

ANALYZE STYLE

Annotate: Mark an example of irony in paragraph 6.

Interpret: What point does Louv make through the use of irony?

remunerative (rĭ-myōō´nər-ə-tĭv):yielding suitable compensation, profitable.

[1] **disassociating** (dĭs-ə-sō´sē-āt-ĭng): removing from association.

SUMMARIZE

Annotate: Mark two significant details about the research that the author cites in paragraph 9.

Analyze: How do these details support the author's key idea that children ought to reconnect with nature?

mental, physical, and spiritual health directly to our association with nature—in positive ways. Several of these studies suggest that thoughtful exposure of youngsters to nature can even be a powerful form of therapy for attention-deficit disorders and other maladies. As one scientist puts it, we can now assume that just as children need good nutrition and adequate sleep, they may very well need contact with nature.

10   Reducing that deficit[2]—healing the broken bond between our young and nature—is in our self-interest, not only because aesthetics or justice demands it, but also because our mental, physical, and spiritual health depends upon it. The health of the earth is at stake as well. How the young respond to nature, and how they raise their own children, will shape the configurations and conditions of our cities, homes—our daily lives. . . .

11   . . . I am encouraged to find that many people now of college age—those who belong to the first generation to grow up in a largely de-natured environment—have tasted just enough nature to intuitively understand what they have missed. This yearning is a source of power. These young people resist the rapid slide from the real to the virtual, from the mountains to the Matrix. They do not intend to be the last children in the woods.

12   My sons may yet experience what author Bill McKibben has called "the end of nature," the final sadness of a world where there is no escaping man. But there is another possibility: not the end of nature, but the rebirth of wonder and even joy. Jackson's obituary for the American frontier was only partly accurate: one frontier did disappear, but a second one followed, in which Americans romanticized, exploited, protected, and destroyed nature. Now that frontier—which existed in the family farm, the woods at the end of the road, the national parks, and in our hearts—is itself disappearing or changing beyond recognition. But, as before, one relationship with nature can evolve into another. . . .

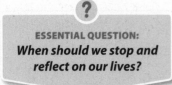

ESSENTIAL QUESTION:
When should we stop and reflect on our lives?

Review your notes and add your thoughts to your **Response Log.**

---

[2] **deficit** (dĕf´ ĭ-sĭt): inadequacy or insufficiency.

COLLABORATIVE DISCUSSION

What is your reaction to Louv's concluding thoughts? Share your ideas with a partner.

Assessment Practice

Answer these questions about *Last Child in the Woods* before moving on to the next selection.

1. What event caused Louv to begin thinking about how children relate to nature?

   - (A) the birth of his child
   - (B) a conversation with his child
   - (C) taking his child on a camping trip
   - (D) looking at his child's science textbook

2. What was Louv's childhood like?

   - (A) playing outside and going fishing
   - (B) going to camp and studying nature
   - (C) wandering the streets of his small town
   - (D) playing video games and being with friends

3. What is the main thing Louv thinks people ought to do?

   - (A) clean up the environment
   - (B) give children books about nature
   - (C) help children reconnect with nature
   - (D) work to make the world a better place

Test-Taking Strategies

from

Walden

Essay by **Henry David Thoreau**

© Houghton Mifflin Harcourt Publishing Company • Image Credits: ©Gabriel Negron/Alamy

NOTICE & NOTE

As you read, use the side margins to make notes about the text.

Note Thoreau's observations about "modern life" and the connection between humans and nature.

from Where I Lived, and What I Lived For

SUMMARIZE

Annotate: Mark the title of this section of the essay.

Interpret: What is the most important idea the writer expresses in paragraph 1? How does the title help you identify this idea?

1   When first I took up my abode in the woods, that is, began to spend my nights as well as days there, which, by accident, was on Independence day, or the fourth of July, 1845, my house was not finished for winter, but was merely a defense against the rain, without plastering or chimney, the walls being of rough weather-stained boards, with wide chinks, which made it cool at night. The upright white hewn studs and freshly planed door and window casings gave it a clean and airy look, especially in the morning, when its timbers were saturated with dew, so that I fancied that by noon some sweet gum would exude from them. . . .

2   I was seated by the shore of a small pond, about a mile and a half south of the village of Concord and somewhat higher than it, in the midst of an extensive wood between that town and Lincoln, and about two miles south of that our only field known to fame, Concord Battle Ground; but I was so low in the woods that the opposite shore, half a mile off, like the rest, covered with wood, was my most distant horizon. For the first week, whenever I looked out on the pond it impressed me like a tarn[1] high up on the side of a mountain, its bottom far above the surface of other lakes, and, as the sun arose, I saw it throwing off its nightly clothing of mist, and here and there, by degrees, its soft ripples or its smooth reflecting surface was revealed, while the mists, like ghosts, were stealthily withdrawing in every direction into the woods, as at the breaking up of some nocturnal conventicle.[2] The very dew seemed to hang upon the trees later into the day than usual, as on the sides of mountains. . . .

3   I went to the woods because I wished to live deliberately, to front only the essential facts of life, and see if I could not learn what it had to teach, and not, when I came to die, discover that I had not lived. I did not wish to live what was not life, living is so dear; nor did I wish to practice resignation, unless it was quite necessary. I wanted to live deep and suck out all the marrow of life, to live so sturdily and Spartan-like[3] as to put to rout all that was not life, to cut a broad swath and shave close, to drive life into a corner, and reduce it to its lowest terms, and, if it proved to be mean, why then to get the whole and genuine meanness of it, and publish its meanness to the world; or if it were sublime, to know it by experience, and be able to give a true account of it in my next excursion. For most men, it appears to me, are in a strange uncertainty about it, whether it is of the devil or of God, and have *somewhat hastily* concluded that it is the chief end of man here to "glorify God and enjoy him forever."

4   Still we live meanly, like ants; though the fable tells us that we were long ago changed into men; like pygmies we fight with cranes; it is error upon error, and clout upon clout, and our best virtue has for its occasion a **superfluous** and evitable[4] wretchedness. Our life is frittered away by detail. An honest man has hardly need to count more than his ten fingers, or in extreme cases he may add his ten toes, and lump the rest. Simplicity, simplicity, simplicity! I say, let your affairs be as two or three, and not a hundred or a thousand; instead of a million count half a dozen, and keep your accounts on your thumbnail. In the midst of this chopping sea of civilized life, such are the clouds and storms and quicksands and thousand-and-one items to be allowed for, that a man has to live, if he would not founder and go to the bottom and not make his port at all, by dead reckoning, and he must be a great calculator indeed who succeeds. Simplify, simplify.

ANALYZE STYLE

Annotate: Mark an example of personification and an example of a simile in paragraph 2.

Analyze: How does this figurative language support a key idea in the paragraph?

superfluous
(so͝o-pûr′flo͞o-əs) *adj.* unnecessary.

---

[1] **tarn:** a small mountain lake or pool.
[2] **conventicle:** a secret or unlawful religious meeting.
[3] **Spartan-like:** in a simple and disciplined way; like the inhabitants of the ancient city-state of Sparta.
[4] **evitable:** avoidable.

Annotate: Mark the very long sentence in paragraph 5.

Analyze: What is the effect of placing this sentence in this paragraph?

5

Instead of three meals a day, if it be necessary eat but one; instead of a hundred dishes, five; and reduce other things in proportion. . . .

Why should we live with such hurry and waste of life? We are determined to be starved before we are hungry. Men say that a stitch in time saves nine, and so they take a thousand stitches today to save nine to-morrow. As for *work*, we haven't any of any consequence. We have the Saint Vitus' dance,[5] and cannot possibly keep our heads still. If I should only give a few pulls at the parish bell-rope, as for a fire, that is, without setting the bell, there is hardly a man on his farm in the outskirts of Concord, notwithstanding that press of engagements which was his excuse so many times this morning, nor a boy, nor a woman, I might almost say, but would forsake all and follow that sound, not mainly to save property from the flames, but, if we will

[5] **Saint Vitus' dance:** a disorder of the nervous system, characterized by rapid, jerky, involuntary movements.

confess the truth, much more to see it burn, since burn it must, and we, be it known, did not set it on fire,—or to see it put out, and have a hand in it, if that is done as handsomely; yes, even if it were the parish church itself. Hardly a man takes a half hour's nap after dinner, but when he wakes he holds up his head and asks, "What's the news?" as if the rest of mankind had stood his sentinels. Some give directions to be waked every half hour, doubtless for no other purpose; and then, to pay for it, they tell what they have dreamed. After a night's sleep the news is as indispensable as the breakfast. "Pray tell me any thing new that has happened to a man any where on this globe,"—and he reads it over his coffee and rolls, that a man has had his eyes gouged out this morning on the Wachito River; never dreaming the while that he lives in the dark **unfathomed** mammoth cave of this world, and has but the rudiment of an eye himself.

ANALYZE STYLE

Annotate: Mark an example of hyperbole in paragraph 5.

Analyze: What is Thoreau exaggerating in this sentence? What effect does this exaggeration have on the reader?

unfathomed
(ŭn-făth´əmd) *adj.* located at the deepest place.

Walden **307**

6   For my part, I could easily do without the post-office. I think that there are very few important communications made through it. To speak critically, I never received more than one or two letters in my life—I wrote this some years ago—that were worth the postage. The penny-post is, commonly, an institution through which you seriously offer a man that penny for his thoughts which is so often safely offered in jest. And I am sure that I never read any memorable news in a newspaper. If we read of one man robbed, or murdered, or killed by accident, or one house burned, or one vessel wrecked, or one steamboat blown up, or one cow run over on the Western Railroad, or one mad dog killed, or one lot of grasshoppers in the winter,—we never need read of another. One is enough. . . .

7   Let us spend one day as deliberately as Nature, and not be thrown off the track by every nutshell and mosquito's wing that falls on the rails. Let us rise early and fast, or break fast, gently and without **perturbation;** let company come and let company go, let the bells ring and the children cry,— determined to make a day of it. . . .

8   Time is but the stream I go a-fishing in. I drink at it; but while I drink I see the sandy bottom and detect how shallow it is. Its thin current slides away, but eternity remains. I would drink deeper; fish in the sky, whose bottom is pebbly with stars. I cannot count one. I know not the first letter of the alphabet. I have always been regretting that I was not as wise as the day I was born. The intellect is a cleaver; it discerns and rifts its way into the secret of things. I do not wish to be any more busy with my hands than is necessary. My head is hands and feet. I feel all my best faculties concentrated in it. My instinct tells me that my head is an organ for burrowing, as some creatures use their snout and fore-paws, and with it I would mine and burrow my way through these hills. I think that the richest vein is somewhere hereabouts; so by the divining rod and thin rising vapors I judge; and here I will begin to mine.

perturbation
(pûr-tər-bā´shən) *n.* disturbance or agitation.

SUMMARIZE

Annotate: Mark the last sentence of the text.

Interpret: What does Thoreau mean when he says "the richest vein is somewhere hereabouts"? What key idea does this statement convey?

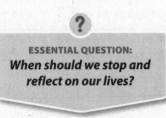

ESSENTIAL QUESTION:
When should we stop and reflect on our lives?

Review your notes and add your thoughts to your **Response Log.**

COLLABORATIVE DISCUSSION

What is one similarity and one difference you notice between Louv's and Thoreau's writing and ideas? Discuss your ideas with a partner.

Assessment Practice

Answer these questions before moving on to the **Analyze the Texts** section on the following page.

1. Where does Thoreau live during the time described in this essay?

   (A) in the village of Concord

   (B) in the small town of Lincoln

   (C) in a field not far from Lincoln

   (D) in the woods not far from Concord

2. What is Thoreau's main purpose for living there?

   (A) to escape modern life

   (B) to learn what is essential about life

   (C) to be more devoted to God and glorify Him

   (D) to become more like an animal than like a human

3. What are Thoreau's main complaints about human society?

   (A) It is dull and full of empty relationships.

   (B) It is shallow and full of terrifying cruelty.

   (C) It is violent and full of appalling suffering.

   (D) It is rushed and full of meaningless distractions.

Ⓔd
Test-Taking Strategies

Analyze the Texts

Support your responses with evidence from the texts.

NOTICE & NOTE

Review what you **noticed and noted** as you read the text. Your annotations can help you answer these questions.

1. **ANALYZE** How does Louv use contrasts—such as *death* and *rebirth, broken* and *healing*—to develop his essay's main ideas in the excerpt from *Last Child in the Woods*?

2. **EVALUATE** Louv includes both scientific evidence and his own personal experiences in *Last Child in the Woods*. Which of the details best support his ideas about the relationship between humanity and nature? Cite text evidence in the chart.

Scientific Evidence	Personal Experience

3. **SUMMARIZE** How does Thoreau describe his reasons for moving to the woods in the excerpt from *Walden*? How do these reasons relate to his purpose in writing *Walden*?

4. **ANALYZE** What is the metaphor that Thoreau uses to describe "civilized life" in paragraph 4? What meaning does he convey through this figure of speech?

5. **INTERPRET** What does Thoreau mean by saying we should not be "thrown off the track" in paragraph 7 of the excerpt from *Walden*?

6. **COMPARE** Both Louv and Thoreau suggest that people benefit from being closer to nature. Which writer is more effective in conveying this idea? Cite text evidence in your response.

Choices

Here are some other ways to demonstrate your understanding of the ideas in this lesson.

Writing
↳ A Nature Diary

For a week, keep a diary in which you note your interactions with the natural world. Use these suggestions for getting the most out of your journal.

1. Plan out at least three nature outings alone or with a group.

2. Connect your experiences and ideas with those of Louv or Thoreau.

3. Include pictures and illustrations of your experiences.

4. Note how long your experiences are and how much time you spend indoors versus outdoors.

5. At the end of the week, summarize your ideas about nature. Include thoughts on your experiences and anything notable you learned.

As you write and discuss, be sure to use the **Academic Vocabulary** words.

> analogy

> denote

> quote

> topic

> unique

Research
↳ Answer Questions on Transcendentalism

Transcendentalism emphasized living a simple life and celebrating the truth found in nature, emotion, and imagination. Research to answer the following questions about transcendentalism.

- What are the main principles of transcendentalism?

- Who are some notable transcendentalist writers?

- What was the impact of transcendentalism?

Speaking & Listening
↳ Debate

Richard Louv strongly suggests that people are feeling disconnected from nature and that this disconnect has had a harmful effect on their lives. Divide into teams and debate whether you agree with this idea. You may cite details from both Louv and Thoreau, your own experiences, or evidence from other sources. Listen carefully to opposing views and answer questions respectfully.

Expand Your Vocabulary

PRACTICE AND APPLY

Use your understanding of the vocabulary words to answer each question.

1. If Walden Pond was **unfathomed,** was it deep or shallow?

2. Many people experience **perturbation** when listening to the news. Does it make them upset or happy?

3. Thoreau found the post office **superfluous.** Did he think it was necessary or unnecessary?

4. Both essayists suggest nature is **remunerative.** Does this mean it harms or benefits them?

Vocabulary Strategy

↳ Context Clues

Using **context clues**—nearby words, phrases, and sentences—can help you figure out the meanings of unfamiliar words. Consider the context in *Last Child in the Woods* for the word *codified*:

> That lesson is delivered in schools, families, even organizations devoted to the outdoors, and codified into the legal and regulatory structures of many of our communities.

A reader might conclude that *codified* means "written" or "added." However, phrases in the paragraph, such as *legal and regulatory structures* let the reader know that *codified* means "organized and systematized."

PRACTICE AND APPLY

Work with a partner to use context to determine the meanings of the words from *Last Child in the Woods*. Record which context clues were most helpful. Then, check your definitions by using a dictionary.

Word	Context Clues	Meaning
ecologically (paragraph 5)		
maladies (paragraph 10)		

☺Ed

Interactive Vocabulary Lesson: Using Context Clues

Watch Your Language!

Sentence Structure

An essential part of a writer's style is **syntax,** or how the writer arranges words to construct phrases, clauses, and sentences. Many writers use variety in sentence structure and length to create rhythm in their prose. Writers may use simple, compound, complex, and compound-complex sentences. In an informal work, writers may use sentence fragments to add emphasis or create a conversational style. Writers' use of syntax allows them to create unique voices in their writing.

The chart below shows examples of varied syntax from *Last Child in the Woods* and *Walden*.

Varying Syntax for Effect		
Sentence Structure	**Essay**	**Example**
Simple	*Walden*	We are determined to be starved before we are hungry.
Compound	*Walden*	Men say that a stitch in time saves nine, and so they take a thousand stitches today to save nine to-morrow.
Complex	*Last Child in the Woods*	Within the space of a few decades, the way children understand and experience nature has changed radically.
Compound-Complex	*Last Child in the Woods*	Jackson's obituary for the American frontier was only partly accurate: one frontier did disappear, but a second one followed, in which Americans romanticized, exploited, protected, and destroyed nature.
Sentence Fragment	*Walden*	Simplicity, simplicity, simplicity!

PRACTICE AND APPLY

Revise a piece of your own writing so that you include at least one of each type of sentence (including a sentence fragment) from the chart above.

Compare Main Ideas

Even though the authors of *Walden* and *Last Child in the Woods* wrote in very different historical and social contexts, they discuss some of the same issues. Using examples from the works, complete the chart below with

- main, or central, ideas about the effects of technology on people
- main, or central, ideas about the benefits of nature for people
- important images and details that relate to main ideas
- important comparisons that relate to main ideas

	A *from* **Last Child in the Woods**	**B** *from* **Walden**
Effects of Technology		
Benefits of Nature		
Important Images and Details		
Important Comparisons		

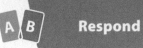

Analyze the Texts

Discuss these questions in your group.

1) **COMPARE** With your group, review the images and details that you cited in your chart. In what ways are the images similar? In what ways are they different? Explain.

2) **INFER** Both essays describe the effects progress and technology have on human beings. According to each, what should be the attitude of people toward technology and toward nature? Cite text evidence in your discussion.

3) **EVALUATE** Would you characterize the diction of each excerpt as formal or informal? In what other ways does the diction affect the tone of each piece? How does each author's diction reflect the purpose of each essay?

4) **ANALYZE** Compare how Thoreau and Louv construct their arguments to best serve their purpose. For example, did they look at cause and effect or did they compare and contrast elements? Which author had the more effective organizational structure?

Collaborate and Present

Now, your group can continue exploring the ideas in these texts by identifying and comparing their main ideas. Follow these steps:

1) **DECIDE ON THE MOST IMPORTANT IDEAS** With your group, review your chart to identify the most important ideas from each essay. Identify points you agree on, and resolve any disagreements through a discussion.

2) **COMPARE MAIN IDEAS** Compare the main ideas of the two essays. Listen actively to the members of your group and ask them to clarify any points you do not understand. Include similarities and differences in the chart.

Similarities	Differences

3) **SYNTHESIZE INFORMATION** What connections did you make between the two pieces? What new understanding about nature and humanity's connection to it emerged from your reading? Record your ideas and any supporting details.

4) **PRESENT TO THE CLASS** Provide a summary of the central ideas of each essay as well as a comparison of those ideas. Consider what new insights you may have learned by synthesizing the information from the two texts. You may adapt the charts you created or prepare other visuals to help convey information to the class.

Collaborate & Compare

Compare Themes

As you read these two short stories, consider how Hawthorne and Poe explore the darker side of Romanticism, with its focus on human suffering and the forces that affect human behavior. Hawthorne examined the psychological effects of sin and guilt, while Poe explored the psychology of first-person narrators who were in dark places, either physically or mentally.

A

The Minister's Black Veil

Short Story
by **Nathaniel Hawthorne**
pages 320–333

B

The Fall of the House of Usher

Short Story
by **Edgar Allan Poe**
pages 341–359

After you have read the stories, you will collaborate with a small group to identify the common themes. You will follow these steps:

- Choose a focus
- Plan elements
- Organize a presentation
- Rehearse
- Present

The Minister's Black Veil

Short Story by **Nathaniel Hawthorne**

Engage Your Brain

Choose one or more of these activities to start connecting with the short story you're about to read.

Extremely Extreme

Ever notice that sometimes humans get so caught up in something that suddenly they've pushed the bounds of normal behavior and taken an interest or idea to the extremes? With a partner, find three examples of extreme behavior in books, movies, the news, or other media. Discuss what motivates people to go to such lengths.

"Clothes Make the Man"

Even Greek and Roman philosophers understood the importance of a fashion statement! Think about an outfit you've seen (or worn) that sent a message. Describe the outfit or draw it on a separate sheet of paper, and then answer the following questions:

- Why choose clothing to get the point across?
- Did the outfit achieve the result the wearer hoped for?

Such a Perverse Fascination

Why do we focus on other people's weaknesses? All of us are less than perfect, but despite acknowledging that fact, we're quick to find fault with others. In a small group, discuss why this is such a universal trait and how we could break the habit.

Analyze Symbols

A symbol is a person, place, thing, or event that represents more than its conventional meaning. Although a symbol may be universal, like a heart representing love, a writer will often creatively adapt it to suggest one or more interpretations. Because it can mean many things, a symbol is an excellent clue to the theme of a story.

The black veil worn by the protagonist is the central symbol of this story. The veil is the source of the main conflict, as seen by the other characters' reactions to the veil. The plot is then advanced by two structural devices:

- **Suspense** is the tension that leaves readers wondering what will happen next and how the central plot will be resolved.

- **Ambiguity** is the uncertainty created when elements in the story aren't clearly defined. The black veil is ambiguous because no one knows what it stands for or why the protagonist wears it.

As you read, pay attention to how Hawthorne uses suspense and ambiguity to suggest some deeper meanings the veil may have.

Analyze Setting

A story's setting can include place, time, mood, social context, or environment. Nathaniel Hawthorne set several of his fictional works in Puritan communities. In "The Minister's Black Veil," the social context actively influences plot events and characters' actions. For example, in Puritan society, the community was thought to be a "pure" working model of Puritan life. Maintaining social order was of primary importance. The meetinghouse was the central community gathering place, and congregation members sat according to social status and gender, with the oldest and most distinguished sitting in front, and men and women sitting on opposite sides. If any individual sinned, he or she was swiftly and publicly punished so that the rest of the community would not be corrupted. Once punished, the individual was shunned or banished.

As you read, use a chart like the one below to track how the setting enhances the author's message about individual and communal sin.

	Examples from Story	Effect on Message
Time and Place		
Mood		
Social Context		

Focus on Genre
↳ **Short Story**

- contains elements such as plot, character, and setting that relate and interact
- uses suspense to maintain readers' interest as the plot is revealed
- may center on a symbol that is central to the story's meaning

© Houghton Mifflin Harcourt Publishing Company

Annotation in Action

This student comments on the use of suspense in "The Minister's Black Veil." As you read, note how Hawthorne adds tension to the plot.

"But what has good Parson Hooper got upon his face?" cried the sexton in astonishment.

All within hearing immediately turned about, and beheld the semblance of Mr. Hooper, pacing slowly his meditative way towards the meetinghouse. With one accord they started, expressing more wonder than if some strange minister were coming to dust the cushions of Mr. Hooper's pulpit.

Suspense! What's the matter? Will the writer tell us?

Expand Your Vocabulary

Put a check mark next to the vocabulary words that you feel comfortable using when speaking or writing.

emblem	☐
pathos	☐
ostentatious	☐
obstinacy	☐
plausibility	☐
mitigate	☐

Turn to a partner and talk about the vocabulary words you already know. Then, use the words you know in a sentence. As you read "The Minister's Black Veil," use the definitions in the side column to help you learn the vocabulary words you don't already know.

Background

Nathaniel Hawthorne (1804–1864) was born in Salem, Massachusetts. Even before college, Hawthorne knew he wanted to write. After graduation, he threw himself into his career, and by 1842, enjoyed moderate success. Although forced to work government jobs, Hawthorne kept writing, winning acclaim for his short stories and his most famous novel, *The Scarlet Letter* (1850).

In the early 1800s, the ideals of Romanticism heavily influenced the arts. Imagination trumped reason, nature embodied the divine, and humans were innately good. Some American Romantics felt these views did not explain human suffering or the conflict between good and evil. Hawthorne, one of these Dark Romantics, was drawn to Puritan ideas of sin, as seen in "The Minister's Black Veil."

The Minister's Black Veil

Short Story by **Nathaniel Hawthorne**

What prompts a kind and conscientious minister to don a black veil and hide his face from sight?

© Houghton Mifflin Harcourt Publishing Company • Image Credits: ©Vintage Visuals/Shutterstock

NOTICE & NOTE

As you read, use the side margins to make notes about the text.

ANALYZE SYMBOLS

Annotate: Mark the word in paragraph 2 that shows something unusual has occurred.

Analyze: How does this word choice build suspense in the story?

1   The sexton stood in the porch of Milford meetinghouse, pulling lustily at the bell rope. The old people of the village came stooping along the street. Children, with bright faces, tripped merrily beside their parents, or mimicked a graver gait, in the conscious dignity of their Sunday clothes. Spruce[1] bachelors looked sidelong at the pretty maidens, and fancied that the Sabbath sunshine made them prettier than on weekdays. When the throng had mostly streamed into the porch, the sexton began to toll the bell, keeping his eye on the Reverend Mr. Hooper's door. The first glimpse of the clergyman's figure was the signal for the bell to cease its summons.

2   "But what has good Parson Hooper got upon his face?" cried the sexton in astonishment.

3   All within hearing immediately turned about, and beheld the semblance[2] of Mr. Hooper, pacing slowly his meditative way towards the meetinghouse. With one accord they started, expressing more

---

[1] **Spruce:** neat and clean.
[2] **semblance:** appearance.

wonder than if some strange minister were coming to dust the cushions of Mr. Hooper's pulpit.

4   "Are you sure it is our parson?" inquired Goodman[3] Gray of the sexton.

5   "Of a certainty it is good Mr. Hooper," replied the sexton. "He was to have exchanged pulpits with Parson Shute of Westbury; but Parson Shute sent to excuse himself yesterday, being to preach a funeral sermon."

6   The cause of so much amazement may appear sufficiently slight. Mr. Hooper, a gentlemanly person about thirty, though still a bachelor, was dressed with due clerical neatness, as if a careful wife had starched his band, and brushed the weekly dust from his Sunday's garb. There was but one thing remarkable in his appearance. Swathed about his forehead, and hanging down over his face, so low as to be shaken by his breath, Mr. Hooper had on a black veil. On a nearer view, it seemed to consist of two folds of crape,[4] which entirely concealed his features, except the mouth and chin, but probably did not intercept his sight, farther than to give a darkened aspect to all living and inanimate things. With this gloomy shade before him, good Mr. Hooper walked onward, at a slow and quiet pace, stooping somewhat and looking on the ground, as is customary with abstracted[5] men, yet nodding kindly to those of his parishioners who still waited on the meetinghouse steps. But so wonder-struck were they that his greeting hardly met with a return.

7   "I can't really feel as if good Mr. Hooper's face was behind that piece of crape," said the sexton.

8   "I don't like it," muttered an old woman, as she hobbled into the meetinghouse. "He has changed himself into something awful, only by hiding his face."

9   "Our parson has gone mad!" cried Goodman Gray, following him across the threshold.

10   A rumor of some unaccountable phenomenon had preceded Mr. Hooper into the meetinghouse, and set all the congregation astir. Few could refrain from twisting their heads towards the door; many stood upright, and turned directly about; while several little boys clambered upon the seats, and came down again with a terrible racket. There was a general bustle, a rustling of the women's gowns and shuffling of the men's feet, greatly at variance[6] with that hushed repose which should attend the entrance of the minister. But Mr. Hooper appeared not to notice the perturbation of his people. He entered with an almost noiseless step, bent his head mildly to the pews on each side, and bowed as he passed his oldest parishioner, a white-haired great-grandsire, who occupied an armchair in the centre of the aisle. It was strange to observe how slowly this venerable man became

Don't forget to **Notice & Note** as you read the text.

ANALYZE SYMBOLS

Annotate: Mark the words in paragraph 6 that describe what is on Mr. Hooper's face.

Interpret: What is the purpose of a veil? What are possible symbolic meanings of the black color?

ANALYZE SETTING

Annotate: Mark the phrases in paragraph 10 that tell you the reaction of the members of the congregation.

Infer: What can you infer about the minister's role in Puritan society from these reactions?

[3] **Goodman:** a title used by Puritans that was equivalent to *mister*.
[4] **crape:** a black, silky fabric worn as a sign of mourning.
[5] **abstracted:** absent-minded; preoccupied.
[6] **at variance:** contrasting.

conscious of something singular in the appearance of his pastor. He seemed not fully to partake of the prevailing wonder till Mr. Hooper had ascended the stairs, and showed himself in the pulpit, face-to-face with his congregation, except for the black veil. That mysterious **emblem** was never once withdrawn. It shook with his measured breath as he gave out the psalm; it threw its obscurity between him and the holy page, as he read the Scriptures; and while he prayed, the veil lay heavily on his uplifted countenance. Did he seek to hide from the dread Being whom he was addressing?

11   Such was the effect of this simple piece of crape, that more than one woman of delicate nerves was forced to leave the meetinghouse. Yet perhaps the pale-faced congregation was almost as fearful a sight to the minister as his black veil to them.

12   Mr. Hooper had the reputation of a good preacher, but not an energetic one: he strove to win his people heavenward by mild persuasive influences, rather than to drive them thither by the thunders of the Word. The sermon which he now delivered was marked by the same characteristics of style and manner as the general series of his pulpit oratory. But there was something, either in the sentiment of the discourse itself, or in the imagination of the auditors, which made it greatly the most powerful effort that they had ever heard from their pastor's lips. It was tinged, rather more darkly than usual, with the gentle gloom of Mr. Hooper's temperament. The subject had reference to secret sin, and those sad mysteries which we hide from our nearest and dearest, and would fain conceal from our own consciousness, even forgetting that the Omniscient[7] can detect them. A subtle power was breathed into his words. Each member of the congregation, the most innocent girl, and the man of hardened breast, felt as if the preacher had crept upon them, behind his awful veil, and discovered their hoarded iniquity[8] of deed or thought. Many spread their clasped hands on their bosoms. There was nothing

emblem
(ĕm´blǝm) *n.* an identifying mark or symbol.

---

[7] **the Omniscient:** God; literally, the all-knowing.
[8] **iniquity:** sinfulness.

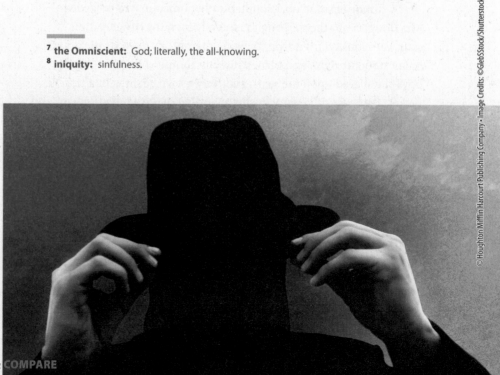

terrible in what Mr. Hooper said; at least, no violence; and yet, with every tremor of his melancholy voice, the hearers quaked. An unsought **pathos** came hand in hand with awe. So sensible were the audience of some unwonted attribute in their minister, that they longed for a breath of wind to blow aside the veil, almost believing that a stranger's visage would be discovered, though the form, gesture and voice were those of Mr. Hooper.

13   At the close of the services, the people hurried out with indecorous[9] confusion, eager to communicate their pent-up amazement, and conscious of lighter spirits the moment they lost sight of the black veil. Some gathered in little circles, huddled closely together, with their mouths all whispering in the centre; some went homeward alone, wrapped in silent meditation; some talked loudly, and profaned[10] the Sabbath day with **ostentatious** laughter. A few shook their sagacious heads, intimating[11] that they could penetrate the mystery; while one or two affirmed that there was no mystery at all, but only that Mr. Hooper's eyes were so weakened by the midnight lamp as to require a shade. After a brief interval, forth came good Mr. Hooper also, in the rear of his flock. Turning his veiled face from one group to another, he paid due reverence to the hoary[12] heads, saluted the middle-aged with kind dignity, as their friend and spiritual guide, greeted the young with mingled authority and love, and laid his hands on the little children's heads to bless them. Such was always his custom on the Sabbath day. Strange and bewildered looks repaid him for his courtesy. None, as on former occasions, aspired to the honor of walking by their pastor's side. Old Squire Saunders, doubtless by an accidental lapse of memory, neglected to invite Mr. Hooper to his table, where the good clergyman had been wont[13] to bless the food almost every Sunday since his settlement. He returned, therefore, to the parsonage, and at the moment of closing the door, was observed to look back upon the people, all of whom had their eyes fixed upon the minister. A sad smile gleamed faintly from beneath the black veil, and flickered about his mouth, glimmering as he disappeared.

14   "How strange," said a lady, "that a simple black veil, such as any woman might wear on her bonnet, should become such a terrible thing on Mr. Hooper's face!"

15   "Something must surely be amiss with Mr. Hooper's intellects," observed her husband, the physician of the village. "But the strangest part of the affair is the effect of this vagary,[14] even on a sober-minded man like myself. The black veil, though it covers only our pastor's face, throws its influence over his whole person, and makes him ghost-like from head to foot. Do you not feel it so?"

pathos
(pā´thŏs) *n.* something that evokes pity or sympathy.

ostentatious
(ŏs-tĕn-tā´shəs) *adj.* conspicuous and vulgar.

NOTICE & NOTE
CONTRASTS AND CONTRADICTIONS

When you notice a sharp contrast between what you would expect and what the character actually does, you've found a **Contrasts and Contradictions** signpost.

Notice & Note: Mark the words in paragraph 13 that show a surprising reaction by the minister.

Analyze: How does this reaction affect the other characters?

---

[9] **indecorous:** undignified; inappropriate.
[10] **profaned:** desecrated; treated irreverently.
[11] **intimating:** revealing.
[12] **hoary:** gray or white due to age.
[13] **wont:** accustomed or used.
[14] **vagary:** oddity.

16 "Truly do I," replied the lady; "and I would not be alone with him for the world. I wonder he is not afraid to be alone with himself!"

17 "Men sometimes are so," said her husband.

18 The afternoon service was attended with similar circumstances. At its conclusion, the bell tolled for the funeral of a young lady. The relatives and friends were assembled in the house, and the more distant acquaintances stood about the door, speaking of the good qualities of the deceased, when their talk was interrupted by the appearance of Mr. Hooper, still covered with his black veil. It was now an appropriate emblem. The clergyman stepped into the room where the corpse was laid, and bent over the coffin, to take a last farewell of his deceased parishioner. As he stooped, the veil hung straight down from his forehead so that, if her eyelids had not been closed forever, the dead maiden might have seen his face. Could Mr. Hooper be fearful of her glance, that he so hastily caught back the black veil? A person, who watched the interview between the dead and the living, scrupled[15] not to affirm that, at the instant when the clergyman's features were disclosed, the corpse had slightly shuddered, rustling the shroud[16] and muslin cap, though the countenance retained the composure of death. A superstitious old woman was the only witness of this prodigy. From the coffin, Mr. Hooper passed into the chamber of the mourners, and thence to the head of the staircase, to make the funeral prayer. It was a tender and heart-dissolving prayer, full of sorrow, yet so imbued with celestial[17] hopes, that the music of the heavenly harp, swept by the fingers of the dead, seemed faintly to be heard among the saddest accents of the minister. The people trembled, though they but darkly understood him, when he prayed

ANALYZE SETTING

Annotate: Mark the words and phrases in paragraph 18 that are spooky or hint at the supernatural.

Synthesize: How does this description reflect what you know about Dark Romanticism?

---

[15] **scrupled:** was reluctant.
[16] **shroud:** a cloth in which people were wrapped before burial.
[17] **celestial:** relating to heaven.

that they, and himself, and all of mortal race might be ready, as he trusted this young maiden had been, for the dreadful hour that should snatch the veil from their faces. The bearers went heavily forth, and the mourners followed, saddening all the street, with the dead before them, and Mr. Hooper in his black veil behind.

19   "Why do you look back?" said one in the procession to his partner.

20   "I had a fancy," replied she, "that the minister and the maiden's spirit were walking hand in hand."

21   "And so had I, at the same moment," said the other. That night, the handsomest couple in Milford village were to be joined in wedlock. Though reckoned a melancholy man, Mr. Hooper had a placid cheerfulness for such occasions, which often excited a sympathetic smile, where livelier merriment would have been thrown away. There was no quality of his disposition which made him more beloved than this. The company at the wedding awaited his arrival with impatience, trusting that the strange awe, which had gathered over him throughout the day, would now be dispelled. But such was not the result. When Mr. Hooper came, the first thing that their eyes rested on was the same horrible black veil, which had added deeper gloom to the funeral, and could portend nothing but evil to the wedding. Such was its immediate effect on the guests, that a cloud seemed to have rolled duskily from beneath the black crape, and dimmed the light of the candles. The bridal pair stood up before the minister. But the bride's cold fingers quivered in the tremulous[18] hand of the bridegroom, and her death-like paleness caused a whisper that the maiden who had been buried a few hours before was come from her grave to be married. If ever another wedding were so dismal, it

[18] **tremulous:** trembling.

© Houghton Mifflin Harcourt Publishing Company • Image Credits: ©CharlinX USA Collection/Alamy; (inset) ©byilwill/Getty Images

Annotate: Mark the words in paragraph 21 that describe the minister's reaction to his own image.

Synthesize: How does this reaction build on the other suspenseful elements in the story?

was that famous one where they tolled the wedding knell.[19] After performing the ceremony, Mr. Hooper raised a glass of wine to his lips, wishing happiness to the new-married couple, in a strain of mild pleasantry that ought to have brightened the features of the guests, like a cheerful gleam from the hearth. At that instant, catching a glimpse of his figure in the looking glass, the black veil involved his own spirit in the horror with which it overwhelmed all others. His frame shuddered—his lips grew white—he spilt the untasted wine upon the carpet—and rushed forth into the darkness. For the Earth, too, had on her Black Veil.

22   The next day, the whole village of Milford talked of little else than Parson Hooper's black veil. That, and the mystery concealed behind it, supplied a topic for discussion between acquaintances meeting in the street, and good women gossiping at their open windows. It was the first item of news that the tavern keeper told to his guests. The children babbled of it on their way to school. One imitative little imp covered his face with an old black handkerchief, thereby so affrighting his playmates that the panic seized himself, and he well-nigh lost his wits by his own waggery.[20]

23   It was remarkable that, of all the busybodies and impertinent people in the parish, not one ventured to put the plain question to Mr. Hooper, wherefore he did this thing. Hitherto, whenever there appeared the slightest call for such interference, he had never lacked advisers, nor shown himself averse to be guided by their judgment. If he erred at all, it was by so painful a degree of self-distrust that even the mildest censure[21] would lead him to consider an indifferent action as a crime. Yet, though so well acquainted with this amiable weakness, no individual among his parishioners chose to make the black veil a subject of friendly remonstrance.[22] There was a feeling of dread, neither plainly confessed nor carefully concealed, which caused each to shift the responsibility upon another, till at length it was found expedient to send a deputation to the church, in order to deal with Mr. Hooper about the mystery, before it should grow into a scandal. Never did an embassy so ill discharge its duties. The minister received them with friendly courtesy, but became silent, after they were seated, leaving to his visitors the whole burden of introducing their important business. The topic, it might be supposed, was obvious enough. There was the black veil, swathed round Mr. Hooper's forehead, and concealing every feature above his placid mouth, on which, at times, they could perceive the glimmering of a melancholy smile. But that piece of crape, to their imagination, seemed to hang down before his heart, the symbol of a fearful secret between him and them. Were the veil but cast aside, they might speak freely of it, but not till then. Thus they sat a considerable time, speechless, confused,

---

[19] **If ever . . . wedding knell:** In Hawthorne's "The Wedding Knell," funeral bells ring during a wedding ceremony.
[20] **waggery:** silly humor.
[21] **censure:** disapproval or criticism.
[22] **remonstrance:** protest.

and shrinking uneasily from Mr. Hooper's eye, which they felt to be fixed upon them with an invisible glance. Finally, the deputies returned abashed to their constituents, pronouncing the matter too weighty to be handled, except by a council of the churches, if, indeed, it might not require a general synod.[23]

24   But there was one person in the village unappalled by the awe with which the black veil had impressed all beside herself. When the deputies returned without an explanation, or even venturing to demand one, she, with the calm energy of her character, determined to chase away the strange cloud that appeared to be settling round Mr. Hooper, every moment more darkly than before. As his plighted wife,[24] it should be her privilege to know what the black veil concealed. At the minister's first visit, therefore, she entered upon the subject, with a direct simplicity, which made the task easier both for him and her. After he had seated himself, she fixed her eyes steadfastly upon the veil, but could discern nothing of the dreadful gloom that had so overawed the multitude: it was but a double fold of crape, hanging down from his forehead to his mouth, and slightly stirring with his breath.

25   "No," said she aloud, and smiling, "there is nothing terrible in this piece of crape except that it hides a face which I am always glad to look upon. Come, good sir, let the sun shine from behind the cloud. First lay aside your black veil: then tell me why you put it on."

26   Mr. Hooper's smile glimmered faintly.

27   "There is an hour to come," said he, "when all of us shall cast aside our veils. Take it not amiss, beloved friend, if I wear this piece of crape till then."

28   "Your words are a mystery too," returned the young lady. "Take away the veil from them, at least."

29   "Elizabeth, I will," said he, "so far as my vow may suffer me. Know, then, this veil is a type and a symbol, and I am bound to wear it ever, both in light and darkness, in solitude and before the gaze of multitudes, and as with strangers, so with my familiar friends. No mortal eye will see it withdrawn. This dismal shade must separate me from the world: even you, Elizabeth, can never come behind it!"

30   "What grievous affliction hath befallen you," she earnestly inquired, "that you should thus darken your eyes forever?"

31   "If it be a sign of mourning," replied Mr. Hooper, "I, perhaps, like most other mortals, have sorrows dark enough to be typified by a black veil."

32   "But what if the world will not believe that it is the type of an innocent sorrow?" urged Elizabeth. "Beloved and respected as you are, there may be whispers that you hide your face under the consciousness of secret sin. For the sake of your holy office, do away this scandal!"

33   The color rose into her cheeks, as she intimated the nature of the rumors that were already abroad in the village. But Mr. Hooper's

ANALYZE SYMBOLS

Annotate: Mark the phrases in paragraphs 31 and 34 that the minister uses to comment on his condition.

Predict: What do these passages suggest about Hawthorne's theme?

[23] **synod:** an assembly or court of church officials.
[24] **plighted wife:** fiancée.

© Houghton Mifflin Harcourt Publishing Company

mildness did not forsake him. He even smiled again—that same sad smile, which always appeared like a faint glimmering of light proceeding from the obscurity beneath the veil.

34 "If I hide my face for sorrow, there is cause enough," he merely replied; "and if I cover it for secret sin, what mortal might not do the same?"

35 And with this gentle but unconquerable **obstinacy** did he resist all her entreaties. At length Elizabeth sat silent. For a few moments she appeared lost in thought, considering, probably, what new methods might be tried to withdraw her lover from so dark a fantasy, which, if it had no other meaning, was perhaps a symptom of mental disease. Though of a firmer character than his own, the tears rolled down her cheeks. But, in an instant, as it were, a new feeling took the place of sorrow: her eyes were fixed insensibly on the black veil, when, like a sudden twilight in the air, its terrors fell around her. She arose, and stood trembling before him.

36 "And do you feel it then at last?" said he mournfully.

37 She made no reply, but covered her eyes with her hand, and turned to leave the room. He rushed forward and caught her arm.

38 "Have patience with me, Elizabeth!" cried he passionately. "Do not desert me, though this veil must be between us here on earth. Be mine, and hereafter there shall be no veil over my face, no darkness between our souls! It is but a mortal veil—it is not for eternity! Oh! you know not how lonely I am, and how frightened to be alone behind my black veil. Do not leave me in this miserable obscurity forever!"

39 "Lift the veil but once, and look me in the face," said she.

40 "Never! It cannot be!" replied Mr. Hooper.

41 "Then, farewell!" said Elizabeth.

42 She withdrew her arm from his grasp and slowly departed, pausing at the door to give one long, shuddering gaze that seemed almost to penetrate the mystery of the black veil. But even amid his grief, Mr. Hooper smiled to think that only a material emblem had separated him from happiness, though the horrors which it shadowed forth must be drawn darkly between the fondest of lovers.

43 From that time no attempts were made to remove Mr. Hooper's black veil or, by a direct appeal, to discover the secret which it was supposed to hide. By persons who claimed a superiority to popular prejudice, it was reckoned merely an eccentric whim, such as often mingles with the sober actions of men otherwise rational, and tinges them all with its own semblance of insanity. But with the multitude, good Mr. Hooper was irreparably a bugbear.[25] He could not walk the streets with any peace of mind, so conscious was he that the gentle and timid would turn aside to avoid him, and that others would make it a point of hardihood to throw themselves in his way. The impertinence

---

obstinacy

(ŏb´stə-nə-sē) *n.* stubbornness.

ANALYZE SYMBOLS

Annotate: Mark the sentences in paragraph 43 that describe Mr. Hooper's inner life beneath the veil.

Analyze: How does the ambiguity over why Mr. Hooper wears the veil affect the meaning of the story?

---

[25] **bugbear:** source of irrational fear.

of the latter class compelled him to give up his customary walk, at sunset, to the burial ground, for when he leaned pensively over the gate, there would always be faces behind the gravestones, peeping at his black veil. A fable went the rounds that the stare of the dead people drove him thence. It grieved him to the very depth of his kind heart to observe how the children fled from his approach, breaking up their merriest sports, while his melancholy figure was yet afar off. Their instinctive dread caused him to feel, more strongly than aught else, that a preternatural[26] horror was interwoven with the threads of the black crape. In truth, his own antipathy to the veil was known to be so great that he never willingly passed before a mirror, nor stooped to drink at a still fountain, lest, in its peaceful bosom, he should be affrighted by himself. This was what gave **plausibility** to the whispers that Mr. Hooper's conscience tortured him for some great crime too horrible to be entirely concealed, or otherwise than so obscurely intimated. Thus, from beneath the black veil there rolled a cloud into the sunshine, an ambiguity of sin or sorrow, which enveloped the poor minister, so that love or sympathy could never reach him. It was said that ghost and fiend consorted with him there. With self-shudderings and outward terrors, he walked continually in its shadow, groping darkly within his own soul, or gazing through a medium that saddened the whole world. Even the lawless wind, it was believed, respected his dreadful secret, and never blew aside the veil. But still good Mr. Hooper sadly smiled at the pale visages of the worldly throng as he passed by.

44   Among all its bad influences, the black veil had the one desirable effect, of making its wearer a very efficient clergyman. By the aid of his mysterious emblem—for there was no other apparent cause— he became a man of awful power, over souls that were in agony for sin. His converts always regarded him with a dread peculiar to themselves, affirming, though but figuratively, that before he brought them to celestial light, they had been with him behind the black veil. Its gloom, indeed, enabled him to sympathize with all dark affections.

---

[26] **preternatural:** inexplicable; supernatural.

plausibility
(plô-zə-bĭl´ĭ-tē) *n.* likelihood; believability.

ANALYZE SETTING

Annotate: Mark the phrases in paragraph 44 that explain the role Mr. Hooper played in political life.

Infer: What can you infer about the role of the clergy in Puritan Massachusetts?

Dying sinners cried aloud for Mr. Hooper, and would not yield their breath till he appeared; though ever, as he stooped to whisper consolation, they shuddered at the veiled face so near their own. Such were the terrors of the black veil, even when Death had bared his visage! Strangers came long distances to attend service at his church, with the mere idle purpose of gazing at his figure, because it was forbidden them to behold his face. But many were made to quake ere they departed! Once, during Governor Belcher's[27] administration, Mr. Hooper was appointed to preach the election sermon. Covered with his black veil, he stood before the chief magistrate, the council, and the representatives, and wrought so deep an impression that the legislative measures of that year were characterized by all the gloom and piety of our earliest ancestral sway.

45   In this manner Mr. Hooper spent a long life, irreproachable[28] in outward act, yet shrouded in dismal suspicions; kind and loving, though unloved, and dimly feared; a man apart from men, shunned in their health and joy, but ever summoned to their aid in mortal anguish. As years wore on, shedding their snows above his sable veil, he acquired a name throughout the New England churches, and they called him Father Hooper. Nearly all his parishioners, who were of a mature age when he was settled, had been borne away by many a funeral: he had one congregation in the church, and a more crowded one in the churchyard; and having wrought so late into the evening, and done his work so well, it was now good Father Hooper's turn to rest.

46   Several persons were visible by the shaded candlelight in the death chamber of the old clergyman. Natural connections[29] he had none. But there was the decorously grave, though unmoved physician, seeking only to **mitigate** the last pangs of the patient whom he could not save.

mitigate
(mĭt´ ĭ-gāt) *v.* to lessen.

----

[27] **Governor Belcher:** Jonathan Belcher (1682–1757), governor of Massachusetts Bay Colony from 1730 until 1741.
[28] **irreproachable:** without fault; blameless.
[29] **Natural connections:** relatives, kin.

There were the deacons, and other eminently pious members of his church. There, also, was the Reverend Mr. Clark, of Westbury, a young and zealous divine, who had ridden in haste to pray by the bedside of the expiring minister. There was the nurse, no hired handmaiden of death, but one whose calm affection had endured thus long, in secrecy, in solitude, amid the chill of age, and would not perish, even at the dying hour. Who, but Elizabeth! And there lay the hoary head of good Father Hooper upon the death pillow, with the black veil still swathed about his brow and reaching down over his face, so that each more difficult gasp of his faint breath caused it to stir. All through life that piece of crape had hung between him and the world: it had separated him from cheerful brotherhood and woman's love, and kept him in that saddest of all prisons, his own heart; and still it lay upon his face, as if to deepen the gloom of his darksome chamber, and shade him from the sunshine of eternity.

47   For some time previous, his mind had been confused, wavering doubtfully between the past and the present, and hovering forward, as it were, at intervals, into the indistinctness of the world to come. There had been feverish turns, which tossed him from side to side and wore away what little strength he had. But in the most convulsive struggles, and in the wildest vagaries of his intellect, when no other thought retained its sober influence, he still showed an awful solicitude lest the black veil should slip aside. Even if his bewildered soul could have forgotten, there was a faithful woman at his pillow, who, with averted eyes, would have covered that aged face, which she had last beheld in the comeliness of manhood. At length the death-stricken old man lay quietly in the torpor[30] of mental and bodily exhaustion, with an imperceptible pulse, and breath that

---

[30] **torpor:** lifelessness, inactivity.

grew fainter and fainter, except when a long, deep, and irregular inspiration[31] seemed to prelude the flight of his spirit.

48   The minister of Westbury approached the bedside.

49   "Venerable Father Hooper," said he, "the moment of your release is at hand. Are you ready for the lifting of the veil, that shuts in time from eternity?"

50   Father Hooper at first replied merely by a feeble motion of his head; then, apprehensive, perhaps, that his meaning might be doubtful, he exerted himself to speak.

51   "Yea," said he, in faint accents, "my soul hath a patient weariness until that veil be lifted."

52   "And is it fitting," resumed the Reverend Mr. Clark, "that a man so given to prayer, of such a blameless example, holy in deed and thought, so far as mortal judgment may pronounce; is it fitting that a father in the church should leave a shadow on his memory that may seem to blacken a life so pure? I pray you, my venerable brother, let not this thing be! Suffer us to be gladdened by your triumphant aspect, as you go to your reward. Before the veil of eternity be lifted, let me cast aside this black veil from your face!"

53   And thus speaking, the Reverend Mr. Clark bent forward to reveal the mystery of so many years. But, exerting a sudden energy that made all the beholders stand aghast, Father Hooper snatched both his hands from beneath the bedclothes and pressed them strongly on the black veil, resolute to struggle, if the minister of Westbury would contend with a dying man.

54   "Never!" cried the veiled clergyman. "On earth, never!"

55   "Dark old man!" exclaimed the affrighted minister, "with what horrible crime upon your soul are you now passing to the judgment?"

56   Father Hooper's breath heaved; it rattled in his throat; but with a mighty effort, grasping forward with his hands, he caught hold of life, and held it back till he should speak. He even raised himself in bed; and there he sat shivering, with the arms of death around him, while the black veil hung down, awful, at that last moment, in the gathered terrors of a lifetime. And yet the faint, sad smile, so often there, now seemed to glimmer from its obscurity, and linger on Father Hooper's lips.

57   "Why do you tremble at me alone?" cried he, turning his veiled face round the circle of pale spectators. "Tremble also at each other! Have men avoided me, and women shown no pity, and children screamed and fled, only for my black veil? What, but the mystery which it obscurely typifies, has made this piece of crape so awful? When the friend shows his inmost heart to his friend; the lover to his best beloved; when man does not vainly shrink from the eye of his Creator, loathsomely treasuring up the secret of his sin; then deem me a monster, for the symbol beneath which I have lived, and die! I look around me, and, lo! On every visage a Black Veil!"

ANALYZE SYMBOLS

Annotate: Mark the phrases that show how the people in Father Hooper's village have acted during his lifetime, as well as phrases that describe how he thinks they should have acted.

Draw Conclusions: What themes do Father Hooper's last words suggest?

---

[31] **inspiration:** inhalation of air into the lungs.

58   While his auditors shrank from one another, in mutual affright, Father Hooper fell back upon his pillow, a veiled corpse, with a faint smile lingering on his lips. Still veiled, they laid him in his coffin, and a veiled corpse they bore him to the grave. The grass of many years has sprung up and withered on that grave, the burial stone is moss-grown, and good Mr. Hooper's face is dust; but awful is still the thought, that it mouldered beneath the Black Veil!

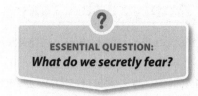

ESSENTIAL QUESTION:
What do we secretly fear?

Review your notes and add your thoughts to your **Response Log.**

COLLABORATIVE DISCUSSION

With a partner, interpret what you think are the real causes of the villagers' discomfort in the minister's presence.

Assessment Practice

Answer these questions before moving on to the **Analyze the Text** section on the following page.

1. What is the topic of the first sermon Mr. Hooper gives when wearing the veil?

   (A) death

   (B) sorrow

   (C) secret sin

   (D) eternal salvation

2. Why does the congregation send a deputation to talk to Mr. Hooper?

   (A) to tell him he is fired

   (B) to ask why he is wearing the veil

   (C) to protest his behavior at the wedding

   (D) to plead with him to marry Elizabeth

3. Which of the following does the story reveal about Puritan beliefs?

   (A) strict separation of church and state

   (B) strong belief in witches and witchcraft

   (C) exclusion of children from Sunday services

   (D) deep concern with sinfulness

Test-Taking Strategies

Analyze the Text

Support your responses with evidence from the text.

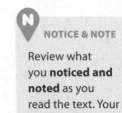

1. **DRAW CONCLUSIONS** Look back at the chart you filled in as you tracked how the setting affects the development of the theme. How do the mood and social context of the story reflect Puritan religious beliefs, values, and ideas? How do these beliefs govern the behaviors of the community? Do you think Hawthorne agrees with these values and behaviors?

2. **ANALYZE** Mr. Hooper's conversation with Elizabeth is the first time that readers learn about the minister from his own words. What insight does this conversation provide about Mr. Hooper's character?

3. **EVALUATE** What evidence in the text hints at or suggests Mr. Hooper's reasons for wearing the black veil? What effect does the ambiguity surrounding the veil add to the overall meaning of the story?

4. **INTERPRET** What does the veil symbolize? How does the meaning of the symbol change over the course of the story? Cite specific details from the story to support your interpretation. Use the chart to help you answer the questions.

Examples from Text	Meaning	Impact

5. **SYNTHESIZE** What themes does the story suggest to you? Cite text evidence in your response.

6. **ANALYZE** Why is it a **Contrast and Contradiction** that no one in the congregation talks to Mr. Hooper about the veil when he first starts wearing it? What might this reaction reveal about Puritan society and beliefs?

Choices

Here are some other ways to demonstrate your understanding of the ideas in this lesson.

Writing
↳ **Argument**

The minister is an ambiguous character: he can be seen as an innocent victim of others' fears, or as a man who isolates himself to protect his moral superiority, or as an example of innate human sinfulness. Examine these text examples to make your decision:

- the first sighting of the minister
- the parishioners' comments after services
- the minister's arrival at the wedding
- the attempt to confront him

When you've decided, write an argument that supports your stance. Include details from the text to support your claims.

> **As you write and discuss, be sure to use the Academic Vocabulary words.**
>
> analogy
>
> denote
>
> quote
>
> topic
>
> unique

Media
↳ **Social Media Story**

Rewrite "The Minister's Black Veil" as a series of tweets or SMS exchanges. You can use abbreviations, acronyms, and, best of all, emojis! If you want to crowdsource your story, you can have your readers offer up some fan fiction or have them comment on what you've written. Share your story on a class social media platform or LAN.

Social & Emotional Learning
↳ **Group Discussion**

As "The Minister's Black Veil" unfolds, it becomes apparent that the relationship between the minister and his congregation is broken. What are possible root causes for this broken relationship? What can be done to mend it? In a small group, address these questions. Consider which characters exhibit the skills below and which could develop them.

- communication
- empathy
- conflict negotiation

At the end of your discussion, sum up your advice to the community.

Expand Your Vocabulary

PRACTICE AND APPLY

Complete each of the following sentence stems in a way that reflects the meaning of the vocabulary word.

1. The painting evoked **pathos** in the viewer because _____ .

2. The **obstinacy** of her response was made clear by _____ .

3. The runner treasured his race number as an **emblem** of _____ .

4. The **ostentatious** display of wealth made visitors uncomfortable because _____ .

5. Proponents of the new law sought to **mitigate** opposition by _____ .

6. The **plausibility** of her statement was supported by _____ .

Vocabulary Strategy
↳ **Nuances in Word Meanings**

 Ed

Interactive Vocabulary Lesson: Denotation and Connotation

When you analyze nuances between words with similar **denotations**, or dictionary meanings, you look for subtle differences in shades of meaning. The **connotation** of a word refers to the feelings or ideas associated with it. For example, consider the connotation of the vocabulary word *ostentatious* in this sentence from "The Minister's Black Veil":

> Some gathered in little circles, huddled closely together, with their mouths all whispering in the centre; some went homeward alone, wrapped in silent meditation; some talked loudly, and profaned the Sabbath day with ostentatious laughter.

The word *ostentatious* carries a negative connotation of disapproval, in contrast to the synonym *loud,* which has a more neutral connotation. This emphasizes the narrator's reproach of the congregants' behavior on what should have been a solemn day of worship.

PRACTICE AND APPLY

Work with a partner to explore nuances in word meanings. Follow these steps:

● List five words from the story that have a strong positive or negative connotation.

● Use a dictionary and a thesaurus to find definitions and synonyms of the words.

● Discuss how synonyms with different connotations would affect meaning.

Watch Your Language!

Appositives and Appositive Phrases

An **appositive** is a noun or pronoun that identifies or renames another noun or pronoun, providing more information about the word it refers to. An **appositive phrase** is simply an appositive and its modifiers.

An appositive or an appositive phrase can be either **essential** or **nonessential**. An **essential appositive** provides information that is necessary to identify what is referred to by the preceding noun or pronoun.

In the following example, the appositive specifies which brother the writer is referring to:

Interactive Grammar Lesson: Appositives and Appositive Phrases

> Essential appositive: **My brother <u>Mychal</u> was always active.**

A **nonessential appositive** provides additional but supplementary information about the preceding noun or pronoun. Nonessential appositives are always set off from the word they refer to by commas or dashes.

> Nonessential appositive: **Elaine, a <u>diligent student</u>, reviewed her extensive notes the night before the test.**

Appositive phrases can be used in place of dependent clauses to make sentences more concise:

> Dependent clause: **The Reverend Mr. Hooper, <u>who was a persuasive but not forceful preacher</u>, delivered sermons that guided rather than scolded.**
>
> Appositive phrase: **The Reverend Mr. Hooper, <u>a persuasive but not forceful preacher</u>, delivered sermons that guided rather than scolded.**

PRACTICE AND APPLY

Find two examples of appositive phrases in "The Minister's Black Veil" and identify whether they are essential or nonessential. Then, write two sentences that include either an appositive or an appositive phrase.

ESSENTIAL QUESTION:
What do we secretly fear?

The Fall of the House of Usher

Short Story by **Edgar Allan Poe**

Engage Your Brain

Choose one or more of these activities to start connecting with the short story you're about to read.

It's So Spooky!

As a class, decide which of the following elements make for the best horror films. Rank them in order of importance. Tally your results, then discuss why you ordered the elements as you did.

- Dark dungeons, cellars, or attics full of discarded junk
- Unexplained occurrences or sounds
- Descriptions of cold and/or wet places
- Plot lines full of suspense and cliffhangers
- Mournful music
- Shadows and tricks of light
- Mysterious or hard-to-know characters
- Villainous characters wielding weapons
- Blood, lots of blood

Emojis to the Rescue

Read the following quotes from one of Edgar Allan Poe's most famous stories. Next to the quote, draw the emoji that corresponds most closely to it. If there isn't an existing emoji you think works, create your own! Then explain your choice of emoji to a classmate.

"I looked upon the scene before me—…upon the bleak walls—upon the vacant eye-like windows—upon a few rank sedges—and upon a few white trunks of decayed trees—with an utter depression of soul."

"[H]e had buried his face in his hands, and I could only perceive that a far more than ordinary wanness had overspread the emaciated fingers through which trickled many passionate tears."

"[T]here *did* stand the lofty and enshrouded figure of the lady Madeline of Usher. There was blood upon her white robes, and the evidence of some bitter struggle upon every portion of her emaciated frame."

It's the Perfect Setting

Imagine you have your own space—could be a house, apartment, office, man cave, or gargantuan walk-in closet—to furnish and decorate as you choose. What does it look like, and how do you use it? What does it say about you as a person? Write a description of that space, then share it with a few classmates.

© Houghton Mifflin Harcourt Publishing Company • Image Credits: ©shaun/iStock/Getty Images

Analyze Mood

Mood is the feeling or atmosphere that a writer creates for the reader. Edgar Allan Poe wanted all of the elements in his stories to work together to create a **unity of effect:** a single powerful and memorable mood. Consider these elements:

- detailed descriptions of setting that create a strong sense of place

- vivid word choices that reflect both the narrator's and other characters' feelings and responses

- sounds created by the words themselves that add a musical or poetic effect and underscore the mood

Use an idea web to identify elements that give you a strong feeling or create a specific atmosphere. Identify the mood. Add more ovals as you discover additional elements that build a unity of effect.

© Houghton Mifflin Harcourt Publishing Company

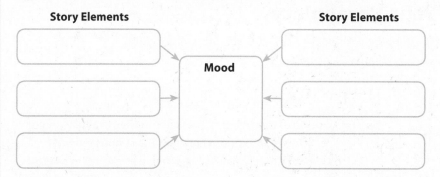

Story Elements   **Story Elements**

Mood

Analyze Allegory

An **allegory** is a story or poem that can be read on one level for its literal meaning and on a second level for its symbolic meaning. Follow these steps to think about how a story works as an allegory:

1. Identify important details, such as settings, characters, or events.

2. Define the literal meaning of each detail.

3. Explain possible symbolic meanings of each detail, such as the idea or feeling that each detail represents.

4. Put the elements together to consider how the entire story works as an allegory that communicates an insight or a message.

As you read, use a chart to analyze details that contribute to Poe's allegory.

Important Story Detail	Literal Meaning	Symbolic Meaning

Focus on Genre
↳ **Short Story**

- presents a fictional narrative, including a plot, setting, characters, and conflict
- combines literary elements to create a specific mood, or atmosphere
- develops themes through both literal and symbolic meanings

Annotation in Action

Here are notes a student took on the opening sentence from "The Fall of the House of Usher." As you read, mark words that create a strong sense of mood.

During the whole of a dull, dark, and soundless day in the autumn of the year, when the clouds hung oppressively low in the heavens, I had been passing alone, on horseback, through a singularly dreary tract of country, and at length found myself, as the shades of the evening drew on, within view of the melancholy House of Usher.

All these d sounds create a pounding, hypnotic rhythm.

Dreary, shades, and melancholy! These descriptive words create the grim mood of the opening.

Expand Your Vocabulary

Put a check mark next to the vocabulary words that you feel comfortable using when speaking or writing.

sojourn	☐
specious	☐
abhorrence	☐
palpable	☐
demeanor	☐
aghast	☐

Turn to a partner and talk about the vocabulary words you already know. Then, talk about horror movies or mysterious television series, using as many of the vocabulary words as you can. As you read "The Fall of the House of Usher," use the definitions in the side column to help you learn the vocabulary words you don't already know.

Background

For **Edgar Allan Poe** (1809–1849), the intensity of imagination provides an escape from the limitations of the exterior, physical world and offers a passage to an inner world that operates quite apart from the rules of reality. "The Fall of the House of Usher," which has been called "the definitive tale of horror," illustrates Poe's unique contribution to American literature as a "Dark Romantic"—his exploration of the dark, often irrational world of the human mind.

In this story, Poe uses many classic Gothic details: a rotting mansion, mysterious illnesses, strange sounds, a person buried alive. The term *Gothic* is used to describe a kind of novel that developed in Germany in the late 1700s and early 1800s. These eerie novels summoned up the mysterious atmosphere suggested by old castles and cathedrals whose dank dungeons and secret passageways might inspire sinister or even supernatural events.

The Fall of the House of Usher

Short Story by **Edgar Allan Poe**

A man visits his friend and finds much more than he bargained for.

NOTICE & NOTE
As you read, use the side margins to make notes about the text.

Son cœur est un luth suspendu;
Sitôt qu'on le touche il résonne.[1]
                              De Béranger.

During the whole of a dull, dark, and soundless day in the autumn of the year, when the clouds hung oppressively low in the heavens, I had been passing alone, on horseback, through a singularly dreary tract of country, and at length found myself, as the shades of the evening drew on, within view of the melancholy House of Usher. I know not how it was—but, with the first glimpse of the building, a sense of insufferable gloom pervaded my spirit. I say insufferable; for the feeling was unrelieved by any of that half-pleasurable, because poetic, sentiment with which the mind usually receives even the sternest natural images of the desolate or terrible. I looked upon the scene before me—upon the mere house, and the simple landscape features of the domain—upon the bleak walls—upon the vacant eye-like windows—upon a few rank sedges[2]—and

---

[1] **Son cœur . . . il résonne:** "His heart is a suspended lute; / Whenever one touches it, it resounds." From "Le Refus" ("The Refusal") by Pierre-Jean de Béranger (1780–1857).
[2] **sedges:** grasslike plants that grow in watery ground.

upon a few white trunks of decayed trees—with an utter depression of soul which I can compare to no earthly sensation more properly than to the after-dream of the reveller upon opium—the bitter lapse into every-day life—the hideous dropping off of the veil. There was an iciness, a sinking, a sickening of the heart—an unredeemed dreariness of thought which no goading of the imagination could torture into aught of the sublime. What was it—I paused to think— what was it that so unnerved me in the contemplation of the House of Usher? It was a mystery all insoluble; nor could I grapple with the shadowy fancies that crowded upon me as I pondered. I was forced to fall back upon the unsatisfactory conclusion, that while, beyond doubt, there *are* combinations of very simple natural objects which have the power of thus affecting us, still the analysis of this power lies among considerations beyond our depth. It was possible, I reflected, that a mere different arrangement of the particulars of the scene, of the details of the picture, would be sufficient to modify, or perhaps to annihilate its capacity for sorrowful impression; and, acting upon this idea, I reined my horse to the precipitous brink of a black and lurid tarn[3] that lay in unruffled lustre by the dwelling, and gazed down—but with a shudder even more thrilling than before—upon the remodelled and inverted images of the gray sedge, and the ghastly tree-stems, and the vacant and eye-like windows.

2   Nevertheless, in this mansion of gloom I now proposed to myself a **sojourn** of some weeks. Its proprietor, Roderick Usher, had been one of my boon companions in boyhood; but many years had elapsed since our last meeting. A letter, however, had lately reached me in a distant part of the country—a letter from him—which, in its wildly importunate nature, had admitted of no other than a personal reply. The MS.[4] gave evidence of nervous agitation. The writer spoke of acute bodily illness—of a mental disorder which oppressed him— and of an earnest desire to see me, as his best and indeed his only personal friend, with a view of attempting, by the cheerfulness of my society, some alleviation of his malady. It was the manner in which all this, and much more, was said—it was the apparent *heart* that went with his request—which allowed me no room for hesitation; and I accordingly obeyed forthwith what I still considered a very singular summons.

3   Although, as boys, we had been even intimate associates, yet I really knew little of my friend. His reserve had been always excessive and habitual. I was aware, however, that his very ancient family had been noted, time out of mind, for a peculiar sensibility of temperament, displaying itself, through long ages, in many works of exalted art, and manifested, of late, in repeated deeds of munificent yet unobtrusive charity, as well as in a passionate devotion to the intricacies, perhaps even more than to the orthodox and easily

sojourn
(sō´jûrn´) *n.* a temporary stay; a brief period of residence.

ANALYZE MOOD

Annotate: In paragraph 2, mark words that describe Roderick Usher's physical and mental condition.

Analyze: How do these descriptions contribute to the mood of the story?

[3] **tarn:** small but deep mountain lake. Its waters are dark from the decomposition of vegetation and because there is no circulation.
[4] **MS.:** abbreviation for "manuscript."

© Houghton Mifflin Harcourt Publishing Company

recognizable beauties, of musical science. I had learned, too, the very remarkable fact, that the stem of the Usher race, all time-honored as it was, had put forth, at no period, any enduring branch; in other words, that the entire family lay in the direct line of descent, and had always, with very trifling and very temporary variation, so lain. It was this deficiency, I considered, while running over in thought the perfect keeping of the character of the premises with the accredited character of the people, and while speculating upon the possible influence which the one, in the long lapse of centuries, might have exercised upon the other—it was this deficiency, perhaps, of collateral issue,[5] and the consequent undeviating transmission, from sire to son, of the patrimony with the name, which had, at length, so identified the two as to merge the original title of the estate in the quaint and equivocal appellation of the "House of Usher"—an appellation which seemed to include, in the minds of the peasantry who used it, both the family and the family mansion.

4   I have said that the sole effect of my somewhat childish experiment—that of looking down within the tarn—had been to deepen the first singular impression. There can be no doubt that the consciousness of the rapid increase of my superstition—for why should I not so term it?—served mainly to accelerate the increase itself. Such, I have long known, is the paradoxical law of all sentiments having terror as a basis. And it might have been for this reason only, that, when I again uplifted my eyes to the house itself, from its image in the pool, there grew in my mind a strange fancy—a fancy so ridiculous, indeed, that I but mention it to show the vivid force of the sensations which oppressed me. I had so worked upon my imagination as really to believe that about the whole mansion and domain there hung an atmosphere peculiar to themselves and their immediate vicinity—an atmosphere which had no affinity with the air of heaven, but which had reeked up from the decayed trees, and the gray wall, and the silent tarn—a pestilent and mystic vapor, dull, sluggish, faintly discernible, and leaden-hued.

5   Shaking off from my spirit what *must* have been a dream, I scanned more narrowly the real aspect of the building. Its principal feature seemed to be that of an excessive antiquity. The discoloration of ages had been great. Minute fungi overspread the whole exterior, hanging in a fine tangled web-work from the eaves. Yet all this was apart from any extraordinary dilapidation. No portion of the masonry had fallen; and there appeared to be a wild inconsistency between its still perfect adaptation of parts, and the crumbling condition of the individual stones. In this there was much that reminded me of the **specious** totality of old wood-work which has rotted for long years in some neglected vault, with no disturbance from the breath of the external air. Beyond this indication of extensive decay, however, the fabric gave little token of instability.

---

[5] **collateral issue:** relatives, such as cousins, who share the same ancestors but who are not in a direct line of descent.

Don't forget to **Notice & Note** as you read the text.

ANALYZE ALLEGORY

Annotate: In paragraph 5, mark the description of a flaw in the House of Usher.

Predict: How might this image have both a literal and a symbolic meaning?

specious
(spē´shəs) *adj.* having the ring of truth or plausibility but actually fallacious.

© Houghton Mifflin Harcourt Publishing Company

Perhaps the eye of a scrutinizing observer might have discovered a barely perceptible fissure, which, extending from the roof of the building in front, made its way down the wall in a zigzag direction, until it became lost in the sullen waters of the tarn.

6   Noticing these things, I rode over a short causeway to the house. A servant in waiting took my horse, and I entered the Gothic archway of the hall. A valet, of stealthy step, thence conducted me, in silence, through many dark and intricate passages in my progress to the *studio* of his master. Much that I encountered on the way contributed, I know not how, to heighten the vague sentiments of which I have already spoken. While the objects around me—while the carvings of the ceilings, the sombre tapestries of the walls, the ebon blackness of the floors, and the phantasmagoric[6] armorial trophies which rattled as I strode, were but matters to which, or to such as which, I had been accustomed from my infancy—while I hesitated not to acknowledge how familiar was all this—I still wondered to find how unfamiliar were the fancies which ordinary images were stirring up. On one of the staircases, I met the physician of the family. His countenance, I thought, wore a mingled expression of low cunning and perplexity. He accosted me with trepidation and passed on. The valet now threw open a door and ushered me into the presence of his master.

7   The room in which I found myself was very large and lofty. The windows were long, narrow, and pointed, and at so vast a distance from the black oaken floor as to be altogether inaccessible from within. Feeble gleams of encrimsoned light made their way through the trellised panes, and served to render sufficiently distinct the more prominent objects around; the eye, however, struggled in vain to reach the remoter angles of the chamber, or the recesses of the vaulted and fretted ceiling. Dark draperies hung upon the walls. The general furniture was profuse, comfortless, antique, and tattered. Many books and musical instruments lay scattered about, but failed to give any vitality to the scene. I felt that I breathed an atmosphere of sorrow. An air of stern, deep, and irredeemable gloom hung over and pervaded all.

8   Upon my entrance, Usher arose from a sofa on which he had been lying at full length, and greeted me with a vivacious warmth which had much in it, I at first thought, of an overdone cordiality—of the constrained effort of the *ennuyé*[7] man of the world. A glance, however, at his countenance convinced me of his perfect sincerity. We sat down; and for some moments, while he spoke not, I gazed upon him with a feeling half of pity, half of awe. Surely, man had never before so terribly altered, in so brief a period, as had Roderick Usher! It was with difficulty that I could bring myself to admit the identity of the wan being before me with the companion of my early boyhood. Yet the character of his face had been at all times remarkable. A

VOCABULARY

Patterns of Word Change:
The word *irredeemable* in paragraph 7 is an adjective formed from the verb *redeem* plus the prefix *ir-* and the suffix *-able*.

Analyze: Why does this form of the word work in the context of the story? How does looking at word changes help you understand this word?

---

[6] **phantasmagoric** (făn-tăz´mə-gôr´ĭk): images appearing to change rapidly, like the events in a dream.

[7] *ennuyé* (än·nwē·yā´) French for "bored" or "jaded."

Don't forget to
Notice & Note as you
read the text.

cadaverousness of complexion; an eye large, liquid, and luminous
beyond comparison; lips somewhat thin and very pallid but of a
surpassingly beautiful curve; a nose of a delicate Hebrew model,
but with a breadth of nostril unusual in similar formations; a finely
moulded chin, speaking, in its want of prominence, of a want of
moral energy; hair of a more than web-like softness and tenuity;—
these features, with an inordinate expansion above the regions of the
temple, made up altogether a countenance not easily to be forgotten.
And now in the mere exaggeration of the prevailing character of these
features, and of the expression they were wont to convey, lay so much
of change that I doubted to whom I spoke. The now ghastly pallor of
the skin, and the now miraculous lustre of the eye, above all things
startled and even awed me. The silken hair, too, had been suffered
to grow all unheeded, and as, in its wild gossamer texture, it floated
rather than fell about the face, I could not, even with effort, connect
its Arabesque expression with any idea of simple humanity.

9   In the manner of my friend I was at once struck with an
incoherence—an inconsistency; and I soon found this to arise
from a series of feeble and futile struggles to overcome an habitual
trepidancy—an excessive nervous agitation. For something of this
nature I had indeed been prepared, no less by his letter, than by
reminiscences of certain boyish traits, and by conclusions deduced
from his peculiar physical conformation and temperament. His
action was alternately vivacious and sullen. His voice varied rapidly
from a tremulous indecision (when the animal spirits seemed utterly
in abeyance) to that species of energetic concision—that abrupt,
weighty, unhurried, and hollow-sounding enunciation—that leaden,
self-balanced and perfectly modulated guttural utterance, which may
be observed in the lost drunkard, or the irreclaimable eater of opium,
during the periods of his most intense excitement.

ANALYZE ALLEGORY

Annotate: In paragraph 8, mark
the description of Usher's hair.

Analyze: How might Usher's
physical appearance have both a
literal and a symbolic meaning?

10 It was thus that he spoke of the object of my visit, of his earnest desire to see me, and of the solace he expected me to afford him. He entered, at some length, into what he conceived to be the nature of his malady. It was, he said, a constitutional and a family evil, and one for which he despaired to find a remedy—a mere nervous affection, he immediately added, which would undoubtedly soon pass off. It displayed itself in a host of unnatural sensations. Some of these, as he detailed them, interested and bewildered me; although, perhaps, the terms and the general manner of their narration had their weight. He suffered much from a morbid acuteness of the senses; the most insipid food was alone endurable; he could wear only garments of certain texture; the odors of all flowers were oppressive; his eyes were tortured by even a faint light; and there were but peculiar sounds, and these from stringed instruments, which did not inspire him with horror.

11 To an anomalous species of terror I found him a bounden slave. "I shall perish," said he, "I *must* perish in this deplorable folly. Thus, thus, and not otherwise, shall I be lost. I dread the events of the future, not in themselves, but in their results. I shudder at the thought of any, even the most trivial, incident, which may operate upon this intolerable agitation of soul. I have, indeed, no **abhorrence** of danger, except in its absolute effect—in terror. In this unnerved, in this pitiable, condition I feel that the period will sooner or later arrive when I must abandon life and reason together, in some struggle with the grim phantasm, Fear."

12 I learned, moreover, at intervals, and through broken and equivocal hints, another singular feature of his mental condition. He was enchained by certain superstitious impressions in regard to the dwelling which he tenanted, and whence, for many years, he had never ventured forth—in regard to an influence whose supposititious force was conveyed in terms too shadowy here to be re-stated—an influence which some peculiarities in the mere form and substance of his family mansion had, by dint of long sufferance, he said, obtained over his spirit—an effect which the *physique* of the gray walls and turrets, and of the dim tarn into which they all looked down, had, at length, brought about upon the *morale* of his existence.

13 He admitted, however, although with hesitation, that much of the peculiar gloom which thus afflicted him could be traced to a more natural and far more **palpable** origin—to the severe and long-continued illness—indeed to the evidently approaching dissolution—of a tenderly beloved sister, his sole companion for long years, his last and only relative on earth. "Her decease," he said, with a bitterness which I can never forget, "would leave him (him the hopeless and the frail) the last of the ancient race of the Ushers." While he spoke, the lady Madeline (for so was she called) passed through a remote portion of the apartment, and, without having noticed my presence, disappeared. I regarded her with an utter astonishment not unmingled with dread; and yet I found it impossible to account for such feelings. A sensation of stupor oppressed me as my eyes

abhorrence
(ăb-hôr´əns) *n.* a feeling of repugnance or loathing.

ANALYZE ALLEGORY

Annotate: In paragraph 12, mark the words that describe the connection between Roderick Usher and his house.

Compare: What is the literal meaning of this connection? How might this connection have a symbolic meaning?

palpable
(păl´pə-bəl) *adj.* capable of being handled, touched, or felt; tangible.

followed her retreating steps. When a door, at length, closed upon her, my glance sought instinctively and eagerly the countenance of the brother; but he had buried his face in his hands, and I could only perceive that a far more than ordinary wanness had overspread the emaciated fingers through which trickled many passionate tears.

14   The disease of the lady Madeline had long baffled the skill of her physicians. A settled apathy, a gradual wasting away of the person, and frequent although transient affections of a partially cataleptical[8]

---

[8] **cataleptical** (kat´ə-lep´tik-əl): Catalepsy is an emotional condition, associated with disorders such as epilepsy and schizophrenia, which may cause the victim to lose sensation and the ability to move the limbs, or even the entire body.

character were the unusual diagnosis. Hitherto she had steadily borne up against the pressure of her malady, and had not betaken herself finally to bed; but on the closing in of the evening of my arrival at the house, she succumbed (as her brother told me at night with inexpressible agitation) to the prostrating power of the destroyer; and I learned that the glimpse I had obtained of her person would thus probably be the last I should obtain—that the lady, at least while living, would be seen by me no more.

15   For several days ensuing, her name was unmentioned by either Usher or myself; and during this period I was busied in earnest endeavors to alleviate the melancholy of my friend. We painted and read together, or I listened, as if in a dream, to the wild improvisations of his speaking guitar. And thus, as a closer and still closer intimacy admitted me more unreservedly into the recesses of his spirit, the more bitterly did I perceive the futility of all attempt at cheering a mind from which darkness, as if an inherent positive quality, poured forth upon all objects of the moral and physical universe in one unceasing radiation of gloom.

16   I shall ever bear about me a memory of the many solemn hours I thus spent alone with the master of the House of Usher. Yet I should fail in any attempt to convey an idea of the exact character of the studies, or of the occupations, in which he involved me, or led me the way. An excited and highly distempered ideality[9] threw a sulphureous lustre over all. His long improvised dirges will ring forever in my ears. Among other things, I hold painfully in mind a certain singular perversion and amplification of the wild air of the last waltz of Von Weber.[10] From the paintings over which his elaborate fancy brooded, and which grew, touch by touch, into vagueness at which I shuddered the more thrillingly, because I shuddered knowing not why—from these paintings (vivid as their images now are before me) I would in vain endeavor to educe more than a small portion which should lie within the compass of merely written words. By the utter simplicity, by the nakedness of his designs, he arrested and overawed attention. If ever mortal painted an idea, that mortal was Roderick Usher. For me at least, in the circumstances then surrounding me, there arose out of the pure abstractions which the hypochondriac contrived to throw upon his canvas, an intensity of intolerable awe, no shadow of which felt I ever yet in the contemplation of the certainly glowing yet too concrete reveries of Fuseli.[11]

17   One of the phantasmagoric conceptions of my friend, partaking not so rigidly of the spirit of abstraction, may be shadowed forth,

---

[9] **distempered ideality:** mental derangement.
[10] **Von Weber:** Carl Maria von Weber (1786–1826), German Romantic composer.
[11] **Fuseli:** Johann Heinrich Füssli (1741–1825), Swiss painter who lived in England and is known for scenes of horror and the supernatural.

Don't forget to
Notice & Note as you
read the text.

although feebly, in words. A small picture presented the interior of an immensely long and rectangular vault or tunnel, with low walls, smooth, white, and without interruption or device. Certain accessory points of the design served well to convey the idea that this excavation lay at an exceeding depth below the surface of the earth. No outlet was observed in any portion of its vast extent, and no torch or other artificial source of light was discernible; yet a flood of intense rays rolled throughout, and bathed the whole in a ghastly and inappropriate splendor.

18   I have just spoken of that morbid condition of the auditory nerve which rendered all music intolerable to the sufferer, with the exception of certain effects of stringed instruments. It was, perhaps, the narrow limits to which he thus confined himself upon the guitar which gave birth, in great measure, to the fantastic character of his performances. But the fervid *facility* of his *impromptus*[12] could not be so accounted for. They must have been, and were, in the notes, as well as in the words of his wild fantasias (for he not unfrequently accompanied himself with rhymed verbal improvisations), the result of that intense mental collectedness and concentration to which I have previously alluded as observable only in particular moments of the highest artificial excitement. The words of one of these rhapsodies I have easily remembered. I was, perhaps, the more forcibly impressed with it as he gave it, because, in the under or mystic current of its meaning, I fancied that I perceived, and for the first time, a full consciousness on the part of Usher of the tottering of his lofty reason upon her throne. The verses, which were entitled "The Haunted Palace," ran very nearly, if not accurately, thus:—

I.

19 In the greenest of our valleys,
      By good angels tenanted,
Once a fair and stately palace—
      Radiant palace—reared its head.
In the monarch Thought's dominion—
      It stood there!
Never seraph[13] spread a pinion[14]
      Over fabric half so fair.

---

12 impromptus (ăn-prônp-tüz´): spontaneous performances.
13 seraph (sĕr´əf): angel.
14 pinion (pĭn´yən): wing.

Annotate: In verses I and II of "The Haunted Palace," mark the words that describe the atmosphere of the palace.

Compare: How does the mood of Usher's poem compare and contrast with the mood of his own home?

II.

20 Banners yellow, glorious, golden,
        On its roof did float and flow
    (This—all this—was in the olden
        Time long ago);
    And every gentle air that dallied,
        In that sweet day,
    Along the ramparts plumed and pallid,
        A winged odor went away.

III.

21 Wanderers in that happy valley
        Through two luminous windows saw
    Spirits moving musically
        To a lute's well-tunèd law;
    Round about a throne, where sitting
        (Porphyrogene!)[15]
    In state his glory well befitting,
        The ruler of the realm was seen.

IV.

22 And all with pearl and ruby glowing
        Was the fair palace door,
    Through which came flowing, flowing, flowing
        And sparkling evermore,
    A troop of Echoes whose sweet duty
        Was but to sing,
    In voices of surpassing beauty,
        The wit and wisdom of their king.

V.

23 But evil things, in robes of sorrow,
        Assailed the monarch's high estate;
    (Ah, let us mourn, for never morrow
        Shall dawn upon him, desolate!)
    And, round about his home, the glory
        That blushed and bloomed
    Is but a dim-remembered story
        Of the old time entombed.

---

15 **Porphyrogene** (pôr-fir´ə-jēn): Poe coined this word from *porphyrogenite,* the name once used to refer to royalty in Byzantine times. (The Greek word *porphyros* means "purple.") *Porphyrogene* means "one born to the purple" or "one of royal blood."

VI.

Don't forget to **Notice & Note** as you read the text.

24 And travellers now within that valley,
   Through the red-litten windows see
Vast forms that move fantastically
   To a discordant melody;
While, like a rapid ghastly river,
   Through the pale door,
A hideous throng rush out forever,
   And laugh—but smile no more.

25   I well remember that suggestions arising from this ballad led us into a train of thought wherein there became manifest an opinion of Usher's which I mention not so much on account of its novelty (for other men* have thought thus), as on account of the pertinacity with which he maintained it. This opinion, in its general form, was that of the sentience[16] of all vegetable things. But, in his disordered fancy, the idea had assumed a more daring character, and trespassed, under certain conditions, upon the kingdom of inorganization.[17] I lack words to express the full extent, or the earnest *abandon* of his persuasion. The belief, however, was connected (as I have previously hinted) with the gray stones of the home of his forefathers. The conditions of the sentience had been here, he imagined, fulfilled in the method of collocation of these stones—in the order of their arrangement, as well as in that of the many *fungi* which overspread them, and of the decayed trees which stood around—above all, in the long undisturbed endurance of this arrangement, and in its reduplication in the still waters of the tarn. Its evidence—the evidence of the sentience—was to be seen, he said, (and I here started as he spoke), in the gradual yet certain condensation of an atmosphere of their own about the waters and the walls. The result was discoverable, he added, in that silent yet importunate and terrible influence which for centuries had moulded the destinies of his family, and which made *him* what I now saw him—what he was. Such opinions need no comment, and I will make none.

26   Our books—the books which, for years, had formed no small portion of the mental existence of the invalid—were, as might be supposed, in strict keeping with this character of phantasm. We pored together over such works as the "Ververt et Chartreuse" of Gresset; the "Belphegor" of Machiavelli; the "Heaven and Hell" of Swedenborg; the "Subterranean Voyage of Nicholas Klimm" by Holberg; the "Chiromancy" of Robert Flud, of Jean D'Indaginé, and of De la Chambre; the "Journey into the Blue Distance" of Tieck; and the "City of the Sun" of Campanella. One favorite volume was a small octavo edition of the "Directorium Inquisitorium," by the Dominican

---

* Watson, Dr. Percival, Spallanzani, and especially the Bishop of Landaff.—See "Chemical Essays," vol. v. [Poe's note]

[16] **sentience** (sen´shəns): consciousness.

[17] **kingdom of inorganization:** world of inorganic objects.

CONTRASTS AND CONTRADICTIONS

When you notice a sharp contrast between what you would expect and what the character actually does, you've found a **Contrasts and Contradictions** signpost.

Notice & Note: Mark the words in paragraph 27 that present the news of Madeline's death.

Draw Conclusions: Why would the narrator—and Roderick Usher—present such major news in this way?

Eymeric de Gironne; and there were passages in Pomponius Mela, about the old African Satyrs and Œgipans,[18] over which Usher would sit dreaming for hours. His chief delight, however, was found in the perusal of an exceedingly rare and curious book in quarto Gothic— the manual of a forgotten church—the *Vigiliæ Mortuorum Secundum Chorum Ecclesiæ Maguntinæ.*[19]

27   I could not help thinking of the wild ritual of this work, and of its probable influence upon the hypochondriac, when, one evening, having informed me abruptly that the lady Madeline was no more, he stated his intention of preserving her corpse for a fortnight (previously to its final interment), in one of the numerous vaults within the main walls of the building. The worldly reason, however, assigned for this singular proceeding, was one which I did not feel at liberty to dispute. The brother had been led to his resolution (so he told me) by consideration of the unusual character of the malady of the deceased, of certain obtrusive and eager inquiries on the part of her medical men, and of the remote and exposed situation of the burial-ground of the family. I will not deny that when I called to mind the sinister countenance of the person whom I met upon the staircase, on the day of my arrival at the house, I had no desire to oppose what I regarded as at best but a harmless, and by no means an unnatural precaution.[20]

28   At the request of Usher, I personally aided him in the arrangements for the temporary entombment. The body having been encoffined, we two alone bore it to its rest. The vault in which we placed it (and which had been so long unopened that our torches, half smothered in its oppressive atmosphere, gave us little opportunity for investigation) was small, damp, and entirely without means of admission for light; lying, at great depth, immediately beneath that portion of the building in which was my own sleeping apartment. It had been used, apparently, in remote feudal times, for the worst purposes of a donjon-keep, and, in later days, as a place of deposit for powder, or some other highly combustible substance, as a portion of its floor, and the whole interior of a long archway through which we reached it, were carefully sheathed with copper. The door, of massive iron, had been, also, similarly protected. Its immense weight caused an unusually sharp, grating sound, as it moved upon its hinges.

29   Having deposited our mournful burden upon tressels within this region of horror, we partially turned aside the yet unscrewed lid of the coffin, and looked upon the face of the tenant. A striking similitude between the brother and sister now first arrested my attention; and Usher, divining, perhaps, my thoughts, murmured out some few words from which I learned that the deceased and himself

ANALYZE MOOD

Annotate: In paragraph 29, mark details about illness and death.

Identify: What mood does the narrator's discussion of death create?

---

[18] **"Ververt et Chartreuse" . . . Satyrs and Œgipans:** The books, authors, and subjects listed have to do with mysticism, magic, and horror.

[19] **Vigiliae Mortuorum . . . Maguntinæ:** Latin for "vigil of the dead."

[20] **harmless . . . precaution:** Usher wishes to be sure his sister's body will not be dissected by doctors. At the time, bodies were sometimes stolen and sold to medical students for dissection and study.

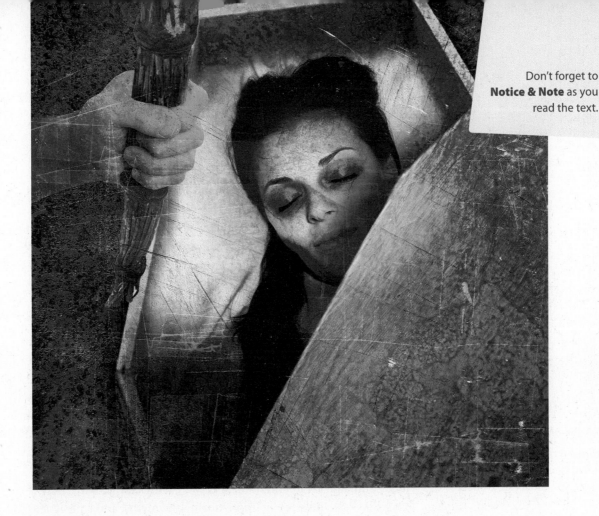

had been twins, and that sympathies of a scarcely intelligible nature had always existed between them. Our glances, however, rested not long upon the dead—for we could not regard her unawed. The disease which had thus entombed the lady in the maturity of youth, had left, as usual in all maladies of a strictly cataleptical character, the mockery of a faint blush upon the bosom and the face, and that suspiciously lingering smile upon the lip which is so terrible in death. We replaced and screwed down the lid, and, having secured the door of iron, made our way, with toil, into the scarcely less gloomy apartments of the upper portion of the house.

30   And now, some days of bitter grief having elapsed, an observable change came over the features of the mental disorder of my friend. His ordinary manner had vanished. His ordinary occupations were neglected or forgotten. He roamed from chamber to chamber with hurried, unequal, and objectless step. The pallor of his countenance had assumed, if possible, a more ghastly hue—but the luminousness of his eye had utterly gone out. The once occasional huskiness of his tone was heard no more; and a tremulous quaver, as if of extreme terror, habitually characterized his utterance. There were times, indeed, when I thought his unceasingly agitated mind was laboring with some oppressive secret, to divulge which he struggled for the necessary courage. At times, again, I was obliged to resolve all into the mere inexplicable vagaries of madness, for I beheld him gazing upon vacancy for long hours, in an attitude of the profoundest

attention, as if listening to some imaginary sound. It was no wonder that his condition terrified—that it infected me. I felt creeping upon me, by slow yet certain degrees, the wild influences of his own fantastic yet impressive superstitions.

31   It was, especially, upon retiring to bed late in the night of the seventh or eighth day after the placing of the lady Madeline within the donjon, that I experienced the full power of such feelings. Sleep came not near my couch—while the hours waned and waned away. I struggled to reason off the nervousness which had dominion over me. I endeavored to believe that much, if not all of what I felt, was due to the bewildering influence of the gloomy furniture of the room—of the dark and tattered draperies, which, tortured into motion by the breath of a rising tempest, swayed fitfully to and fro upon the walls, and rustled uneasily about the decorations of the bed. But my efforts were fruitless. An irrepressible tremor gradually pervaded my frame; and, at length, there sat upon my very heart an incubus[21] of utterly causeless alarm. Shaking this off with a gasp and a struggle, I uplifted myself upon the pillows, and, peering earnestly within the intense darkness of the chamber, hearkened—I know not why, except that an instinctive spirit prompted me—to certain low and indefinite sounds which came, through the pauses of the storm, at long intervals, I knew not whence. Overpowered by an intense sentiment of horror, unaccountable yet unendurable, I threw on my clothes with haste (for I felt that I should sleep no more during the night), and endeavored to arouse myself from the pitiable condition into which I had fallen, by pacing rapidly to and fro through the apartment.

32   I had taken but few turns in this manner, when a light step on an adjoining staircase arrested my attention. I presently recognized it as that of Usher. In an instant afterward he rapped, with a gentle touch, at my door, and entered, bearing a lamp. His countenance was, as usual, cadaverously wan—but, moreover, there was a species of mad hilarity in his eyes—an evidently restrained *hysteria* in his whole **demeanor**. His air appalled me—but any thing was preferable to the solitude which I had so long endured, and I even welcomed his presence as a relief.

33   "And you have not seen it?" he said abruptly, after having stared about him for some moments in silence—"you have not then seen it?—but, stay! you shall." Thus speaking, and having carefully shaded his lamp, he hurried to one of the casements, and threw it freely open to the storm.

34   The impetuous fury of the entering gust nearly lifted us from our feet. It was, indeed, a tempestuous yet sternly beautiful night, and one wildly singular in its terror and its beauty. A whirlwind had apparently collected its force in our vicinity; for there were frequent and violent alterations in the direction of the wind; and the exceeding density of the clouds (which hung so low as to press upon the turrets

© Houghton Mifflin Harcourt Publishing Company

---

[21] **incubus** (ĭn´kyə-bəs)**:** nightmare. In medieval times, it was believed that nightmares were caused by demons (incubi) who tormented the sleeping.

VOCABULARY

Patterns of Word Change: The adverb *cadaverously* in paragraph 32 combines the noun *cadaver* with suffixes *-ous* and *-ly*.

Identify Patterns: Why is this form of the word correct in this sentence? How does looking at word changes help you understand words that include the base word *cadaver*?

demeanor (dĭ-mē´nər) *n.* the way in which a person behaves; deportment.

ANALYZE ALLEGORY

Annotate: In paragraph 34, mark details that describe the clouds outside the House of Usher.

Analyze: What type of weather do the clouds literally represent? How might the clouds reflect a symbolic meaning related to nature?

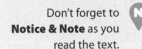

of the house) did not prevent our perceiving the life-like velocity with which they flew careering from all points against each other, without passing away into the distance. I say that even their exceeding density did not prevent our perceiving this—yet we had no glimpse of the moon or stars, nor was there any flashing forth of the lightning. But the under surfaces of the huge masses of agitated vapor, as well as all terrestrial objects immediately around us, were glowing in the unnatural light of a faintly luminous and distinctly visible gaseous exhalation which hung about and enshrouded the mansion.

35   "You must not—you shall not behold this!" said I, shuddering, to Usher, as I led him, with a gentle violence, from the window to a seat. "These appearances, which bewilder you, are merely electrical phenomena not uncommon—or it may be that they have their ghastly origin in the rank miasma of the tarn.[22] Let us close this casement;—the air is chilling and dangerous to your frame. Here is one of your favorite romances. I will read, and you shall listen:—and so we will pass away this terrible night together."

36   The antique volume which I had taken up was the "Mad Trist" of Sir Launcelot Canning;[23] but I had called it a favorite of Usher's more in sad jest than in earnest; for, in truth, there is little in its uncouth and unimaginative prolixity which could have had interest for the lofty and spiritual ideality of my friend. It was, however, the only book immediately at hand; and I indulged a vague hope that the excitement which now agitated the hypochondriac, might find relief (for the history of mental disorder is full of similar anomalies) even in the extremeness of the folly which I should read. Could I have judged, indeed, by the wild overstrained air of vivacity with which he hearkened, or apparently hearkened, to the words of the tale, I might well have congratulated myself upon the success of my design.

37   I had arrived at that well-known portion of the story where Ethelred, the hero of the Trist, having sought in vain for peaceable admission into the dwelling of the hermit, proceeds to make good an entrance by force. Here, it will be remembered, the words of the narrative run thus:

38   "And Ethelred, who was by nature of a doughty[24] heart, and who was now mighty withal, on account of the powerfulness of the wine which he had drunken, waited no longer to hold parley with the hermit, who, in sooth, was of an obstinate and maliceful turn, but, feeling the rain upon his shoulders, and fearing the rising of the tempest, uplifted his mace outright, and, with blows, made quickly room in the plankings of the door for his gauntleted hand; and now pulling therewith sturdily, he so cracked, and ripped, and tore all asunder, that the noise of the dry and hollow-sounding wood alarumed and reverberated throughout the forest."

---

[22] **rank miasma . . . tarn:** The decomposing matter of the tarn could have given rise to swamp gas or electrical discharges, resulting in frightening optical illusions.

[23] **"Mad Trist" of Sir Launcelot Canning:** a book invented by Poe for this story.

[24] **doughty** (dou´tē): courageous.

At the termination of this sentence I started and, for a moment, paused; for it appeared to me (although I at once concluded that my excited fancy had deceived me)—it appeared to me that, from some very remote portion of the mansion, there came, indistinctly to my ears, what might have been, in its exact similarity of character, the echo (but a stifled and dull one certainly) of the very cracking and ripping sound which Sir Launcelot had so particularly described. It was, beyond doubt, the coincidence alone which had arrested my attention; for, amid the rattling of the sashes of the casements, and the ordinary commingled noises of the still increasing storm, the sound, in itself, had nothing, surely, which should have interested or disturbed me. I continued the story:

40

"But the good champion Ethelred, now entering within the door, was sore enraged and amazed to perceive no signal of the maliceful hermit; but, in the stead thereof, a dragon of a scaly and prodigious demeanor, and of a fiery tongue, which sate in guard before a palace of gold, with a floor of silver; and upon the wall there hung a shield of shining brass with this legend enwritten—

41   Who entereth herein, a conqueror hath bin;

42   Who slayeth the dragon, the shield he shall win.

43   And Ethelred uplifted his mace, and struck upon the head of the dragon, which fell before him, and gave up his pesty breath, with a shriek so horrid and harsh, and withal so piercing, that Ethelred had fain to close his ears with his hands against the dreadful noise of it, the like whereof was never before heard."

44   Here again I paused abruptly, and now with a feeling of wild amazement—for there could be no doubt whatever that, in this instance, I did actually hear (although from what direction it proceeded I found it impossible to say) a low and apparently distant, but harsh, protracted, and most unusual screaming or grating sound—the exact counterpart of what my fancy had already conjured up for the dragon's unnatural shriek as described by the romancer.

45   Oppressed, as I certainly was, upon the occurrence of this second and most extraordinary coincidence, by a thousand conflicting sensations, in which wonder and extreme terror were predominant, I still retained sufficient presence of mind to avoid exciting, by any observation, the sensitive nervousness of my companion. I was by no means certain that he had noticed the sounds in question; although, assuredly, a strange alteration had, during the last few minutes, taken place in his demeanor. From a position fronting my own, he had gradually brought round his chair, so as to sit with his face to the door of the chamber; and thus I could but partially perceive his features, although I saw that his lips trembled as if he were murmuring inaudibly. His head had dropped upon his breast—yet I knew that he was not asleep, from the wide and rigid opening of the eye as I caught a glance of it in profile. The motion of his body, too, was at variance with this idea—for he rocked from side to side with a gentle yet constant and uniform sway. Having rapidly taken notice of all this, I resumed the narrative of Sir Launcelot, which thus proceeded:

ANALYZE MOOD

Annotate: In paragraph 40, mark details that create a mood in the "Mad Trist," the story the narrator reads aloud.

Compare: How does the mood of the "Mad Trist" compare with the mood created by the rest of the story about Roderick Usher?

Don't forget to
Notice & Note as you
read the text.

46   "And now, the champion, having escaped from the terrible fury
of the dragon, bethinking himself of the brazen shield, and of the
breaking up of the enchantment which was upon it, removed the
carcass from out of the way before him, and approached valorously
over the silver pavement of the castle to where the shield was upon the
wall; which in sooth tarried not for his full coming, but fell down at
his feet upon the silver floor, with a mighty great and terrible ringing
sound."

47   No sooner had these syllables passed my lips, than—as if a shield
of brass had indeed, at the moment, fallen heavily upon a floor of
silver—I became aware of a distinct, hollow, metallic, and clangorous,
yet apparently muffled, reverberation. Completely unnerved, I
leaped to my feet; but the measured rocking movement of Usher was
undisturbed. I rushed to the chair in which he sat. His eyes were bent
fixedly before him, and throughout his whole countenance there
reigned a stony rigidity. But, as I placed my hand upon his shoulder,
there came a strong shudder over his whole person; a sickly smile
quivered about his lips; and I saw that he spoke in a low, hurried, and
gibbering murmur, as if unconscious of my presence. Bending closely
over him, I at length drank in the hideous import of his words.

48   "Not hear it?—yes, I hear it, and *have* heard it. Long—long—
long—many minutes, many hours, many days, have I heard it—yet
I dared not—oh, pity me, miserable wretch that I am!—I dared
not—I dared not speak! We have put her living in the tomb! Said I
not that my senses were acute? I now tell you that I heard her first
feeble movements in the hollow coffin. I heard them—many, many
days ago—yet I dared not—I dared not speak! And now—to-night—
Ethelred—ha! ha!—the breaking of the hermit's door, and the death-
cry of the dragon, and the clangor of the shield—say, rather, the
rending of her coffin, and the grating of the iron hinges of her prison,
and her struggles within the coppered archway of the vault! Oh!
whither shall I fly? Will she not be here anon? Is she not hurrying to
upbraid me for my haste? Have I not heard her footstep on the stair?
Do I not distinguish that heavy and horrible beating of her heart?
Madman!"—here he sprang furiously to his feet, and shrieked out his
syllables, as if in the effort he were giving up his soul—*"Madman! I tell
you that she now stands without the door!"*

49   As if in the superhuman energy of his utterance there had been
found the potency of a spell, the huge antique panels to which the
speaker pointed threw slowly back, upon the instant, their ponderous
and ebony jaws. It was the work of the rushing gust—but then without
those doors there *did* stand the lofty and enshrouded figure of the
lady Madeline of Usher. There was blood upon her white robes,
and the evidence of some bitter struggle upon every portion of her
emaciated frame. For a moment she remained trembling and reeling
to and fro upon the threshold—then, with a low moaning cry, fell
heavily inward upon the person of her brother, and in her violent and
now final death-agonies, bore him to the floor a corpse, and a victim
to the terrors he had anticipated.

© Houghton Mifflin Harcourt Publishing Company

NOTICE & NOTE
AGAIN AND AGAIN

When you notice certain events,
images, or words recurring over a
portion of the story, you've found
an **Again and Again** signpost.

Notice & Note: Mark the words
that describe what the narrator
hears when he stops reading for
the third time.

Draw Conclusions: Why might
the author bring up these sound
interruptions so many times?

aghast
(ə-găst´) *adj.* struck by shock, terror, or amazement.

50 From that chamber, and from that mansion, I fled **aghast**. The storm was still abroad in all its wrath as I found myself crossing the old causeway. Suddenly there shot along the path a wild light, and I turned to see whence a gleam so unusual could have issued; for the vast house and its shadows were alone behind me. The radiance was that of the full, setting, and blood-red moon which now shone vividly through that once barely-discernible fissure of which I have before spoken as extending from the roof of the building, in a zigzag direction, to the base. While I gazed, this fissure rapidly widened— there came a fierce breath of the whirlwind—the entire orb of the satellite burst at once upon my sight—my brain reeled as I saw the mighty walls rushing asunder—there was a long tumultuous shouting sound like the voice of a thousand waters—and the deep and dank tarn at my feet closed sullenly and silently over the fragments of the "HOUSE OF USHER."

COLLABORATIVE DISCUSSION

With a partner, discuss whether all the events in this story actually take place, or whether some of them occur only in the minds of the characters.

Review your notes and add your thoughts to your **Response Log.**

Assessment Practice

Answer these questions before moving on to the **Analyze the Text** section on the following page.

1. Why does the narrator come to visit the House of Usher?

   (A) He wants to see Madeline, whom he has secretly loved for years.

   (B) Roderick wrote to him, requesting help during a stressful time.

   (C) He hopes to inherit the House of Usher after its owners pass away.

   (D) As a doctor, he plans to cure Madeline of her emotional disorder.

2. Roderick Usher's appearance is

   (A) severe and handsome

   (B) icy and unemotional

   (C) wild and ungroomed

   (D) pleasant and open

3. What finally happens to the House of Usher?

   (A) It breaks apart and sinks without a trace.

   (B) It burns to the ground, leaving only a stone tomb.

   (C) It becomes legendary within the region for being haunted.

   (D) It is swept away by a powerful storm.

Test-Taking Strategies

Analyze the Text

Support your responses with evidence from the text.

(1) **COMPARE** Does the mood of the story stay the same throughout, or does it change from beginning to end? Explain.

(2) **INFER** Why might Poe have decided to make Roderick and Madeline *twins*—not just brother and sister?

(3) **DRAW CONCLUSIONS** What role does Madeline play in the story? Consider how the news of her death is delivered in the **Contrasts and Contradictions** signpost in paragraph 27. How does this new event reflect Madeline's position in the story?

(4) **ANALYZE** How do sounds contribute to the events and mood of the story? Think about the repetition of sounds in the **Again and Again** signpost in paragraph 47, as well as other descriptions of sounds throughout the tale, beginning in the first sentence.

(5) **CONNECT** In paragraph 11, Roderick claims that he has "no abhorrence of danger" but will eventually "abandon life and reason together, in some struggle with the grim phantasm, Fear." Does his prediction come true?

(6) **ANALYZE** Poe said that the poem "The Haunted Palace" is meant to suggest a disordered brain. How might the whole story be read as an allegory of a journey into the human mind? Complete the chart by describing the literal and symbolic meanings of each story element.

Element	Literal Meaning	Symbolic Meaning
Roderick's appearance		
the narrator's presence		
Madeline's death		
the final fall of the house		

(7) **EVALUATE** Is Poe's story from 1839 still frightening to audiences today? Why or why not?

© Houghton Mifflin Harcourt Publishing Company

Choices

Here are some other ways to demonstrate your understanding of the ideas in this lesson.

Writing
↳ Retelling

Poe chooses to have a third party tell the story of the Ushers' demise. How might the story be different if someone else narrated? Retell the story from Roderick's or Madeline's point of view. Think about

- how shifting the point of view changes the perception of events
- how a different character might describe the setting
- what feelings and emotions Roderick or Madeline might reveal

> As you write and discuss, be sure to use the **Academic Vocabulary** words.
>
> analogy
>
> denote
>
> quote
>
> topic
>
> unique

Social & Emotional Learning
↳ Recommendations

Self-Awareness In Poe's day, mental illness was not clearly defined. People with bipolar disorder or depression would have been described as "suffering from melancholy," which is how Poe describes Roderick. In the story, there are outward signs of Roderick's inner turmoil. Find two or three examples, and think about how he could learn to recognize his emotions and ask for help when he needs it. Write down your recommendations for skills he could develop to help manage his mental state.

Speaking & Listening
↳ Debate

The literary critic Cleanth Brooks dismissed "The Fall of the House of Usher" as an "essentially meaningless" exercise in horror for its own sake. Do you agree or disagree with this opinion? Find one classmate who agrees with you and two who don't. Work together to hold a debate.

1. State your position and find examples from the text to support your argument.

2. Anticipate rebuttals and counterclaims from your opponents.

3. Plan your rebuttals and counterclaims for their argument.

4. Conclude with a summary of your argument and clear reasons why it holds up.

Expand Your Vocabulary

PRACTICE AND APPLY

Answer the questions to show your understanding of the vocabulary words.

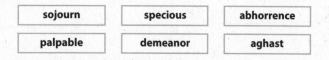

sojourn	specious	abhorrence
palpable	demeanor	aghast

1. How might taking a **sojourn** change your perspective?

2. What is an example of a **specious** argument?

3. What gestures or facial expressions suggest **abhorrence**?

4. When might you experience a **palpable** change?

5. Does a person's **demeanor** always reflect what he or she feels?

6. What situation from a horror film might make a character **aghast**?

Vocabulary Strategy

↳ **Patterns of Word Change**

When you read, you can use patterns of word change to understand related words. Notice how adding suffixes changes the meaning of the verb *pervade*.

> **🙂Ed**
>
> **Interactive Vocabulary Lesson: Patterns of Word Change**

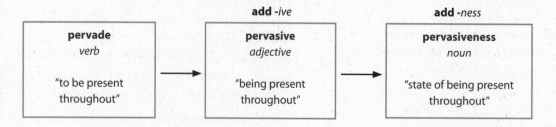

add -*ive*   add -*ness*

| **pervade** *verb* "to be present throughout" | → | **pervasive** *adjective* "being present throughout" | → | **pervasiveness** *noun* "state of being present throughout" |

PRACTICE AND APPLY

Locate these words in the story: *excessive* (paragraph 3), *endurable* (paragraph 10), and *reduplication* (paragraph 25).

Use patterns of word change to identify two related words for each one. Describe how prefixes or suffixes change the word's meaning. Use a dictionary if needed.

Watch Your Language!

Adjective Clauses

Adjective clauses are like extra-long adjectives. Instead of just one word, an adjective clause is a subordinate clause that modifies a noun or pronoun. Writers use adjective clauses to add detailed descriptions that help readers visualize characters, settings, and events.

Use	Adapted Examples
Many adjective clauses begin with a relative pronoun, such as *who* or *which*.	Ethelred, _who was by nature of a doughty heart_, waited no longer. The adjective clause modifies the noun *Ethelred*. The writer spoke of a mental disorder _which oppressed him._ The adjective clause modifies the noun *disorder*.
Some adjective clauses begin with pronouns like *when* or *where*.	During the whole of a dull, dark, and soundless day, _when the clouds hung oppressively low in the heavens. . . ._ The adjective clause modifies the noun *day*.

"Real hungry? Should be, 'Really hungry.' Adjectives take adverbs."

PRACTICE AND APPLY

Combine the sentences to include an adjective clause introduced by the word in parentheses.

1. I was startled by the flickering shadow. It disappeared when the candle blew out. (*which*)

2. The tomb was guarded by a silent woman. She neither spoke nor moved. (*who*)

3. We met in the garden. Every living thing had long ago died. (*where*)

4. An icy chill climbed my spine. The scraping sound echoed in the attic. (*when*)

Write a paragraph describing a frightening or mysterious setting. Include adjective clauses to provide descriptive details.

Compare Themes

Both "The Minister's Black Veil" and "The Fall of the House of Usher" are short stories that develop themes about fear and darkness. The writers use some similar literary elements to develop different themes.

In a small group, complete the chart below to examine the two short stories. Be sure to support your ideas with text evidence.

	A **"The Minister's Black Veil"**	**B** **"The Fall of the House of Usher"**
Setting: How does the story setting help the writer develop a theme?		
Title Symbol: How does the title of the story reflect a symbol that readers learn how to interpret?		
Unity of Effect: How do the story elements combine to create a single effect?		
Allegory: What theme is suggested by interpreting the story on a symbolic level?		

Analyze the Texts

Discuss these questions in your group.

(1) COMPARE How do both stories address fear? Do the objects of fear in each story actually exist, or are they merely created within the minds of the fearful?

(2) EVALUATE Hawthorne's story is told by a third-person narrator; Poe's is told by an unnamed first-person narrator. How effective is each point of view? Would another point of view have been more effective?

(3) CRITIQUE Which story is more realistic? Is a realistic story always more effective?

(4) DRAW CONCLUSIONS Which story's theme is more universal? Why?

Collaborate and Present

Your group can continue exploring the ideas in these texts by collaborating on a multimedia presentation. Follow these steps:

(1) CHOOSE A FOCUS With your group, decide what theme or themes you would like to compare in your presentation.

(2) PLAN ELEMENTS Consider how you will enhance your ideas with media elements. Draft a line or two of text to explain each of your key ideas. Then find or create audio, video, or graphic elements to illustrate and extend your ideas.

Idea/Text	Media (Audio, Video, Graphics)

(3) ORGANIZE A PRESENTATION Decide how you will present your ideas. Consider these two organizations:

- **Work by Work:** Analyze one story completely. Then draw comparisons as you analyze the second story.

- **Element by Element:** Choose one element, such as setting, and analyze its role in both stories. Then compare other key elements, such as central characters, conflicts, or symbols.

(4) REHEARSE As you rehearse, pay attention to the pace and flow of your presentation. Look for ways to create interest by varying media types, changing narrators, and using pauses or audio for effect.

(5) PRESENT Remember your rehearsal notes as you share your presentation with the class.

Reader's Choice

Continue your exploration of the Essential Questions for this unit by doing some independent reading. Read the titles and descriptions shown. Then mark the texts that interest you.

? **ESSENTIAL QUESTIONS:**
Review the four Essential Questions for this unit on page 249.

Short Reads   Available on ⊙Ed

These texts are available in your ebook. Choose one to read and rate. Then defend your rating to the class.

from **Nature** *and* from **Self-Reliance**
Essays by Ralph Waldo Emerson

How can you live as an individual, relate to nature, and be your own boss?

Rate It ☆☆☆☆☆

The Pointlessness of Unplugging
Article by Casey N. Cep

What happens when people unplug from their digital devices?

Rate It ☆☆☆☆☆

The Raven
Poem by Edgar Allan Poe

Does the raven help a grieving man burdened by painful memories? Or is it just a creepy bird?

Rate It ☆☆☆☆☆

The Feather Pillow
Short Story by Horacio Quiroga

Follow the rapid decline of a young bride as her husband tries to find out what's killing her.

Rate It ☆☆☆☆☆

Pastoral
Poem by Jennifer Chang

Transport yourself to a field of flowers and hidden creatures.

Rate It ☆☆☆☆☆

Long Reads

Here are three recommended books that connect to this unit.
For additional options, ask your teacher, school librarian, or peers.
Which titles spark your interest?

Fahrenheit 451

Novel by **Ray Bradbury**

In this dystopian society, Guy's job is to hunt down and burn books. He does not question this task until Clarisse comes along. He begins pilfering books until he is discovered and must run for his life.

X: A Novel

Novel by **Ilyasah Shabazz** and **Kekla Magoon**

Malcolm does not believe his parents when they tell him he can achieve anything. He searches for meaning by immersing himself in the city's nightlife, only to face new dangers.

A Paradise Built in Hell

Nonfiction by **Rebecca Solnit**

People will surprise you when given the opportunity. Solnit examines the challenges disasters wreak on society and how people come together to overcome them.

Extension
↳ **Connect & Create**

ON A RELATED MATTER A common theme in this unit is how we relate to the larger world. Was this a theme in the text you chose? With someone who read the same text, create an ad that promotes the message of the text to a larger audience. Share your ad on a class website.

STOP AND SMELL THE FLOWERS Several texts in this unit encourage readers to take time out and reflect. In the texts you read independently, was the central idea related to being present in the moment? Pick one of the texts and write a journal entry from the perspective of the main character or subject about his or her efforts to be mindful.

NOTICE & NOTE

- Pick one of the texts and annotate the Notice & Note signposts you find.

- Then use the **Notice & Note Writing Frames** to help you write about the significance of the signposts.

- Compare your findings with those of other students who read the same text.

Notice & Note Writing Frames

Write an Explanatory Essay

Writing Prompt

Using ideas, information, or examples from texts in this unit, write an explanatory essay for your school newspaper that explains how the way we interact socially affects individuals and groups.

Manage your time carefully so that you can

- generate ideas to include in your essay;
- plan your essay;
- draft your essay; and
- revise and edit your essay.

Be sure to

- clearly state the main idea of your essay;
- provide clear examples to support your ideas;
- use precise language in your explanations; and
- check that your essay flows logically from one idea to the next.

> ### Review the
> ### Mentor Text
>
> For an example of a well-written explanatory essay that you can use as a mentor text and inspiration for your essay, review
>
> - *from* **Last Child in the Woods** (pages 300–303)
>
> Review your notes and annotations about this text. Think about how the author describes the situations and brings them to life.

Consider Your Sources

Review the list of texts in the unit and choose at least three that you may want to use as support or inspiration for your explanatory essay.

As you review potential sources, consult the notes you made in your **Response Log** and make additional notes about ideas that might be useful as you write your essay. Consider how the writers structured their texts, used descriptive language, and employed other techniques you may want to use.

UNIT 3 SOURCES

- [ ] *from* **Song of Myself**
- [ ] **My Friend Walt Whitman**
- [ ] **Poems by Emily Dickinson**
- [ ] **In the Season of Change**
- [ ] *from* **Last Child in the Woods**
- [ ] *from* **Walden**
- [ ] **The Minister's Black Veil**
- [ ] **The Fall of the House of Usher**

Analyze the Prompt

Review the prompt to make sure you understand the assignment.

1. Mark the sentence in the prompt that identifies the topic of your explanatory essay. Rephrase the sentence in your own words.

2. Then, look for words that indicate the purpose and audience of your essay. Write a sentence describing each.

Find a Purpose

As you respond, consider the two most common purposes of an explanatory essay:

- to **analyze** complex ideas and relationships

- to **explain** the importance of the ideas or relationships

---

What is my topic? What is my writing task?

What is my purpose?

Who is my audience?

Review the Rubric

Your explanatory essay will be scored using a rubric. As you write, focus on the characteristics of a high-scoring essay as described in the chart. You will learn more about these characteristics as you work through the lesson.

Purpose, Focus, and Organization	Evidence and Elaboration	Conventions of Standard English
The response includes: • A strongly maintained controlling idea • Skillful use of transitions to connect ideas • Logical progression of ideas, including strong introduction and conclusion • Appropriate style and tone	The response includes: • Effective use of evidence and sources • Effective use of elaboration • Clear and effective expression of ideas • Appropriate academic and domain-specific vocabulary • Varied sentence structure	The response may include: • Some minor errors in usage but no patterns of errors • Correct punctuation, capitalization, sentence formation, and spelling • Command of basic conventions

1 PLAN YOUR EXPLANATORY ESSAY

Develop a Thesis

Think through how you feel about how interactions with others—for example, in person, via text, or online—affects relationships between individuals and groups. Compare and contrast your ideas with those in the unit texts. Then develop a thesis statement.

Draft Your Thesis

The **thesis**, or controlling idea, of an essay should be a clearly stated single sentence that tells the reader what you are going to be writing about. It usually appears near the end of the first paragraph.

How do we interact with others?	
What effect does the way we interact have on people?	
Possible thesis ideas	

Identify Support

An effective explanatory essay is logical and well reasoned with supporting facts and evidence. Your thesis and ideas should be supported by the following:

- facts
- concrete details
- expert analysis
- quotations

Use the chart to help you plan your supporting ideas.

Explanatory Essay Planning Chart	
Thesis	
Ideas from background reading (summaries, paraphrases, possible quotes)	
Ideas from class discussions and your own experience	

Supporting Details

Your essay should include **supporting details** for your thesis and ideas. Review your notes on the texts and any additional background information that might help you develop your ideas. Note examples and quotations that can add to your readers' understanding of your topic.

Help with Planning

Consult **Interactive Writing Lesson: Writing Informative Texts**

Source	Examples/Quotations

Organize Ideas

Now organize your notes and materials in a way that will help you draft your explanatory essay. Keep in mind that a well-written essay presents ideas in a **logical, coherent** order. You'll use paragraph breaks and transitional words and phrases to maintain a logical flow.

Use the table below to organize your ideas and create coherence.

Put Your Paragraphs in Order

There are a couple of common ways to order body paragraphs in an essay. Experiment with these and decide which is best for your essay:

- Start with the *most important idea* and follow with the next most important and so on.
- Start with the *least important idea* and build the following paragraphs to the most important idea.

INTRODUCTION AND THESIS	• Clearly state your thesis in the first paragraph. • Include an attention-grabbing detail, quote, or question.
BODY PARAGRAPHS (DEVELOPING IDEAS)	• Use two or three paragraphs to support your thesis. • Introduce your ideas and choose facts, details, quotations, or other information as supporting evidence. • Make sure each paragraph logically flows into the next.
TRANSITIONS	• Use transitional words and phrases to connect ideas and paragraphs. • Clarify the relationships between ideas with phrases like *Due to, Another reason,* and *Subsequently.* • Keep chronology and your reader in mind. Use words like *next, previously,* and *meanwhile.*
CONCLUSION	• Restate your thesis and its significance. • Close by including an insight to give your readers something new to think about.

2 DEVELOP A DRAFT

Now it is time to draft your essay. Look at how professional writers craft their essays—you can use similar techniques in your own writing.

Add Structure

EXAMINE THE MENTOR TEXT

Notice how the author of *Last Child in the Woods* (pages 300–302) uses elements of different structures to convey ideas in his writing.

from
Last Child in the Woods
Essay by Richard Louv

The author shows changes in **chronological order.**

> Americans around my age, baby boomers or older, enjoyed a kind of free, natural play that seems, in the era of kid pagers, instant messaging, and video games, like a quaint artifact. Within the space of a few decades, the way children understand and experience nature has changed radically. The polarity of the relationship has reversed. Today, kids are aware of the global threats to the environment—but their physical contact, their intimacy with nature, is fading. That's exactly the opposite of how it was when I was a child.

The author explains the **cause** of children's changing relationship to nature.

The author makes a direct **comparison**.

APPLY TO YOUR DRAFT

Use the frames to practice adding different types of organizational structures to your draft, whether at the beginning of or within a paragraph.

Try These Suggestions

Remember to use elements of the following organizational structures in your essay:

- **Chronological Order**—a structure that shows the order in which events occur
- **Cause and Effect**—a structure that shows how an event results from another event
- **Compare and Contrast**—a structure that focuses on similarities and differences

Chronological	In the past . . . ,	but now . . .
Cause and effect	Because . . . ,	the result was . . .
Compare and contrast	By comparing/contrasting . . . ,	the writer shows . . .

Elaborate on Ideas

EXAMINE THE MENTOR TEXT

Support your ideas in your essay with information like relevant facts, definitions, quotations from authors and experts, pop culture references, or other concrete details. Richard Louv uses recognizable examples from history and pop culture to introduce and elaborate on his ideas.

ⓄEd

Drafting Online

Check your assignment list for a writing task from your teacher.

The author uses a reference to **history** to show the difference between his attitude and his children's attitude toward nature.

> Nobody in the 1950s talked about acid rain or holes in the ozone layer or global warming. But I knew my woods and my fields. . . .
>
> . . . A recent television ad depicts a four-wheel-drive SUV racing along a breathtakingly beautiful mountain stream—while in the backseat two children watch a movie on a flip-down video screen, oblivious to the landscape and water beyond the windows.

The author refers to a **pop culture** TV ad that shows children ignoring nature.

APPLY TO YOUR DRAFT

To develop your explanatory essay, support your ideas with a variety of details. Think of or search for details from history, pop culture references, and memorable quotations that may add interest to your essay.

Historical Details

Pop Culture References

Memorable Quotations

3 REVISE YOUR EXPLANATORY ESSAY

Experienced writers understand how important revising is—it's where the real work of writing happens. Use this guide to help you revise your explanatory essay.

REVISION GUIDE		
Ask Yourself	**Prove It**	**Revise It**
Introduction Does my thesis statement clearly explain my purpose?	Circle your thesis statement.	If needed, **reword** your thesis statement to clarify the topic and purpose.
Evidence Do I provide enough evidence for my thesis? Is it clear how the support connects to my thesis?	**Highlight** the evidence you used. **Check** (✔) that it clearly connects to and supports your thesis.	**Add** additional evidence where needed. **Elaborate** on how your evidence supports your thesis to make the connection clear.
Organization Are my ideas and paragraphs organized clearly?	**Number** each paragraph and note the order in which your ideas are presented. **Put a star** (★) beside transitional words and phrases.	**Reorder** the sentences in your paragraphs for logical flow. **Add** or **reword** transitional language for clarity.
Elaboration Have I elaborated on my ideas?	**Underline** details that elaborate on your ideas.	**Add** references from history or pop culture, or other details that elaborate on ideas.
Style Are my word choices precise and clear? Is the style and tone objective?	**Cross out** (✗) unclear words or phrases. **Put a check mark** (✔) beside any informal language.	**Reword** instances of unclear or informal language.
Conclusion Does my conclusion logically wrap up the ideas I presented?	Circle parts of your conclusion that connect back to your thesis.	**Revise** your conclusion to make the connection to your thesis clearer.

APPLY TO YOUR DRAFT

Consider the following as you look for opportunities to improve your writing:

- Add an interesting fact or quotation to get the reader's attention.
- Don't assume what your reader knows—provide the details and background they need to understand your essay.
- Use precise language to convey your ideas.
- Correct any errors in grammar and punctuation.

Peer Review in Action

Once you have finished revising your explanatory essay, you will exchange papers with a partner in a **peer review**. During a peer review, you will give suggestions to improve your partner's draft.

Read the introduction from a student's draft and examine the comments made by his peer reviewer to see how it's done.

First Draft

"We Are Socializing—You Just Don't See It"
By Victor Tran, Panhandle High School

Parents and teachers may believe that teens are more isolated. We might not be meeting in person. But we are actually socializing all the time. There are more opportunities for us to just shoot the breeze. People who don't know what it's like to be us just don't see it.

> Can you include words that show how your ideas relate?

> This idea seems a bit general. Can you clarify your thesis?

Now read the revised introduction. Notice how the writer improved his draft by revising based on his peer reviewer's comments.

Revision

"We Are Socializing—You Just Don't See It"
By Victor Tran, Panhandle High School

"Why are you always inside? You should be with your friends." I hear this all the time. In the past, when people were in their bedroom they were reading a book, listening to music, or just daydreaming. But just because we are inside doesn't mean we are alone. Why? Because today whole worlds are available to us online: We are texting with friends, communicating through apps, and hanging out virtually. As one contemporary writer puts it, "teens aren't addicted to social media, they are addicted to each other." So while adults think we are isolated, thanks to technology, we are engaged with others all the time.

> Good job! These words show how and why things have changed over time.

> You incorporated a reference to pop culture and clarified your thesis. What an improvement!

APPLY TO YOUR DRAFT

During your peer review, give each other specific suggestions for how to make your explanatory essay more effective. Use your revision guide to help you.

When receiving feedback from your partner, listen attentively and ask questions to make sure you fully understand the revision suggestions.

 Ed

Help with Revision

Find a **Peer Review Guide** and **Student Models** online.

4 EDIT YOUR EXPLANATORY ESSAY

Apply the finishing touches to your draft. Edit your essay to check for proper use of standard English conventions and to correct any misspellings or grammatical errors.

Interactive Grammar Lesson: Semicolons and Colons

Watch Your Language!

USE SEMICOLONS

Authors sometimes use punctuation in a distinctive way that defines their style. Emily Dickinson punctuates her poems with dashes, almost like breaths of air. Richard Louv uses semicolons to string together compound and compound-complex sentences. The formal style of his lengthy sentences creates a slower rhythm for his prose. Semicolons can connect two related ideas and clarify their connections.

Read the following sentences from *Last Child in the Woods*.

> But my son was serious; he felt he had missed out on something important.
> I knew my woods and my fields; I knew every bend in the creek and dip in the beaten dirt paths.

The semicolon joins two closely related ideas. In the first example, the second half of the sentence explains the first. In the second example, the two independent clauses are parallel and rhythmic.

APPLY TO YOUR DRAFT

Now apply what you have learned about semicolons to your own work.

1. **Read your essay aloud.** Listen to your word choices.

2. **Check the rhythm of your sentences.** Change two short related sentences into one with a semicolon.

3. **Exchange drafts** with a peer and review your writing, checking the conventions and grammar.

5 PUBLISH YOUR EXPLANATORY ESSAY

Share It!

Finalize your explanatory essay for your school newspaper. You may also use your essay as inspiration for other projects.

Semicolons

- A **semicolon** separates **two independent clauses.** Both should be able to stand on their own as complete sentences.

- A **semicolon** separates **two independent clauses linked by a conjunction,** if the clauses already contain internal commas.

Ways to Share

- **Host a roundtable discussion** between classmates about the way we communicate and how that impacts society.

- **Create a social media story** using images that reflect the main ideas in your essay.

- **Record a podcast** on your essay topic, using voice and sound to bring your ideas to life. Share it with the class.

Reflect & Extend

Here are some other ways to show your understanding of the ideas in Unit 3.

Reflect on the Essential Questions

Think about the Essential Question you identified as most intriguing on page 250. Has your answer to the question changed after reading the texts in this unit? Discuss your ideas.

You can use these sentence starters to help you reflect on your learning:

- **I think differently now because . . .**
- **I want to learn more about . . .**
- **I was surprised by . . .**

Project-Based Learning
↳ Create an Illustration

You've read about the relationship between the individual and society. Now, with a group of classmates, create an illustration about this topic.

Here are some questions to ask yourself as you get started:

- What interests me most about the individual and society?
- What message or information do I want my illustration to communicate?
- How can I use images to help convey a compelling view on the individual and society?

Media Project

To find more help with this task online, access **Create an Illustration.**

Writing
↳ Write an Argument

Develop an argument on whether individuals have an obligation to make a contribution to the well-being of society. Should activities such as community service or contributions to charity be required? Or should individuals be allowed to decide on their own?

- Make a claim about whether contributions for the good of society should be required.
- Consult sources for evidence, such as examples, statistics, or quotations, that supports your claim. You may also find relevant details in the texts in this unit.
- Address the opposing view with a counterargument.
- Consider including a call to action. What do you want your readers to do after reading your argument?

Resources

HMH *Into Literature* Resources 🙂Ed

For more instruction and practice, access the *Into Literature* Resources and Interactive Lessons.

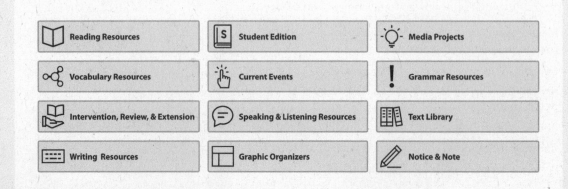

Reading Resources

Student Edition

Media Projects

Vocabulary Resources

Current Events

Grammar Resources

Intervention, Review, & Extension

Speaking & Listening Resources

Text Library

Writing Resources

Graphic Organizers

Notice & Note

Response Log

Use this Response Log to record information
from the texts that relates to or comments on the
Essential Questions in Unit 1.

? Essential Question	Details from Texts
What connects people to certain places?	
What values and beliefs shape who we are?	
What does it mean to be a stranger in a strange land?	
What happens when cultures collide?	

Response Log

Use this Response Log to record information from the texts that relates to or comments on the **Essential Questions** in Unit 2.

? Essential Question	Details from Texts
What does oppression look like?	
How do we gain our freedom?	
How can we share power and build alliances?	
How do we reach our goals?	

Response Log

Use this Response Log to record information from the texts that relates to or comments on the **Essential Questions** in Unit 3.

? Essential Question	Details from Texts
How can we be true to ourselves?	
How do we relate to the world around us?	
What do we secretly fear?	
When should we stop and reflect on our lives?	

Response Log

Use this Response Log to record information from the texts that relates to or comments on the **Essential Questions** in Unit 4.

? Essential Question	Details from Texts
When is self-determination possible?	
What causes divisions between people?	
How do we respond to defeat?	
What is the price of progress?	

Response Log

Use this Response Log to record information from the texts that relates to or comments on the **Essential Questions** in Unit 5.

? Essential Question	Details from Texts
How much do we control our lives?	
Why do humans cause harm?	
What are the consequences of change?	
What makes a place unique?	

Response Log

Use this Response Log to record information from the texts that relates to or comments on the **Essential Questions** in Unit 6.

? Essential Question	Details from Texts
How do we deal with rejection or isolation?	
Can anyone achieve the American Dream?	
When should personal integrity come before civic duty?	
What would we do if there were no limits?	

Using a Glossary

A glossary is an alphabetical list of vocabulary words. Use a glossary just as you would a dictionary—to determine the meanings, parts of speech, pronunciation, and syllabification of words. (Some technical, foreign, and more obscure words in this book are defined for you in the footnotes that accompany many of the selections.)

Many words in the English language have more than one meaning. This glossary gives the meanings that apply to the words as they are used in the selections in this book.

The following abbreviations are used to identify parts of speech of words:

adj. adjective   *adv.* adverb   *n.* noun   *v.* verb

Each word's pronunciation is given in parentheses. A guide to the pronunciation symbols appears in the Pronunciation Key below. The stress marks in the Pronunciation Key are used to indicate the force given to each syllable in a word. They can also help you determine where words are divided into syllables.

For more information about the words in this glossary or for information about words not listed here, consult a dictionary.

Pronunciation Key

Symbol	Examples	Symbol	Examples	Symbol	Examples
ă	pat	m	mum	ûr	urge, term, firm, word, heard
ā	pay	n	no, sudden* (sŭd´n)	v	valve
ä	father, hard	ng	thing	w	with
âr	care	ŏ	pot	y	yes
b	bib	ō	toe	z	zebra, xylem
ch	church	ô	caught, paw	zh	vision, pleasure, garage
d	deed, milled	oi	noise	ə	about, item, edible, gallop, circus
ě	pet	ŏŏ	took	ər	butter
ē	bee	ōō	boot		
f	fife, phase, rough	ŏŏr	lure		
g	gag	ôr	core	**Sounds in Foreign Words**	
h	hat	ou	out		
hw	which	p	pop	KH	German ich, ach; Scottish loch
ĭ	pit	r	roar	N	French bon (bôN)
ī	pie, by	s	sauce	œ	French feu, œuf; German schön
îr	pier	sh	ship, dish	ü	French tu; German über
j	judge	t	tight, stopped		
k	kick, cat, pique	th	thin		
l	lid, needle* (nēd´l)	th	this		
		ŭ	cut		

*In English the consonants *l* and *n* often constitute complete syllables by themselves.

Stress Marks

The strongest, or primary, stress of a word is indicated by a mark (´). Syllables with weaker stress and words of one syllable show no stress mark.

Glossary of Academic Vocabulary

adapt (ə-dăpt´) *v.* to make something suitable for a particular situation; to adjust to an environment.

ambiguous (ăm-bĭg´yoō-əs) *adj.* open to more than one interpretation.

analogy (ə-năl´ə-jē) *n.* a similarity in some respects between things that are otherwise dissimilar or a comparison based on such similarity.

clarify (klăr´ə-fī) *v.* to make clear or easier to understand.

coherent (kō-hîr´ənt) *adj.* holding together in an orderly, logical, or consistent way.

confirm (kən-fûrm´) *v.* to support or establish the certainty or validity of; to verify.

contemporary (kən-tĕm´pə-rĕr-ē) *adj.* belonging to the same period of time; of about the same age; current or modern.

contrary (kŏn´trĕr-ē) *adj.* opposite or opposed in character or purpose.

definitely (dĕf´ə-nĭt-lē) *adv.* in a clearly defined manner; explicitly; precisely; decidedly.

denote (dĭ-nōt´) *v.* to mark; to indicate; to serve as a symbol or name for the meaning of; to signify.

deny (dĭ-nī´) *v.* to declare untrue; to assert to be false; to refuse to believe.

device (dĭ-vīs´) *n.* something made for a specific purpose; a literary technique used to achieve a certain effect.

displace (dĭs-plās´) *v.* to move or force from one place or position to another.

dynamic (dī-năm´ĭk) *adj.* characterized by change, movement, or activity.

format (fôr´măt) *n.* a plan for the organization and arrangement of a specified production.

founder (foun´dər) *n.* someone who sets up, establishes, or provides the basis for something.

global (glō´bəl) *adj.* spherical in shape; worldwide; total.

ideological (ī-dē-ə-lŏj´ĭ-kəl) *adj.* based on ideas, beliefs, or doctrines.

implicit (ĭm-plĭs´ĭt) *adj.* implied or understood though not directly expressed.

infinite (ĭn´fə-nĭt) *adj.* having no boundaries or limits; immeasurably great or large.

publication (pŭb-lĭ-kā´shən) *n.* the act of making public in printed or electronic form; the product of this act.

quote (kwōt) *v.* to repeat or copy words from a source such as a book, usually with an acknowledgment of the source; to give a quotation; *n.* a quotation.

revise (rĭ-vīz´) *v.* to alter or edit; to reconsider and change or modify.

revolution (rĕv-ə-loō´shən) *n.* the overthrow and replacement of a government, often through violent means.

simulated (sĭm´yə-lā-tĭd) *adj.* made in resemblance of or as a substitute for another; performed or staged in imitation of a real event or activity.

somewhat (sŭm´wŏt, -hwŏt, -wŭt, -hwŭt) *adv.* to some extent or degree.

topic (tŏp´ĭk) *n.* the subject of a speech, essay, discussion, or conversation.

unify (yoō´nə-fī) *v.* to make into or become a unit; to consolidate.

unique (yoō-nēk´) *adj.* being the only one of its kind; remarkable or extraordinary.

virtual (vûr´choō-əl) *adj.* existing or resulting in essence or effect though not in actual form; existing in the mind.

Glossary of Critical Vocabulary

abandonment (ə-băn´dən-mĕnt) *n.* a lack of restraint or inhibition.

abdicate (ăb´dĭ-kāt) *v.* to relinquish or cede responsibility for.

abhor (ăb-hôr´) *v.* to regard with horror or loathing; to detest.

abhorrence (ăb-hôr´əns) *n.* a feeling of repugnance or loathing.

abject (ăb´jĕkt) *adj.* miserable and submissive.

abstraction (ăb-străk´shən) *n.* something that is not part of the concrete, material world.

acrid (ăk´rĭd) *adj.* unpleasantly sharp, pungent, or bitter to the taste or smell.

adamant (ăd´ə-mənt) *adj.* inflexible and insistent, unchanging.

affect (ə-fĕkt´) *v.* to cause or influence.

affluence (ăf´lōō-əns) *n.* wealth.

aghast (ə-găst´) *adj.* struck by shock, terror, or amazement.

anomalous (ə-nŏm´ə-ləs) *adj.* unusual.

apprehension (ăp-rĭ-hĕn´shən) *n.* fear or anxiety; dread.

archaic (är-kā´ĭk) *adj.* relating to, being, or characteristic of a much earlier period.

artifice (är´tə-fĭs) *n.* a clever means to an end.

atrocious (ə-trō´shəs) *adj.* evil or brutal.

augment (ôg-mĕnt´) *v.* to make (something already developed or well underway) greater, as in size, extent, or quantity.

automation (ô-tə-mā´shən) *n.* the automatic operation or control of equipment, a process, or a system.

belatedly (bĭ-lā´tĭd-lē) *adv.* done too late or when overdue.

bravado (brə-vä´dō) *n.* a show of bravery or defiance, often in order to make a false impression or mislead someone.

cabal (kə-băl´) *n.* a group united in a secret plot.

calamity (kə-lăm´ĭ-tē) *n.* an event that brings terrible loss or lasting distress.

caliber (kăl´ə-bər) *n.* level of ability.

capacity (kə-păs´ĭ-tē) *n.* ability to hold or have something; function or role.

cardinal (kär´dn-əl) *adj.* most important; prime.

catalyst (kăt´l-ĭst) *n.* a substance, usually used in small amounts relative to the reactants, that modifies and increases the rate of a reaction without being consumed in the process.

cede (sēd) *v.* to yield or give away.

circumlocution (sûr-kəm-lō-kyōō´shən) *n.* the use of unnecessarily wordy language.

circumvent (sûr-kəm-vĕnt´) *v.* to avoid or get around by artful maneuvering.

clave (klāv) *v. Archaic* past tense of *cleave:* to cling; to adhere.

codify (kŏd´ĭ-fī) *v.* to arrange or systematize.

compelled (kəm-pĕld´) *v.* forced (a person) to do something; drove or constrained.

composed (kəm-pōzd´) *adj.* self-possessed; calm.

conceivable (kən-sēv´ə-bəl) *adj.* able to be formed or developed in the mind.

configuration (kən-fĭg-yə-rā´shən) *n.* arrangement of parts or elements.

conjure (kŏn´jər) *v.* to influence or effect by or as if by magic.

conquistador (kŏng-kē´stə-dôr, kŏn-kwĭs´tə-dôr) *n.* a 16th-century Spanish soldier-explorer who took part in the defeat of the Indian civilizations of Mexico, Central America, or Peru.

consolation (kŏn-sə-lā´shən) *n.* act of giving comfort.

constitute (kŏn´stĭ-tōot) *v.* to amount to; to equal.

contrive (kən-trīv´) *v.* to plan skillfully; to design.

contrived (kən-trīvd´) *adj.* obviously planned or calculated; not spontaneous or natural.

conventional (kən-vĕn´shə-nəl) *adj.* based on or in accordance with general agreement, use, or practice; customary.

copious (kō´pē-əs) *adj.* extensive.

defection (dē-fĕkt´shŭn) *n.* the abandonment of one social or political group in favor of another.

delicacy (dĕl´ĭ-kə-sē) *n.* something pleasing and appealing, especially a choice food.

delinquency (dĭ-lĭng´kwən-sē) *n.* shortcoming or misbehavior.

delinquent (dĭ-lĭng´kwənt) *adj.* failing to do what law or duty requires.

demeanor (dĭ-mē´nər) *n.* the way in which a person behaves; deportment.

demurred (dĭ-mûrd´) *v.* disagreed politely or politely refused to accept a request or suggestion.

deprecate (dĕp´rĭ-kāt) *v.* to express disapproval.

deprive (dĭ-prīv´) *v.* to keep from possessing or enjoying; to deny.

diligence (dĭl´ə-jəns) *n.* consistent, thorough effort and dedication.

discord (dĭs´kôrd) *n.* disagreement or conflict.

disposed (dĭ-spōzd´) *adj.* having a preference, disposition, or tendency.

disposition (dĭs-pə-zĭsh´ən) *n.* character or temperament.

distinction (dĭ-stĭngk´shən) *n.* difference in quality.

divers (dī´vərz) *adj.* various; several.

efface (ĭ-fās´) *v.* to rub or wipe out; to erase.

elusive (ĭ-lōo´sĭv) *adj.* difficult to define.

emblem (ĕm´bləm) *n.* an identifying mark or symbol.

engross (ĕn-grōs´) *v.* to completely engage the attention or interest.

eradicate (ĭ-răd´ĭ-kāt) *v.* to tear up by the roots; to eliminate.

establish (ĭ-stăb´lĭsh) *v.* to formally set up; to institute.

estrangement (ĭ-strānj´mənt) *n.* the condition of being detached or withdrawn; alienation.

eviscerate (ĭ-vĭs´ə-rāt) *v.* to remove the necessary or important parts of.

exclusive (ĭk-sklōo´sĭv) *adj.* not allowing something else.

expedience (ĭk-spē´dē-əns) *n.* a self-interested means to an end.

extenuating (ĭk-stĕn´yōo-ā-tĭng) *adj.* serving to make a fault or an offense seem less serious.

extortionist (ĭk-stôr´shən-ĭst) *n.* one who obtains something by force or threat.

extremity (ĭk-strĕm´ĭ-tē) *n.* the outermost or farthest point or portion; the hand or foot.

façade (fə-säd´) *n.* false or misleading appearance.

facile (făs´əl) *adj.* easy to make or understand.

felicity (fĭ-lĭs´ĭ-tē) *n.* great happiness.

ferry (fĕr´ē) *v.* to transport (people or goods) by vehicle.

fixed (fĭkst) *adj.* firmly in position; stationary.

formidable (fôr´mĭ-də-bəl) *adj.* difficult and intimidating.

frantically (frăn´tĭk-lē) *adv.* excitedly, with strong emotion or frustration.

gape (gāp, găp) *v.* to stare wonderingly or stupidly, often with the mouth open.

grope (grōp) *v.* to reach about uncertainly; to feel one's way.

illumination (ĭ-lōo-mə-nā´shən) *n.* awareness or enlightenment.

imperative (ĭm-pĕr´ə-tĭv) *adj.* of great importance; essential.

impertinent (ĭm-pûr´tn-ənt) *adj.* rude; ill-mannered.

impunity (ĭm-pyōō´nĭ-tē) *n.* exemption from punishment, penalty, or harm.

inclination (ĭn-klə-nā´shən) *n.* a characteristic disposition or tendency to act in a certain way; a propensity.

incorrigible (ĭn-kôr´ĭ-jə-bəl) *adj.* incapable of being reformed or corrected.

indigenous (ĭn-dĭj´ə-nəs) *adj.* native to a land.

induced (ĭn-dōōst´) *v.* led or moved, as to a course of action, by influence or persuasion.

ineffable (ĭn-ĕf´ə-bəl) *adj.* beyond description; inexpressible.

infinitesimal (ĭn-fĭn-ĭ-tĕs´ə-məl) *adj.* immeasurably or incalculably minute.

infraction (ĭn-frăk´shən) *n.* the act or instance of infringing, as of a law or rule; a violation.

ingenious (ĭn-jēn´yəs) *adj.* having great inventive skill and imagination.

inhumanity (ĭn-hyōō-măn´ĭ-tē) *n.* lack of pity or compassion.

insurgency (ĭn-sûr´jən-sē) *n.* rebellion or revolt.

intangible (ĭn-tăn´jə-bəl) *adj.* unable to be defined or understood.

interminable (ĭn-tûr´mə-nə-bəl) *adj.* seemingly endless.

internalize (ĭn-tûr´nə-līz) *v.* to take in and make an integral part of one's attitudes or beliefs.

invest (ĭn-vĕst´) *v.* to grant or endow.

malign (mə-līn´) *v.* to make evil, harmful, and often untrue statements about (someone).

metaphysical (mĕt-ə-fĭz´ĭ-kəl) *adj.* based on speculative or abstract reasoning.

miscellany (mĭs´ə-lā-nē) *n.* a collection of various items, parts, or ingredients, especially one composed of diverse literary works.

mitigate (mĭt´ĭ-gāt) *v.* to lessen.

narcotic (när-kŏt´ĭk) *adj.* inducing sleep or stupor; causing narcosis.

noblesse oblige (nō-blĕs´ ō-blēzh´) *n.* the responsibility of people in a high social position to behave in a noble fashion.

oblige (ə-blīj´) *v.* to compel or require (someone) to do something.

obstinacy (ŏb´stə-nə-sē) *n.* stubbornness.

ostensibly (ŏ-stĕn´sə-blē) *adv.* apparently.

ostentatious (ŏs-tĕn-tā´shəs) *adj.* conspicuous and vulgar.

palpable (păl´pə-bəl) *adj.* capable of being handled, touched, or felt; tangible.

panic (păn´ĭk) *n.* sudden, overpowering feeling of fear.

parity (păr´ĭ-tē) *n.* equality; being equivalent.

patent (păt´nt) *n.* an official document granting ownership.

pathos (pā´thŏs) *n.* something that evokes pity or sympathy.

peril (pĕr´əl) *n.* imminent danger.

perturbation (pûr-tər-bā´shən) *n.* disturbance or agitation.

pigmentation (pĭg-mən-tā´shən) *n.* coloration of tissues by pigment.

platoon (plə-tōōn´) *n.* a subdivision of a company of troops consisting of two or more squads or sections and usually commanded by a lieutenant.

plausibility (plô-zə-bĭl´ĭ-tē) *n.* likelihood; believability.

pliable (plī´ə-bəl) *adj.* easily bent or shaped; easily influenced, persuaded, or controlled.

poignant (poin´yənt) *adj.* physically or mentally painful.

polarity (pō-lăr´ĭ-tē) *n.* separation to opposite sides.

ponder (pŏn´dər) *v.* to think about (something) with thoroughness and care.

posse (pŏs´ē) *n.* a group of civilians temporarily authorized by officials to assist in pursuing fugitives.

Glossary of Critical Vocabulary

postulate (pŏs´chə-lāt) *v.* to assume or assert the truth, reality, or necessity of, especially as a basis of an argument.

presaging (prĕs´ĭj-ĭng) *adj.* predicting.

pristine (prĭs´tēn) *adj.* pure or unspoiled.

project (prə-jĕkt´) *v.* to communicate or put forth.

proposition (prŏp-ə-zĭsh´ən) *n.* a plan suggested for acceptance; a proposal.

protrude (prō-trōōd´) *v.* to stick out or bulge.

provision (prə-vĭzh´ən) *n.* food supply.

provocation (prŏv-ə-kā´shən) *n.* the act of provoking or inciting.

recalcitrant (rĭ-kăl´sĭ-trənt) *adj.* uncooperative and resistant of authority.

reckless (rĕk´lĭs) *adj.* acting or done with a lack of care or caution.

reckoning (rĕk´ə-nĭng) *n.* a settlement of accounts.

recompense (rĕk´əm-pĕns) *n.* payment in return for something, such as a service.

regenerate (rĭ-jĕn´ə-rāt) *v.* to form, construct, or create anew.

regimen (rĕj´ə-mən) *n.* a system or organized routine of behavior.

remunerative (rĭ-myōō´nər-ə-tĭv) *adj.* bringing in money or profit.

reparations (rĕp-ə-rā´shəns) *n.* compensation or payment from a nation for damage or injury during a war.

rudiment (rōō´də-mənt) *n.* basic form.

sceptical (skĕp´tĭ-kəl) *adj.* marked by or given to doubt; questioning.

segregated (sĕg´rĭ-gāt-əd) *adj.* separated; isolated.

sentiment (sĕn´tə-mənt) *n.* a thought, view, or attitude, especially one based mainly on emotion instead of reason.

settlement (sĕt´l-mənt) *n.* a small community in a sparsely populated area.

sliver (slĭv´ər) *n.* a small narrow piece, portion, or plot.

sojourn (sō´jûrn´) *n.* a temporary stay; a brief period of residence.

specious (spē´shəs) *adj.* having the ring of truth or plausibility but actually fallacious.

specter (spĕk´tər) *n.* a ghostly apparition; a phantom.

stem (stĕm) *v.* to have or take origin or descent.

stoically (stō´ĭk-lē) *adv.* without showing emotion or feeling.

straits (strāts) *n.* a position of difficulty, distress, or extreme need.

strive (strīv) *v.* to struggle or fight forcefully; to contend.

subservience (səb-sûr´vē-əns) *n.* the condition of being subordinate in capacity or function.

summarily (sə-mĕr´ə-lē) *adv.* quickly and without ceremony.

sundry (sŭn´drē) *adj.* various or assorted.

superfluous (sŏō-pûr´flōō-əs) *adj.* unnecessary.

systematize (sĭs´tə-mə-tīz) *v.* to form something into an organized plan or scheme.

tableau (tăb´lō) *n.* a dramatic scene or picture.

tepid (tĕp´ĭd) *adj.* lukewarm; indifferent.

tidings (tī´dĭngs) *n.* information or news.

timid (tĭm´ĭd) *adj.* lacking self-confidence; shy.

transient (trăn´zē-ənt) *adj.* temporary; short-term.

transition (trăn-zĭsh´ən) *n.* process of change.

trifling (trī´flĭng) *adj.* frivolous; inconsequential.

truculent (trŭk´yə-lənt) *adj.* eager for a fight; fierce.

tyrannical (tĭ-răn´ĭ-kəl) *adj.* characteristic of a tyrant or tyranny; despotic and oppressive.

unalienable (ŭn-āl´yə-nə-bəl) *adj.* impossible to be taken away.

unassailable (ŭn-ə-sā´lə-bəl) *adj.* undeniable.

undulation (ŭn-jə-lā´shən) *n.* a regular rising and falling or movement to alternating sides; movement in waves.

unfathomed (ŭn-făth´əmd) *adj.* located at the deepest place.

unimpeded (ŭn-ĭm-pēd´əd) *adj.* not delayed or obstructed in its progress.

unremitting (ŭn-rĭ-mĭt´ĭng) *adj.* constant; never stopping.

vacant (vā´kənt) *adj.* blank, expressionless.

vanquish (văng´kwĭsh) *v.* to defeat in a contest or conflict.

venture (vĕn´chər) *v.* to risk or dare.

vindicate (vĭn´dĭ-kāt) *v.* to demonstrate or prove the validity of; to justify.

virtuous (vûr´chōō-əs) *adj.* having or showing virtue, especially moral excellence.

virulent (vîr´yə-lənt) *adj.* extremely hostile or malicious.

volatile (vŏl´ə-tl) *adj.* evaporating readily at normal temperatures and pressures.

watershed (wô´tər-shĕd) *n.* a turning point; a crucial dividing line.

wring (rĭng) *v.* to obtain through force or pressure.

Index of Skills

A

absurdity, 549

Academic Vocabulary, 2, 21, 37, 51, 61, 77, 91, 109, 128, 143, 155, 159, 173, 187, 201, 213, 229, 250, 267, 275, 287, 295, 311, 335, 361, 380, 395, 405, 418, 437, 455, 471, 485, 497, 518, 545, 559, 571, 583, 593, 605, 623, 642, 663, 673, 687, 803, 815, 825, 835, 855, 867, 877, 885, 897, 909

act, 691

actions, 691, 693

active voice, 95, 122

actor portrayals, 157

adjective clauses, 363

adverb clause, 473

Again and Again (Notice & Note), 15, 20, 357, 360, 601, 670, 672

Aha Moment (Notice & Note), 579, 582, 660, 662

allegory, 339, 694

    analyze, 339, 343, 345, 346, 354

    compare themes, 364

alliteration, 206, 289

allusion, 387, 460, 479, 546, 817, 871

    analyze, 479, 481

    write, 485

ambiguity, 177, 318

analysis, literary, 61, 545, 784

analyze

    allegory, 339, 343, 345, 346, 354

    allusion, 479, 481

    Analyze Media, 158, 814

    Analyze Text and Media, 418, 807, 812, 813

    Analyze the Image, 1, 127, 249, 379, 517, 641

    Analyze the Text, 20, 36, 50, 60, 76, 90, 95, 108, 111, 142, 154, 172, 186, 200, 212, 215, 228, 233, 266, 274, 286, 294, 310, 315, 334, 360, 365, 394, 404, 436, 454, 470, 475, 484, 496, 501, 544, 558, 570, 582, 592, 604, 622, 626, 662, 672, 686, 730, 754, 784, 802, 824, 834, 854, 866, 876, 884, 896, 908, 913

argument, 135, 138, 139, 387, 390

author's purpose, 218, 221, 224, 227, 596, 602, 610, 612, 618, 620, 676, 679, 682, 683, 684

blank verse, 667, 669

character, 25, 487, 490, 491, 525, 528, 529, 532, 535, 539, 542, 693, 696, 700, 708, 714, 720, 724, 733, 737, 739, 741, 743, 750, 755, 758, 760, 777, 787, 794, 859, 862

counterarguments, 563, 567

development of ideas, 41, 48, 269, 272, 888, 891, 893, 901, 904

figurative language, 55, 58, 279, 282, 283, 829, 831

form, 830, 832

free verse, 257, 260, 263, 587, 590

genre characteristics, 627

graphic novel, 675, 678, 680, 681

ideas and events, 161, 163, 165, 168, 441, 443, 445, 451, 452

idioms, 221, 230

imagery, 1, 56, 147, 151, 289, 291, 587, 590, 879, 881

irony, 575, 580

language, 64, 67, 69, 74, 667, 669

letters, 399

literary analysis, 61

literary devices, 694, 699, 718, 727, 748, 793, 798, 799, 871, 874

mood, 339, 342, 350, 352, 356

myth, 9, 12, 14, 17

perspective, 888, 892, 894

persuasive techniques, 387, 391

plot, 25, 33, 177, 179, 182, 184, 423, 425, 428, 431, 434, 487, 492, 693, 705, 710, 723, 733, 745, 752, 762, 765, 766, 770, 773, 775, 785, 788, 791, 795, 797

point of view, 177, 183, 423, 426, 427, 432, 575, 577, 578, 580

primary sources, 81, 84, 88

reasoning, 837, 840, 842, 845, 847, 849

rhetoric, 460, 464, 468, 817, 820, 822

rhythm, 478, 480, 482

satire, 548, 552, 553, 555

setting, 318, 321, 324, 329, 525, 528, 530, 533, 537, 538, 542, 649, 651, 652, 659

sound devices, 206, 208, 210, 289, 292

speaker, 478, 481

structure, 41, 44, 46, 147, 151, 161, 164, 191, 194, 195, 197, 280, 283, 284, 290, 292, 563, 565, 566, 859, 865, 872, 873, 901, 906

structure and purpose, 269, 271

student model, 121, 243, 375, 511, 637, 923

style, 99, 100, 106, 298, 301, 305, 306, 307

symbols, 318, 320, 321, 326, 327, 328, 332

theme, 25, 27, 28, 57, 98, 102, 105, 206, 210, 258, 261, 262, 264, 279, 284, 545, 880, 882

tone, 142, 218, 220, 223, 226, 399, 401, 402, 441, 444, 448, 449, 450, 549, 551, 554, 556, 588, 589, 879, 882

writing prompt, 115, 237, 369, 505, 631, 917

anaphora, 561

animation, 157

annotate. *See* Annotation in Action

Annotation in Action, 10, 26, 42, 56, 65, 82, 99, 136, 148, 162, 178, 192, 207, 219, 258, 270, 280, 290, 299, 319, 340, 388, 400, 410, 424, 442, 461, 479, 488, 526, 550, 564, 576, 588, 597, 611, 650, 668, 694, 818, 830, 838, 860, 872, 880, 889, 902

antagonist, 693

antonyms, 891, 898

appeals, 474

    emotional, 460 (pathos), 474

    ethical, 387, 460 (ethos)

    logical, 142, 460 (logos), 474

    rhetorical, 460

    to time and place, 387, 460 (kairos)

Apply to Your Draft

    argument, 508, 509, 510, 511, 512

    explanatory essay, 372, 373, 374, 375, 376

    informative essay, 118, 119, 120, 121, 122

    personal narrative, 920, 921, 922, 923, 924

    research report, 240, 241, 242, 243, 244

    short story, 634, 635, 636, 637, 638

appositive, 337

    essential, 337

    nonessential, 337

appositive phrase, 337

archaic vocabulary, 84, 94

archetypes, 9

argument, write an, 335, 376, 925

    address opposing claims, 507, 509

    consider sources, 504

    develop claim, 506

    develop draft, 508–509

    edit, 512

    identify support, 506

    mentor text use, 504, 508, 509

    organize ideas, 507

    persuasive letter, 229

    plan, 506–507

    publish, 512

    refer to sources, 508

    Reflect & Extend, 247, 377, 639

revise, 510–511
rubric, 505
student model, 511
writing prompt, 504
argumentative writing, 563
arguments
adapt for debate, 513
analyze, 135, 138, 139, 387, 390
compare, 458, 474
counterarguments, 563, 567
evaluate, 460, 462, 463, 467, 475
genre elements, 460
purposes, 505
ars poetica, 830, 835
genre elements, 829
write an, 835
article
genre elements, 563
respond to, 571
Assessment Practice, 7, 19, 35, 49, 59, 75,
89, 103, 107, 133, 141, 153, 171, 185,
199, 209, 211, 225, 227, 255, 265, 273,
285, 293, 303, 309, 333, 359, 385, 393,
403, 417, 435, 453, 465, 469, 483, 495,
523, 543, 557, 569, 581, 591, 603, 621,
647, 661, 671, 685, 729, 753, 783, 801,
823, 833, 853, 865, 875, 883, 895, 907
assonance, 289
audience, 81, 218
informative essay, 115
personal narrative, 917
audio recording, 807
author's perspective, 632, 888
author's purpose, 81, 218, 596, 676
analyze, 218, 221, 224, 227, 596, 602, 610,
612, 618, 620, 676, 679, 682, 683, 684
compare, 62
determine, 157
explanatory essay, 369
autobiographical essay, 888
autobiography, 191, 487

B

balanced sentences, 397
bias, 409
Big Questions (Notice & Note), 905
blank verse, 667
analyze, 667, 669
genre elements, 667
blocking, 807
blog writing, 909

C

call to action, 387, 474
capitalization, 573
captions, 675
casting, 807
cataloging, 257

cause, 269
cause and effect, 269, 372, 454
central ideas, 64
determine, 64, 67, 68, 81, 84, 87, 135, 137,
610, 613, 614, 617, 619, 817, 819, 821
characterization, 859
analyze, 487
direct, 487, 693
indirect, 487, 693
characters
analyze, 25, 487, 490, 491, 525, 528, 529,
532, 535, 539, 542, 693, 696, 700, 708,
714, 720, 724, 733, 737, 739, 741, 743,
750, 755, 758, 760, 777, 787, 794,
859, 862
archetypes, 9
dialogue and, 805
motivation, 525
character sketch, 497
chronological order, 161, 239, 372, 441,
633, 919
cite evidence
Analyze Text and Media, 418
Analyze the Text, 50, 60, 154, 172, 501,
544, 558, 582, 730, 754, 824, 834,
884, 896
claims, 387, 470, 474, 506, 837
counterclaim, 507, 509
develop, 506
opposing claims, 507, 509
class discussion, 143
class presentation, 215, 315, 627
clauses, 79
adverb, 473
dependent, 79
independent, 473
noun, 407
relative, 473
subordinate, 79, 473
climax, 693
coherent order, 371
Collaborate & Compare, 62, 96, 204, 216,
296, 314, 316, 458, 476, 500–501, 594,
608, 886, 912
Collaborate and Debate, 913
Collaborate and Discuss, 475
Collaborate and Present, 95, 111, 215, 233,
315, 365, 627
Collaborate and Share, 501
collaborative discussion, 7, 18, 34, 48, 59,
74, 88, 102, 106, 133, 141, 153, 170,
185, 199, 211, 224, 227, 255, 264, 273,
284, 292, 308, 333, 359, 385, 393, 403,
417, 434, 453, 464, 469, 482, 494, 523,
543, 557, 569, 580, 591, 602, 621, 647,
660, 670, 684, 753, 801, 810, 823, 833,
865, 874, 882, 894, 906
collage, 287, 835
mixed-media, 109
collective nouns, 189

colons, 665
commas, 439
comparative essay, 213
compare, 886, 912. *See also* Collaborate &
Compare across genres
Analyze Text and Media, 418
Analyze the Text, 60, 95, 111, 154, 172,
233, 266, 310, 315, 360, 365, 394, 470,
475, 544, 622, 626, 884, 913
arguments, 458, 474
author's purpose, 62
genres, 594, 626
ideas, 886, 912
important details, 214
main ideas, 296, 315
poems, 96, 110, 155, 213, 485
structure, 476, 500
themes, 204, 214, 215, 316, 364
tone, 216, 232
compare-and-contrast essay, 91, 155, 372
compare-and-contrast structure, 239
comparison and contrast, 161
complex sentences, 203, 313, 473
complications, 693
compound-complex sentence, 313, 473
compound sentences, 203, 313, 473, 638
compound subject
plural, 189
singular, 189
concession, 563
conclusions, 837
draw. *See* draw conclusions
conflict, 693
external, 487
internal, 487, 859
conjunctions
coordinating, 638
subordinating, 79
connect
Analyze the Text, 20, 172, 212, 294, 360,
592, 884
make connections, 2, 128, 250, 256, 380,
518, 642
to the modern day, 213
Connect & Create, 235, 367
connotation, 336, 821, 826, 868, 871
connotative meaning, 498
consonance, 289
contested usage, 203, 231
context clues, 30, 38, 312, 456, 572
contrast
Analyze the Text, 95, 212, 215, 501, 913
Contrasts and Contradictions (Notice &
Note), 169, 172, 323, 352, 360, 702, 730,
781, 784, 802
coordinating conjunctions, 638
costuming, 807
counterarguments, analyze, 563, 567
counterclaims, develop, 507, 509

© Houghton Mifflin Harcourt Publishing Company

© Houghton Mifflin Harcourt Publishing Company

Index of Titles and Authors

Acknowledgments

Excerpt from *1491: New Revelations of the Americas Before Columbus* by Charles C. Mann, map by Nick Springer and Tracy Pollack of Springer Cartographics LLC. Text and illustration copyright © 2005, 2006, 2011 by Charles C. Mann. Reprinted by permission of Alfred A. Knopf, an imprint of the Knopf Doubleday Publishing Group, a division of Penguin Random House LLC, Granta Publications, and Roam Agency on behalf of Charles C. Mann.

"Ambush" from *The Things They Carried* by Tim O'Brien. Text and audio copyright © 1990 by Tim O'Brien. Reproduced by permission of Houghton Mifflin Harcourt Publishing Company, HarperCollins Publishers Ltd, and Janklow and Nesbit Associates.

Excerpts from *The American Heritage Dictionary of The English Language, Fifth Edition*. Text copyright © 2016 by Houghton Mifflin Harcourt Publishing Company. Reprinted by permission of Houghton Mifflin Harcourt Publishing Company.

"Balboa" from *Tales of the New World* by Sabina Murray. Text copyright © 2011 by Sabina Murray. Reprinted by permission of Grove/Atlantic, Inc. Any third-party use of this material, outside of this publication, is prohibited.

"Because I could not stop for Death," "Much Madness is divinest Sense," "The Soul selects her own Society," and "Tell all the Truth but tell it slant" from *The Poems of Emily Dickinson* edited by Thomas H. Johnson. Text copyright © 1951, 1955, renewed 1979, 1983 by the President and Fellows of Harvard College. Text copyright 1914, 1918, 1919, 1924, 1929, 1930, 1932, 1935, 1937, 1942 by Martha Dickinson Bianchi. Text copyright © 1952, 1957, 1958, 1963, 1965 by Mary L. Hampson. Reprinted by permission of The Belknap Press of Harvard University Press, Cambridge, Mass.

"Building the Transcontinental Railroad" from *The Chinese in America: A Narrative History* by Iris Chang. Text copyright © 2003 by Iris Chang. Reprinted by permission of Viking Books, an imprint of Penguin Publishing Group, a division of Penguin Random House LLC. All rights reserved. Any third-party use of this material, outside of this publication, is prohibited. Interested parties must apply directly to Penguin Random House LLC for permission.

"Casualties and Costs of the Civil War" by The Gilder Lehrman Institute of American History. Copyright © 2017. Reprinted by permission of The Gilder Lehrman Institute of American History.

The Crucible by Arthur Miller. Text copyright © 1952, 1953, 1954 by Arthur Miller, renewed © 1980, 1981, 1982 by Arthur Miller. Reprinted by permission of Viking Books, an imprint of Penguin Publishing Group, a division of Penguin Random House LLC and The Wylie Agency LLC.

"A Desperate Trek Across America" by Andrés Reséndez from *American Heritage*, Fall 2008, Vol. 58, Issue 5. Text copyright © 2008 by American Heritage Publishing. Reprinted by permission of American Heritage Publishing via Copyright Clearance Center.

Excerpt from *Fast Food Nation* by Eric Schlosser. Text copyright © 2001 by Eric Schlosser. Reprinted by permission of Houghton Mifflin Harcourt, Penguin Books Ltd, Random House Audio Publishing Group, a division of Penguin Random House LLC, and Janklow & Nesbit Associates on behalf of the author.

"First Verse" from *Buffalo Head Solos* by Tim Seibles. Text copyright © 2002 by Tim Seibles. Reprinted by permission of the author.

"The Fourth Industrial Revolution Is Here: Are You Ready?" (retitled from "Why Everyone Must Get Ready for the 4th Industrial Revolution") by Bernard Marr from Forbes.com, April 5, 2016. Text copyright © 2016 by Bernard Marr. Reprinted by permission of Bernard Marr.

"In the Season of Change" by Teresa Palomo Acosta. Text copyright © 1994 by Teresa Palomo Acosta. Reproduced by permission of the author.

From "Introduction" from *Last Child in the Woods* by Richard Louv. Text copyright © 2005 by Richard Louv. Reprinted by permission of Algonquin Books of Chapel Hill. All rights reserved.

"The Latin Deli: An Ars Poetica" by Judith Ortiz Cofer from *The Americas Review*, vol. 19, no. 1. Text Copyright © 1991 by Arte Público Press – University of Houston. Reprinted by permission of Arte Público Press – University of Houston.

Excerpt from *Lean In: Women, Work, and the Will to Lead* by Sheryl Sandberg. Text copyright © 2013 by Lean In Foundation. Reprinted by permission of Alfred A. Knopf, an imprint of the Knopf Doubleday Publishing Group, a division of Penguin Random House LLC, William Morris Endeavor Entertainment, LLC, and The Random House Group Limited.

"The Lowest Animal" from *Letters from the Earth* by Mark Twain, edited by Bernard DeVoto. Text copyright © 1938, 1944, 1946, 1959, 1962 by The Mark Twain Company. Copyright 1942 by The President and Fellows of Harvard College. Reprinted by permission of HarperCollins Publishers.

"My Dungeon Shook: Letter to My Nephew on this One Hundredth Anniversary of the Emancipation" by James Baldwin. Text copyright © 1962, 1963 by James Baldwin. Copyright renewed. Originally published in *The Progressive*. Collected in *The Fire Next Time*, published by Vintage Books. Reprinted by arrangement with the James Baldwin Estate.

"My Friend Walt Whitman" from *Blue Pastures* by Mary Oliver. Text copyright © 1995 by Mary Oliver. Reprinted by permission of Houghton Mifflin Harcourt.

"New Orleans" from *She Had Some Horses* by Joy Harjo. Text copyright © 2008, 1983 by Joy Harjo. Reprinted by permission of W. W. Norton & Company, Inc.

From *Of Plymouth Plantation 1620–1647* by William Bradford, edited by Samuel Eliot Morison, New York: Alfred A. Knopf, 1952.

"One Today: A Poem for Barack Obama's Presidential Inauguration Jan. 21, 2013" from *One Today: A Poem for Barack Obama's Presidential Inauguration January 21, 2013* by Richard Blanco. Text copyright © 2013. Reprinted by permission of the University of Pittsburgh Press.

Acknowledgments

"A Rose for Emily" from *Collected Stories of William Faulkner* by William Faulkner. Text copyright 1930, renewed 1958 by William Faulkner. Reprinted by permission of Random House, an imprint and division of Penguin Random House LLC, W. W. Norton & Company, Inc., and Curtis Brown Ltd, London on behalf of The Estate of William Faulkner.

"Runagate Runagate" from *Collected Poems of Robert Hayden* by Robert Hayden, edited by Frederick Glaysher. Text copyright © 1966 by Robert Hayden. Reprinted by permission of Liveright Publishing Corporation.

"A Soldier for the Crown" from *Soulcatcher and Other Stories* by Charles Johnson. Text copyright © 1998 by Charles Johnson. Reprinted by permission of the WGBH Educational Foundation.

Excerpt from "Speech on the Vietnam War, New York City, April 4, 1967" by Martin Luther King, Jr. Text copyright © 1967 by Dr. Martin Luther King, Jr., renewed © 1991 by Coretta Scott King. Reprinted by permission of Writers House on behalf of the Heirs of the Estate of Martin Luther King, Jr.

Excerpt from *They Called Us Enemy* by George Takei. Copyright © 2019 by George Takei. Reprinted by permission of Top Shelf Productions / IDW Publishing.

"Thomas Jefferson: The Best of Enemies" from *Time Magazine*, July 5, 2004, by Ron Chernow. Text copyright © 2004 by TIME, Inc. Reprinted by permission of TIME, Inc. All rights reserved.

"The Universe as Primal Scream" from *Life on Mars* by Tracy K. Smith. Text copyright © 2011 by Tracy K. Smith. Reprinted with the permission of The Permissions Company, Inc. on behalf of Graywolf Press, Minneapolis, Minnesota. www.graywolfpress.org.

Excerpt from *The Warmth of Other Suns: The Epic Story of America's Great Migration* by Isabel Wilkerson. Text copyright © 2010 by Isabel Wilkerson. Reprinted by permission of Random House, an imprint and division of Penguin Random House LLC, and ICM Partners.

"World, in hounding me, what do you gain?" by Sor Juana Inés de la Cruz, from *A Sor Juana Anthology*, translated by Alan S. Trueblood. Copyright © 1988 by the President and Fellows of Harvard College. Published by Harvard University Press, Cambridge, MA. Reprinted by permission of the publisher.

"World on the Turtle's Back" from *The Great Tree and the Longhouse: The Culture of the Iroquois* by Hazel W. Hertzberg. Text copyright © 1966 by American Anthropological Association. Not for sale or further reproduction. Reprinted by permission of American Anthropological Association.